In My Father's House

IN MY FATHER'S HOUSE

Africa in the Philosophy of Culture

KWAME ANTHONY APPIAH

New York   Oxford   OXFORD UNIVERSITY PRESS

Oxford University Press

Oxford   New York   Toronto
Delhi   Bombay   Calcutta   Madras   Karachi
Kuala Lumpur   Singapore   Hong Kong   Tokyo
Nairobi   Dar es Salaam   Cape Town
Melbourne   Auckland   Madrid

and associated companies in
Berlin   Ibadan

Copyright © 1992 by Kwame Anthony Appiah

First published in 1992 by Oxford University Press, Inc.,
200 Madison Avenue, New York, New York 10016

First issued as an Oxford University Press paperback, 1993

Oxford is a registered trademark of Oxford University Press

Library of Congress Cataloging-in-Publication Data
Appiah, Anthony.
In my Father's house : Africa in the philosophy
of culture / Kwame Anthony Appiah.
p. cm.   Includes bibliographical references and index.
ISBN 0–19–506851–3
1. Africa—Culture—Philosophy.
2. Africa—Intellectual life—20th century.
I. Title.
DT352.4.A66   1992   960—dc20
91–23386
ISBN 0–19–506852–1 (pbk.)

2 4 6 8 10 9 7 5 3 1

Printed in the United States of America

For

Gyamfi, Anthony, Per Kodjo,
Tomiwa, Lamide, Tobi, Mame Yaa,
Maggie, and Elizabeth

and in memory of my father
Joe Appiah, *1918–90*

Abusua-dua yɛntwa

Preface

My first memories are of a place called "Mbrom," a small neighborhood in Kumasi, capital of Asante, as that kingdom turned from being part of the British Gold Coast colony to being a region of the Republic of Ghana. Our home was opposite my grandparent's house—where scores of her kinsfolk and dependents lived under the direction of my stepgrandmother, "Auntie Jane," who baked bread for hundreds of people from Mbrom and the surrounding areas—down the street from many cousins of various, usually obscure, degrees of affinity. Near the center of the second largest city in Ghana, behind our hibiscus hedge in the "garden city of West Africa," our life was essentially a village life, lived among a few hundred neighbors; out from that village we went to the other little villages that make up the city.

We could go higher up the hill, to Asante New Town, to the palace of the Asante king, Prempeh II, whose first wife, my great-aunt, always called me "Akroma-Ampim" (the name of our most illustrious ancestor) or "Yao Antony" (the name of the great-uncle and head of the family from whom I acquired my anglicized name, "Anthony"). Or we could travel in another cultural direction to the campus of the Kwame Nkrumah University of Science and Technology—known always as "Tech"—where I went to primary school, and where many of my friends' parents were professors.

Some worlds—the world of the law courts where my father went, dressed in his dark European suits, carrying the white wig of the British barrister (which he wore after independence as in the colonial period), a rose from the garden (my mother's garden) always in his buttonhole; the world of parliament, where he went in the first years I can remember, an opponent now of his old friend Nkrumah—some worlds we knew of only because our parents spoke of them. Others—the world of the little church, Saint George's, where we went to Sunday school with Baptists and Copts and Catholics and Methodists and Anglicans, from other parts of the country, other parts of the continent, other parts of the world—we knew inside and out, knew because they were central to our friendships, our learning, our beliefs.

In our house, my mother was visited regularly by Muslim Hausa traders from what we called (in a phrase that struck my childhood ear as wonderfully mysterious, exotic in its splendid vagueness) "the North." These men knew she was interested in seeing and, sometimes, in buying the brass weights the Asante had used for weighing gold; goldweights they had collected from villages all over the region, where they were being sold by people who had no use for them anymore, now that paper and coin had replaced gold dust as currency. And as she collected them, she heard more and more of the folklore that went with them; the proverbs that every figurative goldweight elicited; the folktales, *Ananseasεm*, that the proverbs evoked. My father told us these Ananse stories, too, some of them picked up when he was a political prisoner under Nkrumah (there was little else to do in prison but spin yarns). Between his stories and the cultural messages that came with the goldweights, we gathered the sort of sense of a cultural tradition that comes from growing up in it. For us it was not Asante tradition but the webwork of our lives. We loved the stories—my sisters now read the ones that my mother has published to my nephews in Gaborone and in Lagos; my godchildren read them here in America—and we grew to love the goldweights and the carvings that the traders brought.

And the family we grew into (an "extended" family, our English friends would have said, though we would have thought of their conceptions of family as "contracted") gave us an immense social space in which to grow.

But we also went from time to time to my mother's native country, to England, to stay with my grandmother in the rural West Country, returning the visits she had made to us. And the life there—perhaps this is only because it is also part of my earliest memories—seems, at least now, to have been mostly not too different. My grandmother lived next door to my aunt (my mother's sister) and her family, in the village where my aunt was born, just as my father lived next to his father. And so, by an odd cultural reversal, my father lived opposite and close to his patrilineal kin (in matrilineal Asante), while my aunt and her children lived next to their matrilineal kin (in patrilineal England). But it was my father's matriclan and my English grandfather's matriclan—descendants of the eight sisters, of whom one was my great-grandmother—that I came to know best over the years.

If my sisters and I were "children of two worlds," no one bothered to tell us this; we lived in one world, in two "extended" families divided by several thousand miles and an allegedly insuperable cultural distance that never, so far as I can recall, puzzled or perplexed us much. As I grew older, and went to an English boarding school, I learned that not everybody had family in Africa and in Europe; not everyone had a Lebanese uncle, American and French and Kenyan and Thai cousins. And by now, now that my sisters have married a Norweigan and a Nigerian and a Ghanaian, now that I live in America, I am used to seeing the world as a network of points of affinity.

This book is dedicated to nine children—a boy born in Botswana, of Norwegian and Anglo-Ghanaian parents; his brothers, born in Norway and in Ghana; their four cousins, three boys in Lagos, born of Nigerian and Anglo-Ghanaian parents, and a girl in Ghana; and two girls, born in New Haven, Connecticut, of an African-American father and a "white" American mother. These children, my nephews and my godchildren, range in appearance from the color and hair of my father's Asante kinsmen to the Viking ancestors of my Norwegian brother-in-law; they have names from Yorubaland, from Asante, from America, from Norway, from England. And watching them playing together and speaking to each other in their various accents, I, at least, feel a certain hope for the human future.

These children represent an eye to posterity, but this book is also dedicated to my father, who died while I was revising the final manuscript and became the closest of my ancestors. Long before he fell ill, I had decided to name this book for him: it was from him, after all, that I inherited the world and the problems with which this book is concerned. From him I inherited Africa, in general; Ghana, in particular; Asante and

Kumasi, more particularly yet. His Christianity (his and my mother's) gave me *both* the biblical knowledge that means that for me the phrase "in my father's house . . ." must be completed "there are many mansions," *and* the biblical understanding that, when Christ utters those words at the Last Supper, he means that there is room enough for all in heaven; *his* Father's house. Even my father, who loved Ghana as much as anyone, would, of course, have resisted the assimilation of Ghana to heaven; though he might have been tempted to claim that the Kumasi of his youth was as close to heaven as anywhere on earth. But he would not deny—no one who knows these places could deny—that there is plenty of room in Africa, in Ghana, even in Asante, for all sorts and conditions of men and women; that at each level, Africa is various.

Two other crucial intellectual legacies from my father inform this book. One is his Pan-Africanism. In 1945 my father was with Nkrumah and Du Bois at the Pan-African Congress in Manchester; in 1974 he was one of the very few from the 1945 congress (he himself met no other) who attended the congress, hosted by Julius Nyerere, in Dar es Salaam. By then Du Bois and Nkrumah were gone: in 1972 my father had flown to Guinée to negotiate the return of Nkrumah's body for a Ghanaian state funeral; his office, in those days, in Christiansborg Castle in Accra, was a few short steps from Du Bois's grave. My father was, I think, as complete a Pan-Africanist as either of them; yet he also taught us, his children, to be as completely untempted by racism as he was. And he was able, despite his antiracism—despite what I am inclined to call his complete unracism, since racism was never a temptation he had to resist—to find it natural, when he was a delegate from Ghana to the UN to seek solidarity in Harlem, where he went to church most Sundays and made many lifelong friends. My father is my model for the possibility of a Pan-Africanism without racism, both in Africa and in its diaspora—a concrete possibility whose conceptual implications this book is partly intended to explore.

The second legacy is my father's multiple attachment to his identities: above all as an Asante, as a Ghanaian, as an African, and as a Christian and a Methodist. I cannot claim to participate fully in any of these identities as he did; given the history we do not share, he would not have expected me to. But I have tried in this book, in many places, to examine the meaning of one or another, and, by the end, all of these identities, and to learn from his capacity to make use of these many identities without, so far as I could tell, any significant conflict.

I could say more about my father's multiple presences in this book; but, in the end, I would rather that the book should show what I have learned from him than that I should catalog my debts at the start.

I say all this in part because in thinking about culture, which is the subject of this book, one is bound to be formed—morally, aesthetically, politically, religiously—by the range of lives one has known. Others will disagree with much that I have to say, and it is right that those who disagree, as those who agree with me, should know, as we say in America, "where I am coming from." This is especially important because the book is about issues that are bound to be deeply personally important for anyone with my history; for its theme is the question how we are to think about Africa's contemporary cultures in the light both of the two main external determinants of her recent cultural history—European and Afro–New World conceptions of Africa—and of her own endogenous cultural traditions. I believe—this is one of the central goals of the academy, which is my vocation—that we should think carefully about the issues that matter to us most. When I argue that ideological decolonization is bound to fail if it neglects either endogenous "tradition" or exogenous "Western" ideas, and that many African (and African-American) intellectuals have failed to find a negotiable middle way, I am talking about friends and neighbors and I am talking about how *we* deal with *our* shared situation. It would be foolhardy to suppose and unpersuasive to claim that in such a situation it is always one's dispassionate reason that triumphs, that one can pursue the issues with the impartiality of the disinterested. Precisely because I am aware of these other forces, I expect that sometimes along the way my history has not only formed my judgment (which I delight in) but distorted it (which, of course, I do not); to judge whether it has, you will need to know something of that history, and I want you to know, not least because only through the responses of readers will *I* learn of my distortions.

But it is also important to testify, I think, to the practical reality of the kind of intercultural project whose theoretical ramifications I explore in these essays: to show how easy it is, without theory, without much conscious thought, to live in human families that extend across the boundaries that are currently held to divide our race. It may help to have a thumb-nail sketch of the territory that lies before us.

Africa's intellectuals have long been engaged in a conversation with each other and with Europeans and Americans, about what it means to be African. At the heart of these debates on African identity are the seminal works of politicians, creative writers, and philosophers from Africa and her diaspora. In this book, I draw on the writings of these African and African-American thinkers to explore the possibilities and pitfalls of an African identity in the late twentieth century.

The essays fall into four clusters, and, as I look over them with hindsight, I detect a central preoccupation in each.

In the two opening essays, which form the first cluster, I explore the role of racial ideology in the development of Pan-Africanism. I focus, more particularly, on the ideas of the African-American intellectuals who initiated Pan-Africanist discourse. My archetypes are Alexander Crummell, in Chapter 1, and W. E. B. Du Bois, in Chapter 2; and I argue in examining their work that the idea of the Negro, the idea of an African race, is an unavoidable element in that discourse, and that these racialist notions are grounded in bad biological—and worse ethical—ideas, inherited from the increasingly racialized thought of nineteenth-century Europe and America.

The next two essays are united in asking how questions about African identity figure in African literary life: and they do so by exploring the ideas of critics and literary theorists in Chapter 3 and of a major writer—Wole Soyinka—in Chapter 4. The burden of these essays is that the attempt to construct an African literature rooted in African traditions has led both to an understating of the diversity of African cultures, and to an attempt to censor the profound entanglement of African intellec-tuals with the intellectual life of Europe and the Americas.

The pair of chapters that follows—cluster three—is motivated by an essentially philosophical preoccupation with the issues of reason and modernity. In thinking about modern African philosophy, in Chapter 5, and "traditional" religion, in Chapter 6, I rely on a view of the central role of reason in African life before and after colonialism; and I suggest a view of modernization in Africa that differs, as a result, from the standard Weberian view. The upshot here is not so easily reduced to a formula: but my theme is that an ideal of reasonableness (conceived, in a specific sense, transculturally) has a central role to play in thinking about Africa's future. To one side lies parochialism; to the other, false claims to universality.

The final set of chapters raise more explicitly questions of politics and identity. Chapter 7 leads us through the art market and some contemporary novels to the emergence of an unsentimental form of African humanism that can undergird our resistance to tyranny. I explore the meaning of the African nation-state and the forms of social organization that both challenge and enable it, in Chapter 8. In Chapter 9, I take up in a more theoretical way the general question of identities—racial, ethnic, national, Pan-African—and what the power of identities at each of these levels reveals about the possibilities for politics and the role of intellectuals in political life.

It is in this political sphere that so many of the issues raised in this book come together. Rejecting the rhetoric of descent requires a rethinking of Pan-Africanist politics; literature and its criticism are more explicitly preoccupied in Africa than in Europe and North America with political questions; and modernization and its meaning are the major policy questions facing our political institutions. Naturally, therefore, there is no easy separation of the issues; and naturally, also, political questions surface again and again throughout the book. More surprising, I think, is the persistent recurrence of questions of race; of the racialist history that has dogged Pan-Africanism from its inception.

But, that said, I would want to resist the reduction of this book to a single theme. For the situation of the African intellectual is as complex and multifarious a predicament as a human being can face in our time, and in addressing that situation I would not want to bury the many stories in a single narrative. This claim has become a postmodernist mannerism: but it strikes me as, in fact, also a very old and sane piece of wisdom. Wittgenstein used to quote Bishop Butler's remark that "everything is what it is and not another thing." There is a piece of Akan wordplay with the same moral "Esono ɛsono, na ɛsono sosono," . . . which being translated reads "The elephant is one thing and the worm another."

One final plea: a collection of essays of this sort, which is both interdisciplinary (ranging over biology, philosophy, literary criticism and theory, sociology, anthropology, and political and intellectual history) and intercultural (discussing African, American, and European ideas), is bound to spend some of its time telling each of its readers something that he or she already knows. Whatever your training and wherever you live, gentle reader, imagine your fellow readers and their areas of knowledge and ignorance before you ask why I have explained what does not need explaining to *you*. When you find me ignoring what you judge important, or getting wrong what you have gotten right, remember that no one in our day can cover all these areas with equal competence and that that does not make trying any less worthwhile, and recall, above all, that these are, as Bacon (no mean essayist himself) said, "but essaies—that is dispersed Meditations."

Kumasi, Asante   K. A. A.
July 1991

Acknowledgments

I have learned much on the topics discussed in this book over many years from long—though, sadly, infrequent—conversations with Kwasi Wiredu, Kwame Gyekye, and Robin Horton, and, more recently, with Abiola Irele and Valentin Mudimbe, as well as from reading their works; and from talking to my parents, Joe and Peggy Appiah, and my sisters Ama, Adwoa, and Abena.

I am very grateful, too, to Ali Mazrui, Chris Miller, Dick Bjornson, and Kwasi Wiredu for reading the manuscript at a late stage and for the useful suggestions they made. Numerous more specific debts are acknowledged in the notes.

But my main debts are to Henry Louis Gates, Jr.—''Skip''—my fellow-student at Cambridge, my colleague at Yale and Cornell and Duke, my friend throughout; and to Henry Finder, who has listened to and argued with me every step of the way these last few years, and who must now feel he knows my arguments as well as—perhaps better than—I do myself. Skip provided the occasion for my first thoughts on many of these topics, both through our ongoing conversation—now a decade and a half long—on questions about Africa and Afro-America, and by demanding contributions to three collections he has edited. Henry has joined this conversation for the last few years, broadening its scope. Without the two Henrys this would have been a very different book; in fact, without them, I doubt I would have ventured to write a book on these subjects at all.

I began constructing an ancestor of this book at the Cornell Society for the Humanities in 1985. I finished it in the extremely congenial surroundings of the National Humanities Center as an Andrew W. Mellon Fellow: I am delighted to acknowledge and give thanks for the support of the Society, the Center, and the Mellon Foundation. I am grateful, too, to many of my fellow Fellows in both places—especially Wole Soyinka and Gayatri Spivak at Cornell—for stimulation and encouragement they did not know they were providing; to the two Directors, Jonathan Culler and Bob Connor; and to the staffs of both institutions who remained thoroughly congenial while eliminating almost all our material worries.

Contents

In My Father's House

ONE

The Invention
of Africa

"Africa for the Africans!" I cried. . . . "A free and independent state in Africa. We want to be able to govern ourselves in this country of ours without outside interference."[1]
KWAME NKRUMAH

On 26 July 1860, Alexander Crummell, African-American by birth, Liberian by adoption, an Episcopalian priest with a University of Cambridge education, addressed the citizens of Maryland county, Cape Palmas. Though Liberia was not to be recognized by the United States for another two years, the occasion was, by Crummell's reckoning, the thirteenth anniversary of her independence. So it is particularly striking that his title was "The English Language in Liberia" and his theme that the Africans "exiled" in slavery to the New World had been given by divine providence "at least this one item of compensation, namely, the possession of the Anglo-Saxon tongue."[2] Crummell, who is widely regarded as one of the fathers of African nationalism, had not the slightest doubt that English was a language superior to the "various tongues and dialects" of the indigenous African populations; superior in its euphony, its conceptual resources, and its capacity to express the "supernal truths" of Christianity. Now, over a century later, more than half of the population of black Africa lives in countries where English is an official language, and the same providence has decreed that almost all the rest of Africa should be governed in French or Arabic or Portuguese.

Perhaps the Reverend Crummell would have been pleased with this news, but he would have little cause to be sanguine. For—with few exceptions outside the Arabic-speaking countries of North Africa—the language of government is the first language of a very few and is securely possessed by only a small proportion of the population; in most of the anglophone states even the educated elites learned at least one of the hundreds of indigenous languages as well as—and almost always before—English. In francophone Africa there are now elites, many of whom speak French better than any other language, and who speak a variety of French particularly close in grammar, if not always in accent, to the language of metropolitan France. But even here, French is not confidently possessed by anything close to a majority.

These differences between francophone and anglophone states derive, of course, from differences between French and British colonial policy. For, though the picture is a good deal too complex for convenient summary, it is broadly true that the French

3

colonial policy was one of assimilation—of turning "savage" Africans into "evolved" black Frenchmen and women—while British colonial policy was a good deal less interested in making the black Anglo-Saxons of Crummell's vision.

Yet despite these differences, both francophone and anglophone elites not only use the colonial languages as the medium of government but know and often admire the literature of their ex-colonizers, and have chosen to make a modern African literature in European languages. Even after a brutal colonial history and nearly two decades of sustained armed resistance, the decolonization in the midseventies of Portuguese Africa left a lusophone elite writing African laws and literature in Portuguese.

This is not to deny that there are strong living traditions of oral culture—religious, mythological, poetic, and narrative—in most of the "traditional" languages of sub-Saharan Africa, or to ignore the importance of a few written traditional languages. But to find their way out of their own community, and acquire national, let alone international, recognition, most traditional languages—the obvious exception being Swahili—have to be translated. Few black African states have the privilege of corresponding to a single traditional linguistic community. And for this reason alone, most of the writers who have sought to create a national tradition, transcending the ethnic divisions of Africa's new states, have had to write in European languages or risk being seen as particularists, identifying with old rather than new loyalties. (An interesting exception is Somalia, whose people have the same language and traditions but managed, nevertheless, to spend a decade after independence in which their official languages were English, Italian, and Arabic.)[3]

These facts are reflected in many moments; let me offer just two: one, when the decision of the Kenyan writer Ngugi wa Thiong'o to write in his mother tongue, Gikuyu, led many even within his nation to see him—wrongly, in my view—as a sort of Gikuyu imperialist (and that is no trivial issue in the context of interethnic relations in Kenya); the other, when the old "Haute Volta" found an "authentic" name by fashioning itself as "Burkina Faso," taking words from two of the nation's languages—while continuing, of course, to conduct much of its official business in French. In a sense we have used Europe's languages because in the task of nation building we could not afford politically to use each other's.

It should be said that there are other more or less honorable reasons for the extraordinary persistence of the colonial languages. We cannot ignore, for example, on the honorable side, the practical difficulties of developing a modern educational system in a language in which none of the manuals and textbooks have been written; nor should we forget, in the debit column, the less noble possibility that these foreign languages, whose possession had marked the colonial elite, became too precious as marks of status to be given up by the class that inherited the colonial state. Together such disparate forces have conspired to ensure that the most important body of writing in sub-Saharan Africa even after independence continues to be in English, French, and Portuguese. For many of its most important cultural purposes, most African intellectuals, south of the Sahara, are what we can call "europhone."

This linguistic situation is of most importance in the cultural lives of African intellectuals. It is, of course, of immense consequence to the citizens of African states generally that their ruling elites are advised by and in many cases constituted of europhone intellectuals. But a concern with the relations of "traditional" and "modern" conceptual worlds, with the integration of inherited modes of understanding and newly acquired theories, concepts, and beliefs, is bound to be of especial importance in the lives of those of us who think and write about the future of Africa in terms that are largely borrowed from elsewhere. We may acknowledge that the truth is the property of no culture, that we should take the truths we need wherever we find them. But for truths to become the basis of national policy and, more widely, of national life, they must be believed, and whether or not whatever new truths we take from the West *will* be believed depends in large measure on how we are able to manage the relations between our conceptual heritage and the ideas that rush at us from worlds elsewhere. Crummell's peroration is most easily available to us in a collection of his writings first published in 1862 and entitled *The Future of Africa*. It is a mark of the success of a picture of the world that he shared, that few of the readers of this book in the last hundred years—few, that is, of the Europeans, Americans, and Africans equipped with the English to read it—will have found anything odd in this title, its author's particular interest in Africa's future, or of his claim to speak for a continent. It is a picture that Crummell learned in America and confirmed in England; though it would have astonished most of the "native" population of Liberia, this picture has become in our century the common property of much of humankind. And at its root is an understanding of the world that we will do well to examine, to question, perhaps, in the end, to reject.

At the core of Crummell's vision is a single guiding concept: race. Crummell's "Africa" is the motherland of the Negro race, and his right to act in it, to speak for it, to plot its future, derived—in his conception—from the fact that he too was a Negro. More than this, Crummell held that there was a common destiny for the people of Africa—by which we are always to understand the black people[4]—not because they shared a common ecology, nor because they had a common historical experience or faced a common threat from imperial Europe, but because they belonged to this one race. What made Africa one for him was that it was the home of the Negro, as England was the home of the Anglo-Saxon, or Germany the home of the Teuton. Crummell was one of the first people to speak *as* a Negro in Africa, and his writings effectively inaugurated the discourse of Pan-Africanism.

Ethnocentrism, however much it distresses us, can no longer surprise us. We can trace its ugly path through Africa's own recent history. Still, it *is,* at least initially, surprising that even those African-Americans like Crummell, who initiated the nationalist discourse *on* Africa in Africa, inherited a set of conceptual blinders that made them unable to see virtue in Africa, even though they needed Africa, above all else, as a source of validation. Since they conceived of the African in racial terms, their low opinion of Africa was not easily distinguished from a low opinion of the Negro, and they left us, through the linking of race and Pan-Africanism, with a burdensome legacy.

The centrality of race in the history of African nationalism is both widely assumed and often ignored. There were many colonial students from British Africa gathered in London in the years after the Second World War—a war in which many Africans died in the name of liberty—and their common search for political independence from a single metropolitan state naturally brought them together. They were brought together too by the fact that the British—those who helped as well as those who hindered—saw them all as Africans, first of all. But they were able to articulate a common vision of postcolonial Africa through a discourse inherited from prewar Pan-Africanism, and that discourse was the product, largely, of black citizens of the New World.

Since what bound those African-American and Afro-Caribbean Pan-Africanists together was the partially African ancestry they shared, and since that ancestry mattered in the New World through its various folk theories of race, a racial understanding of their solidarity was, perhaps, an inevitable development; this was reinforced by the fact that a few crucial figures—Nkrumah among them—had traveled in the opposite direction to Crummell, seeking education in the black colleges of the United States. The tradition on which the francophone intellectuals of the postwar era drew, whether articulated by Aimé Césaire, from the New World, or Léopold Senghor from the Old, shared the European and American view of race. Like Pan-Africanism, negritude begins with the assumption of the racial solidarity of the Negro.

In the prewar era, colonial Africans experienced European racism to radically different degrees in differing colonial conditions, and had correspondingly different degrees of preoccupation with the issue. But with the reality of Nazi racism open to plain view—a reality that still exhausts the resources of our language—it was easy in the immediate postwar era for anyone to see the potentialities for evil of race as an organizing principle of political solidarity. What was hard to see was the possibility of giving up race as a notion altogether. Could anything be more real than Jewishness in a world where to be Jewish meant the threat of the death camp? In a world where being a Jew had come to have a terrible—racial—meaning for everyone, racism, it seemed, could be countered only by accepting the categories of race. For the postwar Pan-Africanists the political problem was what to do about the situation of the Negro. Those who went home to create postcolonial Africa did not need to discuss or analyze race. It was the notion that had bound them together in the first place. The lesson the Africans drew from the Nazis—indeed from the Second World War as a whole—was not the danger of racism but the falsehood of the opposition between a humane European "modernity" and the "barbarism" of the nonwhite world. We had known that European colonialism could lay waste African lives with a careless ease; now we knew that white people could take the murderous tools of modernity and apply them to each other.

What race meant to the new Africans affectively, however, was not, on the whole, what it meant to educated blacks in the New World. For many African-Americans, raised in a segregated American society and exposed to the crudest forms of discrimination, social intercourse with white people was painful and uneasy. Many of the Africans, on the other hand (my father among them) took back to their homes European wives and warm memories of European friends; few of them, even from the "settler" cultures of East and southern Africa, seem to have been committed to ideas of racial separation or to doctrines of racial hatred. Since they came from cultures where black people were in the majority and where lives continued to be largely controlled by indigenous moral and cognitive conceptions, they had no reason to believe that they were inferior to white people and they had, correspondingly, less reason to resent them.

This fact is of crucial importance in understanding the psychology of postcolonial Africa. For though this claim, will, I think, be easily accepted by most of those who experienced, as I did, an African upbringing in British Africa in the later twentieth century, it will seem unobvious to outside observers, largely, I believe, on the basis of one important source of misunderstanding.

It will seem to most European and American outsiders that nothing could be a more obvious basis for resentment than the experience of a colonized people forced to accept the swaggering presence of the colonizer. It will seem obvious, because a comparison will be assumed with the situation of New World blacks.

My own sense of that situation came first, I think, from reading the copy of Fernando Henriquez's *Family and Color in Jamaica* that George Padmore, the West Indian Pan-Africanist, gave my parents as a wedding present. And one cannot read Eldridge Cleaver's *Soul on Ice,* for example, without gathering a powerful sense of what it must be to belong to stigmatized subculture, to live in a world in which everything from your body to your language is defined by the "mainstream" as inferior. But to read the situation of those colonial subjects who grew to adulthood before the 1950s in this way is to make an assumption that Wole Soyinka has identified in a passage I shall discuss in Chapter 4—the assumption of the "potential equality *in every given situation* of the alien culture and the indigenous, on the actual soil of the latter."[5] And what undercuts this assumption is the fact that the experience of the vast majority of these citizens of Europe's African colonies was one of an essentially shallow penetration by the colonizer.

If we read Soyinka's own *Aké,* a childhood autobiography of an upbringing in prewar colonial Nigeria—or the more explicitly fictionalized narratives of his countryman, Chinua Achebe—we shall be powerfully informed of the ways in which even those children who were extracted from the traditional culture of their parents and grandparents and thrust into the colonial school were nevertheless fully enmeshed in a primary experience of their own traditions. The same clear sense shines through the romanticizing haze of Camara Laye's *L'Enfant noir.* To insist in these circumstances on the alienation of (Western-)educated colonials, on their incapacity to appreciate and value their own traditions, is to risk mistaking both the power of this primary experience and the vigor of many forms of cultural resistance to colonialism. A sense that the colonizers overrate the extent of their cultural penetration is consistent with anger or hatred or a longing for freedom, but it does not entail the failures of self-confidence that lead to alienation.

When I come, in Chapter 3, to discuss colonial and postcolonial *intellectuals,* I shall have more to say about the small class of educated people whose alienation is a real phenomenon (one powerfully characterized by Frantz Fanon). But the fact is that most of us who were raised during and for some time after the colonial era are sharply aware of the ways in which the colonizers were never as fully in control as our elders allowed them to appear. We all experienced the persistent power of our own cognitive and moral traditions: in religion, in such social occasions as the funeral, in our experience of music, in our practice of the dance, and, of course, in the intimacy of family life. Colonial authority sought to stigmatize our traditional religious beliefs, and we conspired in this fiction by concealing our disregard for much of European Christianity in those "syncretisms" I shall be discussing later; the colonial state established a legal system whose patent lack of correspondence with the values of the colonized threatened not those values but the colonial legal system.

An anecdote may illustrate this claim. In the midseventies I was driving with a (white) English friend in the Ghanaian city of Takoradi. My friend was at the wheel. We stopped at a road junction behind a large timber truck, and the driver, who failed to see us in his rearview mirror, backed toward us. My English friend sounded our horn, but the driver went on backing—until he hit and broke our windscreen. It was a crowded area near the docks, and there were many witnesses. It was plain enough whose fault—in the sense of the legal system—the accident was. Yet none of the witnesses was willing to support our version of the story.

In other settings, one might have assumed that this was a reflection of racial solidarity. But what these witnesses said made it plain that their judgment had a different basis, one whose nearest Euro-American counterpart would have been not race but class solidarity. For them the issue was one between a person (a foreigner, and therefore someone with money) who could afford to pay for his own wind-screen, and another person (the truck driver) who was an employee who would lose his job and his livelihood if he were found guilty of a traffic infraction. The formal system of state authority was likely, in the view of our witnesses, to penalize the truck driver—who had done nothing more serious than to damage a piece of property—in a way they judged out of all proportion to his offense. And so, without coordination, they "conspired" to undercut the formal legal system.[6]

This legal system was Ghana's—the system of an independent postcolonial national state. But it was essentially the colonial system, with its British-imposed norms. In the ten years following this episode, the "Peoples' Revolution" of Jerry Rawlings attempted to dismantle much of this system, with a great deal of popular support; it did so, I believe, precisely because it was clear that that system failed utterly to reflect popular norms.

I do not, myself, believe that the notions of right and responsibility implicit in the way in which the Ghanaian legal system of the midseventies, operating under ideal conditions, would have settled the issue, would have been wrong. But that is only to mark my distance from the moral conceptions operative in the streets of Takoradi. (Still, I am *not* so far removed from the reality of the Ghanaian legal system—or legal systems in general—as to believe that there was any guarantee that the case would be formally adjudicated by ideal standards.)

Legal systems—such as those of France or Britain or the United States—that have evolved in response to a changing local political morality are undergirded by a kind of popular consensus that has been arrived at through a long history of mutual accommodation between legal practice and popular norm. Anyone who has wit-nessed such an act of spontaneous and uncomplicated opposition to a state whose operations are *not* grounded in such a consensus can easily imagine how colonial subjects were able to fashion similar acts of resistance.

And so, to repeat my point, it was natural that those colonials who returned to Africa after the Second World War were, by and large, less alienated than many

Europeans and Americans have assumed. It is plain that such figures as Kenyatta and Nkrumah, Kaunda and Nyerere, experienced Western culture fully only when they visited Europe and America; each lived at home comfortably rooted in the traditions of his *ethnos*.

Indeed, to speak of "resistance" in this phase of colonial culture is already to overstate the ways in which the colonial state was invasive. My anecdote comes from urban Takoradi in the late twentieth century; in matters, such as family life, where the state was unable effectively to intervene; in rural areas (at least where there were no plantations); among the indigenous traditional ruling classes and among those who escaped substantial exposure to colonial education even in the cities; before the increasingly deeper penetrations of an alien modernity, the formal colonial system could, for most purposes, be ignored.

A proper comparison in the New World is not with the urban experience of *Soul on Ice* but with the world that Zora Neale Hurston records and reflects, both in her more ethnographic writings and in her brilliant novel, *Their Eyes Were Watching God*—a black world on which the white American world impinged in ways that were culturally marginal even though formally politically overwhelming. There are many moments of cultural autonomy in black America that achieve, against far greater ideological odds than ever faced the majority of Africa's colonized peoples, an equally resilient sense of their own worth.

What the postwar generation of British Africans took from their time in Europe, therefore, was not a resentment of "white" culture. What they took, instead, from their shared experience was a sense that they, as Africans, had a great deal in common: they took it for granted, along with everybody else, that this common feeling was connected with their shared "African-ness," and they largely accepted the European view that this meant their shared race.

For the citizens of French Africa, a different situation led to the same results. For the French *evolués*, of whom Léopold Senghor is the epitome, there would be no question of a cultural explanation of their difference from Europe: for culturally, as *assimilation* required, they were bound to believe that, whatever else they might be also, they were at least French. It is a tale that is worth the frequent retelling it has borne that African children in the French Empire read textbooks that spoke of the Gauls as "nos ancêtres."

Of course, the claim of a Senegalese child to a descent from Astérix was bound to be conceived figuratively; and, as Camara Laye showed in *L'Enfant noir*, colonial pedagogy failed as notably in francophone as in anglophone Africa fully to deracinate its objects. In whatever sense the Gauls were their ancestors, they knew they were— and were expected to remain—"different." To account for this difference, they, too, were thrown back on theories of race.

And so it is that Senghor, first president of Senegal, architect of its independence, exponent of negritude, is also a member of the Académie Française, a distinguished French poet, a former member of the French National Assembly. So it is that this most cultivated of Frenchmen (culturally, if not juridically, speaking) is also, in the eyes of millions of Frenchmen and francophone Africans—as, of course, he is in his own—a spokesman for the Negro race.

For the generation that theorized the decolonization of Africa, then, "race" was a central organizing principle. And, since these Africans largely inherited their conception of "race" from their New World precursors, we shall understand Pan-Africanism's profound entanglement with that conception best if we look first at how it is handled in the work of the African-American intellectuals who forged the links between race and Pan-Africanism. The tale has often been told in the francophone case—the centrality of race in the archaeology of Négritude can hardly be ignored—but it has its anglophone counterpart.[7]

In Chapter 2, therefore, I examine this issue in the work of W. E. B. Du Bois, and I begin with a discussion of the paper on " The Conservation of Races," which he delivered to the American Negro Academy in the year in which it was founded by Alexander Crummell.

Crummell's use of the term *race* was less theoretically articulated—and thus more representative—than Du Bois's. Nevertheless, he did offer a definition—many years after his celebration of the English language in Liberia—that will be found echoed later in Du Bois: "a RACE, i.e. a compact, homogeneous population of one blood ancestry and lineage."[8] Like Du Bois he believed that

> races have their individuality. That individuality is subject at all times to all the laws of race-life. That race-life, all over the globe, shows an invariable proclivity, and in every instance, to integration of blood and permanence of essence.[9]

Or, as he says, elsewhere,

> there are certain tendencies, seen for over 200 years in our population, which indicate settled, determinate proclivities, and which show, if I mistake not, the destiny of races. . . . the principle of race is one of the most persistent things in the constitution of man.[10]

There is no reason to believe that Crummell would ever explicitly have endorsed any very specific view about the biological character of racial difference; or wondered, as Du Bois came to, whether there was a "permanence of essence." Though he always assumes that there are races, and that membership in a race entails the possession of certain traits and dispositions, his notion of *race*—like that of most of the later Pan-Africanists—is not so much thought as felt. It is difficult, therefore, to establish some of the distinctions we need when we ask ourselves what is bound to seem an important question: namely, whether, and in what sense, the Pan-Africanist movement, and Crummell as its epitome, should be called "racist."

It is as well to be clear at the start that, however inchoate the form of race theory that Crummell adopted, it represents something that was new in the nineteenth century. That the specific form race theory took was new does not, of course, mean that it had no historical antecedents, but it is important to understanding what was distinctive in the racial theory of Crummell that we remember both its continuities with and its distance from its forbears. Almost as far back as the earliest human writings, after all, we can find more-or-less well-articulated views about the differences between "our own kind" and the people of other cultures. These doctrines, like modern theories of race, have often placed a central emphasis on physical appearance in defining the

"Other," and on common ancestry in explaining why groups of people display differences in their attitudes and aptitudes.

If we call any group of human beings of common descent living together in some sort of association, however loosely structured, a "people," we can say that every human culture that was aware of other peoples seems to have had views about what accounted for the differences—in appearance, in customs, in language—between them. This is certainly true of the two main ancient traditions to which Euro-American thinkers in general (like Crummell, in particular) have looked back—those of the classical Greeks and the ancient Hebrews. Thus, we find Hippocrates in the fifth century B.C.E. in Greece seeking to explain the (supposed) superiority of his own people to the peoples of (western) Asia by arguing that the barren soils of Greece had forced the Greeks to become tougher and more independent. Such a view attributes the characteristics of a people to their environment, leaving open the possibility that their descendants could change, if they moved to new conditions.

While the general opinion in Greece in the few centuries on either side of the beginning of the common era appears to have been that both the black "Ethiopians" to the south and the blonde "Scythians" to the north were inferior to the Hellenes, there was no general assumption that this inferiority was incorrigible. Educated Greeks, after all, knew that in both the *Iliad* and the *Odyssey* Homer had described Zeus and other Olympians feasting with the "Ethiopians," who offered pious hecatombs of sheep and oxen to the immortals, and there are arguments in the works of the pre-Socratic Sophists to the effect that it is individual character and not skin color that determines a person's worth.[11]

The Greeks identified peoples by their characteristic appearance, both in such biological features as skin, eye, and hair color, and in such cultural matters as hairstyles, the cut of beards, and modes of dress. And while they had a low opinion of most non-Greek cultures—they called foreigners "barbarians," folk etymology had it, because their speech sounded like a continuous "bar bar . . ."—they respected many individuals of different appearance (and, in particular, skin color) and as-sumed, for example, that they had acquired a good deal in their culture from the darker-skinned people of Egypt. Once the Romans captured control of the Mediterra-nean world, and inherited Greek culture, much the same view can be found in their authors, a pattern that continues beyond the climax of the Roman Empire into the period of imperial decline.

In the Old Testament, on the other hand, as we might expect, what is thought to be distinctive about peoples is not so much appearance and custom as their relationship, through a common ancestor, to God. So, in *Genesis,* Jehovah says to Abraham: "Go your way out of your country and from your relatives and from the house of your father and to the country that I shall show you; and I shall make a great people of you and I will make your name great" (Gen. 12:1–2). And from this founding moment—this covenant between Abraham and Jehovah—the descendants of Abraham have a special place in history. It is, of course, Abraham's grandson, Jacob who takes the name of Israel, and his descendants thus become the "people of Israel."

The Old Testament is full of names of peoples. Some of them are still familiar—Syrians, Philistines, and Persians; some of them are less so—Canaanites, Hittites, and Medes. Many of these groups are accounted for in the genealogies of the peoples of the earth and are explicitly seen as descending ultimately not only from the first human couple, Adam and Eve, but more particularly from Noah's three sons. Just as the Israelites are "sons of Shem," the children of Ham and of Japheth account for the rest of the human "family."

But while these different peoples are taken to have different specific characteristics and ancestries, the fundamentally theocentric perspective of the Old Testament requires that what *essentially* differentiates them all from the Hebrews is that they do not have the special relationship to Jehovah of the children, the descendants, of Israel. There is very little hint that the early Jewish writers developed any theories about the relative importance of the biological and the cultural inheritances by which God made these different peoples distinct. Indeed, in the theocentric framework it is God's covenant that matters and the very distinction between environmental and inherited characteristics is anachronistic.

When the prophet Jeremiah asks, "Can an Ethiopian change his skin? Or a leopard its spots?" (Jer. 13:23), the suggestion that the inherited dark skin of Africans was something they could not change did not necessarily imply that the "nature" of Africans was in other ways unchangeable, that they inevitably inherited special moral or intellectual traits along with their skin color.

If there is a normal way that the Bible explains the distinctive characters of peoples, it is by telling a story in which an ancestor is blessed or cursed. This way of thinking is operative in the New Testament also and became, ironically, the basis of later arguments in Christian Europe (at the beginning of the eleventh century of the common era) for anti-Semitism. For when "the Jews" in the Gospel of Matthew choose Barabbas over Christ in response to Pilate's offer to release one or other of them they reply: "His blood be upon us and upon our children" (Matt. 27:25). In effect, "the Jews" here curse themselves.

The Greeks, too, plainly had notions about some clans having the moral characteristics they have by virtue of blessings and curses on their ancestors. *Oedipus the King,* after all, is driven to his fate because of a curse on his family for which he himself is hardly responsible, a curse that continued into the next generation in *Seven against Thebes.* But even here it is never a question of the curse operating by making the whole lineage *wicked,* or by otherwise changing its fundamental nature. Fate operates on people because of their ancestry, once their lineage is cursed. And that, so far as explanations go, is more or less the end of the matter.

I am insisting on the fact that the Greek conception of cultural and historical differences between peoples was essentially environmental and the Jewish conception was essentially a matter of the theological consequences of covenants with (or curses on) ancestors. And the reason should be obvious if we think for a moment about the passages from Crummell quoted earlier: neither the environmentalism of the Greeks nor the theocentric Hebrew understanding of the significance of being one people is an idea that we should naturally apply in understanding Crummell's use of the idea of race. To the extent that we think of Crummell's racial ideology as modern, as involving ideas that *we* understand, we will suppose that he believed the "settled, determinate proclivities," reflect a race's *inherited* capacities.

Indeed, even if Crummell thought (as he surely did) that it was part of God's plan for the world that the heirs to the Anglo-Saxons should rule it, he would *not* have thought of this divine mission as granted them because some ancestor had pleased God and been blessed with an hereditary reward (or, for that matter, because the ancestors of the "darker races" had offended God and been cursed). For by Crummell's day a distinctively modern understanding of what it was to be a people— an understanding in terms of our modern notion of race—was beginning to be forged: that notion had at its heart a new scientific conception of biological heredity, even as it carried on some of the roles played in Greek and Jewish thought by the idea of a people. But it was also interwoven with a new understanding of a people as a nation and of the role of culture—and, crucially (as we shall see in Chapter 3), of literature— in the life of nations.

If we are to answer the question whether Crummell was racist, therefore, we must first seek out the distinctive content of nineteenth-century racism. And we shall immediately see that there are many distinct doctrines that compete for the term *racism,* of which I shall try to articulate what I take to be the crucial three. (So I shall be using the words *racism* and *racialism* with the meanings I stipulate: in some dialects of English they are synonyms, and in most dialects their definition is less than precise.) The first doctrine is the view—which I shall call *racialism*—that there are heritable characteristics, possessed by members of our species, which allow us to divide them into a small set of races, in such a way that all the members of these races share certain traits and tendencies with each other that they do not share with members of any other race. These traits and tendencies characteristic of a race constitute, on the racialist view, a sort of racial essence; it is part of the content of racialism that the essential heritable characteristics of the "Races of Man" account for more than the visible morphological characteristics—skin color, hair type, facial features—on the basis of which we make our informal classifications. Racialism is at the heart of nineteenth-century attempts to develop a science of racial difference, but it appears to have been believed by others—like Hegel, before then, and Crummell and many Africans since—who have had no interest in developing scientific theories.

Racialism is not, in itself, a doctrine that must be dangerous, even if the racial essence is thought to entail moral and intellectual dispositions. Provided positive moral qualities are distributed across the races, each can be respected, can have its "separate but equal" place. Unlike most Western-educated people, I believe—and I shall argue in the essay on Du Bois—that racialism is false, but by itself, it seems to be a cognitive rather than a moral problem. The issue is how the world is, not how we would want it to be.

Racialism is, however, a presupposition of other doctrines that have been called "racism," and these other doctrines have been, in the last few centuries, the basis of a great deal of human suffering and the source of a great deal of moral error.

One such doctrine we might call *extrinsic racism:* extrinsic racists make moral distinctions between members of different races because they believe that the racial essence entails certain morally relevant qualities. The basis for the extrinsic racists' discrimination between people is their belief that members of different races differ in respects that *warrant* the differential treatment—respects, like honesty or courage or intelligence, that are uncontroversially held (at least in most contemporary cultures) to be acceptable as a basis for treating people differently. Evidence that there are no such differences in morally relevant characteristics—that Negroes do not necessarily lack intellectual capacities, that Jews are not especially avaricious—should thus lead people out of their racism if it is purely extrinsic. As we know, such evidence often fails to change an extrinsic racist's attitudes substantially, for some of the extrinsic racist's best friends have always been Jewish. But at this point—if the racist is sincere—what we have is no longer a false doctrine but a cognitive incapacity.

This cognitive incapacity is not, of course, a rare one. Many of us are unable to give up beliefs that play a part in justifying the special advantages we gain from our positions in the social order. Many people who express extrinsic racist beliefs—many white South Africans, for example—are beneficiaries of social orders that deliver advantages to them in virtue of their "race," so that their disinclination to accept evidence that would deprive them of a justification for those advantages is just an instance of this general phenomenon. So, too, evidence that access to higher education is as largely determined by the quality of our earlier educations as by our own innate talents, does not, on the whole, undermine the confidence of college entrants from private schools in England or the United States or Ghana. Many of them continue to believe in the face of this evidence that their acceptance at "good" universities shows them to be better intellectually endowed (and not just better prepared) than those who are rejected. It is facts such as these that give sense to the notion of false consciousness, the idea that an ideology can protect us from facing up to facts that would threaten our position.

My business here is not with the psychological or (perhaps more importantly) the social processes by which these defenses operate, but it is important, I think, to see the refusal of some extrinsic racists to accept evidence against their beliefs as an instance of a widespread phenomenon in human affairs. It is a plain fact, to which theories of ideology must address themselves, that our species is prone both morally and intellectually to partiality in judgment. An inability to change your mind in the face of evidence is a cognitive incapacity; it is one that all of us surely suffer from in some areas of belief. But it is not, as some have held, a tendency that we are powerless to alter. And it may help to shake the convictions of those whose incapacity derives from this sort of ideological defense if we show them how their reaction fits into this general pattern. It is, indeed, because it generally *does* fit this pattern that we call such views *racism*—the suffix *-ism* indicating that what we have in mind is not simply a theory but an ideology. It would be odd to call someone brought up in a remote corner of the world with false and demeaning views about white people a rac*ist* if she would give up these beliefs quite easily in the face of evidence.

I said that the *sincere* extrinsic racist may suffer from a cognitive incapacity. But some who espouse extrinsic racist doctrines are simply insincere *intrinsic* racists. For *intrinsic racists,* on my definition, are people who differentiate morally between members of different races, because they believe that each race has a different moral status, quite independent of the moral characteristics entailed by its racial essence. Just as, for example, many people assume that the bare fact that they are biologically related to another person—a brother, an aunt, a cousin—gives them a moral interest in that person, so an intrinsic racist holds that the bare fact of being of the same race is a reason for preferring one person to another. For an intrinsic racist, no amount of evidence that a member of another race is capable of great moral, intellectual, or cultural achievements, or has characteristics that, in members of one's own race, would make them admirable or attractive, offers any ground for treating that person as she would treat similarly endowed members of her own race. Just so, some sexists are "intrinsic sexists," holding that the bare fact that someone is a woman (or man) is a reason for treating her (or him) in certain ways.

There are some who will want to object already that my discussion of the content of racist moral and factual beliefs underplays something absolutely crucial to the character of the psychological and sociological reality of racism—something that I touched on when I mentioned that extrinsic racist utterances are often made by people who suffer from what I called a "cognitive incapacity." It will be as well to state here explicitly, as a result, that most real-live contemporary racists exhibit a systematically distorted rationality—precisely the kind of systematically distorted rationality that we often recognize in ideology. And it is a distortion that is especially striking in the cognitive domain: extrinsic racists, however intelligent or otherwise well informed, often fail to treat evidence against the theoretical propositions of extrinsic racism dispassionately. Like extrinsic racism, intrinsic racism can also often be seen as ideological, but, since scientific evidence is not going to settle the issue, a failure to see that it is wrong represents a *cognitive* incapacity only according to certain controversial views about the nature of morality.[12] What makes intrinsic racism similarly ideological is not so much the failure of inductive or deductive rationality that is so striking in, say, official Afrikaner theory, but the connection that it, like extrinsic racism, has with the interests—real or perceived—of the dominant group.

There are interesting possibilities for complicating the distinctions I have drawn: some racists, for example, claim, like Crummell, that they discriminate between people because they believe that God requires them to do so. Is this an extrinsic racism, predicated upon the combination of God's being an intrinsic racist and the belief that it is right to do what God wills? Or is it intrinsic racism, because it is based on the belief that God requires these discriminations because they are right? (This distinction has interesting parallels with the *Euthyphro*'s question: is an act pious because the gods love it, or do they love it because it is pious?) Nevertheless, I believe that the contrast between racialism and racism and the identification of two potentially overlapping kinds of racism provide us with the skeleton of an anatomy of racial attitudes. With these analytical tools in hand, we can address, finally, the question of Alexander Crummell's racism.

Certainly, Crummell was a racialist (in my sense), and he was also (again, in my sense) a racist. But it was not always clear whether his racism was extrinsic or intrinsic. Despite the fact that he had such low opinions and such high hopes of the Negro, however, we may suspect that the racism that underlay his Pan-Africanism would, if articulated, have been fundamentally intrinsic, and would therefore have survived the discovery that what he believed about the connection between race and moral capacity was false. It is true that he says in discussing "The Race Problem in America" that "it would take generations upon generations to make the American people homogeneous in blood and essential qualities," implying, some might think, that it is the facts of racial difference—the "essential" moral difference, the difference of "qualities"—between the members of the different races that require a different moral response.[13] But all this claim commits him to by itself is racialism: to the present existence of racial differences. And in other places—as when he is discussing "The Relations and Duties of Free Colored Men in America to Africa"— he speaks of the demands that Africa makes on black people everywhere as "a natural call,"[14] as a "grand and noble work laid out in the Divine Providence,"[15] as if the different moral status of the various races derives not from their different moral characters but from their being assigned different tasks by God. On this view, there could be an allocation of morally different tasks without any special difference in moral or cognitive capacity.

Crummell's model here, like that of most nineteenth-century black nationalists, was, of course, the biblical history of the Jews: Jehovah chose the children of Israel and made a covenant with them as his people and that was what gave them a special moral role in history. But, as I argued earlier, he did not give them any special biological or intellectual equipment for their special task.

If it is not always clear whether Crummell's racism was intrinsic or extrinsic, there is certainly no reason why we should expect to be able to settle the question. Since the issue probably never occurred to him in these terms, we cannot suppose that he must have had an answer. In fact, given the definition of the terms I offered, there is nothing barring someone from being both an intrinsic and an extrinsic racist, holding both that the bare fact of race provides a basis for treating members of your own race differently from others and that there are morally relevant characteristics that are differentially distributed among the races. Indeed, for reasons I shall discuss in a moment, *most* intrinsic racists are likely to express extrinsic racist beliefs, so that we should not be surprised that Crummell seems, in fact, to have been committed to both forms of racism.

I mentioned earlier the powerful impact that Nazi racism had on educated Africans in Europe after the war; since then our own continent has been continually reminded by the political development of apartheid in the Republic of South Africa of the threat that racism poses to human decency. Nobody who lives in Europe or the United States—nobody, at least, but a hermit with no access to the news media— could fail to be aware of these threats either. In these circumstances it no doubt seems politically inopportune, at best, and morally insensitive, at worst, to use the same term—*racism*—to describe the attitudes we find in Crummell and many of his Pan-Africanist heirs. But this natural reaction is based, I believe, on confusions.

What is peculiarly appalling about Nazi racism is not that it presupposed, as all racism does, false (racialist) beliefs; not simply that it involved a moral fault—the failure to extend equality of consideration to our fellow creatures; but that it led to oppression, first, and then to mass slaughter. And though South African racism has not led to killings on the scale of the Holocaust—even if it has both left South Africa judicially executing more (mostly black) people per head of population than most other countries and led to massive differences between the life chances of white and nonwhite South Africans—it *has* led to the systematic oppression and the economic exploitation of people who are not classified as "white," and to the infliction of suffering on citizens of all racial classifications, not least by the police state that is required to maintain that exploitation and oppression.

Part of our resistance, therefore, to calling the racial ideas of Crummell by the same term that we use to describe the attitudes of many Afrikaners surely resides in the fact that Crummell never for a moment contemplated using race as a basis for inflicting harm. Indeed, it seems to me that there is a significant pattern in the rhetoric of modern racism, which means that the discourse of racial solidarity is usually expressed through the language of *intrinsic* racism, while those who have used race as the basis for oppression and hatred have appealed to *extrinsic* racist ideas. This point is important for understanding the character of contemporary Pan-Africanism.

The two major uses of race as a basis for moral solidarity that are most familiar both in Africa and in Europe and America are varieties of Pan-Africanism and Zionism. In each case it is presupposed that a "people," Negroes or Jews, has the basis for a shared political life in their being of a single race. There are varieties of each form of "nationalism" that make the basis lie in shared traditions, but however plausible this may be in the case of Zionism, which has, in Judaism, the religion, a realistic candidate for a common and nonracial focus for nationality, the peoples of Africa have a good deal less culturally in common than is usually assumed. I shall return to this issue in later essays, but let me say here that I believe the central fact is this: what blacks in the West, like secularized Jews, have mostly in common is the fact that they are perceived—both by themselves and by others—as belonging together in the same race, and this common race is used by others as the basis for discriminating against them. ("If you ever forget you're a Jew, a goy will remind you.") The Pan-Africanists responded to their experience of racial discrimination by accepting the racialism it presupposed. Without the background of racial notions, as I shall argue in the second essay, this original intellectual grounding of Pan-Africanism disappears.

Though race is indeed at the heart of the Pan-Africanist's nationalism, however, it seems that it is the fact of a shared race, not the fact of a shared racial character, that provides the basis for solidarity. Where racism is implicated in the basis for national solidarity, it is intrinsic, not extrinsic. It is this that makes the idea of fraternity one that is naturally applied in nationalist discourse. For, as I have already observed, the moral status of close family members is not normally thought of in most cultures as depending on qualities of character: we are supposed to love our brothers and sisters in spite of their faults and not because of their virtues. Crummell, once more a representative figure, takes the metaphor of family and literalizes it in these startling words: "Races, like families, are the organisms and ordinances of God; and race feeling, like family feeling, is of divine origin. The extinction of race feeling is just as possible as the extinction of family feeling. Indeed, a race *is* a family."[16]

It is the assimilation of "race feeling" to "family feeling" that makes intrinsic racism seem so much less objectionable than extrinsic. For this metaphorical identification reflects the fact that, in the modern world (unlike the nineteenth century), intrinsic racism is acknowledged almost exclusively as the basis of feelings of community. So that we can, surely, share a sense of what Crummell's friend and fellow-worker Edward Blyden called "the poetry of politics" that is "the feeling of race," the feeling of "people with whom we are connected."[17] The racism here is the basis of acts of supererogation, the treatment of others better than we otherwise might, better than moral duty demands of us.

This is, I insist, a contingent fact. There is no logical impossibility in the idea of racialists whose moral beliefs lead them to feelings of hatred against other races while leaving no room for love of members of their own. Nevertheless, most racial hatred is in fact expressed through extrinsic racism: most people who have used race as the basis for harm to others have felt the need to see the others as independently morally flawed. It is one thing to espouse fraternity without claiming that your brothers and sisters have any special qualities that deserve recognition, another to espouse hatred of others who have done nothing to deserve it. There is a story told—one of many in a heroic tradition of Jewish humor under duress—of an old Jewish man bullied by a pair of Nazis on the street in Berlin in the 1930s. "Who do you think is responsible for all our problems, Jew?" says one of the bullies. The old man pauses for a moment and replies "Me, I think it is the pretzel makers." "Why the pretzel makers?" says the Nazi and the answer comes back: "Why the Jews?" Any even vaguely objective observer in Germany under the Nazis would have been led to ask this question. But Hitler had a long answer to it—an extended, if absurd, list of accusations against the Jewish "race."

Similarly, many Afrikaners—like many in the American South until recently—have a long list of extrinsic racist answers to the question why blacks should not have full civil rights. Extrinsic racism has usually been the basis for treating people worse than we otherwise might, for giving them less than their humanity entitles them to. But this, too, is a contingent fact. Indeed, Crummell's guarded respect for white people derived from a belief in the superior moral qualities of Anglo-Saxons.

Intrinsic racism is, in my view, a moral error. Even if racialism were correct, the bare fact that someone was of another race would be no reason to treat them worse—or better—than someone of my race. In our public lives, people are owed treatment independently of their biological characters: if they are to be differently treated there must be some morally relevant difference between them. In our private lives, we are morally free to have "aesthetic" preferences between people, but once our treatment of people raises moral issues, we may not make arbitrary distinctions. Using race in itself as a morally relevant distinction strikes most of us as obviously arbitrary. Without associated moral characteristics, why should race provide a better basis than hair color or height or timbre of voice? And if two people share all the properties morally relevant to some action we ought to do, it will be an error—a failure to apply the Kantian injunction to universalize our moral judgments—to use the bare facts of race as the basis for treating them differently. No one should deny that a common ancestry might, in particular cases, account for similarities in moral character. But then it would be the moral similarities that justified the different treatment.

It is presumably because most people—outside the South African Nationalist Party and the Ku Klux Klan—share this sense that intrinsic racism requires arbitrary distinctions that they are largely unwilling to express it in situations that invite moral criticism. But I do not know how I would argue with someone who was willing to announce an intrinsic racism as a basic moral idea.

It might be thought that such a view should be regarded not as an adherence to a (moral) proposition so much as the expression of a taste, analogous, say, to the food prejudice that makes most English people unwilling to eat horse meat and most Westerners unwilling to eat the insect grubs that the !Kung people find so appetizing.

The analogy does at least this much for us, namely, to provide a model of the way that extrinsic racism can be a reflection of an underlying intrinsic prejudice. For, of course, in most cultures food prejudices are rationalized: Americans will say insects are unhygienic, and Asante people that cats must taste horrible. Yet a cooked insect is no more health-threatening than a cooked carrot, and the unpleasant taste of cat meat, far from justifying our prejudice against it, probably derives from that prejudice.

But there the usefulness of the analogy ends. For intrinsic racism, as I have defined it, is not simply a taste for the company of one's "own kind" but a moral doctrine, a doctrine that is supposed to underlie differences in the treatment of people in contexts where moral evaluation is appropriate. And for moral distinctions we cannot accept that "de gustibus non disputandum." We do not need the full apparatus of Kantian ethics to require that morality be constrained by reason.

A proper analogy would be with someone who thought that we could continue to kill cattle for beef, even if cattle exercised all the complex cultural skills of human beings. I think it is obvious that creatures that share our capacity for understanding as well as our capacity for pain should not be treated the way we actually treat cattle; that "intrinsic speciesism" would be as wrong as racism. And the fact that most people think it worse to be cruel to dolphins than to frogs suggests that they may agree with me. The distinction in attitudes surely reflects a belief in the greater richness of the mental life of large mammals. Still, as I say, I do not know how I would *argue* against someone who could not see this; someone who continued to act on the contrary belief might, in the end, simply have to be locked up.

If, as I believe, intrinsic racism is a moral error, and extrinsic racism entails false beliefs, it is by no means obvious that racism is the worst error that our species has made in our time. What was wrong with the Nazi genocide was that it entailed the sadistic murder of innocent millions; that said, it would be perverse to focus too much attention on the fact that the alleged rationale for that murder was "race." Stalin's mass murders, or Pol Pot's, derive little moral advantage from having been largely based on nonracial criteria.

Pan-Africanism inherited Crummell's intrinsic racism. We cannot say it inherited it *from* Crummell, since in his day it was the common intellectual property of the West. We can see Crummell as emblematic of the influence of this racism on black intellectuals, an influence that is profoundly etched in the rhetoric of postwar African nationalism. It is striking how much of Crummell or Blyden we can hear, for example, in Ghana's first prime minister, Kwame Nkrumah, as he reports, in the *Autobiography of Kwame Nkrumah,* a speech made in Liberia in 1952, nearly a century after the speech of Crummell's with which I began:

> I pointed out that it was providence that had preserved the Negroes during their years of trial in exile in the United States of America and the West Indes; that it was the same providence which took care of Moses and the Israelites in Egypt centuries before. "A greater exodus is coming in Africa today," I declared, "and that exodus will be established when there is a united, free and independent West Africa. . . ."
>
> "Africa for the Africans!" I cried. . . . "A free and independent state in Africa. We want to be able to govern ourselves in this country of ours without outside interference."[18]

There is no difficulty in reading this last paragraph from Nkrumah as the epigraph to a discussion of Alexander Crummell. For Nkrumah, as for Crummell, African-Americans who came to Africa (as Du Bois came to Ghana at Nkrumah's invitation) were going back—providentially—to their natural, racial, home.

If we are to escape from racism fully, and from the racialism it presupposes, we must seek other bases for Pan-African solidarity. In Chapter 3—on African literary criticism—I offer a number of suggestions for thinking about modern African writing, suggestions that attempt to elaborate an understanding of the ways in which African writers are formed in shared ways by the colonial and the postcolonial situation; African literature in the metropolitan languages, I shall argue, reflects in many subtle ways the historical encounter between Africa and the West. Then, in Chapter 4, and more fully in Chapter 9, I will argue that there are bases for common action in our shared situation: the Organization of African Unity can survive the demise of the Negro race.

The politics of race that I have described—one that derived from commonplaces of European nationalism—was central to Crummell's ideology. But his nationalism differed from that of his European predecessors and contemporaries in important ways, which emerge if we explore the politics of language with which I began. Crummell's engagement with the issue of the transfer of English to the African Negro runs counter to a strong tradition of European nationalist philosophy. For Herder, prophet of German nationalism and founding philosopher of the modern ideology of nationhood, the spirit of a nation was expressed above all in its language, its *Sprachgeist*. And, since, as Wilson Moses has observed, there is much of Herder in Crummell, we might expect to see Crummell struggling with an attempt to find in the traditional languages of Africa a source of identity.[19] But Crummell's adoption of this Herderian tenet was faced with insuperable obstacles, among them his knowledge of the variety of Africa's languages. By Crummell's day the nation had been fully racialized: granted his assumption that the Negro was a single race, he could not have sought in language the principle of Negro identity, just because there were too many languages. As I shall show in Chapter 3, in discussing African literary criticism, the politics of language has continued to exercise Africans, and there have, of course, been many writers, like Ngugi, who have had a deeper attachment to our mother tongues.

There is no evidence, however, that Crummell ever agonized over his rejection of Africa's many "tongues and dialects," and for this there is, I think, a simple explanation. For Crummell, as "The English Language in Liberia" makes clear, it is not English as the *Sprachgeist* of the Anglo-Saxons that matters; it is English as the vehicle of Christianity and—what he would have seen as much the same thing— civilization and progress.

For Crummell inherited not only the received European conception of race but, as I have said, the received understanding both of the nature of civilization and of the African's lack of it. Crummell's use of the term *civilization* is characteristic of educated Victorian Englishmen or Americans. Sometimes he seems to have in mind only what anthropologists would now call "culture": the body of moral, religious, political, and scientific theory, and the customary practices of a society. In this sense, of course, it would have been proper, even for him, to speak of African civilizations.

But he also uses the term—as we ordinarily use the word *culture*—not descriptively, in this way, but evaluatively; what he valued was the body of true belief and right moral practice that he took to characterize Christianity—or, more precisely, his own form of Protestantism. This double use of the term is, of course, not accidental. For a civilization—in the descriptive sense—would hardly be worthy of the name if it failed to acknowledge the "supernal truths"; our interest in culture, in the descriptive, anthropological sense, derives largely from our sense of its value. Crummell shared with his European and American contemporaries (those of them, at least, who had any view of the matter at all) an essentially negative sense of traditional culture in Africa as anarchic, unprincipled, ignorant, defined by the absence of all the positive traits of civilization as "savage"; and savages hardly have a culture at all. Civilization entailed for Crummell precisely "the clarity of the mind from the dominion of false heathen ideas."[20] Only if there had been in traditional cultures anything Crummell thought worth saving might he have hoped, with Herder, to find it captured in the spirit of the languages of Africa.

It is tremendously important, I think, to insist on how natural Crummell's view was, given his background and education. However much he hoped for Africa, however much he gave it of his life, he could not escape seeing it above all else as heathen and as savage. Every book with any authority he ever read about Africa would have confirmed this judgment. And we can see how inescapable these beliefs were when we reflect that every one of the ideas I have traced in Crummell can also be found in the writings of the same Edward W. Blyden I cited earlier, a man who was, with Africanus Horton (from the Old World) and Martin Robinson Delany (from the New) one of the three contemporaries of Crummell's who could also lay claim to the title of "Father of Pan-Africanism."

Like Crummell, Blyden was a native of the New World and a Liberian by adoption; like Crummell, he was a priest and a founder of the tradition of Pan-Africanism; for a while, they were friends and fellow workers in the beginnings of Liberia's modern system of education. Blyden was a polyglot scholar: his essays include quotations in the original languages from Dante, Virgil, and Saint-Hilaire; he studied Arabic with a view "to its introduction into Liberia College," where he was one of the first professors; and, when he became the Liberian ambassador to Queen Victoria, he came into "contact—epistolary or personal—with . . . Mr. Gladstone, . . . Charles Dickens [and] Charles Sumner."[21] His views on race are Crummell's—and, one might add, Queen Victoria's, Gladstone's, Dickens' and Sumner's: "Among the conclusions to which study and research are conducting philosophers, none is clearer than this—that each of the races of mankind has a specific character and specific work."[22] For Blyden, as for Crummell, Africa was the proper home of the Negro, and the African-American was an exile who should "return to the land of his fathers . . . AND BE AT PEACE."[23] Like Crummell, Blyden believed that "English is undoubtedly, the most suitable of the European languages for bridging over the numerous gulfs between the tribes caused by the great diversity of languages or dialects among them."[24]

It is, perhaps, unsurprising then that Blyden also largely shared Crummell's extreme distaste for the traditional—or, as he would have said, "pagan"—cultures of

Africa. Outside the areas where Islam had brought some measure of exogenous civilization, Blyden's Africa is a place of "noisy terpischorean performances," "Fetichism" and polygamy; it is, in short, in "a state of barbarism."[25] Blyden argued, however, that "there is not a single mental or moral deficiency now existing among Africans—not a single practice now indulged in by them—to which we cannot find a parallel in the past history of Europe";[26] and he had a great deal of respect for African Islam. But, in the end, his view, like Crummell's, was that Africa's religions and politics should give way to Christianity (or, at second best, Islam) and republicanism.[27]

Literate people of my generation, both in Africa and, to a lesser extent, in the West, may find it hard to recover the overwhelmingly negative conception of Africans that inhabited the mainstream of European and American intellectual life by the first years of Europe's African empires. As Blyden expressed the matter with commendable restraint in *Fraser's Magazine* in 1875: "It is not too much to say that the popular literature of the Christian world, since the discovery of America, or, at least for the last two hundred years, has been anti-Negro."[28] I could choose from thousands upon thousands of texts that Crummell and Blyden could have read to "remind" us of this; let me offer one emblematic proof text, whose words have a special irony.

Even in that monument of Enlightenment reasonableness, the *Encyclopédie*—a text that he would probably have stigmatized as the work of a cynical deism—Crummell could have read the following of the people of the Guinea coast:

> The natives are idolaters, superstitious, and live most filthily; they are lazy, drunken rascals, without thought for the future, insensitive to any happening, happy or sad, which gives pleasure to or afflicts them; they have no sense of modesty or restraint in the pleasures of love, each sex plunging on the other like a brute from the earliest age.[29]

If Crummell had opened the encyclopedia at the article on *Humain espèce,* he would have read—in a passage whose original tone of condescension I will not try to translate—that "les Nègres sont grands, gros, bien faits, mais niais & sans genie." We must struggle to remind ourselves that this is the same *Encyclopédie,* the same "Dictionnaire Raisonée des Sciences" that had condemned African slavery as "repugnant to reason" and had argued that to recognize the status of slave in Europe would be "to decide, in Cicero's words, the laws of humanity by the civil law of the gutter."[30] The racial prejudice that the nineteenth century acquired and developed from the Enlightenment did not derive simply from ill feeling toward Africans. And Crummell's and Blyden's desire to help Africans was no less genuine for their inability to see any virtue in our cultures and traditions.

Crummell did not need to read these words in the encyclopedia; his mind was formed by the culture that had produced them. Even after he had lived in Africa, he believed his experience confirmed these judgments.

> Africa is the victim of her heterogeneous idolatries. Africa is wasting away beneath the accretions of moral and civil miseries. Darkness covers the land and gross darkness the people. Great social evils universally prevail. Confidence and security

are destroyed. Licentiousness abounds everywhere. Moloch rules and reigns throughout the whole continent, and by the ordeal of Sassywood, Fetiches, human sacrifices and devil-worship, is devouring men, women, and little children.

Though Crummell's vision of Africa thus differed little from that of the *Encyclopédie* about a century earlier, he had a different analysis of the problem: "They have not the Gospel. They are living without God. The Cross has never met their gaze. . . ."[31]

Crummell's view of a "native religion" that consisted of "the ordeal of Sassywood, Fetiches, human sacrifices and devil-worship" in the African "darkness" was, as I say, less subtle than Blyden's. Blyden wrote:

> There is not a tribe on the continent of Africa, in spite of the almost universal opinion to the contrary, in spite of the fetishes and greegrees which many of them are supposed to worship—there is not, I say, a single tribe which does not stretch out its hands to the Great Creator. There is not one who does not recognize the Supreme Being, though imperfectly understanding His character—and who does perfectly understand his character? They believe that the heaven and the earth, the sun, moon, and stars, which they behold, were created by an Almighty personal Agent, who is also their Maker and Sovereign, and they render to Him such worship as their untutored intellects can conceive. . . . There are no atheists or agnostics among them.[32]

But the differences here are largely differences of tone: for Crummell also wrote—in a passage Blyden quotes—of "the yearning of the native African for a higher religion."[33] What these missionaries, who were also nationalists, stressed, time and time again, was the openness of Africans, once properly instructed, to monotheism; what impressed them both, despite the horrors of African paganism, was the Africans' natural religiosity.[34]

It is tempting to see this view as yet another imposition of the exile's distorting vision; in the New World, Christianity had provided the major vehicle of cultural expression for the slaves. It could not be denied them in a Christian country—and it provided them with solace in their "vale of tears," guiding them through "the valley of the shadow." Once committed to racialist explanations, it was inevitable that the rich religious lives of New World blacks should be seen as flowing from the nature of the Negro—and thus projected onto the Negro in Africa. Yet there is some truth in this view that Crummell and Blyden shared: in a sense, there truly were "no atheists and agnostics in Africa." Unfortunately for the prospects of a Christian Africa, molded to Crummell's or to Blyden's ambitions, the religiosity of the African—as we shall see later—was something that it was easy for Western Christians to misunderstand.[35]

In a marvelous poem, the Cape Verdian Onésima Silveira writes:

> The people of the islands want a different poem
> For the people of the islands;
> A poem without exiles complaining
> In the calm of their existence.[36]

We can take this stanza as an emblem of the challenge the African Pan-Africanists of the postwar era posed to the attitude to Africa that is epitomized in Crummell. Raised in Africa, in cultures and traditions they knew and understood as insiders, they could not share a sense of Africa as a cultural vacuum. However impressed they were by the power of western technology, they were also engaged with the worlds of their diverse traditions. Daily evidences in their upbringing—in medicine, in farming, in spirit possession, in dreams, in "witchcraft, oracles and magic"—of the existence around them of the rich spiritual ontology of ancestors and divinities could not so easily be dismissed as heathen nonsense. The "exiles" of the New World could show their love of Africa by seeking to eliminate its indigenous cultures, but the heirs to Africa's civilizations could not so easily dispose of their ancestors. Out of this situation grew an approach whose logic I shall describe in my discussion of Du Bois; the new Africans shared Crummell's—and Europe's—conception of themselves as united by their race, but they sought to celebrate and build upon its virtues, not to decry and replace its vices. The best-known manifestation of this logic is in negritude; but it also had its anglophone manifestations in, for example, Nkrumah's cult of the "African personality" or J. B. Danquah's celebration of his own religious traditions in *The Akan Doctrine of God.*[37] These celebrators of the African race may have spoken of the need to Christianize or Islamize Africa, to modernize, so to speak, its religion. But the conception they had of what this meant at the level of metaphysics was quite different from that of Crummell and the European missions. To trace out this difference is to follow one important element in the change in Pan-Africanism's understanding of cultural politics that occurred after the Second World War, when it finally became an African movement. And that, as I say, is an inquiry I shall return to later.

Though it thus became possible to value Africa's traditions, the persistence of the category of race had important consequences. For part of the Crummellian conception of race is a conception of racial psychology, and this—which manifests itself sometimes as a belief in characteristically African ways of thinking—has also lead to a persistent assumption that there are characteristically African beliefs. The psychology of race has led, that is, not only to a belief in the existence of a peculiar African *form* of thinking but also to a belief in special African *contents* of thought. The Beninois philosopher Paulin Hountondji has dubbed this view that Africa is culturally homogeneous—the belief that there is some central body of folk philosophy that is shared by black Africans quite generally—"unanimism." He has had no difficulty in assembling a monstrous collection of African unanimist texts.

Yet nothing should be more striking for someone without preconceptions than the extraordinary diversity of Africa's peoples and its cultures. I still vividly recall the overwhelming sense of difference that I experienced when I first traveled out of western to southern Africa. Driving through the semiarid countryside of Botswana into her capital, Gaborone, a day away by plane from the tropical vegetation of Asante, no landscape could have seemed more alien. The material culture of the Batswana, too, struck me as quite radically different from that of Asante. In Gaborone, unlike Asante, all men dressed in shirts and trousers, most women in skirts and blouses, and most of these clothes were unpatterned, so that the streets lacked the color of the flowing Asante "cloth"; the idioms of carving, of weaving, of pottery, and of dance were all unfamiliar. Inevitably, in such a setting, I wondered what, in Botswana, was supposed to follow from my being African. In conversations with Ghanaian doctors, judges, lawyers, and academics in Botswana—as well as in

Zimbabwe and Nigeria—I have often heard echoes of the language of the colonizers in our discussions of the culture of the "natives."

It is easy to see how history can make you, on the one hand, say, a citizen of Ivory Coast or of Botswana; or, on the other, say, anglophone or francophone. But what, given all the diversity of the precolonial histories of the peoples of Africa, and all the complexity of colonial experiences, does it mean to say that someone is African? In Chapter 4, I look at one answer that has been given to this important question: the answer of Wole Soyinka, Nigeria's leading playwright and man of letters, and, perhaps, the creative artist who has written most persuasively on the role of the intellectual and the artist in the life of the nations of contemporary Africa.

But Soyinka's answer to the question "What is Africa?" is one among others. In Chapter 5 I explore the responses of some contemporary African philosophers. I argue that there remains in much of this work an important residue of the ideology represented by Du Bois—a residue that is translated, however, to what we can call a metaphysical level. Nevertheless, as we shall see, this work provides useful hints as to the directions in which we should move in answering this fundamental question.

Now I am confident in rejecting any homogenizing portrait of African intellectual life, because the ethnographies and the travel literature and the novels of parts of Africa other than my home are all replete with examples of ways of life and of thought that strike me as thoroughly pretheoretically different from life in Asante, where I grew up.

Compare Evans-Pritchard's famous Zande oracles,[38] with their simple questions and their straightforward answers, with the fabulous richness of Yoruba oracles, whose interpretation requires great skill in the hermeneutics of the complex corpus of verses of Ifa; or our own Asante monarchy, a confederation in which the king is primus inter pares, his elders and paramount chiefs guiding him in council, with the more absolute power of Mutesa the First in nineteenth-century Buganda; or the enclosed horizons of a traditional Hausa wife, forever barred from contact with men other than her husband, with the open spaces of the women traders of southern Nigeria; or the art of Benin—its massive bronzes—with the tiny elegant goldweight figures of the Akan. Face the warrior horsemen of the Fulani jihads with Shaka's Zulu impis; taste the bland foods of Botswana after the spices of Fanti cooking; try understanding Kikuyu or Yoruba or Fulfulde with a Twi dictionary. Surely differences in religious ontology and ritual, in the organization of politics and the family, in relations between the sexes and in art, in styles of warfare and cuisine, in language—surely all these are fundamental kinds of difference?

As Edward Blyden—who for all his sentimentality of race, was a shrewder observer than Crummell—once wrote:

> There are Negroes and Negroes. The numerous tribes inhabiting the vast continent
> of Africa can no more be regarded as in every respect equal than the numerous
> peoples of Asia or Europe can be so regarded. There are the same tribal or family
> varieties among Africans as among Europeans . . . there are the Foulahs inhabit-
> ing the region of the Upper Niger, the Housas, the Bornous of Senegambia, the
> Nubas of the Nile region, of Darfoor and Kordofan, the Ashantees, Fantees,
> Dahomians, Yorubas, and that whole class of tribes occupying the eastern and
> middle and western portions of the continent north of the equator. Then there are

the tribes of Lower Guinea and Angola . . . all these differing in original bent
and traditional instincts. . . . Now it should be evident that no short description
can include all these people, no single definition, however comprehensive, can
embrace them all. Yet writers are fond of selecting the prominent traits of single
tribes with which they are best acquainted, and applying them to the whole race.[39]

But we shall have ample opportunity in later chapters to look at evidence of Africa's
cultural diversity.

Whatever Africans share, we do not have a common traditional culture, common
languages, a common religious or conceptual vocabulary. As I shall argue in Chapter
2, we do not even belong to a common race; and since this is so, unanimism is not
entitled to what is, in my view, its fundamental presupposition. These essentially
negative claims will occupy much of the argument of the next few essays. But in the
final essays of this book I shall move in a positive direction. I shall try to articulate an
understanding of the present state of African intellectual life that does not share even
at a metaphysical level these assumptions that have been with us since early Pan-
Africanism. Africans share too many problems and projects to be distracted by a
bogus basis for solidarity.

There is a familiar tale of a peasant who is stopped by a traveler in a large car and
asked the way to the capital. ''Well,'' she replies, after pondering the matter a while,
''if I were you, I wouldn't start from here.'' In many intellectual projects I have often
felt sympathy with this sentiment. It seems to me that the message of the first four
chapters in this book is that we must provide an understanding of Africa's cultural
work that does not ''start from here.''

And so, in hopes of finding a different, more productive, starting point, I turn, at
the end of Chapter 5, to the recent work of some African philosophers who have
begun to develop an understanding of the situation of the intellectual in neocolonial
culture—an understanding that is not predicated on a racial vision.

Finally, beginning in Chapter 6, I sketch my own view of Africa's current cultural
position. I shall argue for a different account of what is common to the situation of
contemporary African intellectuals—an account that indicates why, though I do not
believe in a homogeneous Africa, I do believe that Africans can learn from each
other, as, of course, we can learn from all of humankind.

And I want to insist from the start that this task is thus not one for African
intellectuals alone. In the United States, a nation that has long understood itself
through a concept of pluralism, it can too easily seem unproblematic to claim that the
nations of Africa—even Africa itself—could be united not in spite of differences but
through a celebration of them. Yet American pluralism, too, seems to be theorized in
part through a discourse of races. In his important book, *Beyond Ethnicity: Consent
and Descent in American Culture,* Werner Sollors has developed an analysis of the
current American climate in terms of an analytical dualism of descent (the bonds of
blood) and consent (the liberating unities of culture).

The heart of the matter is that in the present climate consent-conscious Americans
are willing to perceive ethnic distinctions—differentiations which they seemingly
base exclusively on descent, no matter how far removed and how artificially

selected and constructed—as powerful and crucial; and that writers and critics pander to that expectation . . . and even the smallest symbols of ethnic differentiation . . . are exaggerated out of proportion to represent major cultural differences, differences that are believed to defy comparison or scrutiny.[40]

Like Africans, Americans need, I believe, to escape from some of the misunderstandings in modern discourse about descent and consent epitomized in the racialism of Alexander Crummell. American by descent, African by consent, Alexander Crummell has something to teach his heirs on both continents. Indeed, because the intellectual projects of our one world are essentially everywhere interconnected, because the world's cultures are bound together now through institutions, through histories, through writings, he has something to teach the one race to which we *all* belong.

TWO

Illusions of Race

If this be true, the history of the world is the history, not of individuals, but of groups, not of nations, but of races . . .[1]

W. E. B. Du Bois

Alexander Crummell and Edward Wilmot Blyden began the intellectual articulation of a Pan-Africanist ideology, but it was W. E. B. Du Bois who laid both the intellectual and the practical foundations of the Pan-African movement. Du Bois's life was a long one, and his intellectual career—which he called the "autobiography of a race concept"[2]—encompassed almost the whole period of European colonial control of Africa. It is hard to imagine a more substantial rupture in political ideas than that which separates the division of Africa at the Congress of Berlin from the independence of Ghana, yet Du Bois was a teenager when the former happened in 1884, and, in 1957, he witnessed—and rejoiced in—the latter. And, as we shall see, there is an astonishing consistency in his position throughout the years. Not only did Du Bois live long, he wrote much; if any single person can offer us an insight into the archaeology of Pan-Africanism's idea of race, it is he.

Du Bois's first extended discussion of the concept of race is in "The Conservation of Races," a paper he delivered to the American Negro Academy in the year it was founded by Alexander Crummell. The "American Negro," he declares, "has been led to . . . minimize race distinctions" because "back of most of the discussions of race with which he is familiar, have lurked certain assumptions as to his natural abilities, as to his political, intellectual and moral status, which he felt were wrong." And he goes on: "Nevertheless, in our calmer moments we must acknowledge that human beings are divided into races," even if "when we come to inquire into the essential differences of races, we find it hard to come at once to any definite conclusion."[3] For what it is worth, however, "the final word of science, so far, is that we have at least two, perhaps three, great families of human beings—the whites and Negroes, possibly the yellow race."[4]

Du Bois is not, however, satisfied with the "final word" of the late-nineteenth-century science. For, as he thinks, what matter are not the "grosser physical differences of color, hair and bone" but the "differences—subtle, delicate and elusive, though they may be—which have silently but definitely separated men into groups."

> While these subtle forces have generally followed the natural cleavage of common blood, descent and physical peculiarities, they have at other times swept across and

28

ignored these. At all times, however, they have divided human beings into races, which, while they perhaps transcend scientific definition, nevertheless, are clearly defined to the eye of the historian and sociologist.

If this be true, then the history of the world is the history, not of individuals, but of groups, not of nations, but of races. . . . What then is a race? It is a vast family of human beings, generally of common blood and language, always of common history, traditions and impulses, who are both voluntarily and involuntarily striving together for the accomplishment of certain more or less vividly conceived ideals of life.[5]

We have moved, then, away from the "scientific"—that is, biological and anthropological—conception of race to a sociohistorical notion. And, by this sociohistorical criterion—whose breadth of sweep certainly encourages the thought that no biological or anthropological definition is possible—Du Bois considers that there are not three but eight "distinctly differentiated races, in the sense in which history tells us the word must be used."[6] The list is an odd one: Slavs, Teutons, English (in both Great Britain and America), Negroes (of Africa and, likewise, America), the Romance race, Semites, Hindus, and Mongolians.

Du Bois continues:

The question now is: What is the real distinction between these nations? Is it physical differences of blood, color and cranial measurements? Certainly we must all acknowledge that physical differences play a great part. . . . But while race differences have followed along mainly physical lines, yet no mere physical distinction would really define or explain the deeper differences—the cohesiveness and continuity of these groups. The deeper differences are spiritual, psychical, differences—undoubtedly based on the physical, but infinitely transcending them.[7]

The various races are

striving, each in its own way, to develop for civilization its particular message, its particular ideal, which shall help guide the world nearer and nearer that perfection of human life for which we all long, that "one far off Divine event."[8]

For Du Bois, then, the problem for the Negro is the discovery and expression of the message of his or her race.

The full, complete Negro message of the whole Negro race has not as yet been given to the world. . . .

The question is, then: how shall this message be delivered; how shall these various ideals be realized? The answer is plain: by the development of these race groups, not as individuals, but as races. . . . For the development of Negro genius, of Negro literature and art, of Negro spirit, only Negroes bound and welded together, Negroes inspired by one vast ideal, can work out in its fullness the great message we have for humanity. . . .

For this reason, the advance guard of the Negro people—the eight million people of Negro blood in the United States of America—must soon come to realize that if they are to take their place in the van of Pan-Negroism, then their destiny is *not* absorption by the white Americans.[9]

And so Du Bois ends by proposing his *Academy Creed,* which begins with words that echo down almost a century of American race relations:

1. We believe that the Negro people, as a race, have a contribution to make to civilization and humanity, which no other race can make.
2. We believe it is the duty of the Americans of Negro descent, as a body, to maintain their race identity until this mission of the Negro people is accomplished, and the ideal of human brotherhood has become a practical possibility.[10]

What can we make of this analysis and prescription? On the face of it, Du Bois's argument in "The Conservation of Races" is that "race" is not a "scientific"—that is, biological—but a sociohistorical concept. Sociohistorical races each have a "message" for humanity, a message that derives, in some way, from God's purpose in creating races. The Negro race has still to deliver its full message, and so it is the duty of Negroes to work together—through race organizations—so that this message can be delivered.

We do not need the theological underpinnings of this argument. What is essential is the thought that Negroes, by virtue of their sociohistorical community, can achieve, through common action, worthwhile ends that will not otherwise be achieved. On the face of it, then, Du Bois's strategy here is the antithesis of a classic dialectic in the reaction to prejudice. The thesis in this dialectic—which Du Bois reports as the American Negro's attempt to "minimize race distinctions"—is the denial of difference. Du Bois's antithesis is the acceptance of difference along with a claim that each group has its part to play, that the white and the Negro races are related not as superior to inferior but as complementaries; the Negro message is, with the white one, part of the message of humankind. What he espouses is what Sartre once called—in negritude—an "antiracist racism."[11]

I call this pattern a classic dialectic, and, indeed, we find it in feminism also. On the one hand, a simple claim to equality, a denial of substantial difference; on the other, a claim to a special message, revaluing the feminine "Other" not as the "helpmeet" of sexism but as the New Woman.

Because this *is* a classic dialectic, my reading of Du Bois's argument is a natural one. To confirm this interpretation we must establish that what Du Bois attempts, despite his own claims to the contrary, is not the transcendence of the nineteenth-century scientific conception of race—as we shall see, he relies on it—but rather, as the dialectic requires, a revaluation of the Negro race in the face of the sciences of racial inferiority. We can begin by analyzing the sources of tension in Du Bois's allegedly sociohistorical conception of race, which he explicitly sets over against the "scientific" conception. The tension is plain enough in his references to "common blood"; for this, dressed up with fancy craniometry, a dose of melanin, and some measure for hair curl, is what the scientific notion amounts to. If he has fully transcended the scientific notion, what is the role of this talk of "blood"?

We may leave aside for the moment the common "impulses" and the voluntary and involuntary "strivings." For these must be due either to a shared biological inheritance, "based on the physical, but infinitely transcending" it; or to a shared history; or, of course, to some combination of these. If Du Bois's notion is purely sociohistorical, then the issue is common history and traditions; otherwise, the issue is, at least in part, a common biology. We shall only know which when we understand the core of Du Bois's conception of race.

The claim that a race generally shares a common language is also plainly inessential: the "Romance" race is not of common language, nor, more obviously, is the Negro. And "common blood" can mean little more than "of shared ancestry," which is already implied by Crummellian talk of a "vast *family*." At the center of Du Bois's conception, then, is the claim that a race is "a vast family of human beings, always of a common history [and] traditions."[12] So, if we want to understand Du Bois, our question must be: What is a "family . . . of common history"?

We already see that the scientific notion, which presupposes common features in virtue of a common biology derived from a common descent, is not fully transcended. It is true that a family can have adopted children, kin by social rather than biological law. By analogy, therefore, a vast human family might contain people joined together not by biology but by an act of choice. But it is plain enough that Du Bois cannot have been contemplating this possibility: like all of his contemporaries, he would have taken it for granted that race is a matter of birth. Indeed, to understand the talk of "family," we must distance ourselves from *all* of its sociological meaning. A family is usually defined culturally through either patrilineal or matrilineal descent alone.[13] But if an individual drew a "conceptual" family tree back over five hundred years and assumed that he or she was descended from each ancestor in only one way, the tree would have more than a million branches at the top. Although, in fact, many individuals would be represented on more than one branch—that far back, we are all going to be descended from many people by more than one route—it is plain, as a result, that a matri- or patrilineal conception of our family histories drastically underrepresents the biological range of our ancestry.

Biology and social convention go startlingly different ways. Let's pretend, secure in our republicanism, that the claim of the queen of England to the throne depends partly on a single line from one of her ancestors nine hundred years ago. If there were no overlaps in her family tree, there would be more than fifty thousand billion such lines, though, of course, there have never been anywhere near that many people on the planet; even with reasonable assumptions about overlaps, there are millions of such lines. We chose one line, even though most of the population of England is probably descended from William the Conqueror by *some* uncharted route. Biology is democratic: all parents are equal. Thus to speak of two people being of common ancestry is to require that somewhere in the past a large proportion of the branches leading back in their family trees coincided.[14]

Already, then, Du Bois requires, as the scientific conception does, a common ancestry (in the sense just defined) with whatever—if anything—this biologically entails. Yet apparently this does not commit him to the scientific conception, for there are many groups of common ancestry—ranging, at its widest, from humanity in general to the narrower group of Slavs, Teutons, and Romance people taken together—that do not, for Du Bois, constitute races. Thus, Du Bois's "common history," which must be what is supposed to distinguish Slav from Teuton, is an essential part of his conception. The issue now is whether a common history is something that could be a criterion that distinguishes one group of human beings—extended in time—from another. Does adding a notion of common history allow us to make the distinctions between Slav and Teuton, or between English and Negro? The answer is no.

Consider, for example, Du Bois himself. As the descendant of Dutch ancestors, why does not the history of Holland in the fourteenth century (which he shares with all people of Dutch descent) make him a member of the Teutonic race? The answer is straightforward: the Dutch were not Negroes, Du Bois is. But it follows from this that the history of Africa is part of the common history of African-Americans not simply because African-Americans are descended from various peoples who played a part in African history but because African history is the history of people of the same race.

My general point is this: just as to recognize two events at different times as part of the history of a single individual, we have to have a criterion of identity for the individual at each of those times, independent of his or her participation in the two events, so, when we recognize two events as belonging to the history of one race, we have to have a criterion of membership of the race at those two times, independently of the participation of the members in the two events. To put it more simply: sharing a common group history cannot be a *criterion* for being members of the same group, for we would have to be able to identify the group in order to identify *its* history. Someone in the fourteenth century could share a common history with me through our membership in a historically extended race only if something accounts for their membership in the race in the fourteenth century and mine in the twentieth. That something cannot, on pain of circularity, be the history of the race.[15]

There is a useful analogy here, which I relied on a moment ago, between the historical continuity of races and the temporal continuity of people. Du Bois's attempt to make sense of racial identity through time by way of a figurative "long memory" subserves the same function as John Locke's attempt—in his *Essay Concerning Human Understanding*—to make literal memory the core of the soul's identity through time. For Locke needed to have an account of the nature of the soul that did not rely on the physical continuity of the body, just as Du Bois wanted to rely on something more uplifting than the brute continuity of the germ plasm. Locke's view was that two souls at different times were, in the philosopher's jargon, "time slices" of the same individual if the later one had memories of the earlier one. But, as philosophers since Locke have pointed out, we cannot tell whether a memory is evidence of the rememberer's identity, even if what is "remembered" really did happen to an earlier person, unless we know already that the rememberer and the earlier person are one. For it is quite conceivable that someone should think that they recall something that actually happened to somebody else. I have simply applied this same strategy of argument against Du Bois. History may have made us what we are, but the choice of a slice of the past in a period before your birth as your own history is always exactly that: a choice. The phrase the "invention of tradition" is a pleonasm.[16]

Whatever holds Du Bois's races conceptually together, then, it cannot be a common history. It is only because they are already bound together that members of a race at different times can share a history at all. If this is true, Du Bois's reference to a common history cannot be doing any work in his individuation of races. And once we have stripped away the sociohistorical elements from Du Bois's definition of race, we are left with his true criterion.

Consequently, not only the talk of language, which Du Bois admits is neither necessary (the Romance race speaks many languages) nor sufficient (African-Americans generally speak the same language as other Americans) for racial identity, must be expunged from the definition; now we have seen that talk of common history and traditions must go too. We are left with common descent and the common impulses and strivings, which I put aside earlier. Since common descent, and the characteristics that flow from it are part of the nineteenth-century scientific conception of race, these impulses are all that is left to do the job that Du Bois had claimed for a sociohistorical conception: namely, to distinguish his conception from the biological one. Du Bois claims that the existence of races is ''clearly defined to the eye of the historian and sociologist.''[17] Since common ancestry is acknowledged by biology as a criterion, whatever extra insight is provided by sociohistorical understanding can only be gained by observation of the common impulses and strivings. Reflection suggests, however, that this cannot be true. For what common impulses—whether voluntary or involuntary—do Romance people share that the Teutons and the English do not?

Du Bois had read the historiography of the Anglo-Saxon school, which accounted for the democratic impulse in America by tracing it to the racial tradition of the Anglo-Saxon moot. He had read American and British historians in earnest discussion of the ''Latin'' spirit of Romance peoples, and perhaps he had believed some of it. Here, then, might be the source of the notion that history and sociology can observe the differing impulses of races.

In all these writings, however, such impulses are allegedly discovered to be the a posteriori properties of racial and national groups, not to be criteria of membership of them. It is, indeed, because the claim is a posteriori that historical evidence is relevant to it. And if we ask which common impulses that history has detected allow us to recognize the Negro, we shall see that Du Bois's claim to have found in these impulses a criterion of identity is mere bravado. If, without evidence about his or her impulses, we can say who is a Negro, then it cannot be part of what it is to be a Negro that he or she has them; rather it must be an a posteriori claim that people of a common race, defined by descent and biology, have impulses, for whatever reason, in common. Of course, the common impulses of a biologically defined group may be historically caused by common experiences, common history. But Du Bois's claim can only be that biologically defined races happen to share, for whatever reason, common impulses. The common impulses cannot be a criterion of membership of the group. And if that is so, we are left with the scientific conception.

How, then, is it possible for Du Bois's criteria to issue in eight groups, while the scientific conception issues in three? The reason is clear from the list. Slavs, Teutons, English, Hindus, and Romance peoples each live in a characteristic geographical region. (American English—and, for that matter, American Teutons, American Slavs, and American Romance people—share recent ancestry with their European ''cousins'' and thus share a mildly more complex relation to a place and its languages and traditions.) Semites (modulo such details as the Jewish Diaspora and the westward expansion of the Islamized Arabs) and Mongolians (this is the whole population of eastern Asia) share a (rather larger) geographical region also. Du Bois's talk of common history conceals his superaddition of a geographical criterion: your history is, in part, the history of people who lived in the same place.[18]

The criterion Du Bois is actually using amounts, then, to this: people are members of the same race if they share features in virtue of being descended largely from people of the same region. Those features may be physical (hence African-Americans are Negroes) or cultural (hence Anglo-Americans are English). Focusing on one sort of feature—"grosser differences of color, hair and bone"—you get "whites and Negroes, possibly the yellow race," the "final word of science, so far." Focusing on a different feature—language or shared customs—you get Teutons, Slavs, and Romance peoples. The tension in Du Bois's definition of race reflects the fact that for the purposes of European historiography (of which his Harvard and University of Berlin trainings had made him aware), it was the latter that mattered, but for purposes of American social and political life it was the former.

The real difference in Du Bois's conception, therefore, is not that his definition of race is at odds with the scientific one: it is rather, as the dialectic requires, that he assigns to race a different moral and metaphysical significance from the majority of his white contemporaries. The distinctive claim is that the Negro race has a positive message, a message that is not only different but valuable. And that, it seems to me, is the significance of the sociohistorical dimension; for the strivings of a race are, as Du Bois viewed the matter, the stuff of history: "The history of the world is the history, not of individuals, but of groups, not of nations, but of races, and he who ignores or seeks to override the race idea in human history ignores and overrides the central thought of all history."[19] By studying history, we can discern the outlines of the message of each race.

We have seen that, for the purpose that concerned him most—namely for understanding the status of the Negro—Du Bois was thrown back on the "scientific" definition of race, which he officially rejected. But the scientific definition (Du Bois's uneasiness with which is reflected in his remark that races "perhaps transcend scientific definition") was itself already threatened as he spoke at the first meeting of the Negro Academy. In the latter nineteenth century most thinking people (like many even today) believed that what Du Bois called the "grosser differences" were a sign of an inherited racial essence, which accounted for the intellectual and moral deficiency of the "lower" races. In "The Conservation of Races" Du Bois elected, in effect, to admit that color was a sign of a racial essence but to deny that the cultural capacities of the black-skinned, curly-haired members of humankind—the capacities determined by their essence—were inferior to those of the white-skinned, straighter-haired ones. But the collapse of the sciences of racial inferiority led Du Bois to repudiate the connection between cultural capacity and gross morphology, to deny the familiar "impulses and strivings" of his earlier definition. We can find evidence of this change of mind in an article in the August 1911 issue of *The Crisis,* the journal of the American National Association for the Advancement of Colored People, which he edited vigorously through most of the early years of the century.

> The leading scientists of the world have come forward . . . and laid down in categorical terms a series of propositions[20] which may be summarized as follows:
> 1. (a) It is not legitimate to argue from differences in physical characteristics to differences in mental characteristics. . . .
> 2. The civilization of a . . . race at any particular moment of time offers no index to its innate or inherited capacities.[21]

The results have been amply confirmed since then. And we do well, I think, to remind ourselves of the current picture.

The evidence in the contemporary biological literature is, at first glance, misleading. For despite a widespread scientific consensus on the underlying genetics, contemporary biologists are not agreed on the question whether there are any human races. Yet, for our purposes, we can reasonably regard this issue as terminological. What most people in most cultures ordinarily believe about the significance of "racial" difference is quite remote from what the biologists *are* agreed on, and, in particular, it is not consistent with what, in the last essay, I called *racialism*. Every reputable biologist will agree that human genetic variability between the populations of Africa or Europe or Asia is not much greater than that within those populations, though how much greater depends, in part, on the measure of genetic variability the biologist chooses. If biologists want to make interracial difference seem relatively large, they can say that "the proportion of genic variation attributable to racial difference is . . . 9–11%."[22] If they want to make it seem small, they can say that, for two people who are both "Caucasoid," the chances of differing in genetic constitution at one site on a given chromosome have recently been estimated at about 14.3 percent, while for any two people taken at random from the human population the same calculations suggest a figure of about 14.8 percent. The underlying statistical facts about the distribution of variant characteristics in human populations and subpopulations are the same, whichever way you express the matter. Apart from the visible morphological characteristics of skin, hair, and bone, by which we are inclined to assign people to the broadest racial categories—black, white, yellow—there are few genetic characteristics to be found in the population of England that are not found in similar proportions in Zaire or in China, and few too (though more) that are found in Zaire but not in similar proportions in China or in England. All this, I repeat, is part of the consensus.

A more familiar part of the consensus is that the differences between peoples in language, moral affections, aesthetic attitudes, or political ideology—those differences that most deeply affect us in our dealings with each other—are not to any significant degree biologically determined.

This claim will, no doubt, seem outrageous to those who confuse the question whether biological difference accounts for our differences with the question whether biological similarity accounts for our similarities. Some of our similarities as human beings in these broadly cultural respects—the capacity to acquire human languages, for example, or the ability to smile—*are* to a significant degree biologically determined. We can study the biological basis of these cultural capacities, and give biological explanations of features of our exercise of them. But if biological difference between human beings is unimportant in these explanations—and it is— then racial difference, as a species of biological difference, will not matter either. We can see why if we attend to the underlying genetics.

Human characteristics are genetically determined,[23] to the extent that they are determined, by sequences of DNA in the chromosome—in other words, by genes.[24] A region of a chromosome occupied by a gene is called a *locus*. Some loci are occupied in different members of a population by different genes, each of which is called an *allele;* and a locus is said to be *polymorphic* in a population if there is at least a pair of alleles for it. Perhaps as many as half the loci in the human population are polymorphic; the rest, naturally enough, are said to be *monomorphic.*

Many loci have not just two alleles but several, and each has a frequency in the population. Suppose a particular locus has n alleles, which we can just call 1, 2, and so on up to n; then we can call the frequencies of these alleles $x_1, x_2, \ldots, x_n$. If you consider two members of a population chosen at random and look at the same locus on one chromosome of each of them, the probability that they will have the same allele at that locus is just the probability that they will both have the first allele (x_1^2), plus the probability that they'll both have the second (x_2^2) $\ldots$ plus the probability that they will both have the nth (x_n^2). We can call this number the *expected homozygosity* at that locus, for it is just the proportion of people in the population who would be homozygous at that locus—having identical alleles at that locus on each of the relevant chromosomes—provided the population was mating at random.[25]

Now if we take the average value of the expected homozygosity for all loci, polymorphic and monomorphic (which geneticists tend to label J), we have a measure of the chance that two people, taken at random from the population, will share the same allele at a locus on a chromosome taken at random. This is a good measure of how similar a randomly chosen pair of individuals should be expected to be in their biology, *and* a good guide to how closely—on the average—the members of the population are genetically related.

I can now express simply one measure of the extent to which members of those human populations we call races differ more from each other than they do from members of the same race. For the value of J for "Caucasoids"—estimated, in fact, largely from samples of the English population[26]—is estimated to be about 0.857, while that for the whole human population is estimated at 0.852. The chances, in other words, that two people taken at random from the human population will have the same characteristic at a random locus are about 85.2 percent, while the chances for two (white) people taken from the population of England are about 85.7 percent. And since 85.2 is 100 minus 14.8, and 85.7 is 100 minus 14.3, this is equivalent to what I said previously: the chances of two people who are both "Caucasoid" differing in genetic constitution at one site on a given chromosome are about 14.3 percent, while, for any two people taken at random from the human population, they are about 14.8 percent.

The conclusion is obvious: given only a person's race, it is hard to say what his or her biological characteristics (apart from those that human beings share) will be, except in respect of the "grosser" features of color, hair, and bone (the genetics of which is, in any case, rather poorly understood)—features of "morphological differentiation," as the evolutionary biologist would say. As Nei and Roychoudhury express themselves, somewhat coyly, "The extent of genic differentiation between human races is not always correlated with the degree of morphological differentiation."[27] This may seem relatively untroubling to committed racialists. Race, they might say, is at least important in predicting morphological difference. But that, though true, is not a biological fact but a logical one, for Nei and Roychoudhury's races are defined by their morphology in the first place. The criterion for excluding from an American "Caucasoid" sample people with black skins is just the "gross" morphological fact that their skins are black. But recent immigrants of eastern European ancestry would be included in the sample, while dark-skinned people whose ancestors for the last ten generations had largely lived in the New World would be excluded.

To establish that this notion of race is relatively unimportant in explaining biological differences between people, where biological difference is measured in the proportion of differences in loci on the chromosome, is not yet to show that race is unimportant in explaining cultural difference. It could be that large differences in intellectual or moral capacity are caused by differences at very few loci, and that at these loci, all (or most) black-skinned people differ from all (or most) white-skinned or yellow-skinned ones. As it happens, there is little evidence for any such proposition and much against it. But suppose we had reason to believe it. In the biological conception of the human organism, in which characteristics are determined by the pattern of genes in interaction with environments, it is the presence of the alleles (which give rise to these moral and intellectual capacities) that accounts for the observed differences in those capacities in people in similar environments. So the characteristic racial morphology—skin and hair and bone—could be a sign of those differences only if it were (highly) correlated with those alleles. Since there are no such strong correlations, even those who think that intellectual and moral character are strongly genetically determined must accept that *race* is at best a poor indicator of capacity.

When I defined *racialism* in Chapter 1, I said that it was committed not just to the view that there are heritable characteristics, which constitute "a sort of racial essence," but also to the claim that the essential heritable characteristics account for more than the visible morphology—skin color, hair type, facial features—on the basis of which we make our informal classifications. To say that biological races existed because it was possible to classify people into a small number of classes according to their gross morphology would be to save racialism in the letter but lose it in the substance. The notion of race that was recovered would be of no biological interest—the interesting biological generalizations are about genotypes, phenotypes, and their distribution in geographical populations. We could just as well classify people according to whether or not they were redheaded, or redheaded and freckled, or redheaded, freckled, and broad-nosed too, but nobody claims that this sort of classification is central to human biology.

There are relatively straightforward reasons for thinking that large parts of humanity will fit into no class of people who can be characterized as sharing not only a common superficial morphology but also significant other biological characteristics. The nineteenth-century dispute between monogenesis and polygenesis, between the view that we are descended from one original population and the view that we descend from several, is over. There is no doubt that all human beings descend from an original population (probably, as it happens, in Africa), and that from there people radiated out to cover the habitable globe. Conventional evolutionary theory would predict that as these populations moved into different environments and new characters were thrown up by mutation, some differences would emerge as different characteristics gave better chances of reproduction and survival. In a situation where a group of people was isolated genetically for many generations, significant differences between populations could build up, though it would take a very extended period before the differences led to reproductive isolation—the impossibility of fertile breeding—and thus to the origin of a new pair of distinct species. We know that there is no such reproductive isolation between human populations, as a walk down any street in New York or Paris or Rio will confirm, but we also know that none of the major human population groups have been reproductively isolated for very many generations. If I may be excused what will sound like a euphemism, at the margins there is always the exchange of genes.

Not only has there always been some degree of genetic linkage of this marginal kind; human history contains continued large-scale movements of people—the "hordes" of Attila the Hun, the Mediterranean jihads of the newly Islamized Arabs, the Bantu migrations—that represent possibilities for genetic exchange. As a consequence, all human populations are linked to each other through neighboring populations, *their* neighbors, and so on. We might have ended up as a "ring species," like the gulls of the *Larus argentatus* and *Larus fuscus* groups that circumscribe the North Pole, where there is inbreeding between most neighboring populations but reproductive isolation of the varieties that form the beginning and end of the chain of variation, but we did not.[28]

The classification of people into "races" would be biologically interesting if both the margins and the migrations had not left behind a genetic trail. But they have, and along that trail are millions of us (the numbers obviously depending on the criteria of classification that are used) who can be fitted into no plausible scheme at all. In a sense, trying to classify people into a few races is like trying to classify books in a library: you may use a single property—size, say—but you will get a useless classification, or you may use a more complex system of interconnected criteria, and then you will get a good deal of arbitrariness. No one—not even the most compulsive librarian!—thinks that book classifications reflect deep facts about books. Each of them is more or less useless for various purposes; all of them, as we know, have the kind of rough edges that take a while to get around. And nobody thinks that a library classification can settle which books we should value; the numbers in the Dewey decimal system do not correspond with qualities of utility or interest or literary merit.

The appeal of race as a classificatory notion provides us with an instance of a familiar pattern in the history of science. In the early phases of theory, scientists begin, inevitably, with the categories of their folk theories of the world, and often the criteria of membership of these categories can be detected with the unaided senses. Thus, in early chemistry, color and taste played an important role in the classification of substances; in early natural history, plant and animal species were identified largely by their gross visible morphology. Gradually, as the science develops, however, concepts are developed whose application requires more than the unaided senses; instead of the phenomenal properties of things, we look for "deeper," more theoretical properties. The price we pay is that classification becomes a more specialized activity; the benefit we gain is that we are able to make generalizations of greater power and scope. Few candidates for laws of nature can be stated by reference to the colors, tastes, smells, or touches of objects. It is hard for us to accept that the colors of objects, which play so important a role in our visual experience and our recognition of everyday objects, turn out neither to play an important part in the behavior of matter nor to be correlated with properties that do. Brown, for example, a color whose absence would make a radical difference to the look of the natural world, is hard to correlate in any clear way with the physical properties of reflecting surfaces.[29]

This desire to save the phenomena of our experience by way of objects and properties that are hidden from our direct view is, of course, a crucial feature of the natural sciences. At the heart of this project, as Heisenberg—one of the greatest physicists of our and any time—once pointed out, is a principle that he ascribed to Democritus:

> Democritus' atomic theory . . . realizes that it is impossible to explain rationally the perceptible qualities of matter except by tracing these back to the behaviour of entities which themselves no longer possess these qualities. If atoms are really to explain the origin of colour and smell of visible material bodies, then they cannot possess properties like colour and smell.[30]

The explanation of the phenotypes of organisms in terms of their genotypes fits well into this Democritean pattern. In the same way, nineteenth-century race science sought in a heritable racial essence an explanation of what its proponents took to be the observed phenomena of the differential distribution in human populations both of morphological and of psychological and social traits. What modern genetics shows is that there is no such underlying racial essence. There was nothing wrong with the Democritean impulse, only with the particular form it took and the prejudices that informed—perhaps one should say ''deformed''—the theorists' views of the phenomena.

The disappearance of a widespread belief in the biological category of the Negro would leave nothing for racists to have an attitude toward. But it would offer, by itself, no guarantee that Africans would escape from the stigma of centuries. Extrinsic racists could disappear and be replaced by people who believed that the population of Africa had in its gene pool fewer of the genes that account for those human capacities that generate what is valuable in human life; fewer, that is, than in European or Asian or other populations. Putting aside the extraordinary difficulty of defining which genes these are, there is, of course, no scientific basis for this claim. A confident expression of it would therefore be evidence only of the persistence of old prejudices in new forms. But even this view would be, in one respect, an advance on extrinsic racism. For it would mean that each African would need to be judged on his or her own merits. Without some cultural information, being told that someone is of African origin gives you little basis for supposing anything much about them. Let me put the claim at its weakest: in the absence of a racial essence, there could be no guarantee that some particular person was not more gifted—in some specific respect—than any or all others in the populations of other regions.[31]

It was earlier evidence, pointing similarly to the conclusion that ''the genic variation within and between the three major races of man . . . is small compared with the intraracial variation''[32] and that differences in morphology were not correlated strongly with intellectual and moral capacity, that led Du Bois in *The Crisis* to an explicit rejection of the claim that biological race mattered for understanding the status of the Negro:

> So far at least as intellectual and moral aptitudes are concerned we ought to speak of civilizations where we now speak of races. . . . Indeed, even the physical characteristics, excluding the skin color of a people, are to no small extent the direct result of the physical and social environment under which it is living. . . . These physical characteristics are furthermore too indefinite and elusive to serve as a basis for any rigid classification or division of human groups.[33]

This is straightforward enough. Yet it would be too swift a conclusion to suppose that Du Bois here expresses his deepest convictions. After 1911 he went on to advocate Pan-Africanism, as he had advocated Pan-Negroism in 1897, and whatever African-Americans and Africans, from Asante to Zulu, share, it is not a single civilization.

Du Bois managed to maintain Pan-Africanism while officially rejecting talk of race as anything other than a synonym for color. We can see how he did this if we turn to his second autobiography, *Dusk of Dawn,* published in 1040.

In *Dusk of Dawn*—the "essay toward the autobiography of a race concept"—Du Bois explicitly allies himself with the claim that race is not a "scientific" concept.

> It is easy to see that scientific definition of race is impossible; it is easy to prove that physical characteristics are not so inherited as to make it possible to divide the world into races; that ability is the monopoly of no known aristocracy; that the possibilities of human development cannot be circumscribed by color, nationality or any conceivable definition of race.[34]

But we need no scientific definition, for

> All this has nothing to do with the plain fact that throughout the world today organized groups of men by monopoly of economic and physical power, legal enactment and intellectual training are limiting with determination and unflagging zeal the development of other groups; and that the concentration particularly of economic power today puts the majority of mankind into a slavery to the rest.[35]

Or, as he puts it pithily a little later, "the black man is a person who must ride 'Jim Crow' in Georgia."[36]

Yet, just a few pages earlier, he has explained why he remains a Pan-Africanist, committed to a political program that binds all this indefinable black race together. This passage is worth citing extensively.

Du Bois begins with Countee Cullen's question—What is Africa to me?—and replies:

> Once I should have answered the question simply: I should have said "fatherland" or perhaps better "motherland" because I was born in the century when the walls of race were clear and straight; when the world consisted of mut[u]ally exclusive races; and even though the edges might be blurred, there was no question of exact definition and understanding of the meaning of the word. . . .
>   Since [the writing of "The Conservation of Races"] the concept of race has so changed and presented so much of contradiction that as I face Africa I ask myself:

what is it between us that constitutes a tie which I can feel better than I can explain? Africa is of course my fatherland. Yet neither my father nor my father's father ever saw Africa or knew its meaning or cared overmuch for it. My mother's folk were closer and yet their direct connection, in culture and race, became tenuous; still my tie to Africa is strong. On this vast continent were born and lived a large portion of my direct ancestors going back a thousand years or more. The mark of their heritage is upon me in color and hair. These are obvious things, but of little meaning in themselves; only important as they stand for real and more subtle differences from other men. Whether they do or not, I do not know nor does science know today.

But one thing is sure and that is the fact that since the fifteenth century these ancestors of mine and their descendants have had a common history; have suffered a common disaster and have one long memory. The actual ties of heritage between the individuals of this group vary with the ancestors that they have in common with many others: Europeans and Semites, perhaps Mongolians, certainly American Indians. But the physical bond is least and the badge of color relatively unimportant save as a badge; the real essence of this kinship is its social heritage of slavery; the discrimination and insult; and this heritage binds together not simply the children of Africa, but extends through yellow Asia and into the South Seas. It is this unity that draws me to Africa.[37]

This passage is affecting, powerfully expressed. We should like to be able to follow it in its conclusions. But, since it seduces us into error, we should begin distancing ourselves from the appeal of its argument by noticing how it echoes our earlier text. Color and hair are unimportant save "as they stand for real and more subtle differences," Du Bois says here, and we recall the "subtle forces" that "have generally followed the natural cleavage of common blood, descent and physical peculiarities" of "The Conservation of Races." There it was an essential part of the argument that these subtle forces—impulses and strivings—were the common property of those who shared a "common blood"; here, Du Bois does "not know nor does science" whether this is so. But if it is not so, then, on Du Bois's own admission, these "obvious things" are "of little meaning." And if they are of little meaning, then his mention of them marks, on the surface of his argument, the extent to which he cannot quite escape the appeal of the earlier conception of race.

Du Bois's yearning for the earlier conception that he has now prohibited himself accounts for the pathos of the chasm between the unconfident certainty that Africa is "of course" his fatherland and the concession that it is not the land of his father or his father's father. What use is such a fatherland? What use is a motherland with which even your mother's connection is "tenuous"? What does it matter that a large portion of his ancestors have lived on that vast continent, if there is no subtler bond with them than brute—that is, culturally unmediated—biological descent and its entailed "badge" of hair and color?

Even in the passage that follows his explicit disavowal of the scientific conception of race, the references to "common history"—the "one long memory," the "social heritage of slavery"—only lead us back into the now-familiar move to substitute for the biological conception of race a sociohistorical one. And that, as we have seen, is simply to bury the biological conception below the surface, not to transcend it. Because he never truly "speaks of civilization," Du Bois cannot ask if there is not in American culture—which undoubtedly *is* his—an African residue to take hold of and rejoice in, a subtle connection mediated not by genetics but by intentions, by meaning. Du Bois has no more conceptual resources here for explicating the unity of the Negro race—the Pan-African identity—than he had in "The Conservation of Races" half a century earlier. A glorious non sequitur must be submerged in the depths of the argument. It is easily brought to the surface.

If what Du Bois has in common with Africa is a history of "discrimination and insult," then this binds him, on his own account, to "yellow Asia and . . . the South Seas" also. How can something he shares with the whole nonwhite world bind him to a part of it? Once we interrogate the argument here, a further suspicion arises that the claim to this bond is based on a hyperbolic reading of the facts. The "discrimination and insult" that we know Du Bois experienced in his American childhood and as an adult citizen of the industrialized world were different in character from that experienced by, say, Kwame Nkrumah in colonized West Africa, and were absent altogether in large parts of "yellow Asia." What Du Bois shares with the nonwhite world is not insult but the *badge* of insult, and the badge, without the insult, is just the very skin and hair and bone that it is impossible to connect with a scientific definition of race.

Du Bois's question deserves a more careful answer than he gives it. What *does* cement together people who share a characteristic—the "badge of insult"—on the basis of which some of them have suffered discrimination? We might answer: "Just that; so there is certainly something that the nonwhite people of the world share." But if we go on to ask what harm exactly a young woman in Mali suffers from antiblack race prejudice in Paris, this answer misses all the important details. She *does* suffer, of course, because, for example, political decisions about North-South relations are strongly affected by racism in the metropolitan cultures of the North. But this harm is more systemic, less personal, than the affront to individual dignity represented by racist insults in the postindustrial city. If she is an intellectual, reflecting on the cultures of the North, she may also feel the meditated sense of insult: she may know, after all, that if she were there, in Paris, she would risk being subjected to some of the same discriminations; she may recognize that racism is part of the reason why she could not get a visa to go there; why she would not have a good time if she did.

Such thoughts are certainly maddening, as African and African-American and black European intellectuals will avow, if you ask them how they feel about the racist immigration policies of Europe or the institutionalized racism of apartheid. And they are thoughts that can be had by any nonwhite person anywhere who knows—in a phrase of Chinua Achebe's—"how the world is moving."[38] The thought that if *I* were there now, I would be a victim strikes at you differently, it seems to me, from the thought—which can enrage any decent white human being—that if I were there and *if I were not white,* I would be a victim.[39] Yet we should always remember that this thought, too, has led many to an identification with the struggle against racism.

The lesson, I think, of these reflections must be that there is no one answer to the question what identifications our antiracism may lead us into. Du Bois writes as if he has to choose between Africa, on the one hand, and "yellow Asia and . . . the South Seas," on the other. But that, it seems to me, is just the choice that racism imposes on us—and just the choice we must reject.

I made the claim in Chapter 1 that there are substantial affinities between the racial doctrines of Pan-Africanism and other forms of nationalism rooted in the nineteenth century, in particular, with Zionism. Since we cannot forget what has been done to Jews in the name of race in this century, this claim is bound to invite controversy. I make it only to insist on the ways in which the Pan-Africanism of the African-American creators of black nationalist rhetoric was not untypical of European and American thought of its day, even of the rhetoric of the victims of racism. With Du Bois's position laid out before us, the comparison can be more substantially articulated.

But, given the sensitivity of the issue, I am bound to begin with caveats. It is no part of my brief to argue that Zionism has to be racialist—not the least because, as I shall be arguing finally, the Pan-Africanist impetus can also be given a nonracialist foundation. Nor is it my intention to argue for the claim that the origins of modern Zionism are *essentially* racialist, or that racialism is central to the thought of all the founders of modern Zionism. It seems to me, as I have said, that Judaism—the religion—and the wider body of Jewish practice through which the various communities of the Diaspora have defined themselves allow for a cultural conception of Jewish identity that cannot be made plausible in the case of Pan-Africanism. As evidence of this fact, I would simply cite the way that the fifty or so rather disparate African nationalities in our present world seem to have met the nationalist impulses of many Africans, while Zionism has, of necessity, been satisfied by the creation of a single state.

But despite these differences, it is important to be clear that there were Jewish racialists in the early story of modern Zionism; that they were not marginal figures or fringe madmen; and that they, like Crummell and, later, Du Bois, developed a nationalism rooted in nineteenth-century theories of race. It is important in the practical world of politics because a racialized Zionism continues to be one of the threats to the moral stability of Israeli nationalism; as witness the politics of the late Rabbi Meir Kahane. But it is theoretically important to my argument, because, as I say, it is central to my view that Crummell's inchoate *theoria,* which Du Bois turned to organized theory, was thoroughly conventional.

Now, of course, to establish that Crummell's view was conventional, we should need no more than to cite the historical writings of the first academic historians in the United States, with their charming fantasies of Puritan democracy as part of a continuous tradition derived from the Anglo-Saxon moot, or the works of British Anglo-Saxon historiography, which traced the evolution of British institutions back to Tacitus's Teutonic hordes; and I shall, indeed, take up some of the issues raised in these writings at the start of Chapter 3. But *that* comparison would leave out part of what is so fascinating about the thought of these early nationalists. For, however anachronistic our reaction, our surprise at Crummell and those of his Zionist contemporaries that shared his racialized vision is that they, as victims of racism, endorsed racialist theories.

So that when we read ''The Ethics of Zionism'' by Horace M. Kallen, published in the *Maccabaean* in New York in August 1906, we may feel the same no-doubt-anachronistic astonishment.[40] Kallen's essay was based on a lecture he had given to a gathering of an American Zionist organization (the *Maccabaean* was its official publication). He says: "It is the race and not the man who, in the greater account of human destiny, struggles, survives or dies, and types of civilization have always reflected the natural character of the dominant races."[41] And we remember Du Bois's "the history of the world is the history, not of individuals . . . but of races." He asks: "What then has the Jew done for civilization? What is his place in the evolution of the human race? What is his moral worth to humanity?"[42] And we are reminded of Du Bois's races each "struggling . . . to develop for civilization its particular message."

There are, of course, instructive differences between Kallen's "ethics" and Du Bois's. Part of the historical divergence between African-American and Jewish-American conceptions of identity is revealed when Kallen explicitly rejects a religious or cultural conception of Jewish identity:

> Here is an intensely united people of relatively unmixed blood, and intense race consciousness, sojourning in all parts of the earth, in some manner successfully, and the natural object of hatred of those among whom it lives. To avoid the effect of this hatred many of the race have tried to eliminate all resemblances between themselves and it. Their languages are as various as the countries in which they live; they proclaim their nationalities as Russian, English, French, Austrian, or American and relegate their racial character to a sectarian label. "We", they say, "are not Jews but Judaists.[")][43]
> . . . our duty i[s] to Judaize the Jew.[44]

For this argument presupposes as its antagonist a purely cultural nationalism of a kind that was to develop fully among African-Americans only later. Kallen saw "Cultur-Zionism" of this sort as not "much better than assimilation,"[45] which, of course, he actively opposed also. But this resistance to assimilation could not be part of Du Bois's position, either: assimilation, which some took to be a possibility for a brief moment after the American Civil War, did not become more than a theoretical possibility again—save for the few African-Americans who could "pass for white"—until after the civil rights movement, and then, of course, it was largely rejected in favor of a cultural nationalism of *Roots*.

Nevertheless, mutatis mutandis, the operative ideology here is recognizably Du Bois's; American Jewish nationalism—at least in *this* manifestation—and American black nationalism are (unsurprisingly) part of the same scheme of things.[46]

If Du Bois's race concept seems an all-too-American creation, its traces in African rhetoric are legion. When Kwame Nkrumah addressed the Gold Coast Parliament in presenting the "motion of destiny" accepting the independence constitution, he spoke these words:

> Honourable Members . . . The eyes and ears of the world are upon you; yea, our oppressed brothers throughout this vast continent of Africa and the New World are looking to you with desperate hope, as an inspiration to continue their grim fight against cruelties which we in this corner of Africa have never known—cruelties which are a disgrace to humanity, and to the civilisation which the white man has set himself to teach us.[47]

To a person unencumbered with the baggage of the history of the idea of race, it would surely seem strange that the independence of one nation of black men and women should resonate more with black people than with other oppressed people; strange too that it should be the whiteness of the oppressors—"the white man"—as opposed, say, to their *imperialism,* that should stand out. It should seem a strange idea, even to those of us who live in a world formed by racial ideology, that your freedom from cruelties I have never known should spur me on in my fight for freedom *because we are of the same color.* Yet Du Bois died in Nkrumah's Ghana, led there by the dream of Pan-Africanism and the reality of American racism. If he escaped that racism, he never completed the escape from race. The logic of his argument leads naturally to the final repudiation of race as a term of difference—to speaking "of civilizations where we now speak of races." The logic is the same logic that has led us to speak of gender—the social construction out of the biological facts—where we once spoke of sex, and a rational assessment of the evidence requires that we should endorse not only the logic but the premises of each argument. I have only sketched the evidence for these premises in the case of race, but it is all there in the journals. Discussing Du Bois has been largely a pretext for adumbrating the argument he never quite managed to complete.

In Chapter 1, I distinguished two kinds of racism—intrinsic and extrinsic: Du Bois's theoretical racism was, in my view, extrinsic. Yet, in his heart, it seems to me that Du Bois's feelings were those of an intrinsic racist. He wanted desperately to find in Africa and with Africans a home, a place where he could feel, as he never felt in America, that he belonged. His reason would not allow him to be an intrinsic racist, however; and so he reacted to the challenges to racialism by seeking in more and more exotic ways to defend his belief in the connection between race and morally relevant properties.

The truth is that there are no races: there is nothing in the world that can do all we ask race to do for us. As we have seen, even the biologist's notion has only limited uses, and the notion that Du Bois required, and that underlies the more hateful racisms of the modern era, refers to nothing in the world at all. The evil that is done is done by the concept, and by easy—yet impossible—assumptions as to its application.

Talk of "race" is particularly distressing for those of us who take culture seriously. For, where race works—in places where "gross differences" of morphology are correlated with "subtle differences" of temperament, belief, and intention—it works as an attempt at metonym for culture, and it does so only at the price of biologizing what *is* culture, ideology.

To call it "biologizing" is not, however, to consign our concept of race to biology. For what is present there is not our concept but our word only. Even the biologists who believe in human races use the term *race,* as they say, "without any social implication."[48] What exists "out there" in the world—communities of meaning, shading variously into each other in the rich structure of the social world—is the province not of biology but of the human sciences.

I have examined these issues through the writings of Du Bois, with the burden of his scholarly inheritance, seeking to transcend the system of oppositions whose acceptance would have left him opposed to the (white) norm of form and value. In his early work, Du Bois takes race for granted and seeks to revalue one pole of the opposition of white to black. The received concept is a hierarchy, a vertical structure, and Du Bois wishes to rotate the axis, to give race a "horizontal" reading. Challenge the assumption that there can be an axis, however oriented in the space of values, and the project fails for loss of presuppositions. In his later writings, Du Bois—whose life's work was, in a sense, an attempt at just this impossible project—was unable to escape the notion of race he explicitly rejected. I shall show in later essays that this curious conjunction of a reliance on and a repudiation of race recurs in recent African theorizing.

We may borrow Du Bois's own metaphor: though he saw the dawn coming, he never faced the sun. And it would be hard to deny that he is followed in this by many in Africa—as in Europe and America—today: we all live in the dusk of that dawn.

THREE

Topologies of Nativism

Au delà du refus de toute domination extérieure, c'est la volonté de renouer en profondeur avec l'héritage culturel de l'Afrique, trop longtemps méconnu et refusé. Loin d'être un effort superficiel ou folklorique pour faire revivre quelques traditions ou pratiques ancestrales, il s'agit de construire une nouvelle société dont l'identité n'est pas conférée du dehors.[1]

CARDINAL PAUL ZOUNGRANA

Martin Farquhar Tupper, an Englishman who lived through most of the nineteenth century, was an extremely prolific writer; in his day the verses in his *Proverbial Maxims* were read by millions, and his two novels and many other writings gathered him a respectable public. Nowadays, Tupper is known only to those with a historical interest in popular writers of the nineteenth century or an antiquarian interest in bad verse. But in 1850 Tupper was at the height of his popularity and his powers, and in that year he published these soon-to-be-famous words in a new journal called the *Anglo-Saxon.*

> Stretch forth! stretch forth! from the south to the north,
> From the east to the west,—stretch forth! stretch forth!
> Strengthen thy stakes and lengthen thy cords,—
> The world is a tent for the world's true lords!
> Break forth and spread over every place
> The world is a world for the Saxon race!

The *Anglo-Saxon* lasted only a year, but its tone is emblematic of an important development in the way educated Englishmen and women thought of themselves and of what it was that made them English—a development that was itself part of a wider movement of ideas in Europe and North America. As heirs to the culture of the modern world, a culture so crucially shaped by the ideas that Tupper's poem represents, almost all twentieth-century readers, not merely in Europe and America but throughout the world, are able to take for granted a set of assumptions about what Tupper means by "race." Those assumptions, which amounted to a new theory of race, color our modern understanding of literature—indeed of most symbolic culture—in fundamental ways, and this despite the fact that many of these assumptions have been officially discarded.

Race, nation, literatue: these terms are bound together in the recent intellectual history of the West, and we shall need, as we shall see, to bear this in mind when we turn to Crummell's and Du Bois's postcolonial literary heirs. For while the ideas of racialism are familiar and no one needs to be reminded of the connection between racialism and the sort of imperialism that Tupper celebrated, it is perhaps a less familiar thought that many of those works that are central to the recent history of our understanding of what *literatue* is are also thematically preoccupied with racial issues. But the reason for this is not far to seek: it lies in the dual connection made in eighteenth- and nineteenth-century Euro-American thought between, on the one hand, race and nationality, and, on the other, nationality and literature. In short, the nation is the key middle term in understanding the relations between the concept of *race* and the idea of literature.

The first of these linkages, between nation and race, will surely be the less puzzling, even to an American reader raised in a self-consciously multiracial nation. Since the seventeenth century, Americans have believed that part of what is distinctive about New World culture and politics is the variety of the national (and later the "racial") origins of the peoples who have settled here. America was a new nation, conceived of by the Puritans as the product of the free choice of its immigrants. The Puritan community was established in self-conscious contrast to the European kingdoms and principalities from which the first immigrants came, states where which ruler you were the subject of was a matter of birth. These first immigrants thought of their new community as the product not of descent but of choice; of the bonds, in a familiar phrase, of brotherly love. As John Winthrop put it in 1630 "the ligaments of this body [the Puritan community] which knit [it] together are love."[2] Precisely because Americans from the beginning contrasted their situation as having consented to live together in the New World, with that in the Old World, where people were the hereditary subjects of monarchies, they have always known that European nations conceived of themselves in terms of descent. From this perspective, all that happened was that descent came in the mid-nineteenth century to be understood in terms of *race*.

Yet the increasing identification of race and nation in European—and more particularly in *English*—thought was a complex process. The Anglo-Saxonism of the nineteenth century in Britain—Crummell's Anglo-Saxonism—has its roots deep in the soil of historical argument about the English constitution; in the fascinating process through which a rising commercial class transformed the monarchy in Britain from its feudal roots into the "constitutional monarchy" that was established at the Restoration of 1660. In the arguments that surround this development, a mythology developed in the seventeenth century of a free Anglo-Saxon people, living under parliamentary government in the period before the Norman Conquest of 1066. Increasingly, Anglo-Saxon institutions were seen both to account for the Englishman's "natural love of freedom" and to underlie the "immemorial rights" of free men against the crown.

This mythology was counterposed against the mainstream historiography of the Middle Ages, which traced the *History of the Kings of Britain*—as Geoffrey of Monmouth's seminal work of 1136 was called—to Brutus, grandson of Aeneas of Troy.[3] It was Geoffrey who established the story of King Arthur, son of Utherpendragon, as forever part of British mythology; his work played a significant part in providing a framework within which the different cultural streams—Roman, Saxon, Danish, and Norman—that had come together over the first millennium in Britain could be gathered into a single unifying history.

When Richard Verstegen published his influential *Restitution of Decayed Intelligence* in 1605, he claimed that England's Anglo-Saxon past was the past of a Germanic people, who shared their language and institutions with the Germanic tribes whose great courage and fierce independence Tacitus had described many centuries earlier. Verstegen argued that these tribes were also the ancestors of the Danes and the Normans, whose invasions of Britain had thus not essentially disturbed the unity of the English as a Germanic people. The effect of this argument, of course, was to provide for the seventeenth century what the *History of the Kings of Britain* had provided in the Middle Ages: a framework within which the peoples of England could be conceived as united.

By the eve of the American Revolution, Anglo-Saxon historiography and the study of Anglo-Saxon law, language, and institutions were established scholarly pursuits, and the notion of a free Anglo-Saxon past, whose reestablishment would be an escape from the monarchy's potential to develop into a tyranny, was one that appealed naturally to such figures as Thomas Jefferson. Anglo-Saxonism spread easily to a United States whose dominant culture imagined itself—even after the Revolution—as British. And when Jefferson, himself no mean Anglo-Saxon scholar, designed a curriculum for the University of Virginia, he included the study of the Anglo-Saxon language, because, as he said, reading the "histories and laws left us in that . . . dialect," students would "imbibe with the language their free principles of government."

Jefferson himself also "suspected," as he argued in his *Notes on the State of Virginia*, that the Anglo-Saxon people were superior to blacks "in the endowments both of body and of mind," though he never directly challenged the biblical orthodoxy that Africans were, like all human beings, descended from Adam and Eve. And this language, with its focus on *endowments*, that is, on heredity, and in its linking of the physical bodily inheritance with the endowments of the mind, is one of the earliest statements of what was then a radical view: the view that the cultural inferiority of the nonwhite races flowed from an inherited racial essence.

But Jefferson is, in many ways, not yet the complete racialist. For one thing, his view is not totally generalized, so that he does not have the idea that *every* person belongs to a race with its own distinctive essence and its own place in the order of moral and intellectual endowments. While his attitude toward blacks was less than enthusiastic, his beliefs about the "endowments" of native Americans, who were plainly not of Anglo-Saxon descent, were largely positive, and he actively favored interbreeding to produce a new strain of Americans of "mixed blood." But, in the half century following the *Notes on the State of Virginia*, the generalization of race thinking—to produce the racialism of Crummell and Du Bois—was completed.[4]

In the different circumstances of the New World, where racial slavery had become a central fact of life, Jefferson anticipated an intellectual process that began in Britain only later. In England, Anglo-Saxonist mythology had so far been used largely in arguments within the United Kingdom, arguments that centered on the shift of power from the feudal aristocracy to the rising bourgeoisie. In the period from the end of the Napoleonic Wars to the midcentury, the celebration of the Anglo-Saxon people and their institutions was turned outward to justify the domination of the nonwhite world. And it is the lineaments of this fully racialized nation—what I earlier called the linkage between nation and race—that we recognize so easily in Tupper's verse.

But the deep-rooted character of the second linkage—between nation and literature—will probably be less naturally intelligible. And our starting point for understanding the role of the idea of a national literature in the development of the concept of a national culture must be in the work of the man who developed its first real theoretical articulation (a man I have already mentioned—almost inevitably—in connection with Crummell)—namely, Johann Gottfried Herder.

In his *On the New German Literature: Fragments* of 1767, Herder—who is in some ways the first important philosopher of modern nationalism—proposed the notion that language is not just "a tool of the arts and sciences" but "a part of them." "Whoever writes about the literature of a country," Herder continued, "must not neglect its language." Herder's notion of the *Sprachgeist*—literally, the "spirit" of the language—embodies the thought that language is more than the medium through which speakers communicate. As Hans Kohn, one of the great historians of nationalism, has written, for Herder a

> nationality lived above all in its civilization; its main instrument was its language, not an artificial instrument, but a gift of God, the guardian of the national community and the matrix of its civilization. Thus language, national language, became a sacred instrument; each man could be himself only by thingking and creating in his own language. With the respect for all other nationalities went a respect for their languages.[5]

Herder had, of course, to make a sharp distinction between nations and states because in eighteenth-century Europe there was not even an approximate correlation between linguistic and political boundaries. (It is important to remember that the correlation remains in most parts of the world quite rough-and-ready.) The modern European nationalism that produced, for example, the German and Italian states, involved an attempt to create states to correspond to nationalities: nationalities conceived of as sharing a civilization and, more particularly, a language and literature. Exactly because political geography did not correspond to Herder's nationalities, he was obliged to draw a distinction between the nation as a natural entity and the state as the product of culture, as a human artifice.

The opposition between nature and culture is one of the oldest in Western intellectual history (indeed, Claude Lévi-Strauss, has argued that it is one of the central oppositions of human thought). But this opposition has been understood in radically different ways in different periods. For Herder and his contemporaries, as Hans Kohn makes clear, human nature was still largely a matter of God's intentions for human beings; the nation was natural, as Crummell wrote about a century after Herder's *Fragments* (in a passage I have already cited), because "races, like families, are the organisms and ordinances of God."[6]

But with the increasing influence of the natural sciences in the period since Herder's day, what is natural in human beings—"human nature"—has come increasingly to be thought of in terms of the sciences of biology and anthropology. Inevitably, then, the nation comes more and more to be identified as a biological unit, defined by the shared essence that flows from a common descent; even when, as in the case of Alexander Crummell, the reality of races was also itself seen, theologically— as the Hebrews had seen it—as a product of the divine will.

Superimposing the Herderian identification of the core of the nation with its national literature on the racial conception of the nation, we arrive at the racial understanding of literature that flourishes from the mid-nineteenth century in the work of the first modern literary historians. Hippolyte Taine's monumental *History of English Literature*—perhaps the first modern literary history of English, published in France in the 1860s—begins with the words: "History has been transformed, within a hundred years in Germany, within sixty in France, and that by the study of their literatures."[7] But he is soon telling us that:

> a race, like the Old Aryans, scattered from the Ganges as far as the Hebrides, settled in every clime, and every stage of civilization, transformed by thirty centuries of revolutions, nevertheless manifests in its languages, religions, literatures, philosophies, the community of blood and of intellect which to this day binds its offshoots together.[8]

What is revealed, in short, by the study of literature that has transformed the discipline of history is the "moral state" of the race whose literature it is. It is because of this conception that Taine finds it proper to start his study of English literature with a chapter on the Saxons, so that Taine's *History* begins not in England at all but in Holland:

> As you coast the North Sea from Scheldt to Jutland, you will mark in the first place that the characteristic feature is the want of slope: marsh, waster, shoal; the rivers hardly drag themselves along, swollen and sluggish, with long, black-looking waves.[9]

The "Saxons, Angles, Jutes, Frisians . . . [and] Danes"[10] who occupied this region of Holland at the beginning of the first millennium are, according to Taine, the ancestors of the English, but since they, themselves, are of German descent, Taine also refers, in describing this "race" a few pages later, to some of their traits reported in Tacitus.

It is the conception of the binding core of the English nation as the Anglo-Saxon *race* that accounts for Taine's decision to identify the origins of English literature not in its antecedents in the Greek and Roman classics that provided the models and themes of so much of the best-known works of English "poesy"; not in the Italian models that influenced the drama of Marlowe and Shakespeare; but in *Beowulf,* a poem in the Anglo-Saxon tongue, a poem that was unknown to Spenser and Shakespeare, the first poets to write in a version of the English language that we can still almost understand.

Yet this decision was quite representative. When the teaching of English literature was institutionalized in the English universities in the nineteenth century, students were required to learn Anglo-Saxon in order to study *Beowulf.* Anglo-Saxonism thus played a major role in the establishment of the canon of literary works that are to be studied in both British and American colleges, and the teachers who came from these colleges to the high schools brought the Anglo-Saxon canon with them.

It hardly needs pointing out that explicit Anglo-Saxonism is not exactly in favor; it has succumbed, we may happily say, first to the political and then to the intellectual onslaughts of antiracism. So there is something of a historical irony in the fact that among the most prominent reflections of racially understood ethnicity in literary studies in recent years is in the development of African-American literary criticism. For anyone who has followed the argument so far, it will not be surprising that the persistent stream of African-American nationalist argument—a tradition whose origins can be traced back to well before the rise of racial Anglo-Saxonism—has been accompanied by appeals to an African cultural heritage expressed in black folk music, poetry, and song. Such intellectual pioneers as Du Bois from the latter nineteenth century on attempted to articulate a racial tradition of black letters, in part as a natural expression of the Herderian view of the nation as identified above all else with its expression in "poesy." Many African-American theorists would have agreed with Carlyle—there is another irony in this happy consensus between "niggers" and the author of the "Occasional Discourse on the Nigger Question"—when he wrote in *The Edinburgh Review* in 1831 (in a discussion of a history of German poetry):

> The history of a nation's poetry is the essence of its history, political, scientific, religious. With all these the complete Historian of Poetry will be familiar: the national physiognomy, in its finest traits, and through its successive stages of growth, will be clear to him; he will discern the grand spiritual tendency of every period.

But there is another reason why the identification of a history of black literature has been central not merely to African-American literary criticism but to the culture of African-Americans: namely, that for almost the whole period that there have been people of African descent in the New World, Europeans and Americans of European descent have consistently denied that black people were capable of contributing to "the arts and letters." Starting before the fixing of *race* as a biological concept, influential figures expressed their doubts about the "capacity of the Negro" to produce literature. Even in the Enlightenment, which emphasized the universality of reason, Voltaire in France, Hume in Scotland, and Kant in Germany, like Jefferson in the New World, denied literary capacity to people of African descent. As Hume—surely a philosopher of more than negligible influence—wrote in a famous footnote to his essay *Of National Characters* (1748): "I am apt to suspect the Negroes to be naturally inferior to the Whites. There scarcely ever was a civilized nation of that complexion, nor even any individual, eminent either in action or speculation."[11] And, as we have seen, once race was conceptualized in biological terms, such low opinions of black people would lead easily to the implication that these incapacities were part of an inescapable racial essence.

In response to this long line of antiblack invective, black writers in the United States since the very first African-American poet (Phillis Wheatley, who lived in Boston in the latter part of the eighteenth century) have sought to establish the "capacity of the Negro" by writing and publishing first poetry and then, later—as literature came to be conceived as encompassing the novel, the essay, and the autobiography—in each of these forms.[12] More than this, the major proportion of the published writing of African-Americans, even when not directed to countering racist mythology, has been concerned thematically with issues of race, a fact that is hardly surprising in a country where black people were subjected to racial slavery until the mid-nineteenth century and then treated legally as second-class citizens in many places until the 1960s.

The recognition, especially in recent years, of the role of Anglo-Saxonism, in particular, and racism, more generally, in the construction of the canon of literature studied in American university departments of English has led many scholars to argue for the inclusion of texts by African-Americans in that canon, in part because their initial exclusion was an expression of racism. It has led others to argue for the recognition of an African-American tradition of writing, with its own major texts, which can be studied as a canon of their own.

What has not been so clear—despite the close affiliations of anglophone African and African-American criticisms—is the role of the conjunction of nation and literature in anglophone African criticism; it is to that issue, which I believe we should understand in the context I have just described, that I want to turn now.

Not long ago, I heard the Congolese writer Sony Labou Tansi discuss his ambivalent relation to the French language. Raised first by his Zairian kin in the (Belgian) Congo and then sent to school in (French) Congo-Brazzaville, he arrived at his formal schooling unfamiliar with its (French) language of instruction. He reported, with a strange mildness, the way in which his colonial teachers daubed him with human feces as a punishment for his early grammatical solecisms; then, a moment later, he went on to talk about his own remarkable work as a novelist and playwright in French. Labou Tansi has fashioned out of an experience with such unpromising beginnings a use for a language he ought surely to hate—a language literally shit-stained in his childhood—a use in the project of postcolonial literary nationalism.

In Africa and around the world, so much of our writing and, more especially, of our writing about writing touches on these issues of the nation and its language, on the conjunction captured almost at the start of modern theories of the nation in the Herderian conception of the *Sprachgeist*. For intellectuals everywhere are now caught up—whether as volunteers, draftees, or resisters—in a struggle for the articulation of their respective nations, and everywhere, it seems, language and literature are central to that articulation.

The power of the idea of the nation in the nonindustrialized world is more than a consequence of the cultural hegemony of the Europeans and Americans whose ancestors invented both the idea and most of the world's juridical nationalities. As Ben Anderson has argued—in his elegant *Imagined Communities*—though the national idea was introduced to much of the world by way of contacts with European imperialism, the appeal of the idea to the "natives" soon outran the control and the interests of the metropole. African and Asian intellectuals do not believe in national self-determination simply because it was forced upon them, because it was imposed as a tool of their continued neocolonial domination; rather, the idea of the nation provided—first for the local elite, then for the newly proletarianized denizens of the colonial city, and finally even for a peasantry attempting to come to terms with its increasing incorporation into the world system—a way to articulate a resistance both to the material domination of the world empires and to the more nebulous threat to precolonial modes of thought represented by the Western project of cultural ascendancy.

I began with the tradition that leads through Tupper to the present day not merely because, as we shall see, it informs recent African criticism, but also because I want to insist on the extent to which the issues of language and nation that are so central to the situation I want to discuss in this essay—that of sub-Saharan African writers and critics—are also the problems of European and American criticism. This is not—as it is often presented as being—a voyage into the exotic, a flirtation with a distant Other. Voltaire or one of his philosophe comrades in a European culture before the heyday of the world empires once said that when we travel, what we discover is always ourselves. It seems to me that this thought has, so to speak, become true. In the world after those world empires, a world where center and periphery are mutually constitutive, political life may be conceived of (however misleadingly) in national terms, but what Voltaire might have called the life of the mind cannot. If I seek to locate my discussion of the African situation with a few elements of context, then, it is in part so that others can recognize how much of that situation is familiar territory.

That the territory *is* so familiar is a consequence of the way in which intellectuals from what I will call, with reservations, the Third World, are a historical product of an encounter with what I will continue, with similar reservations, to call the West. As we have seen, most African writers have received a Western-style education; their ambiguous relations to the world of their foremothers and forefathers and to the world of the industrialized countries are part of their distinctive cultural (dis)location, a condition that Abiola Irele has eloquently described in "In Praise of Alienation."

> We are wedged uncomfortably between the values of our traditional culture and those of the West. The process of change which we are going through has created a dualism of forms of life which we experience at the moment less as a mode of challenging complexity than as one of confused disparateness.

Of course, there are influences—some of them (as we shall see) important—that run from the precolonial intellectual culture to those who have received colonial or postcolonial educations in the Western manner. Nevertheless, in sub-Saharan Africa, most literate people are literate in the colonial languages; most writing with a substantial readership (with the important exception of Swahili) is in those languages, and the only writing with a genuinely subcontinental audience and address is in English or in French. For many of their most important cultural purposes, African intellectuals, south of the Sahara, are what I have called "europhone."

There *are* intellectual workers—priests, shamans, griots, for example—in Africa and Asia (and some in South America and Australasia, too) who still operate in worlds of thought that are remote from the influences of Western literate discourse. But we surely live in the last days of that phase of human life in culture; and whether or not we choose to call these people "intellectuals"—and this strikes me as a decision whose outcome is less important than recognizing that it has to be made—

they are surely *not* the intellectuals who are producing the bulk of what we call Third World literature, nor are they articulating what we call literary theory or criticism. Literature, by and large, in sub-Saharan Africa means europhone literature (except in the Swahili culture area, where Swahili and the colonial languages are active together). And what matters in its being europhone is more than its inscription in the languages of the colonizers.

For language here is, of course, a synecdoche. When the colonialists attempted to tame the threatening cultural alterity of the African (whether through what the French called *assimilation* or through the agency of missionary "conversion"), the instrument of pedagogy was their most formidable weapon. So that the problem is not only, or not so much, the English or the French or the Portuguese languages as the cultural imposition that they each represent. Colonial education, in short, produced a generation immersed in the literature of the colonizers, a literature that often reflected and transmitted the imperialist vision.

This is, surely, no new thing: literary pedagogy played a similar role in Roman education in the provinces of that empire, an empire that still provides perhaps our most powerful paradigm of imperialism. John Guillory has recently focused our attention on a standard—dare I say, magisterial—treatment, by R. R. Bolgar in *The Classical Heritage and Its Beneficiaries,* of the process in which "the legions withdraw and are replaced by schools."

> As the protective might of the legions weakened, so the imperial government came
> to rely to an ever greater extent on its intangible assets. . . . Steel was in short
> supply . . . so the provinces were to be grappled to the soul of Rome by hoops of
> a different make.[13]

The role of the colonial (and, alas, the postcolonial) school in the reproduction of Western culture is crucial to African criticism because of the intimate connection between the idea of criticism and the growth of literary pedagogy, for (as John Guillory reminds us in the same place) the role of literature, indeed, the formation of the concept, the institution of "literature," is indissoluble from pedagogy. Roland Barthes expressed the point in a characteristic apothegm: " 'L'enseignement de la littérature' est pour moi presque tautologique. La littérature, c'est ce qui s'enseigne, un point c'est tout. C'est un objet d'enseignement.''[14] Abstracted from its context, this formulation no doubt requires some qualifying glosses. But one cannot too strongly stress the importance of the fact that what we discuss under the rubric of modern African writing is largely what is *taught* in high schools all around the continent. Nor should we ignore the crucial psychological importance of the possibility of such an African writing. The weapon of pedagogy changes hands simply because we turn from reading Buchan and Conrad and Graham Greene to reading Abrahams, Achebe, Armah—to begin an alphabet of writers in the Heinemann African Writer's series, which constitutes in the most concrete sense the pedagogical canon of anglophone African writing. The decolonized subject people write themselves, now, as the subject of a literature of their own. The simple gesture of writing for and about oneself—there are fascinating parallels here with the history of African-American writing—has a profound political significance.

Writing for and about ourselves, then, helps constitute the modern community of the nation, but we do it largely in languages imposed by "the might of the legions." Now that the objects of European imperialism have at last become the subjects of a discourse addressed both to each other and to the West, European languages and European disciplines have been "turned," like double agents, from the projects of the metropole to the intellectual work of post colonial cultural life.

But though officially in the service of new masters, these tools remain, like all double agents, perpetually under suspicion. Even when the colonizer's language is creolized, even when the imperialist's vision is playfully subverted in the lyrics of popular songs, there remains the suspicion that a hostile *Sprachgeist* is at work. Both the complaints against defilement by alien traditions in an alien tongue and the defenses of them as a practical necessity (a controversy that recalls similar debates in situations as otherwise different as, say, the early-twentieth-century Norwegian debate over "New Norwegian" and the nineteenth-century German Jewish debates over Yiddish) seem often to reduce to a dispute between a sentimental Herderian conception of Africa's languages and traditions as expressive of the collective essence of a pristine traditional community, on the one hand, and, on the other, a positivistic conception of European languages and disciplines as mere tools; tools that can be cleansed of the accompanying imperialist—and, more specifically, racist— modes of thought.

The former view is often at the heart of what we can call "nativism": the claim that true African independence requires a literature of one's own. Echoing the debate in nineteenth-century Russia between "Westerners" and "Slavophiles," the debate in Africa presents itself as an opposition between "universalism" and "particular- ism," the latter defining itself, above all else, by its opposition to the former. But there are only two real players in this game: us, inside; them, outside. That is all there is to it.

Operating with this topology of inside and outside—indigene and alien, Western and traditional—the apostles of nativism are able in contemporary Africa to mobilize the undoubted power of a nationalist rhetoric, one in which the literature of one's own is that of one's own nation. But nativists may appeal to identities that are both wider and narrower than the nation: to "tribes" and towns, below the nation-state; to Africa, above. And, I believe, we shall have the best chance of redirecting nativism's power if we challenge not the rhetoric of the tribe, the nation, or the continent but the topology that it presupposes, the opposition it asserts.

Consider, then, that now-classic manifesto of African cultural nationalism, *Toward the Decolonization of African Literature*. This much-discussed book is the work of three Nigerian authors—Chinweizu, Onwuchekwa Jemie, and Ihechukwu Madu- buike—all of them encumbered with extensive Western university educations. Dr. Chinweizu, a widely published poet and quondam editor of the Nigerian literary magazine *Okike*, was an undergraduate at MIT and holds a doctorate from SUNY Buffalo; he has emerged (from a career that included time on the faculty at MIT and at San Jose State) as one of the leading figures in contemporary Nigerian journalism, writing for a long period a highly influential column in *The Guardian* of Lagos. Dr. Jemie holds a doctorate from Columbia University in English and comparative literature, is also a distinguished poet, and has published an introduction to the poetry of Langston Hughes. And Dr. Ihechukwu Madubuike—who has been Nigeria's minister of education—studied at Laval in Canada, the Sorbonne, and SUNY Buffalo. All of these critics have taught in black studies programs in the United States—in their preface they thank the Department of Afro-American Studies at the University of Minnesota and the Black Studies Department at Ohio State University for "supportive clerical help." If their rhetoric strikes responsive chords in the American ear, we shall not find it too surprising.

Not that their language fails to incorporate Nigerian elements. The term *bolekaja*—which means, "Come down, let's fight"—is used in western Nigeria to refer to the "mammy-wagons" that are the main means of popular transportation; it reflects "the outrageous behaviour of their touts." In their preface, Chinweizu, Jemie, and Madubuike call themselves "*bolekaja* critics, outraged touts for the passenger lorries of African literature."

> There comes a time, we believe, in the affairs of men and of nations, when it becomes necessary for them to engage in *bolekaja* criticism for them to drag the stiflers of their life down to earth for a corrective tussle. A little wrestle in the sands never killed a sturdy youth.[15]

And it is clear that it is not really the "sturdy youth" of African criticism that they take to be at risk; for the work of the succeeding chapters is to wrestle the critical ethnocentrism of their Eurocentric opponents to the ground in the name of an Afrocentric particularism. If this is to be a struggle to the death, Chinweizu and his compatriots expect to be the survivors. They assert, for example, that

> most of the objections to thematic and ideological matters in the African novel sound like admonitions from imperialist motherhens to their wayward or outright rebellious captive chickens. They cluck: "Be Universal! Be Universal!"[16]

And they condemn

> the modernist retreat of our poets into privatist universalism [which] makes it quite easy for them to shed whatever African nationalist consciousness they have before they cross the threshold into the sanctum of "poetry in the clouds." And that suits the English literary establishment just fine, since they would much prefer it if an African nationalist consciousness, inevitably anti-British, was not promoted or cultivated, through literature, in the young African elite.[17]

Thus, when the British critic Adrian Roscoe urges African poets to view themselves as "inheritors of a universal tradition of art and letters and not just as the recipients of an indigenous legacy," he reaps the nationalists' scorn.[18] For their central insistence is that "African literature *is* an autonomous entity separate and apart from all other literature. It has its own traditions, models and norms."[19]

Now we should recognize from the start that such polemics can be a salutary corrective to a great deal of nonsense that has been written about African literature, by critics for whom literary merit is gauged by whether a work can be inserted into a Great White Tradition of masterpieces. It is hard not to be irritated by high-handed pronouncements from critics for whom detailed description of locale amounts to mere travelogue, unless, say, the locale is "Wessex" and the author is Thomas Hardy; for whom the evocation of local custom amounts to mere ethnography, unless, say, they are the customs of a northern English mining town and the author is D. H. Lawrence; and for whom the recounting of historical event amounts to mere journalism, unless the event is the Spanish civil war and the author is Hemingway.

What Chinweizu and his colleagues are objecting to, in other words, is the posture that conceals its privileging of one national (or racial) tradition against others in false talk of the Human Condition. It is not surprising, then, that Chinweizu and his colleagues also endorse T. S. Eliot's view that "although it is only too easy for a writer to be local without being universal, I doubt whether a poet or novelist can be universal without being local too."[20] And here, of course, it is plain enough that "universal" is hardly a term of derogation.

Indeed it is characteristic of those who pose as antiuniversalists to use the term *universalism* as if it meant *pseudouniversalism,* and the fact is that their complaint is not with universalism at all. What they truly object to—and who would not?—is Eurocentric hegemony *posing* as universalism. Thus, while the debate is couched in terms of the competing claims of particularism and universalism, the actual ideology of universalism is never interrogated, and, indeed, is even tacitly accepted. Ironically, as we shall see later, the attack on something called "universalism" leads to the occlusion of genuine local difference.

The appeal of this nativist rhetoric is most easily understood in the context of the subcontinent's politico-linguistic geography, a geography I rehearsed at the start of the book. The essential fact to recall here is the association of a europhone elite and a noneurophone populace, for it is this combination that makes for the appeal of nativism. That the European languages—and, in particular, the dialects of them in which elite writing goes on—are far from being the confident possession of the populace does not, of course, distinguish Third World literature—the writings that are taught—from the bulk of contemporary European or American taught writings. But the fact that contemporary African literature operates in a sphere of language that is so readily identifiable as the product of schooling—and schooling that is fully available only to an elite—invites the nativist assimilation of formal literature to the alien. This association is reinforced by the recognition that there is, in Africa as in the West, a body of distinctive cultural production—over the whole range of popular culture—that *does* have a more immediate access to the citizen with less formal education.

So, for example, there are certainly, as I have already once said, strong living practices of oral culture—religious, mythological, poetic, and narrative—in most of the thousand and more languages of sub-Saharan Africa, and there is no doubt as to the importance of the few languages that were already (as we say) reduced to writing before the colonial era. But we must not fall for the sentimental notion that the "people" have held onto an indigenous national tradition, that only the educated bourgeoisie are "children of two worlds." At the level of popular culture, too, the currency is not a holdover from an unbroken stream of tradition; indeed, it is, like most popular culture in the age of mass production, hardly national at all. Popular culture in Africa encompasses the (Americans) Michael Jackson and Jim Reeves; when it picks up cultural production whose sources are geographically African, what it picks up is not usually in any plausible sense traditional. Highlife music is both recognizably West African and distinctly not precolonial; and the sounds of Fela Kuti would have astonished the musicians of the last generation of court musicians in Yorubaland. As they have developed new forms of music, drawing on instrumental repertoires and musical ideas with a dazzling eclecticism, Africa's musicians have also done astonishing things with a language that used to be English. But it is *as* English that that language is accessible to millions around the continent (and around the world).

If we are to move beyond nativist hand waving, the right place to start is by defamiliarizing the concepts with which we think about—and teach—literature. Too often, attempts at cultural analysis are short-circuited by a failure to recall the histories of the analytical terms—*culture, literature, nation*—through which we have come to speak about the postcolonial world. So it is as well to remind ourselves of the original twinning of literature and nationalism, with which I began this essay, and with the ways in which each is essentialized through narratives. We are familiar, from Ernest Renan, with the selective remembering and forgetting of the past that undergirds group identity. And recent historiography has stressed again and again the ways in which the "national heritage" is constructed through the invention of traditions; the careful filtering of the rough torrent of historical event into the fine stream of an official narrative; the creation of a homogeneous legacy of values and experience.[21]

In the specific context of the history of "literature" and its study, recent debates have also left us attuned to the ways in which the factitious "excavation" of the literary canon can serve to solidify a particular cultural identity. The offical constitution of a national history bequeaths us the nation, and the discipline of literary history, as Michel de Certeau has aptly remarked, "transforms the text into an institution"—and so bequeaths us what we call literature.[22]

The late Raymond Williams once noted that as the term *literature* begins to acquire its modern semantic freight, we find "a development of the concept of 'tradition' within national terms, resulting in the more effective definition of 'a national literature.'"[23] As I argued at the start of this essay, "literature" and "nation" could hardly fail to belong together: from the very start they were made for each other. Once the concept of literature was taken up by African intellectuals, the African debate about literary nationalism was inevitable.

So that what we see in *Toward the Decolonization of African Literature* is, in effect, the establishment of a "reverse discourse": the terms of resistance are already given us, and our contestation is entrapped within the Western cultural conjuncture we affect to dispute. The pose of repudiation actually presupposes the cultural institutions of the West and the ideological matrix in which they, in turn, are imbricated. Railing against the cultural hegemony of the West, the nativists are of its party without knowing it.[24] Indeed, the very arguments, the rhetoric of defiance, that our nationalists muster are, in a sense, canonical, time-tested. For they enact a conflict that is *interior* to the same nationalist ideology that provided the category of "literature" its conditions of emergence: defiance is determined less by "indigenous" notions of resistance than by the dictates of the West's own Herderian legacy—its highly elaborated ideologies of national autonomy, of language and literature as their cultural substrate. Nativist nostalgia, in short, is largely fueled by that Western sentimentalism so familiar after Rousseau; few things, then, are less native than nativism in its current forms.

In this debate among African intellectuals we see recapitulated the classic gestures of nation formation in the domain of culture. And surely this is exactly as we should expect. In postcolonial discourse the project of nation formation—what used to be, in the eighteenth century, the attempt to define (and thus to invent) the "national character"—always lies close to the surface. But, as any Americanist would remind us, the emergence of American literature in the nineteenth century was circumscribed by just such concerns, coupled with a strong sense of being at the periphery vis-à-vis the European center. So it is with a sense of recognition that one turns from the rhetoric of postcolonial criticism today to read, say, William Carlos Williams's anxious observation:

> Americans have never recognized themselves. How can they? It is impossible until someone invent the original terms. As long as we are content to be called by somebody's else terms, we are incapable of being anything but our own dupes.[25]

In their ideological inscription, the cultural nationalists remain in a position of counteridentification (to borrow Michel Pêcheux's convenient schematism), which is to continue to participate in an institutional configuration—to be subjected to cultural identities—one officially decries.[26]

Once we lay aside the "universalism" that Chinweizu and others rightly attack as a disguised particularism, we can understand how an Afrocentric particularism—Chinweizu's cultural nationalism—is itself covertly universalist. Nativism organizes its vaunted particularities into a "culture" that is, in fact, an artifact of Western modernity. While Western criteria of evaluation are challenged, the way in which the contest is framed is not. The "Eurocentric" bias of criticism is scrutinized, but not the way in which its defining subject is constructed. For to acknowledge *that* would be to acknowledge that outside is not outside at all, so that the topology of nativism would be irretrievably threatened.

Ideologies succeed to the extent that they are invisible, in the moment that their fretwork of assumptions passes beneath consciousness; genuine victories are won without a shot being fired. Inasmuch as the most ardent of Africa's cultural nationalists participates in naturalizing—universalizing—the value-laden categories of "literature" and "culture," the triumph of universalism has, in the face of a silent nolo contendere, already taken place. The Western emperor has ordered the natives to exchange their robes for trousers: their act of defiance is to insist on tailoring them from homespun material. Given their arguments, plainly, the cultural nationalists do not go far enough; they are blind to the fact that their nativist demands inhabit a Western architecture.

It is as well to insist on a point that is neglected almost as often as it has been made, namely that nativism and nationalism (in all their many senses) are different creatures. Certainly, they fit together uneasily for many reasons. A return to traditions, after all, would never be a return to the contemporary nation-state. Nor could it mean, in Africa (where Pan-Africanism is a favorite form of nationalism) a return to an earlier continental unity, since—to insist on the obvious—the continent was not united in the past. I shall argue in Chapter 9 that various projects of African solidarity have their uses on the continent and in her diaspora: but these forms of "nationalism" look to the future not to the past.

I think that once we see the larger context more clearly, we will be less prone to the anxieties of nativism less likely to be seduced by the rhetoric of ancestral purity. More than a quarter of a century ago, Frantz Fanon exposed the artificiality of nativist intellectuals, whose ersatz populism only estranges them from the *Volk* they venerate. The intellectual

> . . . sets a high value on the customs, traditions, and the appearances of his people, but his inevitable, painful experience only seems to be a banal search for exoticism. The sari becomes sacred, and shoes that come from Paris or Italy are left off in favor of pampooties, while suddenly the language of the ruling power is felt to burn your lips.[27]

Inevitably, though, the "culture that the intellectual leans toward is often no more than a stock of particularisms. He wishes to attach himself to the people, but instead he only catches hold of their outer garments."[28] Fanon does not dismiss the products of the modern cultural worker in the colonial or postcolonial era, but he urges that the native poet who has taken his people as subject "cannot go forward resolutely unless he first realizes the extent of his estrangement from them."[29] Intellectuals betray this estrangement by a fetishistic attitude toward the customs, folklore, and vernacular traditions of their people, an attitude that, Fanon argues, must, in the end, set them against the people in their time of struggle.

One focus of this estrangement that has not, perhaps, been sufficiently appreciated is the very conception of an African identity. Although most discourse about African literature has moved beyond the monolithic notions of negritude or the "African personality," the constructed nature of the modern African identity (like all identities) is not widely enough understood. Terence Ranger has written of how the British colonialist's "own respect for 'tradition' disposed them to look with favour upon what they took to be traditional in Africa."[30] British colonial officers, traveling in the footsteps of Lord Lugard (and with the support of that curious creature, the government anthropologist) collected, organized, and enforced these "traditions," and such works as Rattray's *Ashanti Law and Constitution* had the effect of monumentalizing the flexible operations of precolonial systems of social control as what came to be called "customary law." Ironically, for many contemporary African intellectuals, these invented traditions have now acquired the status of national mythology, and the invented past of Africa has come to play a role in the political dynamics of the modern state.

> The invented traditions imported from Europe not only provided whites with models of command but also offered many Africans models of "modern" behavior. The invented traditions of African societies—whether invented by the Europeans or by Africans themselves in response—distorted the past but became in themselves realities through which a good deal of colonial encounter was expressed.[31]

So it is, Ranger observes, that "those like Ngugi who repudiate bourgeois elite culture face the ironic danger of embracing another set of colonial inventions instead.''[32] The English, who knew all about nations, could extend a similar comprehension to its stand-in, the "tribe," and that could mean inventing tribes where none quite existed before. The point extends beyond the anglophone domain. In Zaire we find that a sweeping linguistic division (between Lingala and Swahili) is a product of recent history, an outcome of worker stratification imposed by the Belgian administration.[33] Indeed, as I argued in Chapter 1, the very invention of Africa (as something more than a geographical entity) must be understood, ultimately, as an outgrowth of European racialism; the notion of Pan-Africanism was founded on the notion of the African, which was, in turn, founded not on any genuine cultural commonality but, as we have seen, on the very European concept of the Negro. "The Negro," Fanon writes, is "never so much a Negro as since he has been dominated by whites."[34] But the reality is that the very category of the Negro is at root a European product: for the "whites" invented the Negroes in order to dominate them. Simply put, the course of cultural nationalism in Africa has been to make real the imaginary identities to which Europe has subjected us.

As John Wisdom used to observe, "every day, in every way, we are getting meta and meta." It was inevitable, in such an age, that the debate should have been translated to a higher register. Certainly the claims of nativism upon literary theory cast in sharp political relief an ongoing debate over the relation between literary theory and particular bodies of texts. We can take as a starting point a recent intervention on this issue by Christopher Miller.

In his "Theories of Africans: The Question of Literary Anthropology," Miller addresses with subtlety and intelligence the problematic nature of the claim that Africa's literatures require their own particular kinds of reading. He proposes, as his title suggests, a kind of literary theory that is driven by the "anthropological" urge to question "the applicability of all our critical terms" and examine "traditional African cultures for terms they might offer."[35]

Miller's argument invites us to focus on two major issues. On the one hand—and this is the direction that his own inquiry takes—the invocation of anthropology as a model for theory is bound to pose questions, at the very least, of tact. As African critics have complained, anthropological reading often grows out of a view of the texts that regards African literature as a sociological datum simply because it does not deserve or require a literary reading. But that invites the more general question of the constitution of an African criticism, which will itself depend, finally, on facing the second problem posed by Miller's piece—namely, the question of the specificity of what is called literary theory to particular text-milieux. Miller's characterization of theory as "self-reflexivity" raises immediately the issue of the complex dependency of what is called literary theory on particular bodies of texts; if we are to begin to find a place for the term *theory* in African literary studies, this is a problem we shall have to address. And, as we shall see, central to this problematic is precisely the issue of what it is to carry out a literary reading.

Yet, to pose the question of theory's textual specificity is to presuppose a historically rather recent—though very powerful and very seductive—conception of what literary theory is or might be. Even as ambitious a study as Georg Lukács's *Die Theorie des Romans* is, finally, a historically conceived account of (some) novels; the work remains, from the viewpoint of this contemporary conception of theory, mere (but not, therefore, unmagnificent) *theoria*. What we have been introduced to, in the last two decades, is an epistemology of reading that is truly imperial: both more fine-grained and more general—more, as it were, "universal"—in scope. The object of study may be the nature of the linguistic act itself (or, alternately, the nature of the "literary") rather than a particular literary formation that is thematically or formally delineated.

This conception of theory has found perhaps its most powerful exemplar in the late Paul de Man: when, for example, he announces that literariness—the property that "emerges" in a literary reading of any text—consists, at least in part, in "the use of language that foregrounds the rhetorical over the grammatical and the logical function."[36] Reading Proust so that "a vast thematic and semiotic network is revealed that structures the entire narrative and that remains invisible to a reader caught in naive metaphorical mystification," de Man remarks that

> the whole of literature would respond in similar fashion, although the techniques and the patterns would have to vary considerably, of course, from author to author. But there is absolutely no reason why analyses of the kind here suggested for Proust would not be applicable, with proper modifications of technique, to Milton or to Dante or to Hölderlin. This will, in fact, be the task of literary criticism in the coming years.[37]

Yet this Euro-American conception of theory de Man represents is riven precisely by these claims to a determined universality. On the one hand is this de Manian conception of literary theory as a discourse about literature in general—a discourse that attempts to characterize textuality itself, rather than to explore this sonnet or that novel. On the other is the equally familiar notion that "theories" should be in a certain sense text-specific—should somehow address, that is, particularly interrelated bodies of writing. We confront the question that Denis Kambouchner has posed so starkly: *"How is generality in literary theory possible?*—or even more simply, if we persist in recognizing generality as the fundamental condition of theoretical discourse: *how is a theory of literature possible?"*[38] And, as Kambouchner argues, to answer this question we must first distinguish two senses of the term *literary theory*.

> In its broader and more diluted sense this term, or title, would denote the totality of texts, theoretical in nature, devoted to literature, without discriminating as to their object, orientation, or validity. In its second stricter and stronger sense, it would designate only the general constitution of a coherent, unified theory.[39]

Consider, now, the tension between proposition and example—the sort of disruptive intertwining de Man himself finds everywhere—in the grand passage cited just now, in which the "whole of literature" mysteriously collapses into the high canonical: Milton, Dante, Hölderlin. The fact is that, despite this talk of the "whole of literature," there is, as Cynthia Chase has argued, a complex interdependency between de Manian literary theory and a specific body of—largely Romantic—texts, which sits uneasily with the claim of epistemological universality that talk of "theory" inevitably implies.[40] In short, those who accept the relevance of poststructuralist thought for European texts from the Enlightenment on have reason to be uncomfortable with their extension to texts from outside this tradition—texts, as

Christopher Miller puts it with perhaps a trace of a smile, "that might not be a rewriting of Hegel (or even of Kant)."[41]

It is hardly outrageous, I think, to suggest that literary theory in Kambouchner's stricter sense, taking for its subject the "text in general," is not, after all, something we need to be especially concerned with if our interest is in the peculiar characteristics of the African written text. It does not follow that we must think the project of literary theory, again in Kambouchner's strong sense, is uninteresting; far from it. To the extent that African writing fails to conform to a literary theory in this strong sense, that is a problem for the theory, revealing it as yet another local principle masquerading as universal, and this is a problem we can begin to address only and precisely by a serious analysis of African texts.

But since this theoretical task is motivated not at all by an interest in the particularities of individual genres and styles, it can take African texts as exemplars only at the cost of ignoring what might matter most to us about them. And, in fact, one can distinguish here, in a way made familiar by methodological discussions of the relations beteen history and sociology, between two fundamental motivations for theoretical activity: the nomothetic and the idiographic. The positivists sought to apply their models of natural scientific explanation to the discipline of history, attempting to force historical explanation into the Procrustean mold of their "deductive-nomological" model; it is a familiar objection that in so doing they ignored the fundamentally different *urges* of historical and scientific explanation.

The deductive-nomological model, you will recall, seeks to see explanation in terms of a reduction of some particular events to be explained to a general pattern: a derivation of this specific pattern of events from the wider pattern of laws of nature. And though there is, no doubt, truth in the claim that one way to understand a historical event is to see it as fitting into a general pattern—perhaps the aftermath of the French Revolution just *is* better understood as part of a pattern that is found also in the Russian Revolution—it is also true that the historian's concern remains often with the particular event. Historians do not need to confirm or discover the patterns that nomothetic sociology seeks to discover, for they may use known patterns to explore the minute particularity of some local configuration of fact. If the *nomothetic* impulse is to seek general patterns, call them laws or what you will, we might gloss the *idiographic* impulse—the chronicler's impulse—as the desire to put our general knowledge to the service of a particular narrative.

This issue is important in the present theoretical conjuncture because we are sometimes said to be in a poststructuralist age, and structuralism began, at least on many accounts, with the application of Saussurean linguistics to the question of the literary text. But—as I once remarked in a discussion of structuralist criticism and African literature—if you think Saussurean linguistics works, it should work for African languages as well as the Indo-European ones that were its model. If you are interested, however, by contrast, in acquainting yourself with the particularities of Twi, surely something like Saussurean linguistics is simply the wrong level, too high a level, of abstraction with which to begin.[42]

What we *should* begin with is a firm contrast between a sense of literary theory— the strict or nomothetic—in which it purports to be a general theory of literature independent of particular text-milieux, and the humbler aims of literary criticism, which is concerned with the specificity of particular texts and literatures and may be concerned with what we value in reading as an encounter with specific texts.

We shall not, of course, dissolve our problem with a definition. On the one hand, there is no such thing as a "naive" reading innocent of all theoretical presumptions; however carefully we distinguish between theory and criticism, we will not be able to eradicate theory from our readings. And, on the other, there is surely something appealing in the notion of African theories for African texts. Indeed, you might think that this possibility exerts an especially strong pull in light of the fact that (as many critics complain) contemporary theory has often sponsored techniques of reading that yield somewhat homogeneous results. Our modern theories are too powerful, prove too much. We have learned to read Baudelaire so as to instantiate the disjunction between rhetoric as trope and rhetoric as persuasion, but it is surely with a feeling of ennui that we greet the same outcome in reading Rilke and Hölderlin and Proust and Wordsworth and Yeats and Nietzsche and Locke and Hegel and Blanchot. Doubtless, then, the particularist's stance has been strengthened by the fact that deconstruction— which, as it has been institutionalized in the United States, is widely identified with "theory" itself—is a mode of reading that seems to share its motto with the Holiday Inn: the best surprise is, apparently, no surprise.

At any rate, theory in the grand sense is surely yielding increasingly to a more particularized historical method. Today, as Marilyn Butler, for example, has suggested, the question is: "How are we to write historical criticism?"[43] And "history" here is—as it should be—the occasion for a more political style of reading. Critics with these sympathies may be more attuned to the distinctive circumstances of composition of postcolonial literatures.

But what exactly—in the postcolonial context—is the content of the nativist's injunction to read literature by means of a theory drawn from the text's own cultural or intellectual inheritance? Initially it would seem that to accept this principle would have wide-ranging consequences for the way we read all literature. For it seems to accord to African literature a deference that we do not accord the high-canonical works of European literature. Most of us are inclined to think that our insights into (say) the cultural production of genre and gender are not to be kept for our own age and region; we do not think that a feminist or marxian reading of Milton is merely an exercise in cultural imperialism (a temporal imperium corresponding to the geographical). A book that is widely regarded as having revitalized modern Wordsworth criticism (I refer to Hartman's study *Wordsworth's Poetry, 1787–1814*) draws extensively on the categories of Jung and of the German phenomenologists—not because anyone supposed these were part of Wordsworth's intellectual climate but because it was thought they might help explicate the nature of Wordsworth's poetic achievements.

Then again, we could indeed replace such a pluralism of critical perspectives with a criticism grounded on the text's (or its author's) own cultural or intellectual foundations, but there would be nothing recherché about that attempt either. J. R. Caldwell's classic *John Keats's Fancy* (the examples are taken almost entirely at random) reads Keats in terms of the categories of associationism, categories that featured large in Keats's own literary and intellectual inheritance and were part of the general intellectual and literary legacy of the eighteenth century. Tony Nuttall has read Wordsworth in terms of Lockean psychology—again, something indigenous to the poet's own intellectual climate; something, so to speak, from the inside.

One trouble with *this* rationale for nativism, though, is precisely that it ignores the multiplicity of the heritage of the modern African writer. To insist on nativism on these grounds would be to ignore plain facts: to ignore the undeniable datum that Soyinka's references to Euripides are as real as his appeal to Ogun (and also to Brazilian syncretisms of Yoruba and Christian religions); or the certainty that, whatever their ethical or legal relations, Ouologuem's *Le Devoir de Violence* is intimately bound up with Graham Greene's *It's a Battlefield;*[44] or Achebe's report, apropos of his reading as a child, that "the main things were the Bible and the Book of Common Prayer and the [English] Hymn Book."[45]

No one should contest the point that an adequate understanding of a work of literature will involve an understanding of its cultural presuppositions. Does it matter to *Madame Bovary* how adultery matters in the France of her day? Then it matters (as we shall see in the next essay) to Soyinka's *Death and the King's Horseman* that the death of the title is a death whose meaning the king's horseman accepts, a death he has chosen. But each of these cases makes a crucial point for us, which is that we do not always need to be told what we do not know. For the text itself may show us.

We could take examples for almost anywhere, but consider, for the sake of example, Okot p'Bitek's wonderful poetic cycle *Song of Lawino,* in which a "traditional" Acoli wife laments the loss of her husband to the White Man's world. Lawino says at one point, as she discusses her feelings about her co-wife, the Europeanized Clementine, Tina for short:

> Forgive me, brother
> Do not think I am insulting
> The woman with whom I share my husband!
> Do not think my tongue
> Is being sharpened by jealousy.
> It is the sight of Tina
> That provokes sympathy from my heart.
> I do not deny that
> I am a little jealous
> It is no good lying,
> We all suffer from a little jealousy.
> It catches you unawares
> Like the ghosts that bring fevers;
> It surprises people
> Like earth tremors:
> But when you see the beautiful woman
> With whom I share my husband
> You feel a little pity for her!
>
> Her breasts are completely shrivelled up,
> They are all folded dry skins,
> They have made nests of cotton wool
> And she folds the bits of cow-hide

In the nests
And calls them breasts!

O! my clansmen
How aged modern women
Pretend to be young girls![46]

Now anyone who reads the poem may wonder whether the device of addressing the narration to a "brother" or a "clansman" comes from Acoli traditional oral poetry, and (for the record) it does. But we do not need to be told after reading this passage that Acoli marriage is polygynous, that Acoli tradition holds that ghosts bring fevers, that the Acoli traditionally expected people to "grow old gracefully." The information is available to us in the poem—and in its extremely popular Acoli original—and we cannot argue that it is there because p'Bitek is addressing foreigners.

Part of what is meant by calling, say, Achebe's *Things Fall Apart* "anthropologizing" is that the narrator tells us so much about the culture that could, in this way, have been shown. I have already suggested one reason why this fact requires careful interpretation, for what I earlier called "the gesture of writing for and about oneself" is not simply a matter of creating texts addressed to a European Other. For those of us raised largely with texts that barely acknowledged the specificity of our existence, each work that simply places before us the world we already know—and this is a point that has been made eloquently by feminism—can provide a moment of self-validation; I shall return later to the role of such recognitions in reading.

To offer such explanations of Achebe's metanarrative is surely not to engage in negative criticism. Nobody thinks that Scott's explication in *Ivanhoe* of the historical realities (as he imagined them) of Anglo-Saxon and Norman culture is irresponsible or unliterary. Achebe's account of Ibo life is to be compared with Scott's tale because each is a form of historical novel. By the time Achebe wrote, the world he was describing was gone, as Gerald Moore has pointed out:

> Achebe had to strive for objectivity in evoking a world he had never known. . . .
> Achebe's childhood as the son of a leading Christian convert had been spent in considerable isolation from the vestiges of traditional culture still surviving around him. It was only as an adult that he gained the orientation which made him frequent the old, the shrines, the festivals, and all other available means towards the recreationof a credible, actual past.[47]

Achebe is acutely conscious of his distance from this world and of the role of colonial pedagogy in enforcing it. As he once wrote: "Here, then, is an adequate revolution for me to espouse—to help my society regain belief in itself and put away the complexes of the years of denigration and self-abasement."[48] If Achebe sometimes tells us too much (and in this there are many worse offenders) he is a skillful shower too.

I have suggested that the context that we need may be presupposed—and thus communicated—by the text to anyone willing to exercise a modicum of effort (the reviews of the 1987 production of Soyinka's *Death and the King's Horseman* in New York should remind us, however, that some European and American critics are not willing to undertake this modest task). But even when the reader or audience *is* willing, there are aspects of context that a reader whose culture is not that of the fiction may fail to grasp, and it seems to me nothing more than commonsensical to provide the alien reader with the needed information.

But, of course, none of this is news. Indeed, the history of the reception of African literature in the West suggests that providing a social context has never been the problem; on the contrary, people have been all too eager to attend to the ethnographic dimension of African literature.[49] And, as I have suggested, it would be another thing altogether to hold that a critical perspective that simulates the author's will guarantee a reading more adequate to the text. Dr. Johnson had undoubted advantages as a reader of his contemporaries, and we benefit from his insights, but that does not mean that we will—or that we should—afford him the last word (oh, how he would have loved that) on the subject.

There is, at all events, a fundamental reason why nativism in theory is unlikely to lead us away from where we already are. Time and time again, cultural nationalism has followed the route of alternate genealogizing. We end up always in the same place; the achievement is to have invented a different past for it. In the fervor of cultural reassertion, as Immanuel Wallerstein has observed, "the antecedents of scientificity were rediscovered under many different names";[50] today certain African intellectuals are doing the same for literary theory. If we start with a conception of hermeneutics borrowed from the Euro-American academy, we may well succeed in producing an "elegant variation," inserting the odd metaphor from indigenous oracle interpretation, say.[51] But the whole exercise puts me in mind of a certain disreputable trading concern I once visited in Harare—a product of the frankly desultory attempts at sanctions against the Republic of South Africa. Their specialty was stamping "Made in Zimbabwe" onto merchandise imported, more or less legally, from the South. Perhaps a few are really fooled, but the overall effect of the procedure is only to provide a thin skein of legitimacy to stretch over existing practices.

For all our gestures of piety toward the household gods cannot disguise the fact that the "intellectual" is the product of a particular social formation—that, as Gayatri Spivak has observed, there is a sense in which the "third-world intellectual" is a contradiction in terms precisely because, as I said at the start, intellectuals from the Third World are a product of the historical encounter with the West. And the problematic from which the theoretical discourse about literature arises is not a universal one—not, at least, until it is *made* universal. Literary theory is not only an intellectual project, it is also a genre; and genres have histories, which is to say times and places. Here again, the covert universalism within the rhetoric of particularism rears its head, for it is surely Eurocentric presumption to insist on a correspondence within African culture to the institutionalized discourses of the West.

But there is another difficulty with this nativism in theory—namely, that (in keeping with the rhetoric of contemporary theory generally) it grounds a politics of reading on a spurious epistemology of reading. And the talk of theoretical adequacy—which is here both the carrot and the stick—is seriously misleading.

In place of this, I think we shall be better off in our choice of theory if we give up the search for Mr. Right and speak, more modestly, of *productive modes of reading*.

Here, especially in approaching these texts for which we lack well-developed *traditions* of reading, we have the opportunity to rethink the whole activity of reflection on writing. So that before I turn, finally, to some of the particulars of African literary production, I want to say a little about an alternative to the epistemology of reading that informs much of our current rhetoric.

To focus on the issue of whether a reading is *correct* is to invite the question "What is it that a reading is supposed to give a correct account *of?*" The quick answer—one that, as we shall immediately see, tells us less than it pretends to—is, of course, "the text." But the text exists as linguistic, as historical, as commercial, as political event. And while each of these ways of conceiving the very same object provides opportunities for pedagogy, each provides different opportunities— opportunities between which we must choose. We are inclined at the moment to talk about this choice as if the purposes by which it is guided were, in some sense, given. But were that true, we would have long agreed on the nature of a literary reading, and there is surely little doubt that the concept of a "literary reading," like the concept of "literature," is what W. B. Gallie used to call an "essentially contested concept." To understand what a reading is, is to understand that what counts as a reading is always up for grabs.

By what purposes, then, should we judge our readings? To offer an answer to this question is not to rise above the contest but to engage in it: to take a stand and to argue for it. And I think it will be clear enough why—at this point, at least—the overwhelming differences between the sociopolitical situations of teachers of litera- ture in Africa, on the one hand, and in the various traditions of the West, on the other, may very well suggest different stands, diferent arguments and thus different conceptions of reading.

Consider, then, these differences (with the United States taken as the specific Western point of contrast). The African teacher of literature teaches students who are, overwhelmingly, the products of an educational system that enforces a system of values that ensures that, in the realm of culture, the West in which they do not live is *the* term of value; the American teacher of literature, by contrast, has students for whom the very same West is the term of value but for whom that West is, of course, fully conceived of as their own. While American students have largely internalized a system of values that prohibits them from seeing the cultures of Africa as sources of value for them—despite ritualized celebrations of the richness of the life of savages— they have also acquired a relativist rhetoric that allows them, at least in theory, to grant that, "for the Other," his or her world is a source of value. American students would thus expect African students to value African culture, *because it is African,* while African students, raised without relativism, expect Americans to value their own culture because it is, by some objective standard, superior. (Obviously these generalizations admit many exceptions.)

These sociological facts, reflexes of asymmetries of cultural power, have pro- found consequences for reading. If one believes that the kinds of cultural inferiority complexes represented in the attitudes of many African students need to be exorcised, then the teaching of literature in the Westernized academy in Africa will require an approach that does three crucial things: first, identify accurately the situation of the modern African text as a product of the colonial encounter (and neither as the simple continuation of an indigenous tradition nor as a mere intrusion from the metropole); second, stress that the continuities between precolonial forms of culture and contemporary ones are nevertheless genuine (and thus provide a modality through which students can value and incorporate the African past); and third, challenge directly the assumption of the cultural superiority of the West, both by undermining the aestheticized conceptions of literary value that it presupposes and by distinguishing sharply between a domain of technological skill in which—once goals are granted—comparisons of efficiency are possible, and a domain of value, in which such comparisons are by no means so unproblematic. (What I have in mind here is an argument that begins with the modest observation that it is surely a very odd idea that there is *one* currency of literary value, an "aesthetic quality," which accounts for our choices in and of reading.) This final challenge—to the assumption of Western cultural superiority—requires us, in the last analysis, to expose the ways in which the systematic character of literary (and, more broadly, aesthetic) judgments of value is the product of certain institutional practices and not something that simply reflects a reality that exists independently of those practices and institutions.

In the American academy, on the other hand, the reading of African writing is reasonably directed by other purposes: by the urge to continue the repudiation of racism; by the need to extend the American imagination—an imagination that regulates much of the world system economically and politically—beyond the narrow scope of the United States; by the desire to develop views of the world elsewhere that respect more deeply the autonomy of the Other, views that are not generated by the local political needs of America's multiple diasporas.

To stress such purposes in reading is to argue that, from the standpoint of an analysis of the current cultural situation—an analysis that is frankly political—certain purposes are productively served by the literary institutions of the academy.

But having made these distinctions, it may be as well to insist that some of our critical materials can be put to use on both sides of the Atlantic. Thus, for example, there are distinctive formal features that arise, as has often been pointed out, from the particular closeness of African readers and writers to living traditions of oral narration. Addressing the incorporation of orality in writing allows us to meet both the need to connect modern African students with their geographical situations, and the concern to expand the American student's imagination of the world.

And—to provide another less-familiar example—African writing raises a set of difficulties that stem from one of the characteristics of the cultural situation of African writers in the colonial languages: namely, the fact that they normally conceive of themselves as addressing a readership that encompasses communities wider than any "traditional" culture. To address these issues productively is to allow students to explore the space of cultural politics: to allow students both African and American to learn to resist facile reductions of modern African cultural production; and so it will be well to exemplify my claims in this specific area.

The most-often-discussed consequences of the situation I have just outlined appear at the thematic level. When authors write in English or French about lives in their own countries in all their specificity, they necessarily find themselves accounting for features of those lives that derive from that specificity. This entails the use of particular concepts of, for example, kinship and family, marriage and status. As we have seen, the presentation of such details has often been read, especially by people outside Africa, as anthropologizing. We are told that Achebe's *Arrow of God,* for example, fails, in part, because it cannot take its setting for granted; that Achebe is always telling us what we need to know, acknowledging the reader's distance from Ibo traditions, and thus, allegedly, identifying the intended reader as a foreigner. I have heard the same point made about Soyinka's dramas, and I confess to finding it difficult to accept. For there are reasons, reasons highly specific to the situation of black African writing in metropolitan languages, why this is a mistake.

There is one trivial reason. Achebe and Soyinka are very consciously writing for Nigerian—and not just Ibo or Yoruba—audiences. The fact that a certain amount of detail is introduced in order to specify a thick description of the cultural milieu simply does not imply a foreign—if that means a non-African—reader. That is the first point.

But it *is,* essentially, trivial because of a second point. To make that point I should begin with a not-to-be-neglected fact: Achebe and Soyinka are popular writers at home. If the presence of these accumulations of allegedly ethnographic detail were indeed a way of identifying an alien reader, why do Nigerian (and more specifically Yoruba or Ibo) readers not find them alienating? The fact is that the accumulation of detail is a device not of alienation but of incorporation. The provision, in traditional narrations, of information already known to the hearer does not reflect a view of the hearer as alien. Otherwise, oral narrations would not consist of twice-told tales. The function of a rehearsal of the familiar in narration often depends precisely on our pleasure in recognizing in a tale what we already know.

The centrality of this issue—of the inscription of the social world out of which one writes—is only an example, of course, of the sort of circumstance we need to be aware of if we are to write intelligently about modern African writing. And it depends essentially upon seeing the writer, the reader, and the work in a cultural—and thus a historical, a political, and a social—setting.

So let me end with an observation that derives from just such a contextualizing grasp, one that identifies the dual sources of the situation of the modern African text. In a passage that provides the epigraph of Chapter 4, Chinua Achebe reflects on the necessity for a modern African writer to examine intelligently the various identities he or she inhabits. And he ends by interrogating his identity as an African in these words: "What does Africa mean to the world? When you see an African what does it mean to a white man?"[52] Notice the presupposition of the second question: the recognition that a specifically African identity began as the product of a European gaze.

Anthropologizing modes of reading would stress the sources of Achebe's "social vision" in an African setting.[53] It seems to me, by contrast, essential to insist that the nationalist dimensions of public history that are central to so much modern African writing are not mere reflexes of the epic mode of oral history and myth; they grow out of the world situation of the African writer and not out of a purely local eccentricity. Achebe is a fine example of someone who draws on the reserves of his native orature, but we misunderstand those uses if we do not see them in their multiple contexts.

We need to transcend the banalities of nativism—its images of purgation, its declarations, in the face of international capital, of a specious "autonomy," its facile topologies. The language of empire—of enter and periphery, identity and difference, the sovereign subject and her colonies—continues to structure the criticism and reception of African literature *in* Africa as elsewhere. And this makes the achievement of critical balance especially difficult to maintain. On the one hand, we find theorists who emphasize the processes of demonization and subjection, the ways in which the "margin" is produced by the "cultural dominant"—Europe defining her sovereignty by insisting on the otherness of her colonies. On the other—Other?—hand, talk about the production of marginality by the culture of the center is wholly inadequate by itself. For it ignores the reciprocal nature of power relations; it neglects the multiform varieties of individual and collective agency available to the African subject; and it diminishes both the achievements and the possibilities of African writing.

The point to be borne in mind here is not that ideologies, like cultures, exist antagonistically, but that they *only* exist antagonistically; domination and resistance are a large part of what they are *for*. In the ferment of present-day African literary debate, it is as well to remember that the very meaning of postcolonial discourse subsists on these conflictual relations. Indeed, they are *the* topos of contemporary African literature.

Yet I, at least, worry about our entrancement with the polarities of identity and difference; partly because the rhetoric of alterity has too often meant the evacuation of specificity; partly because too many African intellectuals, captivated by this Western thematic, seek to fashion themselves as the (image of the) Other. We run the risk of an ersatz exoticism, like the tourist trinkets in the Gifte Shoppes of Lagos and Nairobi.

Nativism invites us to conceive of the nation as an organic community, bound together by the *Sprachgeist,* by the shared norms that are the legacy of tradition, struggling to throw off the shackles of alien modes of life and thought. "Here I am," Senghor once wrote, "trying to forget Europe in the pastoral heart of Sine."[54] But for us to forget Europe is to suppress the conflicts that have shaped our identities; since it is too late for us to escape each other, we might instead seek to turn to our advantage the mutual interdependencies history has thrust upon us.

FOUR

The Myth of an African World

I'm an Ibo writer, because this is my basic culture; Nigerian, African and a writer . . . no, black first, then a writer. Each of these identities does call for a certain kind of commitment on my part. I must see what it is to be black—and this means being sufficiently intelligent to know how the world is moving and how the black people fare in the world. This is what it means to be black. Or an African—the same: what does Africa mean to the world? When you see an African what does it mean to a white man?[1]

CHINUA ACHEBE

The African-Americans whose work I discussed in Chapters 1 and 2 conceived their relation to Africa through the mediating concept of race, a concept they acquired from a Euro-American cultural matrix. As a result, as I have argued, it was inevitable that their answer to the question of the African identity should have been rooted in the romantic racisms that have been so central to the European and American national-isms of the past century and a half; and their thinking provided the starting point for those Africans who took up the banner of a Pan-Africanist black nationalism in the period since the Second World War. The nativism of *Towards the Decolonization of African Literature* is simply the reflection of these forces in the domain of academic literary criticism.

Yet Africans were bound also to start with a deeper knowledge of and sympathy with their local traditions. Blyden and Crummell may have been Liberians, but their sympathies were limited by their American upbringings, and Du Bois, though a Ghanaian at his death, never sought a deep understanding of the cultures among which he lived in his final years. When we turn to the europhone Africans who inherited their mantle, we see a shift in focus, in attitude, in perspective, that is of crucial importance in understanding their cultural politics. If there is one perspective above all that epitomizes these changes in the anglophone world, it is not that of the Christian priest and missionary (like Blyden or Crummell), not that of the sociologist (like Du Bois), not that of the critic (like Chinweizu and his colleagues), but that of the writer. Chinua Achebe has put the matter characteristically concisely:

It is, of course true that the African identity is still in the making. There isn't a final identity that is African. But, at the same time, there *is* an identity coming into existence. And it has a certain context and a certain meaning. Because if somebody meets me, say, in a shop in Cambridge [England], he says "Are you from Africa?"

Which means that Africa means something to some people. Each of these tags has a meaning, and a penalty and a responsibility. All these tags, unfortunately for the black man, are tags of disability. . . .

I think it is part of the writer's role to encourage the creation of an African identity.[2]

There is no better point of entry to the issue of the African intellectuals' articulation of an African identity than through the reflections of our most powerful creative writers. Of these none, I believe, has been a more powerful literary, cultural, and political force, at least in anglophone Africa, than the Nigerian writer Wole Soyinka.

Wole Soyinka writes in English. But this, like many obvious facts, is one whose obviousness may lead us to underrate its importance and its obscurities. For if it is obvious that Soyinka's language is English, it is a hard question whose English he writes. Amos Tutuola accustomed the Western ear to "Nigerian English"; Soyinka's English is "Nigerian" only when he is listening to Nigerians, and then his ear is exact. But with the same precision he captures the language of the colonial, matter and manner; only someone who *listened* would have the British district officer's wife say, as her husband goes off to deal with "the natives" in *Death and the King's Horseman:* "Be careful, Simon, I mean, be clever."[3] Yet the very same text recalls, on occasions, the English of Gilbert Murray's translations from the Greek—Soyinka, we remind ourselves, has translated (or, we had better say, transformed) *The Bacchae*—as here in the first recital of the play:

> Death came calling.
> Who does not know the rasp of reeds?
> A twilight whisper in the leaves before
> The great araba falls.[4]

The resonance is one among a multitude. In reading Soyinka we hear a voice that has ransacked the treasuries of English literary and vernacular diction, with an eclecticism that dazzles without disconcerting, and has found a language that is indisputably his own. For—and this is what matters—however many resonances we hear, Soyinka writes in a way that no contemporary English or American writer could. It is important to understand why this is. For the answer lies at the root of Soyinka's intellectual and literary project.

Though he writes in a European language, Soyinka is not writing, cannot be writing, with the purposes of English writers of the present. And it is for this reason above all that Soyinka's language may mislead. It is exactly because they can have little difficulty in understanding what Soyinka says that Europeans and Americans must learn to be careful in attending to his purposes in saying it. For there is a profound difference between the projects of contemporary European and African writers: a difference I shall summarize, for the sake of a slogan, as the difference between the search for the self and the search for a culture.

The idea that modern European writers have been engaged in the search for the self is a critical commonplace. That it is a commonplace offers us no guarantee that it is true. But there is much to be said for the idea as it is expounded, for example, in Lionel Trilling's argument in his classic essay *Sincerity and Authenticity*.

For Trilling, sincerity was no longer *the* problem for the European writer. Gone is the obsession with the attempt to bring what one is (one's self) and what one appears to be (one's role) into some kind of accommodation: Leavis with his "engagingly archaic . . . seriousness"[5] is the last, late hero of sincerity, and the sin of sins for him is hypocrisy. Enter authenticity, the paradoxically histrionic concern of existentialism and the beat poets, which is also central, to give a measure of its extent, to Proust and psychoanalysis—the obsession with the transcendence of what one seems to be by what one really is, beyond sincerity and hypocrisy. Authenticity is an escape from what society, the school, the state, what *history,* has tried to make of us; the authentic man is Nietzsche, his sin of sins false consciousness. In the world of authenticity, Freud stands as a giant witness to the impossible pain of discovering one's inner, deeper, more real, *simpliciter* one's *authentic,* self.

> The artist—as he comes to be called—ceases to be the craftsman or the performer, dependent upon the approval of the audience. His reference is to himself only, or to some transcendent power which—or who—has decreed his enterprise and alone is worthy to judge it.[6]

The very fact that Trilling's language here will strike many European and American literary critics as old-fashioned is in itself evidence about the character of intellectual life in the industrialized world. (I shall return to this issue—in Chapter 7.) In the years since his death, the language of criticism and of critical theory has changed. But literary historians and historians of ideas in the West are likely to agree that there is in their tradition a sense of the writer as oppositional, whose roots can be traced back at least to the Renaissance. Stephen Greenblatt has argued—in *Renaissance Self-fashioning*—that Renaissance writers fashioned "selves" from "among possibilities whose range was strictly delimited by the social and ideological system in force"[7] so that the sense of a self fashioned *against* the culture is a fiction. Literary history, by the very fact of attempting to give an account of the writer in terms of a history within society, challenges the writer's claim—which we find in Europe at least since romanticism—to be simply oppositional. But it is exactly this pervasive sense of the creative self as oppositional—so pervasive that Greenblatt's work is interesting in part because it challenges it—that I take as the datum in my contrast with contemporary African writers.[8]

We can find this conception articulated in Trilling's preface to *The Opposing Self,* a collection of essays on various European writers from Keats to Orwell. Trilling is discussing Matthew Arnold's oft-cited maxim that literature is a criticism of life. Arnold, Trilling argued, "meant, in short, that poetry is a criticism of life in the same way that the Scholar Gipsy was a criticism of the life of an inspector of elementary schools."

> The Scholar Gipsy *is* poetry—he *is* imagination, impulse and pleasure: he is what virtually every writer of the modern period conceives, the experience of art projected into the actuality and totality of life as the ideal form of the moral life. His existence is intended to disturb us and make us dissatisfied with our habitual life in culture.[9]

Trilling's particular concern with the transition from sincerity to authenticity as moralities of artistic creation is part of a wider and distinctive pattern. Authenticity is but one of the ideas through which the idea of the artist as outsider has been articulated.

For Africa, by and large, this authenticity is a curiosity: though trained in Europe or in schools and universities dominated by European culture, the African writers' concern is not with the discovery of a self that is the object of an inner voyage of discovery. Their problem—though not, of course, their subject—is finding a public role, not a private self. If European intellectuals, though comfortable inside their culture and its traditions, have an image of themselves as outsiders, African intellectuals are uncomfortable outsiders, seeking to develop their cultures in directions that will give them a role.

The relation of African writers to the African past is a web of delicate ambiguities. If they have learned neither to despise it nor to try to ignore it—and there are many witnesses to the difficulty of this decolonization of the mind—they have still to learn how to assimilate and transcend it. They have grown up in families for which the past is, if not present, at least not far below the surface. That past and their people's myths of the past are not things they can ignore. When Ngugi wa Thiong'o says that "the novelist, at his best, must feel himself heir to a continuous tradition," he does not mean, as the Westerner might suppose, a literary tradition: he means, as any African would know, "the mainstream of his people's historical drama."[10] It is this fundamentally sociohistorical perspective that makes the European problem of authenticity something distant and unengaging for most African writers.

We must not overstate the distance from London to Lagos: the concept of authenticity, though often dissociated from its roots in the relation of reader or writer to society, is one that can only be understood against the social background. It is the fact that we are social beings, after all, that raises the problem of authenticity. The problem of who I really am is raised by the facts of what I appear to be, and though it is essential to the mythology of authenticity that this fact should be obscured by its prophets, what I appear to be is fundamentally how I appear to others and only derivatively how I appear to myself. Robinson Crusoe before Friday could hardly have had the problem of sincerity, but we can reasonably doubt that he would have faced issues of authenticity either.

Yet, and here is the crux, for European writers these others who define the problem are "my people," and they can feel that they know who these people are, what they are worth. For African writers the answer is not so easy. They are Asante, Yoruba, Kikuyu, but what does this now mean? They are Ghanaian, Nigerian, Kenyan, but does this yet mean anything? They are black, and what is the worth of the black person? They are bound, that is, to face the questions articulated in my epigraph by Achebe. So that though the European may feel that the problem of who he or she is can be a private problem, the African asks always not "who am I?" but "who are we?" and "my" problem is not mine alone but "ours."

This particular constellation of problems and projects is not often found outside Africa: a recent colonial history, a multiplicity of diverse subnational indigenous traditions, a foreign language whose metropolitan culture has traditionally defined the "natives" by their race as inferior, a literary culture still very much in the making. It is because they share this problematic that it makes sense to speak of a Nigerian writer as an African writer, with the problems of an African writer, and it is because he has attempted with subtlety and intelligence to face some of these common problems that Soyinka deserves the attention of Africans.

I want to try to identify a problem in Soyinka's account of his cultural situation: a problem with the account he offers of what it is to be an African writer de nos jours, a problem that appears in the tension between what his plays show and what he says about them.

We could start in many places in his dramatic oeuvre; I have chosen *Death and the King's Horseman*. "The play," Soyinka says, "is based on events which took place in Oyo, ancient Yoruba city of Nigeria, in 1946. That year, the lives of Elesin (Olori Elesin), his son, and the Colonial District Officer intertwined with the disastrous results set out in the play."[11] The first scene opens with a praise singer and drummers pursuing Elesin Oba as he marches through the marketplace. We gradually discover that he is the "King's Horseman"—whose pride and duty is to follow the dead king to ride with him to the "abode of the gods."[12] In the words of Joseph, the "houseboy" of the British district officer, "It is native law and custom. The King die last month. Tonight is his burial. But before they can bury him, the Elesin must die so as to accompany him to heaven."[13] When a colonial official intervenes to stop Elesin Oba's "ritual suicide," his son, newly returned from England for the king's funeral, dies for him, and the Elesin responds by strangling himself in his cell with the chain with which the colonial police have bound his hands. The district officer's intervention to save one life ends with the loss of two and, as the people of Oyo believe, with a threat to the cosmic order.

The issue is complicated by the fact that Elesin Oba has chosen to marry on the eve of his death—so that, as he puts it, "My vital flow, the last from this flesh is intermingled with the promise of future life."[14] We are aware from the very first scene that this act raises doubts—expressed by Iyaloja, mother of the market—about the Elesin's preparedness for his task. When the Elesin fails, he himself addresses this issue, as he speaks to his young bride:

> First I blamed the white man, then I blamed my gods for deserting me. Now I feel I want to blame you for the mystery of the sapping of my will. But blame is a strange peace offering for a man to bring a world he has deeply wronged, and to its innocent dwellers. Oh little mother, I have taken countless women in my life, but you were more than a desire of the flesh. I needed you as the abyss across which my body must be drawn, I filled it with earth and dropped my seed in it at the moment of preparedness for my crossing. . . . I confess to you, daughter, my weakness came not merely from the abomination of the white man who came violently into my fading presence, there was also a weight of longing on my earth-held limbs. I would have shaken it off, already my foot had begun to lift but then, the white ghost entered and all was defiled.[15]

There are so many possible readings here, and the Elesin's uncertainties as to the meaning of his own failure leave us scope to wonder whether the intervention of the colonizer provides only a pretext. But what is Soyinka's own reading?

In his author's note to the play Soyinka writes:

> The bane of themes of this genre is that they are no sooner employed creatively than
> they acquire the facile tag of "clash of cultures," a prejudicial label, which, quite
> apart from its frequent misapplication, presupposes a potential equality *in every
> given situation* of the alien culture and the indigenous, on the actual soil of the
> latter. (In the area of misapplication, the overseas prize for illiteracy and mental
> conditioning undoubtedly goes to the blurb-writer for the American edition of my
> novel *Season of Anomy* who unblushingly declares that this work portrays the
> "clash between the old values and new ways, between Western methods and
> African traditions"!) . . . I find it necessary to caution the would-be producer of
> this play against a sadly familiar reductionist tendency, and to direct his vision
> instead to the far more difficult and risky task of eliciting the play's threnodic
> essence. . . .
>
> The Colonial Factor is an incident, a catalytic incident merely. . . . The
> confrontation in the play is largely metaphysical.

I find the tone of this passage strained, the claim disingenuous. We may, of course,
make distinctions more carefully than blurb writers and scribblers of facile tags:
Soyinka feels that talk of the clash of cultures suggests that colonizer and colonized
meet on culturally equal terms. We may reject the implication. There is, as Soyinka
says, something so oversimple as to be thoroughly misleading in the claim that the
novel is "about," that it "portrays," the relation between European methods and
African traditions.

Still, it is absurd to deny that novel and play have something to say about that
relationship. The "Colonial Factor" is not a catalytic incident merely; it is a profound
assault on the consciousness of the African intellectual, on the consciousness that
guides this play. And it would be irresponsible, which Soyinka is not, to assert that
novel and play do not imply a complex (and nonreductionist) set of attitudes to the
problem. It is one thing to say (as I think correctly) that the drama in Oyo is driven
ultimately by the logic of Yoruba cosmology, another to deny the existence of a
dimension of power in which it is the colonial state that forms the action.

So that after all the distinctions have been drawn, we still need to ask why Soyinka
feels the need to conceal his purposes. Is it perhaps because he has not resolved the
tension between the desire that arises from his *enracinement* in the European tradition
of authorship to see his literary work as, so to speak, authentic, "metaphysical," and
the desire that he must feel as an African in a once-colonized and merely notionally
decolonized culture to face up to and reflect the problem at the level of ideology? Is it,
to put it briskly, because Soyinka is torn between the demands of a private
authenticity and a public commitment? Between individual self-discovery and what
he elsewhere calls the "social vision"?

It is this problem, central to Soyinka's situation as the archetypical African writer,
that I wish to go on to discuss.

The "social vision" is, of course, the theme of two of the lectures in Soyinka's *Myth,
Literature and the African World,* and it was in this work that the tensions I have
mentioned first caught my attention. Soyinka's essays are clearly not directed
particularly to an African audience (hardly surprising when we remember that they
are based on lectures given in England at Cambridge University). References to Peter

Brook and Brecht, to Robbe-Grillet and Lorca, are intended to help locate the Western reader. Indeed, the introduction of Lorca is glossed with the observation that it is "for ease of reference."[16] And it is clear from the way in which the first chapter (on Yoruba theology and its transformations in African and African-American drama) tells us much that it would be absurd to tell to any Yoruba, and a certain amount that it would be gratuitous to mention for almost any African readership.

Yet, it is intended (and to a large extent this intention is achieved) that *Myth, Literature and the African World* should be a work that, like Soyinka's plays (and unlike, say, Achebe's novels) takes its African—its Yoruba—background utterly for granted. Soyinka is not arguing that modern African writers should be free to draw on African, and, in his case, Yoruba, mythology; rather, he is simply showing us how this process can and does take place. He tells us in his preface, for example, that the literature of the "secular social vision" reveals that the "universal verities" of "the new ideologue" can be "elicited from the world-view and social structure of his own [African] people."[17] I have every sympathy with the way Soyinka tries to take the fact of Africa for granted. But this taking for granted is doubly paradoxical.

First, the readership for his dramatic texts and theoretical writings—*unlike* the audience for his performances—is largely not African. *Myth, Literature and the African World* is largely to be read by people who see Soyinka as a guide into what remains for them from a literary point of view (and this is, of course, a reflection of political realities) the Dark Continent. How can we ask people who are not African, do not know Africa, to take us for granted? And, more importantly, why *should* we? (Observe how odd it would be to praise Norman Mailer—to take a name entirely at random—for taking America for granted.)

It is part of the curious problematic of the African intellectual that taking his culture for granted—as politics, as history, as culture, and, more abstractly yet, as mind—is, absurdly, something that does require an effort. So that, inevitably—and this is the second layer of paradox—what Soyinka does is to take Africa for granted in reaction to a series of self-misunderstandings in Africa that are a product of colonial history and the European imagination, and this despite Soyinka's knowledge that it is Europe's fictions of Africa that we need to forget. In escaping Europe's Africa, the one fiction that Soyinka as theorist cannot escape is that Africans can only take their cultural traditions for granted by an effort of mind.

Yet in Soyinka's plays Yoruba mythology and theology, Yoruba custom and tradition *are* taken for granted. They may be reworked, as Shakespeare reworked English or Wagner German traditions, but there is never any hesitation, when, as in *Death and the King's Horseman,* Soyinka draws confidently on the resources of his tradition. We outsiders need surely have no more difficulty in understanding Soyinka's dramas because they draw on Yoruba culture than we have in understanding Shakespeare because he speaks from within what used to be called the "Elizabethan world picture," and Soyinka's dramas show that he knows this.

I think we should ask what leads Soyinka astray when it comes to his accounting for his cultural situation. And part of the answer must be that he is answering the wrong question. For what he needs to do is not to take an *African* world for granted but to take for granted his own culture—to speak freely not as an African but as a Yoruba and a Nigerian. The right question, then, is not "Why Africa shouldn't take its traditions for granted?'' but ''Why I shouldn't take mine?'' The reason that Africa cannot take an African cultural or political or intellectual life for granted is that there is no such thing: there are only so many traditions with their complex relationships—and, as often, their lack of any relationship—to each other.

For this reason, Soyinka's situation is even more complex than it is likely to appear to the Westerner—or to the African enmeshed in unanimist mythologies. For even if his writing were addressed solely to other Africans, Soyinka could not presuppose a knowledge of Yoruba traditions—and these are precisely what we need to understand if we are to follow the arguments of his first lecture. Even when addressing other Africans, that is, he can only take for granted an interest in his situation, and a shared assumption that he has the right to speak from within a Yoruba cultural world. He cannot take for granted a common stock of cultural knowledge.

These issues are important for my own project in these essays. As I have already said, it is simply a mistake to suppose that Africa's cultures are an open book to each other. That is one reason why, as we saw in Chapter 3, the fact that I explain this or that Asante custom or belief does not by itself show that I am talking for the West. We cannot, therefore, infer a Western audience for Soyinka's—brilliant and original—exposition of Yoruba cosmology. What shows that Soyinka's audience is Western is the sorts of references he makes, the sorts of Yoruba customs he chooses to explain.

Now, of course, the only way that the misunderstandings I have been discussing can be overcome is by acknowledging and transcending them; nothing is to be achieved by ignoring them. And, despite the remarks in the author's note Soyinka knows this well. What I want to argue, however, is that the ''African World'' that Soyinka counterposes as *his* fiction of Africa is one against which we should revolt—and that we should do so, to return to my earlier argument, because it presupposes a false account of the proper relationships between private ''metaphysical'' authenticity and ideology; a false account of the relations between literature, on the one hand, and the African world, on the other.

We can approach Soyinka's presuppositions by asking ourselves a question: what has Yoruba cosmology, the preoccupation of the first lecture of *Myth, Literature and the African World*, to do with African literature? It is not enough to answer that Yoruba cosmology provides both the characters and the mythic resonances of some African drama—notably, of course, Soyinka's—as it does of some of the Afro-Caribbean and African-American drama that Soyinka himself discusses in *Myth, Literature and the African World*. For this is no answer for the Akan writer or reader who is more familiar with Ananse than Esu-Elegba as trickster, and who has no more obligations to Ogun than he does to Vishnu. ''Africa minus the Sahara North''—and this is an observation of Soyinka's—''is still a very large continent, populated by myriad races and cultures.''[18]

It is natural, after reading the first lecture of *Myth, Literature and the African World*, to suppose that Soyinka's answer to our question must be this: ''Yoruba mythology is taken by way of example because, as a Yoruba, it happens to be what I know about.'' In his interesting discussion of the differences (and similarities) between Greek myth and drama and Yoruba, for example, he says: ''that Greek religion shows persuasive parallels with, *to stick to our example*, the Yoruba, is by no means denied"[19]—as if the Yoruba case is discussed as an example of (what else?) the African case. Many other passages would support this interpretation.

Now if this is Soyinka's presupposition—and if it is not, it is certainly a presupposition of his text—then it is one that we must question. For, I would suggest, the assumption that this system of Yoruba ideas is—that it *could* be—typical, is too direct a reaction to the European conception of Africa as what Soyinka elsewhere nicely terms a "metaphysical vacuum":[20] and the correct response to this absurdity is not to claim that what appears to Europe as a vacuum is in fact a uniform medium populated with certain typical metaphysical notions, of which Yoruba conceptions would be one particularization, but rather to insist that it is a plenum richly populated with the metaphysical thought worlds of (in his own harmless hyperbole) "myriad races and cultures."

I do not want to represent Soyinka's apparent position as a kind of Yoruba imperialism of the thought world. The motive is nobler, and I think it is this: Soyinka recognizes that, despite the differences between the histories of British, French, and Portuguese ex-colonies, there is a deep and deeply self-conscious continuity between the problems and projects of decolonized Africans, a continuity that has, as he shows, literary manifestations, and he wants to give an account of that continuity that is both metaphysical and endogenous. The desire to give an account that is endogenous is, I think, primary. As we saw with Du Bois, there is something disconcerting for a Pan-Africanist in the thesis (which I here state at its most extreme) that what Africans have in common is fundamentally that European racism failed to take them seriously, that European imperialism exploited them. Soyinka will not admit the presupposition of Achebe's question: "When you see an African what does it mean to a white man?"—the presuppositon that the African identity is, in part, the product of a European gaze.

I had better insist once more that I do not think that this *is* all that Africans have culturally in common. It is obvious that, like Europe before the Renaissance and much of the modern Third World, African cultures are formed in important ways by the fact that they had until recently no high technology and relatively low levels of literacy. And, despite the introduction of high technology and the rapid growth of literacy, these facts of the recent past are still reflected in the conceptions even of those of us who are most affected by economic development and cultural exposure to the West. I shall return to these issues in the final essays. But even if these economic and technical similarities were to be found only in Africa—and they aren't—they would not, even with the similarities in colonial history, justify the assmuption of metaphysical or mythic unity, except on the most horrifyingly determinist assumptions.

In denying a metaphysical and mythic unity to African conceptions, then, I have *not* denied that "African literature" is a useful category. I have insisted from the very beginning that the social-historical situation of African writers generates a common set of problems. But notice that it is precisely not a metaphysical consensus that creates this shared situation. It is, inter alia, the transition from traditional to modern loyalties; the experience of colonialism; the racial theories and prejudices of Europe, which provide both the language and the text of literary experience; the growth of both literacy and the modern economy. And it is, as I say, because these are changes that were to a large extent thrust upon African peoples by European imperialism, precisely because they are exogenous, that Soyinka, in my view, revolts against seeing them as the major determinants of the situation of the African writer.

Once he is committed to an endogenous account of this situation, what is left by unity in metaphysics? Shaka and Osei Tutu—founders, respectively, of the Zulu and the Asante nations—do not belong in the same narrative, spoke different languages, and had conceptions of kinship (to bow to an ethnographer's idol) that were centrally patrilineal and matrilineal, respectively. Soyinka could have given an account of what they had in common that was racial. But, as I have argued and Soyinka knows well, we have passed the time when black racism is possible as an intelligent reaction to white racism. So, as I say, we are left with common metaphysical conceptions.

Though I think that the appeal of the myth of Africa's metaphysical solidarity is largely due to Soyinka's wish for an endogenous account, there is, I suspect, another reason why he is tempted by this story. Soyinka, the man of European letters, is familiar with the literature of authenticity and the account of it as an exploration of the metaphysics of the individual self, and he is tempted, by one of those rhetorical oppositions that appeal to abstract thinkers, to play against this theme an African exploration of the metaphysics of the community.

But in accepting such an account Soyinka is once more enmeshed in Europe's myth of Africa. Because he cannot see either Christianity or Islam as endogenous (even in their more syncretic forms), he is left to reflect on African traditional religions, and these have always seemed from Europe's point of view to be much of a muchness.

Some threads need tying together. I began this chapter by asserting that the central project of that Pan-African literary culture to which Soyinka belongs could be characterized as the search for a culture—a search for the relation of the author to the social world. I then suggested that we could detect in a preface of Soyinka's a tension between a private "metaphysical" account of his play *Death and the King's Horseman* and its obvious ideological implications. Soyinka, I went on to claim, rejects any obviously "political" account of his literary work, because he wishes to show how an African writer can take Africa for granted in his work, drawing on "the world-view . . . of his own people," and because he wishes to represent what is *African* about his and other African writing as arising endogenously out of Africa's shared metaphysical resources. Most recently I have argued that we cannot accept a central presupposition of this view, namely the presupposition that there is, even at quite a high level of abstraction, *an* African worldview.

My argument will be complete when I have shown why Soyinka's view of African metaphysical solidarity is an answer to the search for a culture, and what, since we must reject his answer, should replace it. To this latter question, I shall offer the beginnings of an answer that is sketched out further in later chapters.

African writers share, as I have said, both a social-historical situation and a social-historical perspective. One aspect of the situation is the growth both of literacy and of the availability of printing. This generates the now-familiar problem of the transition from fundamentally oral to literary cultures, and in doing so it gives rise to that peculiar privacy that is associated with the written and persistent text, a privacy associated with a new kind of property in texts, a new kind of authorial authority, a new kind of creative persona. It is easy to see now that, in generating the category of the individual in the new world of the public—*published*—text, in creating the private "metaphysical" interiority of the author, this social-historical situation tears the writer out of his social-historical perspective; the authorial "I" struggles to displace the "we" of the oral narration.

This struggle is as central to Soyinka's situation as it is to that of African writers generally. At the same time, and again typically, Soyinka, the individual, a Nigerian outside the traditional, more certain world of his Yoruba ancestors, struggles with the Soyinka who experiences the loss of that world, of these gods of whom he speaks with such love and longing in the first lecture. Once again the "I" seeks to escape the persistent and engulfing "we."

And with this dialectic of self-as-whole and self-as-part, we reach the core: for this struggle is, I suggest, the source of the tension in his author's note—the tension between Soyinka's account of his drama and the drama itself. But it is also at the root of the project of *Myth, Literature and the African World*.

For Soyinka's search for a culture has led him, as the title of the book indicates, away from the possibility of a Yoruba or a Nigerian "we" to an African, a continental community. His solution to the problem of what it is that individuates African culture (which he senses as a problem because he realizes that Africans have so much in common) is that African literature is united in its drawing on the resources of an African conception of community growing out of an African metaphysics. The tension in *Myth, Literature and the African World* is between this thesis and the Soyinka of the dramas, implicit in his account of Yoruba cosmology in the first lecture, the Soyinka whose account of Yoruba cosmology is precisely not the Yourba account; who has taken sometimes Yoruba mythology, but sometimes the world of a long-dead Greek, and demythologized them to his own purposes, making of them something new, more "metaphysical," and, above all, more private and individual.

Once we see that Soyinka's account of his literary project is in tension with his literary corpus, we can see why he has to conceal, as I have suggested he does, the ideological role that he sees for the writer. If African writers were to play their social role in creating a new African literature of the "secular social vision" drawing on an African metaphysics, then the colonial experience *would* be a "catalytic incident merely"—it could only be the impetus to uncover this metaphysical solidarity. Furthermore, his own work, viewed as an examination of the "abyss of transition," serves its ideological purpose just by being a *metaphysical* examination, and loses this point when reduced to an account of the colonial experience. Paradoxically, its political purpose—in the creation of an African literary culture, the declaration of independence of the African mind—is served only by concealing its political interpretation.

We cannot, then, accept Soyinka's understanding of the purposes of Africa's literatures today. And yet his *oeuvre* embodies, perhaps more than any other body of modern African writing, the challenge of a new mode of individuality in African intellectual life. In taking up so passionately the heritage of the printed word, he has entered inevitably into the new kind of literary self that comes with print, a self that is the product, surely, of changes in social life as well as in the technology of the word.

This novel self is more individualist and atomic than the self of precapitalist societies; it is a creature of modern economic relations. I do not know that this new conception of the self was inevitable, but it is no longer something that we in Africa could escape even if we wanted to. And if we cannot escape it, let us celebrate it—there is surely a Yoruba proverb with this moral—and celebrate it in the work of Wole Soyinka, who has provided in his plays a literary experience whose individuality is an endless source of insight and pleasure.[21]

FIVE

Ethnophilosophy and Its Critics

By "African philosophy" I mean a set of texts, specifically the set of texts written by Africans themselves and described as philosophical by their authors themselves.[1]

PAULIN HOUNTONDJI

M y epigraph is a definition proposed by the Beninois philosopher Paulin Hountondji—a definition that knowingly sidesteps what has been one of the cruces of philosophical debate in postcolonial black Africa. As we have puzzled over whether philosophers who happen to share a continent should for that reason be classified together, we have wondered, too, what sorts of intellectual activity should be called "philosophy." And, despite Hountondji, we know that not any answer to that question will do. If Sir Isaac Newton had lived in Africa, *Principia* would be, by this criterion, a work of African philosophy: for Newton called this the first great text of modern theoretical physics, a work of natural philosophy. And thousands of books published each year in the United States on astrology or bogus Hindu mysticism would count by an analogous criterion as American philosophy.

Yet there is something to be said for Hountondji's strategy. While philosophers in Africa are seeking a role for themselves—or wondering, perhaps, whether they have any role at all—it may be as well not to rely too much on restrictive definitions. The worst that can be said, after all, against someone who calls a cookbook a contribution to the philosophy of cooking is, perhaps, that *philosophy* is a rather grandiose word.

We do well to be especially careful in applying definitions borrowed from the European philosophical traditions in which contemporary African university philosophers have been trained, because even within these traditions there is a notoriously wide range of opinion about the tasks and the topics of philosophy. And the disagreements within the Western academy about the character of philosophy pale into insignificance when we seek to give a unitary explanation of what makes both Confucius and Plato philosophers or of what makes certain Indian and Chinese and Latin writings all *philosophical* texts.

So that, though we *could* try to approach the question of African philosophy by the method of definitions, asking what "philosophy" means and what it means to be African, settling the issue by definitional fiat is unlikely to be productive. A cookbook might better not be called "the philosophy of cooking," but it might be a good cookbook nevertheless. I suggest we start instead by examining the range of things that have come to be called "African philosophy" and asking which of these activities is worthwhile or interesting—and in what ways.

Since I do not wish to prejudge the issue of what should count as African philosophy, I shall not assume, as Hountondji does, that it has to be written. As we shall see in Chapter 6, there is something to be said for—and a good deal to be said against—a view of written African philosophy as continuous with earlier preliterate forms of intellectual activity. But my concern in these essays is primarily with the situation of African intellectuals.[2] And because, as I have already said, the training of African university philosophers has been in the traditions of the West, we may begin—here as elsewhere in the characterization of African intellectual life—by relating the situation of the contemporary African intellectual to the cultures of their former colonizers. Provided we keep open minds, that need not blind us to the way that philosophy in Africa grows also out of her own indigenous traditions.

Western academic philosophy may have a hard time agreeing on its own definition, but any definition must be responsible to certain facts about the application of the concept. In the Euro-American tradition nothing can count as philosophy, for example, if it does not discuss problems that have a family resemblance to those problems that have centrally concerned those we call "philosophers." And nothing that does address itself to such problems but does so in ways that bear no family resemblance to traditional philosophical methods ought to count either. And the Wittgensteinian notion of family resemblance, here, is especially appropriate because a tradition, like a family, is something that changes from one generation to the next. Just as there may be no way of seeing me as especially like my remote ancestors, even though there are substantial similarities between the members of succeeding generations, so we are likely to be able to see the continuities between Plato and Frege only if we trace the steps in between. Contemporary philosophical discourse in the West is, like all discourse, the product of a history, and it is that history that explains why its many styles and problems hang together.

It would be difficult to give an exhaustive list of the problems that have come to be at the core of the Western tradition. But they can all, I think, be seen as growing out of a history of systematic reflection on widespread, prereflective beliefs about the nature of humankind, about the purposes, and about our knowledge of and our place in the cosmos. When these beliefs are not subjected to systematic and critical analysis we speak of "folk philosophy." But in Western academic philosophy—by contrast, for example, with anthropology or the history of ideas—what is required is not just a concern with the issues that are the topic of folk philosophy but a critical discourse, in which reason and argument play a central role.

We cannot, however, characterize philosophy simply as the discourse that applies to our folk beliefs the techniques of logic and reason. Not only because others—in physics and sociology and literary theory—make such arguments too, but because academic philosophy has come to be defined by a canon of subjects as well as by its argumentative method. If we understand "philosophy" as the tradition to which Plato and Aristotle, Descartes and Hume, Kant and Hegel belong, then at least the following concepts are bound to be regarded as central to that canon: beauty, being, causation, evil, God, gods, good, illusion, justice, knowledge, life, meaning, mind, person, reality, reason, right, truth, understanding, and wrong.

Now, no doubt, not all cultures have exactly these concepts, but all of them will probably have concepts that bear a family resemblance to them. No human being could think about action who did not have a concept like our concept of causation; or think about why things happen in the world without such a concept. No one could have social norms without concepts at least something like *good, evil, right,* and *wrong,* and a society without norms could hardly exist—not simply because the concept of a society is connected with the idea of shared norms but because without common norms it is difficult to conceive of any collective action. Similarly, every culture has had views about what it is to have something like a mind and of its relationship to the body; almost every culture has had a concept that plays some of the roles of concepts of divinity. And even if there were a human culture where nothing like any of these concepts was present, it is hard to make sense of the idea of a culture that did not have *any* crucial organizing concepts.

There is, then, in every culture a folk philosophy, and implicit in that folk philosophy are all (or many) of the concepts that academic philosophers have made central to their study in the West. Of course, there might not be in every society people who pursued a systematic critical conceptual inquiry, but at least in every culture there is work for a philosopher, should one come along, to do.

There are many reasons for supposing that the task might be difficult; many too for doubting that every society would come, without exogenous intervention, to take up the project. But in the actual world, there *has* been an exogenous intervention, and it has left people with Western philosophical trainings in Africa. Because they are Africans rooted to at least some degree in their traditional cultures and, at the same time, intellectuals trained in the traditions of the West, they face a special situation. They may choose to borrow the tools of Western philosophy for their work. But if they wish to pursue such conceptual inquiries in the thought worlds of their own traditions, they are bound to do so with a highly developed awareness of the challenges of Western ideas.

They are bound also to have to make choices within Western traditions. Not only is there a considerable difference in the styles of philosophy in France and in Germany, on the one hand, and in the anglophone world, on the other, but there is in Britain and in North America a wide divergence between the practice—and the metaphilosophical theory—of the dominant Anglo-American tradition and the theory and practice of those whose work is conceived as closer to the traditions that remain strong in France and Germany.[3] That the work of these latter philosophers is often referred to as "Continental" philosophy is a reflection of the essentially English origins of this dichotomization.

When, in the first decades of this century, Frege began to replace Hegel as the tutelary spirit of English philosophy, the ethos of Continental historicist modes of thought was gradually eliminated from the philosophy faculties of English (though, curiously, not from Scottish) universities. In England the most influential body of philosophical practice through the midcentury derived from the transfer, through such figures as Ludwig Wittgenstein and Alfred Ayer, of the logical positivism of the Vienna circle to Oxford and Cambridge into the context provided by the critique of idealism that had been begun by G. E. Moore and Bertrand Russell. The tradition that resulted came to be known as *analytical philosophy*.

This wind from Austria blew less vigorously in the United States, where pragmatism provided an indigenous alternative to the influences of the Vienna circle. But W. V. O. Quine, one of the most potent influences in the formation of the modern idiom of American philosophy, had been influenced, like Alfred Ayer, by his contacts with the Viennese school, even if, as he acknowledged, pragmatism was another of his major influences. While Wittgenstein brought the gospel to Cambridge, the influence of Moritz Schlick, a central figure in the organization of the circle, and, above all, of Rudolf Carnap—from one perspective, the greatest systematic philosopher of the century—also left their impress on American academic philosophy.

For the many who resisted these strains of thought in the United States, the founding figure of their tradition remained not Frege but Hegel, and the most influential of the moderns were not Wittgenstein and Carnap but Husserl and Heidegger. Those in this tradition felt at ease with Sartre, who had introduced into French philosophy the influence of the German phenomenologists and turned it, as he claimed, to good existentialist use. They continued to read Schopenhauer. They rediscovered Nietzsche—decontaminated of his Nazi associations—after the Second World War. The analytical philosophers, meanwhile, were reading Russell and Moore and the early Wittgenstein—and later on Carnap and the later Wittgenstein and Quine—and spending more and more of their time on something called the *philosophy of language*.

Far more striking to the casual observer than the differences in doctrines of these groups—for neither "Continental" nor "analytical" philosophy is easily characterized by a creed—are their differences in method and idiom. They share, of course, a vocabulary of key words that belong to the language of the Western philosophical tradition—*truth* and *meaning,* for example, being familiar lexical presences for each, but they often put these shared words to radically different uses; and words like *being* (for the analyticals), and *reference* (for the Continentals), which were important for the other tradition, became for a period virtually taboo.

For an outsider this fuss may seem simply preposterous: what is at stake, after all, is only the right to the label "philosophy." Why should it matter to anyone (analytic or Continental) whether someone else (Continental or analytic) cares to call what they are doing by this label? But the answer is simple: "philosophy" is the highest-status label of Western humanism. The claim to philosophy is the claim to what is most important, most difficult, most fundamental in the Western tradition. And the enduring power of that claim is reflected in the commonest response from the inquisitive French or British or American stranger who asks what I do: "Philosophy?" Pause. "You must be very clever." To admit to a Western audience that philosophers, like all intellectuals, can be witless as well as smart; and that the questions we ask and answer are hard, but no harder than the questions in physics or literary theory; to admit *that*—our darkest secret—would be to throw away a couple of millennia of cultural capital.

We can characterize the divided house of anglophone academic philosophy not only by its double idiom but also by a double self-image. Analytical philosophers think of themselves as on the side of logic, science, and method against superstition; on the side of a modest and careful search for truth against bombast. For them philosophy is often a technical subject, and a grasp of these technicalities is a condition of professional competence. Continentals believe that the issues they deal with are difficult and important and that their tradition is continuous with the best and deepest of the Western tradition of humanistic scholarship. They are likely to see philosophy as continuous not with the sciences but with literature and the arts. If they complain about the analyticals, they complain that their work is shallow, cold, dry, inconsequential; that they evade the difficulty of the central philosophical questions by reducing them to trivial, often semantic, debates; that they lack a sense of the historical development of the life of reason. And, in return, the analyticals are likely to object that Continentals mistake obscurantism for profundity.

These self- (and other) images are, I suppose, stereotypes. Few, on either "side," express themselves as clearly and strongly as this; most analytical philosophers will agree that there is some interest in, say, Sartre's moral psychology, and most Continentals will agree that analytical philosophy of logic and language, while not nearly as important as it is supposed to be, is often the work of subtle and gifted minds. But though these images are stereotypes, they are not, in my view, caricatures. Bernard Williams, a leading British analytical philosopher, has written recently that analytical philosophy "has no distinctive subject matter."

> What distinguishes analytical philosophy from other contemporary philosophy (though not from much philosophy of other times) is a certain way of going on, which involves argument, distinctions, and, so far as it remembers to try to achieve it and succeeds, moderately plain speech. As an alternative to plain speech, it distinguishes sharply between obscurity and technicality. It always rejects the first, but the second it sometimes finds a necessity. This feature peculiarly enrages some of its enemies. Wanting philosophy to be at once profound and accessible, they resent technicality but are comforted by obscurity.[4]

"A certain way of going on": no choice of phrasing could more vividly display the laid-back tone of much analytical philosophizing, the sense that we shall go further, faster, if we do not make too much fuss. The "enemies" are bound to be enraged by someone who speaks of "a certain way of going on," when what is at issue is philosophical methodology, not least because this conversational tone attempts to claim as natural and uncomplicated what is often, from another point of view, a profoundly challenging philosophical claim. For anyone who has watched the Anglo-American philosophical scene, even from afar, it will not be hard to guess who these "enemies" are.

In the United States this discourse of mutual incomprehension and distaste has become more complicated in the recent years. For many younger philosophers see little point in the labels. There is a tendency more and more to speak—as Williams does here—of differences of idiom and to hope for some sort of common ground. But in the academy, as in politics, true détente requires more than the regular expression of a desire for rapprochement.

The Continentals in the United States, though drawing on the canon of academic philosophy in France and Germany, differed from their literally European cousins in one major respect. For political philosophy, and in particular, various readings of and reactions to Marxism, have never had the central place in the American tradition that they have had in Europe. In Europe, figures such as Althusser and Sartre in France, or Adorno or Habermas in Germany, have developed a philosophical reflection on politics that takes Marxism seriously, however much it is criticized.

Not only have the recent rapprochements made the work of European philosophers increasingly familiar to Anglo-American philosophers, but there is also in Europe a growing interest in the work of the British, North American, and Australian philosophers who constitute the canon of analytical philosophy. Nevertheless, for the first twenty-five years of the postwar era we must recognize two powerful and powerfully distinct philosophical traditions in the West. And it was in those decades that the philosophy departments of anglophone and francophone Africa were established.

Philosophers in African philosophy departments inherited, then, the two warring Western traditions, and one thing that we can say with certainty is that if we accept Paulin Hountondji's proposal we shall have, as a result, to count as African philosophy many texts whose connection with Africa is no more (and, one should no doubt say, no less) profound than the nationality of their authors. This is a consequence Hountondji accepts. His definition, with which I began, is intended to restore ''the simple, obvious truth that Africa is above all a continent and the concept of Africa an empirical, geographical concept and not a metaphysical one.''[5] But the important questions for an African scholar about her involvement with Western academic philosophy are not to be settled by facts of geography. For she will want to ask, first, if there is anything distinctive she can bring to the Western tradition from her history, her culture, her language, and her traditions and, second, what, in Africa, is the teaching and writing of Western-style philosophy for?

Now many contemporary philosophers in the West would treat the question what philosophy is *for* with the special disdain reserved for philistinism. Of course, they have their reasons for doing philosophy, and most believe that the fact that philosophy is studied in their universities is a positive good for their culture. But they are inclined to regard as a complex question what positive good it is. And, since the practice of philosophy is not seriously threatened, however tight the purse strings of the academy are drawn, they do not spend much time on answering it. Granted that philosophy serves some purpose, the task is not to justify it but to do it.

In Africa the question of the usefulness of philosophy is not so easily put aside. Universities compete with other areas of national life for the scarce resources of development. For the politicians, for the populace generally, it is easy to see why it is worth having doctors, engineers, economists, even lawyers; it is easy, too, to believe that the theoretical sciences, from physics to jurisprudence, are inextricably bound up with the applied ones. But the humanities, and above all, philosophy, are not so easily valued. For philosophy as it is practiced in the university is peculiarly remote from the thoughts of ordinary individuals, in Africa as elsewhere, about truth and reason, gods and good, matter and mind.

The worth of any formal philosophy is especially hard to see outside the Islamized regions, because there is no indigenous formal tradition. Muslims have a long history of philosophical writing, much of it written in Africa, so that the study of philosophy can be seen as traditional (and therefore holy) and endogenous (and therefore nationalistic). But in much of black Africa there is no Islamic tradition, indeed no written tradition at all. The sense in which there is a philosophical tradition is, as I suggested earlier, that there is an oral folk philosophy, whose authority lies largely in its purported antiquity, not in the quality of the reasoning—or the evidence—that sustains it, and which is usually unable to treat critical activity as disinterested. Given the not-unreasonable postcolonial skepticism about everything foreign, it is natural that there should be a growing literature, written by Africans trained in Western philosophy, that asks what African philosophy is for.

Not only is this natural, it is surely also salutary; even if this means that much time is taken up, in the words of the Ghanaian philosopher Kwasi Wiredu, "talking *about* African philosophy as distinct from actually doing it."[6]

On Wiredu's conception, which grows out of the Anglo-American tradition, African philosophy may borrow and refine the methods of Western philosophy and apply them to the analysis of the conceptual problems of African life. To do this, on his view, it is necessary first to develop a sympathetic reflective understanding of traditional modes of thought. And, to a large extent, our modes of thought remain (as I shall argue later) much closer to traditional ideas than many are willing to acknowledge. Since the specific ideas of different African cultures vary, each philosopher must speak from within some specific tradition; the project is African only because the philosopher is, say, Akan, and the Akan are geographically African.

But others have sought to make their philosophy African in a different way. They have asked the question "Is there an African philosophy?" and answered it in the affirmative. Since *philosophy* is so equivocal a word, however, there are a number of ways in which the question might be taken.

If it means "Is there folk philosophy in Africa?" the answer is: "Africa has living people and cultures and therefore, of necessity, folk philosophies." But if *African* in *African philosophy* is meant to distinguish a natural kind, there seems no terribly good reason for supposing that the answer should be yes. Why should the Zulu, the Azande, the Hausa, and the Asante have the same concepts or the same beliefs about those matters which the concepts are used to think about and discuss? Indeed, it seems they do not. If similarities are expected, it should be on the basis of the similarities between the economies and social structures of traditional societies or as the result of cultural exchanges; but the cultural exchange across the continent at the level of ideas has been limited by the absence of writing, and the socioeconomic similarities are often exaggerated. Many African societies have as much in common with traditional societies that are not African as they do with each other.

The question may, however, be intended as one about philosophy in the sense of the Western academic canon: the sense in which Socrates or Thales is reputed to be the first Western philosopher. And in this sense the question is more difficult. Certainly the elders of many African societies discuss questions about right and wrong, life and death, the person and immortality. They even discuss the question whether an argument is a good argument or a consideration a weighty consideration.

And this is at least the beginning of philosophy as a reflective activity. But often difficult problems are put aside by appealing to "what the ancestors have said" in a way that is reminiscent of argument from authority in the Middle Ages in Europe. And just as those philosophers in the scholastic tradition who argued that something must be so because "the Philosopher"—Aristotle—had said it was so were arguing badly, so it seems to me that the elders who argue this way are simply making bad arguments. But the idea of a discourse free from the constraints of the authority of tradition is an extraordinarily modern conception in Europe—and it should not be a matter of shame and reproach that those elders who have faced the question whether the ancestors might have been wrong have been, in all probability, quite few. Creative, critical philosophers have been few in the history of the West, and their bravery has often been made easier by their access to a written critical tradition. Oral traditions have a habit of transmitting only the consensus, the accepted view: those who are in intellectual rebellion (and European anthropologists and missionaries have met plenty of these) often have to begin in each generation all over again.

I have already said that there is no reason to think that the folk philosophies of Africa are uniform. What account can we give, then, of the belief that there is a role for something that is importantly African to be done in philosophy? Part of the explanation must lie, as we have seen, in racialism: what more natural reaction to a European culture that claims—with Hume and Hegel—that the intellect is the property of men with white skins, than to insist there is something important in the sphere of the intellect that belongs to black men? If there is white philosophy, why not also black philosophy? The origins of the argument are intelligible—and it is somehow healthier than the view of the apostles of negritude, that black men should give the intellect over to whites and explore the affective realm that is their special property. Unlike Césaire we need not say, "Eia for those who never invented anything."[7]

But black philosophy must be rejected, for its defense depends on the essentially racist presuppositions of the white philosophy whose antithesis it is. Ethnocentrism—which is an unimaginative attitude to one's own culture—is in danger of falling into racism, which is an absurd attitude to the color of someone else's skin.

So that if the argument for an African philosophy is not to be racist, then some claim must be substantiated to the effect that there are important problems of morals or epistemology or ontology that are common in the situation of those on the African continent. And the source of that common problematic, if it cannot be racial, must lie in the African environment or in African history.

Now you might say that I have just *assumed* that an argument for an African philosophy must be an argument that there are problems in philosophy that are either crucially or uniquely raised in the African situation, and that I have assumed this even though it is clear that differences in styles of philosophy are often, as I have said, not so much differences in matter as in method. But these assumptions are surely quite reasonable. For what reasons could there be in the African situation for supposing that we must deal with philosophy in a particular way? The most that can be said is that what our problems are will determine what methods are appropriate—and perhaps the problems that concern us now are so different from European philosophical problems that we will have to develop a radically different methodology. If, however, African philosophy shares neither the problems nor the methods of Western philosophy, one is bound to wonder what the point is of calling the activity "philosophy" at all. There is, surely, no more reason to suppose that every intellectual activity in the West should have an African twin than there is to suppose that we must have African harpsichords or African sonnets.

But, of course, I have left something out of account. "Philosophy," as I said earlier, is the highest-status label of Western humanism. The urge to find something in Africa that "lives up to" the label is, in part, a question of wanting to find something in Africa that *deserves* the dignity; that warrants the respect that we have been taught (in our Western or Westernized schools and colleges) is due to Plato and Aristotle, Kant and Hegel. And part of a proper response to this impulse is to demystify that canonical respect; something that requires only, surely, that we remark the preposterous foundations upon which it is established.

Our textbook histories of Western culture may insist that Plato and Aristotle are at the root of its central insights. But if we ask ourselves what is most valuable in Euro-American culture, we shall surely want to mention, for example, democracy, to which Plato and Aristotle—and, for that matter, Kant and Hegel—were opposed; applied science and technology, to which Plato contributed nothing and Aristotle provided a long false start whose overthrow in the Renaissance finally made possible the scientific revolution; and a literary culture that refers back to Plato and Aristotle almost exclusively in moments of Christian religiosity (which they would have repudiated) or snobbism or hocus-pocus. The point is not that these are authors we should not read—reading them has provided me, as it has provided many others, with some of the greatest pleasures of my reading life—but rather that we should not read them as repositories of forgotten truth or sources of timeless value. Plato and Aristotle are often interesting because they are wicked and wrong; because they provide us with access to worlds of thought that are alien, stretching our conception of the range of human thought; because we can trace, in tracing the history of reflection on their work, a single fascinating strand in the history of the mental life of our species.

Even if the philosophical canon *were* the *fons et origo* of all value in Western culture—and even if there were nothing to match up to it in Africa—what, more than a moment's regret that we can share pride in it only as human beings and not as Africans, would hang on it? Surely not that we would thereby be deprived of some rights against the West? There is no reason to accept the astonishing hyperbole that what is most of value to Westerners (or to anyone else) in their culture—what will justify it at the Last Judgment—is to be found in a few-score philosophical works written over a couple of millennia by a small company of Western European men. It is not as members of the national (or racial or intellectual) community from which these writers sprung that Europeans deserve equality of respect or claim their rights under the United Nations Declaration of Human Rights, and not to belong to that community is, in consequence, no bar to claiming those rights for the rest of us.

If we want to find a place for philosophy in Africa, let us begin with a sense of proportion about its significance; I am all in favor of keeping my job, but not at the price of an ignoble lie.

What projects, then, *should* philosophers concerned with the intellectual health of the continent pursue? Richard Wright has provided an accurate survey of the answers to this question that are currently on offer:

> (1) The thought of the African people is intrinsically valuable and should be studied for that reason, if for no other; (2) it is important to the history of ideas that we discover and understand the relation between (or influence of) African thought and the thought of the Western world. For, if Western civilization had its origin on the African continent . . . the correct pattern of intellectual development . . . will become clear only as we begin to understand the basis and direction of that development . . . (3) it is important in understanding practical affairs that we clearly delineate their underlying philosophical motivation.[8]

The first of these options leads swiftly to what Paulin Hountondji calls "ethnophilosophy," the attempt to explore and systematize the conceptual world of Africa's traditional cultures. It amounts, in effect, to adopting the approach of a folklorist: doing the natural history of traditional folk thought about the central issues of human life.[9]

The founding text of ethnophilosophy is *La Philosophie Bantoue,* a book in which the Belgian missionary Father Placide Tempels sought to characterize the essential features of the thought of the Bantu-speaking peoples of central and southern Africa. Tempels argued that the Bantu way of thought had at its center a notion of Force, a notion that occupied the position of privilege of the notion of Being in Western (by which, as a Catholic, he meant Thomist) thought. I do not myself believe that this way of formulating his claim has been helpful. But Tempels's influential formulation can at least be seen as registering the crucial role played by concepts of agency in many traditional African cultures, in places where the West has come to see only efficient— that is, impersonal—causation. (This is a question I follow up on in Chapter 6.)

Though much ethnophilosophical material is indeed very interesting—at least where it is not, as it too often is, woefully inaccurate—we should go carefully in discussing how to put it to philosophical use. For though anthropology (like travel) may broaden the mind, the kind of analytical work that needs to be done on these concepts is not something that is easily done secondhand, and most anthropological reports—though not, perhaps, the best ones—are pretty philosophically naive. This would be mere carping (there is, after all, too little written about Africa that *is* philosophically serious) were it not for the fact that the view that African philosophy just *is* ethnophilosophy has been largely assumed by those who have thought about what African philosophers should study.

Now the description of someone else's folk philosophy, without any serious analysis of its concepts or any critical reflection on how understanding the world with those concepts allows us to appreciate what may not be appreciated in other conceptual schemes, is surely a mere curiosity. It might, I suppose, lead to intellectual tolerance, but it might just as easily lead to chauvinism or total incomprehension: "So they believe all that; so what? They're wrong, aren't they?"

Of course, where the beliefs are those of our *own* cultures, we cannot make this response. You cannot intelligibly say: "We believe all that; so what? We're wrong, aren't we?" But the fact is that philosophers in Africa are bound, by their position as intellectuals educated in the shadow of the West, to adopt an essentially comparative perspective. Even if it is their own traditions they are analyzing, they are bound to see them in the context of European (and often Islamic) as well as other African cultures. No one can be happy celebrating her own tradition in the knowledge that it makes claims inconsistent with other systems, without beginning to wonder which system is right about which issues. A cozy celebration of one's own conceptual and theoretical resources is a simple impossibility. For one has to live one's life through concepts, and, despite the fact that people everywhere constantly inhabit inconsistent presuppositions, in one life at one time there can sometimes be space for only one system. That system does not have to be either "Western" or "traditional": it can take elements of each and create new ones of its own. But the life of reason requires the integration of elements: if elements in different systems or within the same system are incompatible, something has to go.

Most existing ethnophilosophy is predicated on two major assumptions. The first, which Paulin Hountondji has dubbed "unanimism," is the factual assumption, which I have already rejected, that there is some central body of ideas that is shared by black Africans quite generally. The second is the evaluative assumption that the recovery of this tradition is worthwhile.

Against the dominant stream of ethnophilosophy runs a current of recent work, which explicitly denies one or both of the presuppositions of ethnophilosophy. Hountondji's *African Philosophy: Myth and Reality*—originally published in French, with the subtitle "a critique of ethnophilosophy," in 1976—and Marcien Towa's 1971 *Essai sur la problématique philosophique dans l'Afrique actuelle*,[10] in francophone Africa, and Kwasi Wiredu's 1980 *Philosophy and an African Culture*, in anglophone Africa, are the major texts of this second tradition.

Towa and Wiredu have made a sustained assault on the evaluative assumption: Wiredu, by arguing persuasively that there is no philosophical interest in a recovery and preservation of traditional ideas that is not critical; Towa in suggesting, following Césaire, that the mere accumulation of traditions is a diversion from engagement with the real political issues facing Africa, issues her philosophers ought to articulate and address. Hountondji endorses both these lines of attack, but he combines them with a sustained attack on the unanimism that undergirds the project of ethnophilosophy. I shall return to the work of Hountondji and Wiredu at the end of this essay. But we can examine both the prospects and the pitfalls of ethnophilosophy by examining some representative work in this tradition.

If there is one question, above all, that is almost never satisfactorily addressed by such work, it is what the *point* is of this cataloging of thought worlds. Wiredu has argued that it serves no *philosophical* purpose: what other purposes could it serve? Consider a couple of the papers Richard Wright has collected in *African Philosophy: An Introduction*—John Ayoade's discussion of "Time in Yoruba Thought" and Helaine Minkus's essay, apropos of Ghana, on "Causal Theory in Akwapim Akan Philosophy"—and ask the question as sharply as it can be phrased: since, in Hountondji's words, "African traditions are no more homogeneous than those of any other continent,"[11] why should anyone who is neither from Akwapim nor from Yorubaland take an interest in these papers?

This question is raised particularly urgently for me because the Twi-speaking peoples of Akwapim share most of the concepts and the language of Asante, my home. At the points of divergence between Akwapim beliefs (as reported by Minkus) and Asante beliefs, even an unphilosophical Asante might wish to raise the question Minkus never addresses, the question whether what the Akwapim Akan believe is *true*. Minkus has a paragraph of discussion of the fact that Akan thought—like natural science, Christianity, Islam, and the quantum theory—has features that "insulate it from attack and doubt,"[12] in effect observing that this way of looking at the world has the properties that the great French philosopher-physicist Pierre Duhem, noticed in physical theory. But what conclusions are we supposed to draw from this—the only critical observation she makes?

I shall return to Duhem's thesis in Chapter 6, arguing that its applicability to traditional religion is a mark of certain underlying similarities of Western and traditional—in short, of human—modes of thought. But here I want simply to make the point that since, as I have argued, the African philosopher is bound to adopt an essentially comparative perspective, Minkus, in adopting an essentially descriptive enterprise, stops precisely at the point where the questions that are urgent for us begin.

The beginnings of a more comparative analysis *are* to be found in an interesting paper of Ben Oguah's: "African and Western Philosophy: A Comparative Study." Oguah argues that the materials for reflecting on certain perennial problems of Western philosophy are available in the Fanti conceptual vocabulary. Thus he shows convincingly (as I, at least, would expect) that the concepts necessary to discuss the nature of the person, of other minds, of freedom of the will, of immortality, of rationalism and empiricism—in short of the whole gamut of philosophical questions familiar in the West, exist in the Fanti vocabulary. To organize these concepts and their relations into a coherent system is the task of what the English philosopher Sir Peter Strawson—one of Oguah's teachers—has called "descriptive metaphysics."[13] But, as many philosophers have observed in discussing Strawson's work, though this sort of careful conceptual analysis is indeed a helpful preliminary to the philosophical project, it is surely only a preliminary to the "revisionary metaphysics" that seeks to assess our most general concepts and beliefs, to look for system in them, to evaluate them critically, and, where necessary, to propose and develop new ways of thinking about the world.

More than this, the systematization of what exists prior to the sort of organized, written collaborative discourse that academic philosophy represents inevitably changes the character of our ideas. The image of philosophy presented by British conceptual analysis in the 1950s and 1960s as an activity that takes as its material the raw stuff of everyday conceptual life, merely organizing and articulating it, is false to the experience of doing philosophy. We may agree with J. L. Austin that the structure of the concepts with which people ordinarily operate is highly complex and subtly nuanced, without agreeing that the process of making the implicit explicit leaves the prereflective texture of our thought unchanged.

A simple example will make the point for me. If we were reporting, as ethnographers, the views of rural French men and women, we should have to accept that many of them believe that something of them—their spirit, as we might say—

survives the death of their bodies. But to systematize this sort of view, we should have to decide whether this entity had a location in the ordinary world of space and time. Many of these people, if asked, would be likely, if they took any view of the matter at all, to answer that it did not. We can imagine that, for them, the idea of disembodied existence is essentially subjectively conceived as the having of experiences without the possession of a body. But philosophical reflection stretching back through Wittgenstein to Descartes has led many of us to conclude that this notion is just incoherent. And since anyone with a Western philosophical training knows that there are grounds for thinking it incoherent, there is something less than sane in the intellectual project of recovering this notion without at least considering whether, in the end, it makes sense.

We know there are mystical traditions, in Catholicism or Buddhism, for example, that have at their core a belief in the ultimate unintelligibility of the deepest truths about our human situation; each believes that there are "mysteries in the strict sense." John Skorupski summarizes the Catholic position thus:

> In a nutshell, a "mystery" is a doctrine whose truth cannot be demonstrated but must be taken on faith; a mystery "in the strict sense" is a doctrine such that not merely the fact that it is true, but also the fact that it has definite coherent sense must be taken on faith.[14]

But even in these traditions the class of such mysteries is restricted, and their truth and intelligibility have the sanction not of evidence and argument, it is true, but, in the one case, of divine revelation and, in the other, of a certain kind of contemplative experience.

There is one other crucial example of an acceptance of unintelligibility, which is of importance to an understanding of Western intellectual life—namely, the quantum theory. Here the acceptance of indeterminism requires us also to accept the ultimate inexplicability of certain events—they are simply and irreducibly random—and thus to give up the Laplacean vision of a world whose motions are completely predictable and determined by intelligible laws. But there is a tremendous resistance—epitomized in Einstein's pained exclamation that God does not play dice with the world—to accepting this. And if the ultimate unintelligibility of some aspects of the world is accepted, it is accepted only reluctantly and in the face of very powerful evidence. If science accepts unintelligibility, it is in the name of truth.

In the Catholic tradition too, there is no question but that the truth of the mysteries is conceived of as the source of their importance. Perhaps the Western Catholic, in religious moments, can accept this restricted domain of doctrines beyond our capacity for interpretation, but an intellectual, a university woman or man, formed at least in part in the Western tradition cannot allow the proliferation of unintelligibility. If the Buddhist sage really does simply accept the unknowability of the world, it is an acceptance that most African intellectuals will find as hard as most European ones to share.

Because the issues of truth and intelligibility are thus bound to be central to any intellectual project conceived of by someone with a Western conception of a reflective life, Oguah faces, as a result, the following dilemma. If, on the one hand, his view is that European and Fanti concepts are the same but their beliefs are different, a crucial question, which he hardly raises, is who is right. And if, on the other, the concepts are different, the interesting question is whether the Fanti concepts are more appropriate to the world than European ones, or, if not, at least more appropriate to the problems and form of life of the Fanti. In either case, to refuse to go beyond mere description of the conceptual situation seems at best eccentric, at worst simply irresponsible.

These problems are, of course, problems in the natural and biological sciences or in anthropology or comparative thought. But a philosopher, with a philosopher's training, is at least in a better position to see and say what Fanti concepts are and how they work than many social scientists—in particular if that philosopher is, like Oguah, a Fanti. And, at all events, in the present African situation this preliminary work must be done by somebody, if the inescapable task of deciding who is right— and therefore whether or not to give up traditional Fanti modes of thought— is to be rationally accomplished. Not to address this issue is to leave the outcome in the hands not of reason but of chance; or, perhaps, to leave the intellectual future of the Fanti-speaking peoples, and that of other Africans, to be decided by the fact of the technological superiority of the already hegemonic cultures of the metropolitan world.

There is, therefore, in my view, no possibility of not bringing a Western philosophical training to bear. What we must be careful of is simply projecting Western ideas, along with these Western-derived methods, into the indigenous conceptual framework, and Oguah seems to me not to have successfully negotiated this problem. I want to consider this issue in the context of his interesting discussion of Fanti philosophy of mind, but for reasons that will become clear, I shall begin by saying a little about the philosophical psychology of the Asante people, whose culture and language belong to the same Akan culture area as the Fanti.

According to most traditional Asante people, a person consists of a body (*nipadua*) made from the blood of the mother (the *mogya*); an individual spirit, the *sunsum,* which is the main bearer of one's personality; and a third entity, the ɔkra. The *sunsum* derives from the father at conception. The ɔkra, a sort of life force, departs the body only at the person's last breath; is sometimes, as with the Greeks and Hebrews, identified with breath; and is often said to be sent to a person at birth, as the bearer of one's *nkrabea,* or destiny, from God. The *sunsum,* unlike the ɔkra, may leave the body during life and does so, for example, in sleep, dreams being thought to be the perceptions of a person's *sunsum* on its nightly peregrinations. Since the *sunsum* is a real entity, dreaming that you have committed an offense is evidence that you have committed it, and, for example, a man who dreams that he has had sexual intercourse with another man's wife is liable for the adultery fees that are paid for daytime offenses.[15]

Since Asante-Twi and Fanti-Twi are largely mutually intelligible, it is reasonable, I think, to consider Oguah's account in the light of these Asante conceptions.[16] Oguah asserts that the Fanti conceptual scheme is dualist—in fact, Cartesian. But at least three caveats need to be entered about this claim. First, since Fanti is an Akan language and the word ɔkra, which Oguah translates as "soul" is, of course, the same as the word for what, in Asante, I identified not with the mind but with the life force, we might wonder why there is no mention, in Oguah, of the *sunsum*. There is, of course, no reason why the Fanti should have precisely the tripartite system we find among the Asante (and other Akan peoples in, for example, Akwapim), and there is some tendency among modern Asante speakers as well to use the words ɔkra and *sunsum* almost interchangeably, even while insisting, when asked, on the distinctness of their referents. But Oguah's access, as a contemporary native speaker of Fanti-Twi, is to these terms as mediated by the many Christian influences that have settled in the coastal regions of Ghana, after four centuries of trade and missions from Europe, and over a century of an extensive British cultural presence in the Gold Coast colony. Even if, therefore, there is, for the Fanti, no *sunsum,* we are not free to infer that this is a fact about unadulterated Fanti traditions: it might be the result of Christianization.

I emphatically do not wish to imply that Christian beliefs are *in se* un-African. But the Fanti live on the coast of modern Ghana, and this case allows us to focus on the question whether, in cultures that have exchanged goods, people, and ideas with each other and with Europe (or, in East Africa, with the Middle and Far East) for many centuries, it makes sense to insist on the possibility of identifying some precolonial system of ideas as *the* Fanti tradition. Of course, for a Fanti speaker today the beliefs of her ancestors are surely not intrinsically more valuable than the beliefs of her contemporaries, and it is perfectly reasonable for Oguah to treat the concepts as he finds them—now—in his own culture. But the fact that there is reason to suppose that these beliefs are the product of a history of cultural exchanges, that they are probably not, as the elders sometimes claim, the unadulterated legacy of immemorial tradition, *does* bring into sharp relief the question why these particular beliefs should be granted a special status. If our ancestors believed differently, why should not our descendants? Such reflection is bound to make especially compelling the demand, to which I have returned again and again, for African intellectuals to give a critical—which does *not* mean an unsympathetic—reading of the modes of thought of their less Western-influenced sisters and brothers.

Second, however—and putting aside the question whether this reportage is, by itself, what is needed—the evidence that the Fanti are now dualists, and Cartesian dualists at that, is surely not very compelling. For a Cartesian dualist, mind and body are separate substances, and this doctrine—which I admit to finding less than easy to understand—is not one I would expect to find among the Fanti. The Fanti, for example, according to Oguah's own account, hold that "what happens to the *okra* takes effect in the *honam*"[17]—that is, the body. And Oguah offers no evidence that they find this idea at all problematic. But if that is so, their dualism must be at least in some respects different from Descartes's, since, for a Cartesian, the relation of mind and body *is* felt as problematic.

More than this, there is, as Kwame Gyekye—another distinguished Twi-speaking philosopher—has pointed out, a good deal of evidence that the Akan regard the psychic component of the person as having many rather physical-sounding properties. So that even if there were not these problems with the general notion of the Fanti as Cartesian interactionists, Oguah's insistence that the "*okra,* like the Cartesian soul, is not spatially identifiable,"[18] looks to me like a projection of Western ideas. For if, as I suspect, my Fanti stepgrandmother would have agreed that the ɔkra leaves the body at death,[19] then there is no doubt that at least sometimes—namely, as it leaves the body—it is thought of as having a spatial location; even if, most of the time, it would be thought strange to ask where it was since the answer, for a living person, is obvious—in the body; and for a dead person is likely to be regarded as speculative at best.

But, third, it seems to me that the imputation of philosophical doctrines as specific as Cartesian dualism to a whole people in virtue of their possession of a notion that has some of the characteristics of a Cartesian mind is intrinsically not very plausible. Were Descartes's peasant contemporaries dualists, because they used such words as *penser?* Oguah offers evidence on these issues in the form of proverbs, and this is part of an established tradition in African ethnophilosophy.[20]

I do not myself believe that any of Ghana's Akan peoples are dualist. But I do not think that it makes sense to say they are monists either: like most Westerners—all Westerners, in fact, without a philosophical training—most simply do not have a view about the issue at all.[21] For, as I have argued already, the examination and systematization of concepts may require us to face questions that, prior to reflection, simply have not been addressed. What the Fanti have is a concept—*ɔkra*—ripe for philosophical work. What is needed is someone who does for this concept the sort of work that Descartes did for the concept of the mind, and, in doing this, like Descartes, this Fanti philosopher will be covering new territory.

Ethnophilosophy, then, strikes me as a useful beginning: a point from which to strike out in the direction of negotiating the conceptual lives—which is, in a sense, to say the lives tout court—of contemporary Africans. But, as I have argued, without an impetus toward such interventions (or, worse, as a substitute for them), it is merely a distraction.

In the catalog I cited from the philosopher Richard Wright, both the first option (studying African conceptual systems for their own sake) and the third (studying them because in "understanding practical affairs" we need to "delineate their underlying philosophical motivation") can lead naturally to ethnophilosophy (though, as I shall argue at the end of this chapter, the latter argument can also lead in other directions). Nevertheless, ethnophilosophy is, as Wright's account suggests, only one of the options that have engaged African philosophers. And his second option—or, more precisely, its rationale—strikes me as even more dubious than the project of an uncritical ethnophilosophy.

Consider the passage once more:

> it is important to the history of ideas that we discover and understand the relation between (or influence of) African thought and the thought of the Western world. For, if Western civilization had its origin on the African continent . . . the correct pattern of intellectual development . . . will become clear only as we begin to understand the basis and direction of that development.

It is, of course, crucial, as I have argued myself, that we understand (as the second option proposes) "the relation between (or influence of) African thought and the thought of the Western world." But Wright, like numerous others, takes this as a reason for raising the question whether Egyptian philosophy, as the genuine prehistory of philosophy in Africa, should not be studied in African philosophy departments.

> For, if Western civilization had its origin on the African continent . . . the correct pattern of intellectual development . . . will become clear only as we begin to understand the basis and direction of that development.

I object to this argument not only because I think what matter are answers, not histories of answers, but also because it is absurd to argue that because a thought is African, and the prehistory of European thought lies in Africa, that thought will help us to understand Western thought. Should we conduct a study of Italian peasantry in the twentieth century as a preliminary to the study of Cicero? Or go to the mayor of Athens for understanding of Plato's *Republic?*

The importance of ancient Egyptian philosophy for contemporary African intellectual life has been argued with most vigor in the writings of the Senegalese man of letters Cheikh Anta Diop, whose work makes clear, I think, the motivations of the school. In *The African Origins of Civilization,* Diop summarized his claims: "Ancient Egypt was a Negro civilization. . . . The moral fruit of their civilization is to be counted among the assets of the Black world." Because, "[a]nthropologically and culturally speaking, the Semitic world was born during protohistoric times from the mixture of white-skinned and dark-skinned people in Western Asia . . . [and] all races descended from the Black race,"[22] it followed that the first great human civilization—one from which the Greeks, among others, borrowed much—was a black civilization. Since he had also argued in *L'Unité culturelle de l'Afrique Noire* for the existence of "features common to Negro African civilization,"[23] Diop exhibits, in our own day, the essential elements of the romantic racialism of Crummell and Blyden and Du Bois, and he makes quite explicit the connections between claims about Egyptian philosophy and the projects of Pan-African nationalism. For it is, of course, the historical depth of the alleged tradition, along with its putative negritude, that makes Egyptian thought a suitable vehicle for contemporary racial pride. And since philosophers have succeeded in persuading many in the West that philosophical ideas are central to any culture—a trick that depends on an equivocation between "philosophy," the formal discipline, and "folk philosophy"—and since these men are Western-trained intellectuals, it is natural that they should see in Egyptian philosophy the continent's proudest achievement.

Yet it seems to me that Diop—whose work is clearly among the best in this tradition—offers little evidence that Egyptian philosophy is more than a systematized but fairly uncritical folk philosophy, makes no argument that the Egyptian problematic is that of the contemporary African, and allows for a hovering, if inexplicit, suggestion that the Egyptians are important because the originators of the Pharaonic dynasties were black.

I have never seen any particular point in *requiring* European and American philosophers—*qua* philosophers—to study the pre-Socratics: their work is a mixture of early "science," poetry, and myth, and if it is important for modern philosophy at all it is important partly because it creates the world of texts in which Plato began[24]— or, should we say, took the first faltering steps toward?—the business of systematically reflecting on and arguing about the concepts of folk philosophy, and partly because it has been the subject of sustained attention from philosophers in the Western tradition.[25] No analogous argument exists for the study of ancient Egyptian thought in contemporary Africa: there are no founding texts, there is no direct or continuous tradition.

Even what we might call the historicist view that understanding a concept involves understanding its history does not justify the study of either Greek or Egyptian "philosophy": for the transformations that the conceptual world of Africa and Europe have undergone since, respectively, the fifth century B.C. and the eighteenth dynasty are so great, and our forms of life so different, that the level of understanding to be gleaned by historical research is surely very limited. The understanding of the prehistory of a concept is helpful in present conceptual inquiries only if the prehistory is genuinely and deeply understood, and the distance and the paucity of data from ancient Greece or Egypt are enough to preclude any deep historical understanding, certainly if the study of that history is regarded merely as a propaedeutic. Besides which, the historicist claim is only plausible where there are important social and intellectual continuities between the various stages of society in which a concept is studied. And I deny that this condition is satisfied in the relationship between ancient Egypt and modern Africa, or ancient Greece and modern Europe. Even if I am wrong, I find nothing in Diop to persuade me otherwise.[26]

If Diop and his followers—a group we might call the "Egyptianists"—are right, then ancient Egypt deserves a more central place than it currently has in the study of ancient thought: and if they are right then it should be studied intensely in Africa and Europe and America and Australasia, wherever there is an interest in the ancient world. If European or American or Australasian intellectuals are too blinkered or too deeply chauvinistic to accept this, then maybe these matters will only be studied in Africa. But that would be a matter for regret.

The only paper in Wright's collection that exemplifies the critical analysis that characterizes the best philosophy—the only paper that seems to me to offer a standard for African philosophy to aim at—is Kwasi Wiredu's "How Not to Compare African Thought with Western Thought." In essence what he argues is that the common view that there is something particularly puzzling about African thought about "spirits" derives from a failure to notice that these beliefs are very like beliefs widely held in the European past. His presupposition that what makes a concept interesting is not whose it is but what it is and how it deals with the realities that face those whose concept it is, is one that I find thoroughly sympathetic. We can put the issue between Wiredu and the ethnophilosophers simply enough: analysis and exposition are necessary preliminaries to the critique of concepts, but without the critique the analysis is Othello without the Moor of Venice.

With the exception of Hountondji and Diop, the works I have discussed so far come from the anglophone tradition. And in discussing the structure of African philosophical debate, we have, as I have said, to distinguish the two major distinct traditions of modern philosophical work on the African continent. But I do not think that, so far as the issues that I am discussing are concerned, this divide is now of the same significance, say, as the (diminishing) intellectual gap between London and

Paris. African philosophers are now significantly aware of each other across the anglophone-francophone divide. There is a great deal of ethnophilosophy published in French, for example, in the francophone *Cahiers des religions Africaines* as in the bilingual *Africa,* and it provides material for philosophical reflection. But without the further step of critical reflection on the ethnophilosophical material, this is, as Hountondji (a francophone from Benin) and Wiredu (an anglophone from Ghana) have both insisted, of no direct interest to *philosophy,* in that sense of "philosophy" that distinguishes those who pursue philosophy in the university. And uncritical ethnophilosophy fails, in the end, as I have argued, to face the truly urgent questions that would be faced by a critical tradition.[27]

I do not, however, wish to minimize the importance or deny the intelligibility of one important motivation for the work of the ethnophilosophers: namely, the desire to recover for Africa a history in philosophy, to deny Robin Horton's claim that "Logic or Philosophy"[28] are absent from the continent's traditional thought. But the objection to this strategy has been well stated by Marcien Towa:[29]

> Le concept de philosophie ainsi élargi est coextensif à celui de culture. Il est obtenu par opposition au comportement animal. Il se différencie donc d'un tel comportement mais demeure indiscernible de n'importe quelle forme culturelle: mythe, religion, poésie, art, science, etc.[30]

To make a case for "philosophy" by eliminating what is distinctive in philosophical thinking is to fight for a word only.

Yet, so it seems to me, there *are* reasons for philosophers in Africa to continue to analyze the nature of the precolonial conceptual worlds of our cultures—reasons essentially captured in Wright's formulation of the third option: "It is important in understanding practical affairs that we clearly delineate their underlying philosophical motivation."[31] For (as I shall argue in detail in Chapter 6) some of the common features that there *are* in many of the traditional conceptual worlds of Africa plainly persist in the thinking of most Africans, even after modern schooling in secondary schools and universities. They provide the basis for a common set of African philosophical problems: for where we differ from the West, only a careful examination of the merits of our own traditions can allow us to escape the complementary dangers of adopting too little and too much of the intellectual baggage of our former colonizers.

Wiredu and Hountondji share this belief; in exploring Africa's current philosophical options, it is right to return to them.

Kwasi Wiredu's rejection of ethnophilosophy reflects his opposition to the claim that for philosophy to be acceptably African, its subject matter or its claims or its methods, or all three, must differ from those of philosophy in the cultures that colonized Africa. As we saw in Chapter 4, others have often assumed, where they have not asserted, that the distinctive features of philosophy in Africa will be African—and not Kikuyu or, say, Yoruba—reflecting a continental (or a racial) metaphysical community.

As a believer in the universality of reason, Wiredu holds the relevance of his being African to his philosophy to be both, in one sense, more global and, in another, more local; more local in that, as his title implies, he speaks as a Ghanaian for *an* African culture, more global in that he asks what it is that the particularity of his Ghanaian experience can offer to the philosophical community outside Africa. For Wiredu there are no African truths, only truths—some of them about Africa.

It is with these assumptions that he asks "what a contemporary African philosopher is to make of his background." If his reply to this question has a central theme, it is that modernization, the central project of black Africa, is essentially a philosophical project. Development, he argues, is to be measured by the "degree to which rational methods have penetrated through habits." For Wiredu "the quest for development . . . should be viewed as a continuing world-historical process in which all peoples, Western and non-Western alike, are engaged." Looked at this way, modernization is not "unthinkingly jettisoning" traditional ways of thought and adopting foreign habits, rather it is a process in which "Africans, along with all other peoples, seek to attain a specifically human destiny."

Wiredu's tone in this book is strongly humanist—morally serious but not moralistic. He criticizes the apostles of negritude, observing that people die daily in Ghana because they prefer traditional herbal remedies to Western medicines, so that "any inclination to glorify the unanalytical cast of mind is not just retrograde; it is tragic." He articulates and endorses the communalism of traditional society while deploring the authoritarianism that seems to go with it, saying that "it is important . . . to see what contribution philosophical thinking can make" to the question whether the former can be preserved without the latter.

Wiredu makes explicit the connection between an understanding of tradition and his concern for the possibilities of modernization: "Obviously it is of prime philosophical importance to distinguish between traditional, pre-scientific thought and modern, scientific thought by means of a clearly articulated criterion or set of criteria."[32] While sharing the view that traditional thought involves literal belief in quasi-material agents—he remarks upon the "ubiquity of references to gods and all sorts of spirits"[33]—he thinks it helpful to take the "folk thought" of the West as a model. For, as he claims, what is distinctive in African traditional thought is that it is traditional; there is nothing especially African about it. Wiredu argues that what is called the "traditional" mode of thought is not especially African, and he is highly critical of its rationality. He says, for example, in Chapter 3 of *Philosophy and an African Culture:*

> Many traditional African institutions and cultural practices . . . are based on superstition. By "superstition" I mean a rationally unsupported belief in entities of any sort[34] . . . Folk thought can be comprehensive and interesting on its own account, but its non-discursiveness remains a drawback.[35]

The problem is not with the contents of the beliefs expressed, however, or even whether they are comprehensive, but that they are held superstitiously: "The attribute of being superstitious attaches not to the content of a belief but to its relation to other beliefs."[36] It is this lack of an interest in reasons, with the appeal to "what our ancestors said,"[37] which is part of the "authoritarianism"[38] of traditional thought, that differentiates traditional from scientific thought. So this critique gives rise to an urgent call for the "cultivation of rational enquiry. One illuminating (because fundamental) way of approaching the concept of 'development' is to measure it by the degree to which rational methods have penetrated thought habits."[39]

Wiredu's book is, as I have said, most often seen as belonging with Hountondji's *African Philosophy: Myth and Reality;* a book that collects the major papers in which he has pursued his attack on ethnophilosophy.

Hountondji's makes his major objections to ethnophilosophy in the first three essays, which appear in their original order of publication. Beginning with a recapitulation of Césaire's political critique of Tempels as a "diversion," he moves on to discuss the work of Kagamé, Tempels's major African follower, whose *Philosophie Bantou-Rwandaise de L'Etre* "expressly and from the outset, establishes its point of view in relation to Tempels' work as an attempt by an autochthonous Bantu African to 'verify the validity of the theory advanced by this excellent missionary.'"[40] While endorsing some of Kagamé's specific criticism of Tempels, Hountondji objects to their shared unanimism.

It is in these objections to Kagamé that Hountondji's argument seems weakest. For Kagamé explicitly roots his analysis in *language*. And though it is indeed odd to suppose, with some unanimists, that a people should share the same beliefs on all the major issues in their lives, it is not at all odd to suppose that people who speak the same language should share concepts, and thus those a priori beliefs whose possession is constitutive of a grasp of concepts. If this view—which was just the official theory of ordinary language philosophy and *is* the unofficial assumption of a great deal of conceptual analysis—is wrong, it cannot be refuted by Hountondji's arguments, which show only that a whole people is unlikely to share all their important a posteriori beliefs.

Along with his attack on ethnophilosophy, Hountondji has a plausible and unflattering analysis of its motivations. Ethnophilosophy, he alleges, exists *"for a European public."*[41] It is an attempt to cope with feelings of cultural inferiority by redefining folklore as "philosophy," so as to be able to lay claim to an autochthonous philosophical tradition.

The most original of Hountondji's objections to the ethnophilosophers derives from an essentially Althusserian view of the place of philosophy. The appeal to Althusser—which contrasts rather strikingly with Wiredu's appeals to Dewey—reflects the distinction between francophone and anglophone traditions with which I began. Hountondji cites a passage from *Lenin and Philosophy* where Althusser says that philosophy "has been observed only in places where there is also what is called a science or sciences—in the strict sense of theoretical discipline, i.e. ideating and demonstrative, not an aggregate of empirical results . . ."[42] and then goes on to argue himself that if "the development of philosophy is in some way a function of the development of the sciences, then . . . we shall never have, in Africa, a philosophy in the strict sense, until we have produced a history of science."[43] Hountondji then develops in Althusserian language a version of Wiredu's insistence on the development of that critical tradition, which literacy for the first time makes possible.

This explicit Marxism differentiates Hountondji from Wiredu. For when Wiredu discusses the relationship between philosophical reflection on politics and political life, he is concerned above all to challenge the hegemony of Marxists in African political philosophy. But I take this no-doubt-significant difference between them to be less fundamental for my purposes here than their agreement about what is special about the African philosopher's position.

Hountondji's critique of method and motivation leads naturally on to his prescriptions. His primary prescription is that we should think of African philosophy as being African not (as the ethnophilosophers claim) because it is *about* African concepts or problems, but because (and here he agrees with Wiredu) it is that part of the universal discourse of philosophy that is carried on by Africans. Indeed, this claim is announced in the first—extremely well-known—sentence of the first essay, the sentence with which I began myself: "By 'African philosophy' I mean a set of texts, specifically the set of texts written by Africans themselves and described as philosophical by their authors themselves."[44] This sentence foreshadows the full burden of much of his argument. The definition of African philosophy as simply philosophy written by Africans is the first step in an argument for a discourse in African languages addressed *to* Africans.[45] And the stress on "texts" with "authors" anticipates Hountondji's objection both to the idea of ethnophilosophy as the property of whole communities and to the possibility of an oral tradition of philosophy. Orality is inconsistent with the demands of what Althusser calls "science": writing liberates the individual mind "to make innovations that may shake established ideas and even overthrow them completely."[46]

In rejecting the possibility that there are specially African topics and concepts that deserve philosophical study, Hountondji seems to me to draw too radical a conclusion from his critique of ethnophilosophy.[47] For if philosophers are to contribute—at the conceptual level—to the solution of Africa's real problems, then they need to begin with a deep understanding of the traditional conceptual worlds the vast majority of their fellow nationals inhabit. In this, I believe, it is Wiredu who is right: what is wrong with the ethnophilosophers is that they have never gone beyond this essentially preliminary step. "The test," Wiredu says, "of a contemporary African philosopher's conception of African philosophy is whether it enables him to engage fruitfully in the activity of modern philosophising with an African conscience."[48] Going beyond the descriptive project of ethnophilosophy is the real challenge of philosophers engaged with the problems of contemporary Africa; like Wiredu—and Hountondji—I aspire to a more truly critical discourse. And so, in these final chapters I shall attempt to pursue this elusive discourse further. I begin with two chapters that reflect on rather different ways of thinking about contemporary African intellectual life: one, in the philosophical discourse on "tradition and modernity"; the other, in discussions of the postcolonial condition. In the final chapters I first explore the issues that surround nationalism and attachments to the modern state; then, more speculatively, I sketch the possibilities of a rethought Pan-African identity.[49]

SIX

Old Gods, New Worlds

Bima ya beto ke dya—bambuta me bikisa.
Ce que nous mangeons—les ancêtres nous l'ont indiqué.
Explication: "Nous connaissons ce qui est comestible parce
que les ancêtres nous l'ont montré. Nous ne faisons que
suivre les ancêtres."[1]

MBIEM PROVERB

In coming to terms with what it means to be modern, Western and African intellectuals have interests they should share. For the nature and meaning of modernity is a topos that recurs in the modern Western imagination. Whether in reactionary romanticisms or in Futurist celebrations of the new, whether in a confident optimism in the ameliorative capacities of modern science or a nostalgic longing for the unalienated, unhurried—and, by now, unfamiliar—traditional sense of community, much of Western thought about intellectual and social life is predicated upon an understanding of what it is to be modern, and on reactions, whether positive or negative, to the fact of modernity.

For the African intellectual, of course, the problem is whether—and, if so, how—our cultures are to *become* modern. What is for the West a fait accompli—indeed, we might define modernity as the characteristic intellectual and social formation of the industrialized world—offers most Africans at best vistas of hope, at worst prospects to fear. But, plainly, the question what it is to *be* modern is one that Africans and Westerners may ask together. And, as I shall suggest, neither of us will understand what modernity is until we understand each other.

Since I am a philosopher—and, in consequence, intellectually perverse—I will begin by trying to understand the modern through its antithesis, the traditional. I want to try to expose some natural errors in our thinking about the traditional-modern polarity, and thus help toward an understanding of some of the changes in progress in Africa, and the ways in which they have—and have not—made her more like the West. I want to examine some aspects of traditional culture—understanding this simply to mean culture before the European empires—as it manifested itself in one place in Africa, and then to look at some of the ways in which the experience of colonization and extended interaction with the West has produced a culture in transition from tradition to modernity, a culture that, for want of a better word, I shall call nontraditional.[2]

But I propose to begin in a place whose strangeness for most Europeans and Americans and whose naturalness for many Africans are a measure of the distance between Nairobi and New York; namely, with what, with some unhappiness, I shall call "religion." For one of the marks of traditional life is the extent to which beliefs, activities, habits of mind, and behavior in general are shot through with what Europeans and Americans would call "religion." Indeed, it is because understanding traditional religion is so central to the conceptual issues that modernization raises that philosophical discussion of the status of traditional religion has been so central in recent African philosophy. And the urgency and the relevance of the issue to central questions of public policy is one of the reasons why there is greater excitement to be found in philosophical discussion of religion in Africa than in philosophy of religion in the West.

If I am reluctant to use the term *religion* without qualification, it is because religion in the contemporary West is, by and large, so different from what it is in traditional life that to report it in Western categories is as much to invite misunderstanding as to offer insight. But the examples I want to discuss should help make this point for me. Let us begin, then, with an account of a traditional ceremony.

The place is somewhere in rural Asante. The time is the ethnographic present—which is to say, the past. As we arrive, a male figure dressed in a fiber skirt and with charms about his neck is dancing to the accompaniment of drumming and singing. Suddenly he leaps into a nearby stream and emerges clasping something to his breast. This he places in a brass pan and pounds with clay (which we later discover comes from the sacred river Tano) and the leaves or bark of various plants, some gold dust, and an aggrey bead.

During the pounding, the figure utters words, which we may translate as follows:

> God, Kwame, Upon-whom-men-lean-and-do-not-fall; Earth Goddess, Yaa; Leopard and all beasts and plants of the forest, today is sacred Friday: and you, Ta Kwesi, we are installing you, we are placing you, so that we may have life, that we may not die, that we may not become impotent. To the village head of this village, life; to the young men of the village, life; to those who bear children, life; to the children of the village, life.
>
> Spirits of the trees, we call upon you all, to let you come here now, and let all that is in our heads be placed in this shrine.
>
> When we call upon you in darkness, when we call upon you in the day, if we say to you "Do this for us," that will be what you will do.
>
> And these are the rules that we are placing here for you, god of ours: if a king comes from somewhere and comes to us or our children or our grandchildren, and says he is going to war, and he comes to tell you; and if he is going to fight and will not have a victory, it is necessary that you should tell us; and if he is going and he will have a victory, tell the truth also.

The peroration continues, and the spirit is asked repeatedly to tell the truth about the sources of the evil that make men ill. The priest ends by saying:

> We have taken sheep and a chicken, we have taken palm-wine, which we are about to give you that you may reside in this village and preserve its life. . . .
>
> Perhaps on some tomorrow the King of Asante may come and say "My child So-and-so is sick," or perhaps "Some elder is sick"; or he may send a messenger

to ask you to go with him; and in such a case you may go, and we will not think you
are fleeing from us.

The mouths of all of us speak these things together.

Then the sacrifices of the animals are made, and their blood is allowed to flow into the
brass pan. While this is going on, perhaps some other priest will go into trance and
sing the song of some other minor local spirit.

This account is a rough paraphrase of one that Captain R. S. Rattray published in
the 1920s[3] and, with few modifications, you could find just such a ceremony at the
installation of a spirit—an *obosom*—in a shrine today.

Perhaps there is nothing puzzling in the ritual I have described. I have tried
deliberately to give an account of a series of actions that people outside the culture are
unlikely to believe could possibly succeed, but that all of us could surely at least
imagine believing in. Yet this ritual is part of a religious world that is typical of the
many traditional cultures whose modes of thought have struck Western ethnography
and philosophy as puzzling.

We can begin to see why, if we ask ourselves not what it is that is believed by these
actors but how they could have come to believe it. Most intellectuals outside Asante
think they know, after all, that there are no such spirits. That, for all the requests in the
priest's prayer, no unseen agent will come to inhabit the shrine; no one will answer the
questions "What made this person ill?" or "Would we win if we went to war?" or
"How should we cure the king's elder?" Yet here is a culture where, for at least
several hundred years, people have been setting up just such shrines and asking them
just such questions and asking the spirits they believe are in them to perform just such
tasks. Surely by now they should know, if they are rational, that it won't work?

Now it is the appeal to a notion of rationality in this last question that will lead us
into characteristically philosophical territory: and it is, in part, because of what it tells
us about rationality, about the proper scope and function of reason, that these rituals
are of philosophical significance. And if we press the question how these beliefs can
be sustained in the face of a falsity that is obvious, at least to us, we shall return, in the
end, to the question whether we have really understood what is going on.

It is as well, however, to begin with some distinctions. I have already made what is
the first crucial distinction: between understanding the content of the beliefs involved
in the actions in a religious performance, on the one hand, and understanding how
those beliefs became established in the culture, on the other. But we shall need more
distinctions than this. For we need, I think, to bear in mind at least these three separate
types of understanding: first, understanding the ritual and the beliefs that underlie it;
second, understanding the historical sources of both ritual and belief; and, third,
understanding what sustains them.

One of the advantages of making such distinctions—exactly the sort of distinction
that is often held up as typical of the trivial logic chopping that makes academic
philosophy so unpleasing to those who do not practice it—is that it allows us to set
some questions to one side. So we can say, to begin with, that to understand these
ritual acts what is necessary is what is necessary in the understanding of any acts:
namely to understand what beliefs and intentions underlie them, so that we know
what the actors think they are doing, what they are trying to do. Indeed if we cannot do

this we cannot even say what the ritual is. To say that what is going on here is that these people are inviting a spirit to take up its place in a shrine is already to say something about their beliefs and their intentions. It is to say, for example, that they believe that there is a spirit, Ta Kwesi, and believe too that asking the spirit to do something is a way of getting that spirit to do it; it is to say that they want the spirit to inhabit the shrine.

Perhaps this is obvious; perhaps there are no behaviorists left in the world, or at least in the little portion of it that might read this book. So perhaps I do not need to say that it is not just the performance of certain bodily movements by the priest and the other villagers that makes up this ritual. But it is important to remember that you and I could carry out these very movements in order to demonstrate the form of the ritual, and that if *we* did it in *that* spirit, we should not be inviting anyone—least of all Ta Kwesi—to do anything. It is thus precisely because we think these particular Asante acts are intended in a certain way that we know what is going on is a religious act. What makes it religious is what the people are trying to do.

Any theoretical account of this ritual must begin by trying to understand, therefore, what the beliefs and intentions are that inform it. But that is not, of course, all there is to understanding the ritual. For there are certainly features of it—the use of gold dust and the aggrey bead in making up the contents of the brass pan, for example—that may still remain in need of explanation. We may well discover that though the priest means to put the gold dust into the pot, he does so only because this is, as he might say, part of "how the ancestors called a spirit"—that is, he might have no special reason of his own for using the gold dust.

What does it mean to say that this still needs explaining? The priest does lots of things in the performance of the ritual for no special reason of his own. He raises a stick up and down as he dances, and he does so deliberately: it is part of his intention in dancing to raise the stick up and down. Yet we may find nothing to explain in this.

I think the first step in answering the question "Why does the gold dust need explaining?" is to distinguish between two kinds of things that the priest does in the performance of the ritual. On the one hand, there are such things as the addition of the gold dust, which the priest believes are an essential part of what he is doing. To leave out the gold dust would be to fail to do something that is essential if the performance is to succeed in bringing the spirit to its new shrine. These essential components of the ritual are to be contrasted with what we can call the "accidental" components. Maybe the priest wipes the sweat off his nose as the dancing rises in crescendo, and, when asked, he tells us that this is, of course, something that the ritual could have done without. If the raising of the stick and the wiping of the sweat are accidental to the performance, then that is why we do not need to explain them to understand the ritual. So that part of why the gold dust needs explaining is that it is essential to the ritual action.

Now in saying that the gold dust is essential, we have already given part of its explanation. It is there because without it the act is believed to be less efficacious, perhaps not efficacious at all. But a question remains. Why does adding it make a difference? After all, all of us probably have ancestors, great-grandmothers, for example, who had remedies for the common cold, of which we take little or no notice.

Why should the priest think that this piece of ancestral lore is worth holding onto, especially if he has no idea why the ancestors thought it an essential part of calling a spirit?

Here, I think, many cultural anthropologists will be disposed to say that the gold dust attracts our attention because it plainly symbolizes something. We can make up our own stories. Let us suppose, for the sake of argument, that what it symbolizes is the giving of riches to the spirit, a sort of spiritual sweetener for the contract between village and spirit that is in the making. The plausibility of this suggestion should not distract us from what is problematic in it. For if this *is* why the gold dust is there, why doesn't the priest know it? The obvious answer is that he doesn't know it because he is only carrying out the prescribed form.[4] The people who designed the ritual, the people the priest calls the ancestors, knew why the gold dust was there. They put it there because they thought that part of a proper invitation to a powerful spirit was to give it some of your riches. For to do this is to do what you would do when asking any powerful person for a favor. It is true that spirits have no use for money—the spiritual economy is greased by something other than gold—but in handing over this gold dust you are treating the spirit as you would treat a human being you respect. For these ancestors, then, the handing over of the gold dust is an act whose efficacy depends upon the spirit's recognition that it is an expression of respect.

I do not know if anything like this is true; it would be a hard thing to find out simply because ''the ancestors'' are not around to ask. But notice that this explanation of the presence of the gold dust as symbolic takes us out of the arena of understanding the ritual acts themselves into examining their origins. This resort to origins is not, however, what makes it true that the gold dust functions symbolically. Our priest might himself have been aware that the gold dust functions symbolically in this way. And I shall try in a moment to say a little more about what this means. But it is important to see that treating an element of a ritual as symbolic requires that there be someone who treats it symbolically—and that this someone be either the actor him- or herself, or the originator of the form of ritual action. Finding that the priest does not see the act as symbolic, we needed to look for someone who did. There are more and less sophisticated versions of this sort of symbolist treatment. Durkheim, for example, appears to have thought that religious practices can symbolize social reality because, though the agent is not consciously aware of what they symbolize, he or she may be unconsciously aware of it.[5] Lévi-Strauss, I think, believes something similar. I happen to think that this is a mistake, but whether or not Durkheim was right, he recognized, at least, that a symbol is always somebody's symbol: it is something that means something to someone.

But what is it exactly to use the gold dust as a symbol of respect? We are so familiar with this sort of symbolic act that we do not often reflect upon it. Here again, it is useful to make a distinction. Some symbols, of which words are the paradigm, are purely conventional. It is because there exists a complex interaction of beliefs and intentions between speakers of the same language that it is possible for us to use our words to express our thoughts to each other. This complex background makes it possible for us to refer to objects, and thus to use words to stand for those objects symbolically. But words are not the only purely conventional symbols, and speaking is not the only purely conventional symbolic act. In saluting a superior officer, a soldier expresses his recognition of the officer's superiority. And it is only because such a convention exists that the act of saluting has the meaning it has.

Now the gold dust is not a purely conventional symbol. It is possible to use the gold dust in this context as a symbol of respect, because in other contexts the giving of gold dust is a sign of respect. After all, the reason that giving gold dust to a powerful figure in Asante is a sign of respect is not that there is a convention to this effect. People give gold dust to powerful people because gold dust is money, and money is something that powerful people, like others, have a use for. To give someone money when you need him or her to do something for you is to seek to influence their acts, and thus to acknowledge that they have it in their power to do something for you. They know that you think they have that power because you both know that you would not be giving them the money otherwise. If the giving of gold dust along with a request occurs regularly in contexts where people require something of someone with powers they do not themselves have; and if, as in Asante, to ask someone in a position of power to do something for you is to show respect; then offering gold dust in conjunction with a request becomes a sign of respect—in the simple sense that it is something whose presence gives evidence that the giver respects the receiver.

It is thus not *arbitrary* that the ancestors in my story chose gold dust as a symbol of respect, even though they realized that in placing the gold dust in the pan they were not in fact giving the spirit something that it could use.

Many symbolic ritual acts have this character. They are not arbitrary signs, like words or salutes; they are acts that draw their meaning from the nonritual significance of relevantly similar performances. What makes them symbolic is the recognition by the agents that these acts in ritual contexts do not work in the standard way. The spirit comes not because we have given it some money but because we have done something that shows respect, and giving the gold dust shows respect because outside these ritual contexts the giving of gold dust is standardly accompanied by respect.

I have spent some time discussing the role of this symbol in this ritual because to many it has seemed that it is the distinguishing character of these religious acts that they are symbolic. Clifford Geertz has famously remarked that religion is "a system of symbols."[6] Now it is, of course, an impressive fact about many religious practices and beliefs that they have symbolic elements: the Eucharist is loaded with symbolism, and so is the Passover meal. But I want to argue that the symbolism arises out of the fundmental nature of religious beliefs, and that these fundamental beliefs are not themselves symbolic.

All my life, I have seen and heard ceremonies like the one with which I began. This public, ritual appeal to unseen spirits on a ceremonial occasion is part of a form of life in which such appeals are regularly made in private. When a man opens a bottle of gin, he will pour a little on the earth, asking his ancestors to drink a little and to protect the family and its doings. This act is without ceremony, without the excitement of the public installation of an *obosom* in a new shrine, yet it inhabits the same world. Indeed, it is tempting to say that, just as the public installation of a spirit is like the public installation of a chief, the private libation is like the private pouring of a drink for a relative. The element of ceremonial is not what is essential; what is essential is the ontology of invisible beings. So that in the wider context of Asante life it seems absurd to claim that what was happening, when my father casually poured a few drops from the top of a newly opened bottle of Scotch onto the carpet, involved anything other than a literal belief in the ancestors. The pouring of the drink may have been symbolic: there is no general assumption in Asante that the dead like whiskey. But for the gesture of offering them a portion of a valued drink to make sense, the ancestors who are thus symbolically acknowledged must exist. It is true, as Kwasi Wiredu has expressed the matter, that the proposition "that our departed ancestors continue to hover around in some rarified form ready now and then to take a sip of the ceremonial schnapps is . . . [one] that I have never heard rationally defended."[7] But that it is never rationally defended is not, perhaps, so surprising: it is, after all, not usually rationally *attacked*. (Nor, as I say, do we need to suppose that a literal sip is at stake.) The proposition that there are planets hovering around the sun, larger than the earth, however small they may appear as we ponder the night sky, is not in the usual course of things rationally defended in Europe or America. It is not rationally defended not because anyone thinks there could be no rational defense but because it is taken, now, to be obviously true. And, in traditional Asante culture the existence of disembodied departed spirits is equally uncontroversial. I shall return to this issue later.

If I am right, and it is (as Tylor claimed) a commitment to disembodied agency that crucially defines the religious beliefs that underlie rituals like the one I have described, then there is, of course, an important question that needs to be answered— namely, why in many such rituals symbolism plays so important a part. And the answer is implicit in the account I gave earlier of the relationship between the installation of a chief and the installation of a spirit.

For, as any Asante could tell you, symbolism is a major feature of both of these ceremonies. And though there is a religious component in the installation of a chief, as there is in any public ceremony in Asante, that does not make the installation an essentially religious act. Symbolism is in fact a feature of all major ceremonial occasions in any culture, and the presence of symbolism in religious ceremonial derives from its nature as ceremonial and not from its nature as religious. In private and less ceremonial religious acts in a traditional culture (such as, for example, an appeal at a household shrine to the ancestors), there is still, of course, an element of symbolism. But it is important to recall here that in Asante culture relations with *living* elders where a request is being made in private are also ceremonious. All important contacts between individuals in traditional cultures are ceremonious. When Rattray reported a séance at the Tano shrine in the early part of this century, he described how, when the priest with the shrine "containing" the spirit on his head entered the trance in which he would speak for the spirit, the assembled priests and elders said, "Nana, ma akye" (Sir, good morning), as they would have done if a chief (or an elder) had entered. The formality of the response is somehow less striking to me than its naturalness, the sense it gives that the Tano spirit is simply a being among beings—addressed with ceremony for its status or its power and not because the scene is set apart from the everyday.

And once we have seen that the ritual setting is ceremonious, we need only the further premise that all ceremony has elements of symbolism to complete a syllogism: ritual entails symbolism. I do not myself have theories as to why human beings so closely bind together ceremony and symbolism. It is something many of us begin to do in our play as children, and it is surely as much a part of our natural history as, say, language. But that the prevalence of symbolism in religious ritual in Asante derives from the conception of relations between people and spirits as relations between persons seems to me, in the light of these facts, hard to deny. Case by case, the same claim can be made for religion in most nonliterate cultures—in Africa and elsewhere.

If the emphasis in Western theory on the distinctively symbolic character of traditional religious thought and practice is misleading, it is worth taking a moment to consider why it should have been so pervasive. And the answer lies, I think, in the character of religion in the industrial cultures in which this theorizing about religion takes place.

Christianity is a religion that defines itself by doctrine; heresy, paganism, and atheism have been, as a result, at various times central *topoi* of Christian reflection. In this respect Christianity is not, of course, unique; Islam, too, is defined by its doctrine and, like Christianity, its Book. Islamic evangelists have sometimes held that the simple acceptance of two items of doctrine—that God is one, and that Muhammad is his prophet—was sufficient to constitute conversion, though Christian missionaries have usually insisted on at least token assent to some more complex credo. But these differences seem relatively unimportant when we come to contrast Christianity and Islam, on the one hand, with many of the other systems of ritual, practice, and belief that we call religions. Never has the contrast been more sharply drawn than in a remark of Chinua Achebe's: "I can't imagine Igbos traveling four thousand miles to tell anybody their worship was wrong!"[8]

The extraordinary importance attached to doctrine in the Christian churches is not a modern phenomenon; growing up between Roman and Hellenistic paganism, on the one side and Judaism, on the other, and divided bitterly and regularly from the very beginning on topics that may seem to us wonderfully abstruse, the history of the church is, to a great extent, the history of doctrines. But, though doctrine is indeed central to Christianity in this way, it is important to remember what this means. "Doctrine" does not mean, precisely, beliefs (for it is easy to show, as Keith Thomas does in his marvelous *Religion and the Decline of Magic,* that the character of the actual propositions believed by Christians has changed radically in the last two millennia); rather it means the verbal formulae that express belief. And this has proved something of an embarrassment for many Christians in the world since the scientific revolution.

It is a familiar theme in the history of theology that Christianity has followed in some measure Oscar Wilde's epigram: "Religions die when they are proved true. Science is the record of dead religions."[9] One powerful reaction among Christian intellectuals has been to retreat in the face of science into the demythologization of the doctrines whose central place in the definition of his religious tradition they cannot escape. And—as I think the work of Keith Thomas, among others, shows—it is correct to say that the effect of demythologization has been to treat doctrines that were once taken literally as metaphorical or, to return to my theme, symbolic. This has led us, if I may caricature recent theological history, to the position where the statement that "God is love" can be claimed by serious men—Paul Tillich, for example—to mean something like "Love is tremendously important," and to treating the traditional doctrine of the triumph of the kingdom of God as a "symbolic" way of expressing a confidence that "love will win in the end." And similar demythologizing tendencies can be detected in liberal (or otherwise counternormative) Jewish theology (certainly they are found in Martin Buber). It is not my business to say whether this is a healthy development, though it will no doubt be clear which way my sympathies lie. But even if, as I doubt, this is consistent with the main traditions of Christianity or Judaism, to treat the religious beliefs of traditional cultures as likewise symbolic is radically to misrepresent their character.

The intellectual reformulation of Christianity coexists with a change in the character of Christian lay life, at least insofar as it concerns intellectuals. For educated Christians in Europe prior to the scientific revolution and the growth of industrial capitalism, the belief in spiritual beings—saints, angels, principalities, and powers—had in many respects just the character I claim for traditional Asante religion. Through acts at shrines that Westerners would call magical in Asante, the faithful sought cures for their ills, answers to their questions, guidance in their acts. As technological solutions to illness and a scientific understanding of it have developed, many people (and, especially, many intellectuals) have turned away from this aspect of religion, though, as we should expect, it remains an important part of Christianity in the nonindustrial world and in those—significant—parts of the industrial world where the scientific worldview remains ungrasped.

But in the industrial world, the religious life of intellectuals has turned more and more toward the contemplative, conceived of as spiritual intercourse with God. If God's answer is sought to any questions of a technical character, it is those questions that have remained recalcitrant to scientific management (questions about one's relations with others) and questions that could not even in principle be addressed by science (questions of value). This is itself a very interesting development, but it has driven a great wedge between the religion of the industrial world and the religion of traditional cultures.

There is a further change in the nature of contemplative religion in the West. It connects with the observation I made earlier that symbolism characterizes the ceremonious, and that social relations of importance require ceremony in traditional cultures. As our relations with each other have become less ceremonious, so have our private religious acts. Prayer has become for many like an intimate conversation. But so it is for Asante tradition. It is just that the understanding of intimacy is different.

I have largely been addressing the first group of questions I posed about religious ritual: those about the nature of the ritual and the beliefs that underlie it. I have said little about the origins of these beliefs; in predominantly nonliterate cultures, such questions often cannot be answered because the evidence is lacking. For Christianity or Judaism it is possible to discuss such questions because we have records of the councils of Nicea and Chalcedon, or because we have the extensive traditions of literate Jewish reflection. But if we are to face the question of the rationality of traditional belief we must turn, finally, to my third set of questions: those about what keeps these beliefs, which outsiders judge so obviously false, alive.

It is in asking these questions that some have been led by another route to treating religion symbolically. The British anthropologist John Beattie, for example, has developed a "symbolist" view of Africa's traditional religions, whose "central tenet," as Robin Horton (a philosopher-anthropologist, who is a British subject and a longtime Nigerian resident) puts it, "is that traditional religious thought is basically different from and incommensurable with Western scientific thought"; so that the symbolists avoid "comparisons with science and turn instead to comparisons with symbolism and art."[10]

The basic symbolist thought is neatly (if ironically) captured in this formulation of the Cameroonian philosopher M. Hegba:

> Une première approche des phénomènes de la magie et de la sorcellerie serait de supposer que nous nous trouvons là en face d'un langage symbolique. . . . Un homme qui vole dans les airs, qui se transforme en animal, ou qui se rend invisible à volonté . . . pourraient n'être alors qu'un langage codé dont nous devrions simplement découvrir la clef. Nous serions alors rassurés.[11]

Simply put, the symbolists are able to treat traditional believers as reassuringly rational only because they deny that traditional people mean what they say. Now Robin Horton has objected—correctly—that this tale leaves completely unexplained the fact that traditional people regularly appeal to the invisible agencies of their religions in their explanations of events in what we would call the natural world.[12] Horton could usefully have drawn attention here to a fact that Hegba observes, when he moves from characterizing symbolism to criticizing it, namely that "le langage symbolique et ésoterique est fort en honneur en notre société."[13] It is peculiarly unsatisfactory to treat a system of propositions as symbolic when those whose propositions they are appear to treat them literally *and* display, in other contexts, a clear grasp of the notion of symbolic representation.

I have mentioned Durkheim once already, and it is in his work that we can find the clearest statement of the connection between the urge to treat religion as symbolic and the question why such patently false beliefs survive. For Durkheim cannot allow that religious beliefs are false, because he thinks that false beliefs could not survive. Since if they are false they would not have survived, it follows that they must be true: and since they are not literally true, they must be symbolically true.[14] This argument is based on a misunderstanding of the relationship between the rationality of beliefs, their utility and their truth; it is important to say why.

Rationality is best conceived of as an ideal, both in the sense that it is something worth aiming for and in the sense that it is something we are incapable of realizing. It is an ideal that bears an important internal relation to that other great cognitive ideal, Truth. And, I suggest, we might say that rationality in belief consists in being disposed so to react to evidence and reflection that you change your beliefs in ways that make it more likely that they are true. If this is right, then we can see at once why inconsistency in belief is a sign of irrationality: for having a pair of inconsistent beliefs *guarantees* that you have at least one false belief, as inconsistent beliefs are precisely beliefs that cannot all be true. But we can also see that consistency, as an ideal, is not enough. For someone could have a perfectly consistent set of beliefs about the world, almost every one of which was not only false but obviously false. It is *consistent* to hold, with Descartes in one of his skeptical moments, that all my experiences are caused by a wicked demon, and, to dress the fantasy in modern garb, there is no inconsistency in supporting the paranoid fantasy that the world is "really" a cube containing only my brain in a bath, a lot of wires, and a wicked scientist. But, though consistent, this belief is not rational: we are all, I hope, agreed that reacting to sensory evidence in *this* way does not increase the likelihood that your beliefs will be true.[15]

Now the question of the utility, the survival value, of a set of beliefs is quite separate from that of both their truth and their reasonableness, thus conceived. Anyone who has read Evans-Pritchard's elegant discussion of Zande witchcraft beliefs—to which I shall return later—will remember how easy it is to make sense of the idea that a whole set of false beliefs could nevertheless be part of what holds a community together. But the point does not need laboring: since Freud we can all understand why, for example, it might be more useful to believe that you love someone than to recognize that you do not.

With such an account of reasonableness, we can see why the apparently obvious falsehood of the beliefs of the Asante priest might be regarded as evidence of his unreasonableness. For how could he have acquired and maintained such beliefs if he was following the prescription always to try to change his beliefs in ways that made it more likely that they were true? The answer is simple. The priest acquired his beliefs in the way we all acquire the bulk of our beliefs: by being told things as he grew up. As Evans-Pritchard says of the Zande people, they are "born into a culture with ready-made patterns of belief which have the weight of tradition behind them."[16] And of course, so are we. On the whole, little has happened in his life to suggest they are not true. So too, in our lives.

Now it may seem strange to suggest that accepting beliefs from one's culture and holding onto them in the absence of countervailing evidence can be reasonable, if it can lead to having beliefs that are, from the point of view of Western intellectuals, so wildly false. And this is especially so if you view reasonableness as a matter of trying to develop habits of belief acquisition that make it likely that you will react to evidence and reflection in ways that have a tendency to produce truth. But to think otherwise is to mistake the relatively deplorable nature of our epistemic position in the universe. It is just fundamentally correct that there is no requirement other than consistency that we can place on our beliefs in advance, in order to increase their likelihood of being true; and that a person who starts with a consistent set of beliefs can arrive, by way of reasonable principles of evidence, at the most fantastic untruths. The wisdom of epistemological modesty is, surely, one of the lessons of the history of natural science; indeed, if there is one great lesson of the failure of positivism as a methodology of the sciences, it is surely, as Richard Miller has recently argued, that there are no a priori rules that will guarantee us true theories.[17] The success of what we call "empirical method" seems, in retrospect, to have been, like evolution, the result of capitalizing on a series of lucky chances. If the priest's theory is wrong, we should see this as largely a matter of bad luck, rather than of his having failed culpably to observe the proper rules of an a priori method.

We may also fail to see how reasonable the priest's views should seem, because, in assessing the religious beliefs of other cultures, we start, as is natural enough, from our own. But it is precisely the absence of this, our alien, alternative point of view in traditional culture, that makes it reasonable to adopt the "traditional" worldview. The evidence that spirits exist is obvious: priests go into trance, people get better after the application of spiritual remedies, people die regularly from the action of inimical spirits. The reinterpretation of this evidence, in terms of medical–scientific theories or of psychology, requires that there be such alternative theories and that people have some reason to believe in them; but again and again, and especially in the area of mental and social life, the traditional view is likely to be confirmed. We have theories explaining some of this, the theory of suggestion and suggestibility, for example, and if we were to persuade traditional thinkers of these theories, they might become skeptical of the theories held in their own culture. But we cannot *begin* by asking them to assume their beliefs are false, for they can always make numerous moves in reasonable defense of their beliefs. It is this fact that entitles us to oppose the thesis that traditional beliefs are simply unreasonable.

The classical account of this process of defense in the ethnography of African traditional thought is Evans-Pritchard's *Witchcraft, Oracles and Magic among the Azande*. Toward the end of the book, he says, "It may be asked why Azande do not perceive the futility of their magic. It would be easy to write at great length in answer to this question, but I will content myself with suggesting as shortly as possible a number of reasons."[18] He then lists twenty-two such reasons. He mentions, for example, that since "magic is very largely employed against mystical powers . . . its action transcends experience" and thus "cannot easily be contradicted by experience,"[19] reinforcing a point made a few pages earlier: "We shall not understand Zande magic . . . unless we realize that its main purpose is to combat other mystical powers rather than to produce changes favourable to man in the objective world."[20] He says that the practices of witchcraft, oracles, and magic presuppose a coherent system of mutually supporting beliefs.

> Death is proof of witchcraft. It is avenged by magic. The accuracy of the poison oracle is determined by the king's oracle, which is above suspicion. . . . The results which magic is supposed to produce actually happen after the rites are performed. . . . Magic is only made to produce events which are likely to happen in any case . . . [and] is seldom asked to produce a result by itself but is associated with empirical action that does in fact produce it—e.g. a prince gives food to attract followers and does not rely on magic alone.[21]

And, though he acknowledges that Azande notice failures of their witchcraft, he shows too how they have many ways to explain this failure: there may have been an error in executing the spell, there may be an unknown and countervailing magic, and so on.

   It is the fact that it is possible to make exactly these sorts of moves in defense of traditional religious beliefs that has led some to draw the conclusion that traditional religious belief should be interpreted as having the same purposes as those of modern natural science, which are summarized in the slogan "explanation, prediction, and control." For when scientific procedures fail, scientists do not normally react—as I once heard a distinguished physicist react to an hour in a lab with the allegedly parapsychological phenomena produced by Uri Geller[22]—by saying that we must "begin physics all over again." Rather, they offer explanations as to how the failure could have occurred consistently with the theory. Biochemists regularly ignore negative results, assuming that test tubes are dirty, or that samples are contaminated, or that in preparing the sample they have failed to take some precaution that is necessary to prevent the action of those enzymes that are always released when a cell is damaged. A skeptical Zande could well make the same sorts of observation about these procedures as Evans-Pritchard makes about Azande magic: "The perception of error in one mystical notion in a particular situation merely proves the correctness of another and equally mystical notion."

Philosophers of science have names for this: they say that theory is "underdetermined" by observation, and that observation is "theory-laden." And they mean by underdetermination the fact that French philosopher-physicist Pierre Duhem noticed in the early part of this century: that the application of theory to particular cases relies on a whole host of other beliefs, not all of which can be checked at once. By the theory-ladenness of observation, relatedly, they mean that our theories both contribute to forming our experience and give meaning to the language we use for reporting it. Sir Karl Popper's claim that science should proceed by attempts at falsification, as we all know after reading Thomas Kuhn, is incorrect.[23] If we gave up every time an experiment failed, scientific theory would get nowhere. The underdetermination of our theories by our experience means that we are left even by the most unsuccessful experiment with room for maneuver. The trick is not to give up too soon or go on too long. In science, as everywhere else, there are babies and there is bathwater.

I have suggested we might assimilate the theories that underlie traditional religion and magic to those that are engendered in the natural sciences because both are explanatory systems of belief that share the problem of underdetermination. But there are other routes to this assimilation, and if we are to explore the plausibility of this idea, it will help if we assemble a few more pieces of the evidence.

For the sake of comparison with the ceremony with which I began this chapter, let me describe another ceremony, in which I participated some years ago in Kumasi. It was, as it happens, my sister's wedding, and the legal ceremony occurred in a Methodist church, in the context of a service in the language of the old English prayer book. "Dearly Beloved," it began "we are gathered here together in the sight of God." In the front row sat the king of Asante, his wife, the queen mother, and the king's son, Nana Akyempemhene, as grand a collection of the Asante traditional aristocracy as you could wish for. Afterwards we went back to the private residence of the king, and there we had a party, with the queen mother's drummers playing, and hundreds of members of the royal household.

But, not long after we began, the Catholic archbishop of Kumasi (remember, this is after a *Methodist* ceremony) said prayers, and this was followed (and remember this was a *Catholic* archbishop) by the pouring of libations to my family ancestors, carried out by one of the king's senior linguists. The words addressed to those ancestors were couched in the same idiom as the words of the priest that Rattray heard. And the king of Asante is an Anglican and a member of the English bar; his son, a lawyer then in the Ghanaian Diplomatic Service, has a Ph.D. from Tufts; and the bride and groom met at Sussex University in England (and each had another degree as well) and were, respectively, a medical sociologist and a Nigerian merchant banker. These, then, are modern Africans, not merely in the sense that they are alive now, but they have that essential credential of the modern man or woman—a university's letters after your name. I shall argue, in a moment, that these letters are of more than metaphorical importance.

What are we to make of all of this? Or rather, what are Europeans and Americans to make of it, since it is all so familiar to me—to most contemporary Africans—that I find it hard to recover the sense of contradiction between the elements of this no-doubt remarkable "syncretism."

These ceremonies are what I want to call "nontraditional"—they are not traditional because they coexist both with some degree of belief in the Christianity that came with the colonials, on the one hand, and with some familiarity with the vision of the natural sciences, on the other. But they are not "modern" either—because the meanings attached to these acts are not those of the purely symbolic Eucharist of extreme liberal theology. The question, of course, is how all these elements can coexist, what it is that makes this conceptual melee not a source of intellectual tension and unease but a resource for a tremendous range of cultural activity.

The key to this question is, I think, to be found in following up the idea that we were led to earlier, the idea that traditional religious theory is in certain respects more like modern science than modern religion—in particular, that it shares the purposes of modern natural science, which we may summarize in the slogan "explanation, prediction, and control." It is his systematic development of the analogy between natural science and traditional religion that has made the work of Robin Horton so important in the philosophy of African traditional religions, and it will be useful to begin with him.[24]

Horton's basic point is just the one I made earlier: the fundamental character of these religious systems is that the practices arise from the belief, literal and not symbolic, in the powers of invisible agents. Horton argues persuasively, and I believe correctly, that spirits and such function in explanation, prediction, and control much as do other theoretical entities: they differ from those of natural science in being persons and not material forces and powers, but the logic of their function in explanation and prediction is the same.

Horton's view, then, is that religious beliefs of traditional peoples constitute explanatory theories and that traditional religious actions are reasonable attempts to pursue goals in the light of these beliefs—attempts, in other words, at prediction and control of the world. In these respects, Horton argues, traditional religious belief and action are like theory in the natural sciences and the actions based on it. As Hegba, in the francophone African tradition, says:

> Sans méconnaître ses limites ni freiner la marche vers le progrès, la science et la
> libération, il faut admettre que l'explication africaine des phénomènes de la magie
> et de la sorcellerie est rationelle. Nos croyances populaires sont déconcertantes
> certes, parfois fausses, mais ne serait-ce pas une faute méthodologique grave que
> de postuler l'irrationnel au point de départ de l'étude d'une société?[25]

Horton's thesis is not that traditional religion is a kind of science but that theories in the two domains are similar in these crucial respects. The major *difference* in the contents of the theories, he argues, is that traditional religious theory is couched in terms of personal forces, while natural scientific theory is couched in terms of impersonal forces. The basic claim strikes me as immensely plausible.

Yet there is in the analogy between natural science and traditional religion much to mislead also. A first way in which the assimilation risks being deceptive comes out if we remind ourselves that most of us are quite vague about the theoretical underpinnings of the medical theories that guide our doctors and the physical theories that are used to make and mend our radios. In this we are, of course, like the average nineteenth-century Asante, who was, presumably, quite vague about the bases on which herbalists and priests practiced their arts. In application, in use by nonspecialists in everyday life, our theories about how the world works are often relied on in general outline in a practical way, without much articulation and without any deep investment in the details. In much contemporary African religious practice (and this includes the ceremony I have described) there is (within each community of practice, each sect or cult or community) a great deal more consensus on the proper forms of ritual and liturgical action than there is as to what justifies it; in this, religious practice in Africa differs little enough from religious practice in the contemporary industrialized world. Though the extent of literal belief in invisible agency may be somewhat greater in Africa than in the United States (and is probably much greater than in, say, Britain or Norway), there is both there and here a sense in which religious life can continue and be participated in with little curiosity about the literal beliefs of fellow participants, and little theoretical commitment on our own parts. In insisting on the role of *theory,* here, one is bound, as a result, to seem to be focusing on something that is far from central for those whose religious practices we are discussing, and thus distorting their experience in order to draw the analogy with natural science. But provided we bear in mind that no claim is being made beyond the claim that these religious practices operate on the assumption of a certain theory— that there are spiritual agencies of various kinds—and that this theory allows for explanation and prediction in the sort of way that scientific theories do, I do not think we need be led into misjudging the relative importance of theory and practice in traditional religion in this way.

Still, this worry comes close to a second difficulty with the assimilation of traditional religion and natural science, one Kwasi Wiredu has pointed out—namely, that it is, prima facie, very odd to equate traditional religious belief in West Africa with modern Western scientific theory, when the obvious analogue is traditional Western religious belief.[26] I think it will be obvious from what I have already said that it seems to me that there need be no contest here: for the explanatory function of religious beliefs in traditional Europe seems to me to be identical in its logic with that of scientific theory also.

What *is* misleading is not the assimilation of the logics of explanation of theories from religion and science but the assimilation of traditional religion and natural science as institutions. This is, first of all, misleading because of the sorts of changes that I sketched in Western religious life. For the modern Westerner, as I have shown, to call something "religious" is to connote a great deal that is lacking in traditional religion and not to connote much that is present. But there is a much more fundamental reason why the equation of religion and science is misleading. And it is to do with the totally different social organization of enquiry in traditional and modern cultures. I shall return to this issue at the end of the chapter.

Horton himself is, of course, aware that traditional religious beliefs are certainly unlike those of natural science in at least two important respects. First of all, as I have already insisted, he points out that the theoretical entities invoked are agents and not material forces. And he offers us an account of why this might be. He suggests that this difference arises out of the fundamental nature of explanation as the reduction of the unfamiliar to the familiar. In traditional cultures nature, the wild, is untamed, alien, and a source of puzzlement and fear. Social relations and persons are, on the contrary, familiar and well understood. Explaining the behavior of nature in terms of agency is thus reducing the unfamiliar forces of the wild to the familiar explanatory categories of personal relations.

In the industrial world, on the other hand, industrialization and urbanization have made social relations puzzling and problematic. We move between social environments—the rural and the urban, the workplace and the home—in which different conventions operate; in the new, urban, factory, market environment we deal with people whom we know only through our common productive projects. As a result the social is relatively unfamiliar. On the other hand, our relations with objects in the city are relations that remain relatively stable across all these differing social relations. Indeed, if factory workers move between factories, the skills they take with them are precisely those that depend on a familiarity not with other people but with the workings of material things. It is no longer natural to try to understand nature through social relations; rather, we understand it through machines, through matter whose workings we find comfortably familiar. It is well known that the understanding of gases in the nineteenth century was modeled on the behavior of miniature billiard balls—for nineteenth-century scientists in Europe knew the billiard table better than they knew, for example, their servants. Alienation is widely held to be the characteristic state of modern man: the point can be overstated, but it cannot be denied.

> In complex, rapidly changing industrial societies, the human scene is in flux. Order, regularity, predictability, simplicity, all these seem lamentably absent. It is in the world of inanimate things that such qualities are most readily seen. And this . . . I suggest, is why the mind in quest of explanatory analogies turns most readily to the inanimate. In the traditional societies of Africa we find the situation reversed. The human scene is the locus *par excellence* of order, predictability, regularity. In the world of the inanimate, these qualities are far less evident . . . here, the mind in quest of explanatory analogies turns naturally to people and their relations.[27]

Horton relies here on a picture of the function of scientific theory as essentially concerned to develop models of the unified, simple, ordered, regular underlying features of reality in order to account for the diversity, complexity, disorder, and apparent lawlessness of ordinary experience.[28] His story works so well that it is hard not to feel that there is *something* right about it; it *would* indeed explain the preference for agency over matter, the first of the major differences Horton acknowledges between traditional religion and science.

And yet this *cannot* be quite right. All cultures—in modest mood, I might say, all the cultures I have knowledge of—have the conceptual resources for at least two fundamental sorts of explanation. On the one hand, all have some sort of notion of what Aristotle called "efficient" causation: the causality of push and pull through which we understand the everyday interactions of material objects and forces. On the other, each has a notion of explanation that applies paradigmatically to human action, the notion that the American philosopher Daniel Dennett has characterized as involving the "intentional stance."[29] This sort of explanation relates actions to beliefs, desires, intentions, fears, and so on—the so-called propositional attitudes— and is fundamental (in ways I suggested earlier) to folk psychology. We might say, analogously, that efficient causality is central to what cognitive psychologists now call "naive" or "folk physics."

These kinds of explanation are, of course, interconnected: when I explain the death of the elephant by talking of your need for food, your hunt, your firing the gun, there are elements of folk physics and of folk psychology involved in each stage of this narrative. To say that mechanical explanation is unfamiliar to preindustrial peoples is, of course, to say something true. Mechanical explanation is explanation in terms of machines, which are, of course, exactly what preindustrial cultures do not have. But mechanical explanation is by no means the only kind of nonintentional explanation: there is more to folk physics than a view of machines. And the fact is that the stability of the causal relations of objects in the preindustrial world is surely quite substantial: not only do people make tools and utensils, using the concepts of efficient causation, but their regular physical interactions with the world—in digging, hunting, walking, dancing—are as stable and as well understood as their familial relations. More than this, preindustrial *Homo* is already *Homo faber,* and the making of pots and of jewelry, for example, involve intimate knowledge of physical things and an expectation of regularity in their behavior. Pots and rings and neck- laces break, of course, and they often do so unpredictably. But in this they are not obviously less reliable than people, who, after all, are notoriously difficult to predict also.

What we need to bring back into view here is a kind of explanation that is missing from Horton's story: namely, functional explanation, which we find centrally (but by no means uniquely) in what we might call "folk biology." Functional explanation is the sort of explanation that we give when we say that the flower is there to attract the bee that pollinates it; that the liver is there to purify the blood; that the rain falls to water the crops.

This sort of explanation is missing from Horton's story for a very good reason— namely, that the positivist philosophy of science on which Horton relies sought either to eradicate functional explanation or to reduce it to other sorts of explanation, in large part because it reeked of teleology—of the sort of Aristotelian "final" causation that positivism took to have been shown to be hopeless by the failure of vitalism in nineteenth-century biology. And, surely, what is most striking about the "unscien- tific" explanations that most precolonial African cultures offer is not just that they appeal to agency but that they are addressed to the question "Why?" understood as asking what the event in question was *for.* Evans-Pritchard in his account of Zande belief insists that the Azande do not think that "unfortunate events" ever happen by chance:[30] their frequent appeal to witchcraft—in the absence of other acceptable explanations of misfortune—demonstrates their unwillingness to accept the existence of contingency. But to reject the possibility of the contingent is exactly to insist that everything that happens serves some purpose: a view familiar in Christian tradition in such formulas as "And we know that all things work together for good to them that love God" (Rom. 8:28), or in the deep need people feel—in Europe and America as in Africa—for answers to the question "Why do bad things happen to good people?" Zande witchcraft beliefs depend on an assumption that the universe is in a certain sort of evaluative balance; in short, on the sort of assumption that leads monotheistic theologians to develop theodicies.

What Zande people will not accept, as Evans-Pritchard's account makes clear, is not that "unfortunate events" have no explanation—the granary falls because the termites have eaten through the stilts that support it—but that they are meaningless; that there is no deeper reason why the person sitting in the shade of the granary was injured. And in that sense they share an attitude that we find in Christian theodicy from Irenaeus to Augustine to Karl Barth: the attitude that the cosmos works to a plan. Precolonial African cultures, pre- and nonscientific thinkers everywhere are inclined to suppose that events in the world have meaning; they worry not about the possibility of the unexplained (what has no efficient cause nor agent explanation) but of the meaningless (what has no function, no point). And this marks those who accept the scientific worldview—a minority, of course, even in the industrialized world—from almost all other humans throughout history. For it is a distinctive feature of that scientific worldview that it *accepts* that not everything that happens has a human meaning. To explain *this* difference between scientific and nonscientific visions we need, I think, to begin with the fact that the world, as the sciences conceive of it, extends so hugely far beyond the human horizon, in time as in space. As Alexandre Koyré indicated in the title of his well-known study of the birth of modern celestial physics, the Newtonian revolution took the intellectual path *From the Closed World to the Infinite Universe,* and the Victorian dispute between science and religion had at its center a debate about the age of the earth, with geology insisting that the biblical time scale of thousands of years since the creation radically underestimated the age of our planet. Copernicus turned European scientists away from a geocentric to a heliocentric view of the universe and began a process, which Darwin continued, that inevitably displaced humankind from the center of the natural sciences. A recognition that the universe does not seem to have been made simply for us is the basis of the radically nonanthropocentric character of scientific theories of the world. This nonanthropocentrism is part of the change in view that develops with the growth of capitalism, of science, and of the modern state, the change to which, for example, Weber's account of modernization was addressed, and it contributes profoundly to the sense of the universe as disenchanted that Weberians have taken to be so central a feature of modernity (a claim that makes more sense as a claim about the life of professional intellectuals than as one about the culture as a whole). To these issues I shall return in Chapter 7.

But Horton in his original work made, as I said, a second important claim for difference: he summarized it by calling the cognitive world of traditional cultures "closed" and that of modern cultures "open." "What I take to be the key difference is a very simple one," he writes. "It is that in traditional cultures there is no developed awareness of alternatives to the established body of theoretical tenets; whereas in scientifically oriented cultures, such an awareness is highly developed."[31] And it is here, when we turn from questions about the content and logic of traditional and scientific explanation to the social contexts in which those theories are constructed and mobilized, that Horton's account begins to seem less adequate.

We should begin, however, by agreeing that there clearly are important differences between the social contexts of theory formation and development in precolonial Africa, on the one hand, and post-Renaissance Europe, on the other. Modern science began in Europe just when her peoples were beginning to be exposed to the hitherto unknown cultures of the Orient, Africa, and the Americas. The first vernacular scientific works—Galileo's dialogues, for example—were written in Italy at a time when the Italian trading cities had been for some time at the center of commerce between the Mediterranean, the Near and Far East, the New World, and Africa. In such a climate, it is natural to ask whether the certainties of your ancestors are correct, faced with cultures such as the China Marco Polo reported, whose technical ingenuity was combined with totally alien theories of nature.

This challenge to traditional Western beliefs occurs not only in terms of the theory of nature but also recapitulates Greek discussions of the ways in which matters of value seem to vary from place to place; discussions that lead very naturally to moral as well as scientific skepticism of exactly the kind that we find in the early modern empiricists. And it seems no coincidence that those earlier Greek discussions were prompted by an awareness of the existence of alternative African and Asian worldviews, an awareness to be found in the first historians, such as Herodotus. (Herodotus's account of the Persian Wars begins with an extended discussion of the variety of religious and social customs found within the Persian empire.) It is, in other words, the availability of alternative theories of morals and nature that gives rise to the systematic investigation of nature, to the growth of speculation, and to the development of that crucial element that distinguishes the open society—namely, organized challenges to prevailing theory.

Remember the answer the priest gave to the question about the gold dust: "We do it because the ancestors did it." In the open society this will no longer do as a reason. The early modern natural scientists, the natural philosophers of the Renaissance, stressed often the unreasonableness of appeals to authority. And if modern scholarship suggests that they *over*stressed the extent to which their predecessors were bound by a hidebound traditionalism, it is still true that there *is* a difference—if only in degree—in the extent to which modernity celebrates distance from our predecessors, while the traditional world celebrates cognitive continuity.

Now Horton's account of the sense in which the traditional worldview is closed has—rightly—been challenged. The complexities of war and trade, dominance and clientage, migration and diplomacy, in much of precolonial Africa are simply not consistent with the image of peoples unaware that there is a world elsewhere. As Catherine Coquery-Vidrovitch, a leading French historian of Africa, has pointed out:

In fact, these reputedly stable societies rarely enjoyed the lovely equilibrium presumed to have been disrupted by the impact of colonialism. West Africa, for example, had been seething with activity even since the eighteenth-century waves of Fulani conquest and well before the creation of units of resistance to European influence. . . . The Congolese basin was the site of still more profound upheavals linked to commercial penetration. In such cases the revolution in production rocked the very foundations of the political structure. As for South Africa, the rise of the Zulus and their expansion had repercussions up into central Africa. How far back do we have to go to find the stability alleged to be "characteristic" of the precolonial period: before the Portuguese conquest, before the Islamic invasion, before the Bantu expansion? Each of these great turning points marked the reversal of long-term trends, within which a whole series of shorter cycles might in turn be identified, as, for example, the succession of Sudanic empires, or even such shorter cycles as the periods of recession (1724–1740, 1767–1782, 1795–1811, and so on) and the upswing of the slave-trade economy of Dahomey. In short, the static concept of "traditional" society cannot withstand the historian's analysis.[32]

In particular—as Horton himself has insisted in "A Hundred Years of Change in Kalabari Religion"—African historians can trace changes in religious and other beliefs in many places long before the advent of Christian missionaries and colonial educators. The Yoruba were aware of Islam before they were aware of England, of Dahomey before they heard of Britain. But Yoruba religion has many of the features that Horton proposed to explain by reference to a lack of awareness of just such alternatives.

It is also possible to find first-rate speculative thinkers in traditional societies whose individual openness is not to be denied. I think here of Ogotemmeli, whose cosmology Griaule has captured in *Dieu d'eau,* and Barry Hallen has provided evidence from Nigerian sources of the existence, within African traditional modes of thought, of styles of reasoning that are open neither to Wiredu's stern strictures nor to Horton's milder ones.[33] To begin with, Hallen says, when Yoruba people answer the question "Why do you believe x?" by saying that "this is what the forefathers said,"[34] in the way that Wiredu objects to and Horton also takes to be typical, they are not trying to offer a reasoned justification for believing x. Rather they are

taking the question as one about the origin of a belief or custom. They are giving the same sort of response Westerners would be likely to if asked how they came to believe in shaving the hair off their faces. However if one goes further and asks a Yoruba to explain what a belief "means" a more sophisticated response is often forthcoming.[35]

And, Hallen goes on to argue, in Yoruba culture this more sophisticated response often meets standards for being critical and reflective. Hallen takes as a model Karl Popper's[36] characterization of critical reflection on tradition, a gesture all the more significant given the Popperian provenance of the open-closed dichotomy. This requires:

1. identifying the tradition *as* a tradition;
2. displaying an awareness of its consequences; *and*
3. being aware of at least one alternative and, on some critical basis, choosing to affirm or to reject it.[37]

By this test the Yoruba *babalawo*—the diviner and healer—whom Hallen cites *is* critically appreciative of the tradition he believes in.

Hallen is right, then, to challenge the structure of Horton's original dichotomy of the open and the closed. On the one hand, as I said earlier, there is in post-Kuhnian history and sociology of science a good deal of evidence that these Popperian desiderata are hardly met in physics, the heartland of Western theory. On the other, Horton's original stress on the "closed" nature of traditional modes of thought does look less adequate in the face of Africa's complex history of cultural exchanges and of Hallen's *babalawo,* or in the presence of the extraordinary metaphysical synthesis of the Dogon elder, Ogotemmeli.[38] In a recent book—written with the Nigerian philosopher J. O. Sodipo—Hallen insists on the presence among Yoruba doctors of theories of witchcraft rather different from those of their fellow countrymen.[39] Here, then, among the doctors, speculation inconsistent with ordinary folk belief occurs, and there is no reason to doubt that this *aspect* of contemporary Yoruba culture is, in *this* respect, like many precolonial cultures.

But in rejecting altogether Horton's characterization of the traditional world as "closed," we risk losing sight of something important. Such thinkers as Ogotemmeli are individuals—individuals like Thales and the other early pre-Socratics in the Western tradition—and there is little evidence that their views have a wide currency or impact (indeed, it seems clear that the *babalawos* of Hallen and Sodipo's acquaintance are not especially concerned to *share* or to *spread* their speculations). If "traditional" thought is more aware of alternatives and contains more moments of individual speculation than Horton's original picture suggested, it is also true that it differs from the thought of both theorists and ordinary folk in the industrialized world in its responses to those alternatives and its incorporation of these speculations.

Horton has recently come—in response, in part, to Hallen's critique—to speak not of the closedness of traditional belief systems but, borrowing a term from Wole Soyinka, of their being "accommodative." He discusses work by students of Evans-Pritchard's that not only addresses the kind of static body of belief that is captured in Evans-Pritchard's picture of the Azande thought world but also stresses the dynamic and—as Horton admits—"open" way in which they "devise explanations for novel elements in . . . experience," and "their capacity to borrow, re-work and integrate alien ideas in the course of elaborating such explanations." "Indeed" he continues, "it is this 'open-ness' that has given the traditional cosmologies such tremendous durability in the face of immense changes that the 20th century has brought to the African scene." Horton then contrasts this accommodative style with the "adversary" style of scientific theory, which is characterized by the way in which the main stimulus to change of belief is not "novel experience but rival theory."[40]

And it seems to me that this change from the Popperian terminology of "open" and "closed" allows Horton to capture something important about the difference between traditional religion and science; something to do not with individual cognitive strategies but with social ones. If we want to understand the significance of social organization in differentiating traditional religion and natural science, we can do no better than to begin with those of Evans-Pritchard's answers to the question why the Azande do not see the falsity of their magic beliefs that mention social facts about the organization of those beliefs.

Evans-Pritchard wrote:

> Scepticism, far from being smothered, is recognized, even inculcated. But it is only about certain medicines and certain magicians. By contrast it tends to support other medicines and other magicians.
>   . . . Each man and each kinship group acts without cognizance of the actions of others. People do not pool their ritual experiences.
>   . . . They are not experimentally inclined.[41] . . . Not being experimentally inclined, they do not test the efficacy of their medicines.

And, he added, "Zande beliefs are generally vaguely formulated. A belief, to be easily contradicted by experience . . . must be clearly shared and intellectually developed."[42]

Whatever the practices of imperfect scientists are actually like, none of these things is supposed to be true of natural science. In our official picture of the sciences, skepticism *is* encouraged even about foundational questions—indeed, that is where the best students are supposed to be directed. Scientific researchers conceive of themselves as a community that cuts across political boundaries as divisive as the (late and unlamented) cold war Iron Curtain, and results, "experiences," *are* shared. The scientific community *is* experimentally inclined, and, of course, scientific theory *is* formulated as precisely as possible in order that those experiments can be carried out in a controlled fashion.

That, of course, is the only *official* view. Three decades of work in the history and sociology of science since Thomas Kuhn's iconoclastic *The Structure of Scientific Revolutions* have left us with a picture of science as much more messy and muddled— in short, as a more human business. Yet while this work has had the effect of revising (one is inclined to say "tarnishing") our image of the institutions of scientific research, it has not revised the fundamental recognition that the production of scientific knowledge is organized around competing theoretical positions, and that the demand for publication to establish the success of laboratories and individual scientists exposes each competing theory to review by ambitious countertheorists from other laboratories, with other positions. What we have learned, however (though it should have been obvious all along), is that there are serious limits placed on the range of positions that will be entertained. In 1981, for example, when Rupert Sheldrake's *A New Science of Life* was published, a correspondent in *Nature* suggested it might usefully be burned; this was inconsistent with official ideology because Sheldrake, a former research fellow of the Royal Society who had studied the philosophy of science, had constructed a proposal, which, though provocative, was deliberately couched in terms that made it subject to potential experimental test. Still, it outraged many biologists (and physicists), and if there had not been a challenge from the *New Scientist* magazine to design experiments, his proposal, like most of those regarded as in one way or the other the work of a "crank," would probably simply have been ignored by his professional peers. (There is some conclusion to be drawn from the fact that the copy of Sheldrake's book listed in the catalog at Duke

University appears to be in the divinity school library!) The development of science is not a free-for-all with all the participants cheering each other on with the cry: "And may the best theory win." But science *is*, crucially, adversarial, and the norms of publication and reproducibility of results, even though only imperfectly adhered to, are explicitly intended to lay theories and experimental claims open to attack by one's peers, and thus make competition from the adventurous "young Turk" possible.

More important than the hugely oversimplified contrast between an experimental, skeptical, science and an unexperimental, "dogmatic" traditional mode of thought is the difference in images of knowledge that are represented in the differences in the social organization of inquiry in modern as opposed to "traditional" societies. Scientists, like the rest of us, hold onto theories longer than they may be entitled to, suppress, unconsciously or half consciously, evidence they do not know how to handle, lie a little; in precolonial societies there were, we can be sure, individual doubters who kept their own counsel, resisters against the local dogma. But what is interesting about modern modes of theorizing is that they are organized around an image of constant change: we expect new theories, we reward and encourage the search for them, we believe that today's best theories will be revised beyond recognition if the enterprise of science survives. My ancestors in Asante never organized a specialized activity that was based around this thought. They knew that some people know more than others, and that there are things to be found out. But they do not seem to have thought it necessary to invest social effort in working out new theories of how the world works, not for some practical end (this they did constantly) but, as we say, for its own sake.

The differences between traditional religious theory and the theories of the sciences reside in the social organization of inquiry, as a systematic business, and it is differences in social organization that account, I think, both for the difference we feel in the character of natural scientific and traditional religious theory—they are the products of different kinds of social process—and for the spectacular expansion of the domain of successful prediction and control, an expansion that characterizes natural science but is notably absent in traditional society. Experimentation, the publication and reproduction of results, the systematic development of alternative theories in precise terms, all these ideals, however imperfectly they are realized in scientific practice, are intelligible only in an organized social enterprise of knowledge.

But what can have prompted this radically different approach to knowledge? Why have the practitioners of traditional religion, even the priests, who are the professionals, never developed the organized "adversarial" methods of the sciences? There are, no doubt, many historical sources. A few, familiar suggestions strike one immediately.

Social mobility leads to political individualism, of a kind that is rare in the traditional polity; political individualism allows cognitive authority to shift, also, from priest and king to commoner; and social mobility is a feature of industrial societies.

Or, in traditional societies, accommodating conflicting theoretical views is part of the general process of accommodation necessary for those who are bound to each other as neighbors for life. I remember once discussing differences between Ghana and America in cultural style with a fellow Ghanaian and an American. The American student asked what had struck us both as the most important cultural difference between Ghana and the United States when we first arrived. "You are so aggressive," said my Ghanaian friend. "In Ghana, we would not think that very good manners." Of course, what he had noticed was not aggression but simply a different conversational style. In Ghana, but not in America, it is impolite to disagree, to argue, to confute. And this accommodating approach to conversation is part of the same range of attitudes that leads to theoretical accommodations.

We could think of more differences in social, economic, and ecological background, which together may help to account for this difference in approach to theory; in Chapter 7, I will say something about the significance for this question of the growth of the market economy. But it seems to me that there is one other fundamental difference between traditional West African culture and the culture of the industrial world, and that it plays a fundamental role in explaining why the adversarial style never established itself in West Africa. And it is that these cultures were largely nonliterate.

Now literacy has, as Jack Goody has pointed out in his influential book *The Domestication of the Savage Mind*, important consequences; among them is the fact that it permits a kind of consistency that oral culture cannot and does not demand. Write down a sentence and it is there, in principle, forever; that means that if you write down another sentence inconsistent with it, you can be caught out. It is this fact that is at the root of the possibility of the adversarial style. How often have we seen Perry Mason—on television in Ghana or the United States or England (for television, at least, there is only one world)—ask the stenographer to read back from the record? In the traditional culture the answer can only be: "What record?" In the absence of written records, it is not possible to compare the ancestor's theories in their actual words with ours; nor, given the limitations of quantity imposed by oral transmission, do we have a detailed knowledge of what those theories were. We know more about the thought of Isaac Newton on one or two subjects than we know about the entire population of his Asante contemporaries.

The accommodative style is possible because orality makes it hard to discover discrepancies. And so it is possible to have an image of knowledge as unchanging lore, handed down from the ancestors. It is no wonder, with this image of knowledge, that there is no systematic research: nobody need ever notice that the way that traditional theory is used requires inconsistent interpretations. It is literacy that makes possible the precise formulation of questions that we have just noticed as one of the characteristics of scientific theory, and it is precise formulation that points up inconsistency. This explanation, which we owe to Horton, is surely very plausible.

Given the orality of traditional culture, it is possible to see how the accommodative approach can be maintained. With widespread literacy, the image of knowledge as a body of truths always already given cannot survive. But the recognition of the failures of consistency of the traditional worldview does not automatically lead to science; there are, as I have already observed, many other contributing factors. Without widespread literacy it is hard to see how science could have got started: it is not a sufficient condition for science, but it seems certainly necessary. What else, apart from a lot of luck, accounts for the beginnings of modern science? So many things: the Reformation, itself dependent not merely on literacy but also on printing and the wider dissemination of the Bible and other religious writings, with its transfer of cognitive authority from the Church to the individual; the experience with mechanism, with machinery, in agriculture and warfare; the development off universities. My claim is not that literacy explains modern science (China is a standing refutation of that claim); it is that it was crucial to its possibility. And the very low level of its literacy shaped the intellectual possibilities of precolonial Africa.

For literacy has other significant consequences. Those of us who read and write learn very quickly how different in style written communication is from oral; we learn it so early and so well that we need to be reminded of some of the differences—reminded, in fact, of the differences that are really important. Here is one, whose consequences for the intellectual life of literate peoples are, I think, considerable.

Suppose you found a scrap of paper, which contained the following words: "On Sundays here, we often do what Joe is doing over there. But it is not normal to do it on *this* day. I asked the priest whether it was permissible to do it today and he just did this." A reasonable assumption would be that you were reading a transcription of words someone had spoken. And why? Because all these words—*here, there, this, today,* and even *Joe* and *the priest*—are what logicians call *indexicals.* You need the context in which the sentence is uttered to know what they are referring to.

Every English speaker knows that *I* refers to the speaker, *you* to his or her audience: that *here* and *now* refer to the place and time of the utterance. And when we hear someone speak we are standardly in a position to identify speaker and audience, place and time. But when we write we have to fill in much of what context provides when we speak. We have to do this not only so that we avoid the uncertainty of indexicals but because we cannot assume that our readers will share our knowledge of our situation, and because, if they do not, they cannot ask us. But thinking about this—and trying to rephrase speech into writing to meet these demands—is bound to move you toward the abstract and the universal, and away from the concrete and the particular.

To see why literacy moves you toward universality in your language, consider the difference between the judgments of a traditional oracle and those of experts in a written tradition. A traditional thinker can get away with saying that if three oracles have answered that Kwame has engaged in adultery, then he has. But in a written tradition, all sorts of problems can arise. After all, everybody knows of cases where the oracles have been wrong three times because they were interfered with by witchcraft. To escape this problem, the literate theorist has to formulate principles not just for the particular case but more generally. Rather than saying, "Three oracles have spoken: it is so"—or, as the Akan proverb has it, "Ɔbosom anim, yɛkɔ no mprɛnsa" (One consults a spirit three times)—he or she will have to say something like the following:

> Three oracles constitute good prima facie evidence that something is so; but they may have been interfered with by witchcraft. This is to be revealed by such and such means. If they have been interfered with by witchcraft, it is necessary first to purify the oracle.

And so on, listing those qualifying clauses that we recognize as the mark of written scholarship.

And to see why literacy moves you toward abstraction in your language, listen to traditional proverbs, orally transmitted. Take the Akan proverb "Aba a ɛtɔ nyinaa na ɛfifiri a, anka obi rennya dua ase kwan," which means (literally) "If all seeds that fall were to grow, then no one could follow the path under the trees." Its message is (usually) that if everyone were prosperous, no one would work. But it talks of seeds, trees, paths through the forest. The message is abstract, but the wording is concrete. The concreteness makes the proverb memorable—and in oral tradition all that is carried on is carried on in memory; there are, as I said, no records. But it also means that to understand the message—as I am sure only Twi-speaking people did before I explained it—you have to share with the speaker a knowledge of his or her background assumptions to a quite specific extent. The proverb works because, in traditional societies, you talk largely with people you know; all the assumptions that are needed to unpack a proverb are shared. And it is because they are shared that the language of oral exchange can be indexical, metaphorical, context-dependent.

Write, then, and the demands imposed by the distant, unknown reader require more universality, more abstraction. Because our reader may not share the cultural assumptions necessary to understand them, in contexts where communication of information is central our written language becomes less figurative. And so another nail is beaten into the coffin of the inconsistencies of our informal thought.

For if we speak figuratively, then what we say can be taken and reinterpreted in a new context; the same proverb, precisely because its message is not fixed, can be used again and again. And if we can use it again and again with different messages, we may fail to notice that the messages are inconsistent with each other. After all, the proverb is being used *now* in *this* situation, and why should we think of those other occasions of its use *here* and *now?*

The impulse to abstract and universal and away from figurative language, and the recognition of the failures of consistency of the traditional worldview do not automatically lead to science; there are, as I have already observed, many other contributing factors. But, like literacy itself, these traits of literate cultures, while not sufficient to make for science, are ones it is hard to imagine science doing without.

In characterizing the possibilities of literacy, there is, as we have seen in many of the attempts to oppose tradition and modernity, a risk of overstating the case; our modernity, indeed, consists in part in our wishing to see ourselves as different from our ancestors. The communities of specialized knowledge that produce new physics and new ecology and new chemistry are small worlds of their own, with complex codes and practices into which ephebes are inducted not merely by the transmission of writings. Literate culture is still the culture of people who speak, and the mark of the autodidact, the person who has only book learning, is an unfamiliarity with the context of conversation you need to make a sound professional judgment. Physics textbooks do not tell you how to operate in the sociology and politics of the lab, and nowhere will you find it written exactly what it is about the major theorists in a field that makes their work important. More than this, the kind of checking for consistency that writing (and, now, the computer) makes possible is no guarantee that that possibility will be actualized or that, once inconsistencies are identified (as they seem to have been at the heart of the quantum theory), it will be clear what to do about them.

On the other side, there are many devices for supporting the transmission of a complex and nuanced body of practice and belief without writing. In Asante, for example, the figurative brass weights used for weighing gold dust are associated with proverbs that they represent, in ways that mean that the daily conduct of trade offered reminders of ideas of society and nature; and the same sorts of cultural coding are found in the patterns imprinted on the *Adinkra* cloth, or carved into our stools.

Still, intellectual style in cultures without widely distributed literacy was for that reason radically different from the style of contemporary literate cultures. And, complex as the real story is, the sorts of differences I have been discussing are real and have been important.

Literacy, then, makes possible the "modern" image of knowledge as something that is constantly being remade; what drives the culture to take up this possibility is, I believe, the economic logic of modernity, to whose operations I shall devote attention in the next essay.

Once it *did* start, scientific activity followed the pattern of all other activity in industrial society: it became subject to a division of labor. First a class of scientists; then of biologists, then of zoologists, then of embryologists, in an endless hierarchy of proliferating species. This differentiation has its own important consequences for the nature of science and those theories that are its product.[43] The division of labor in the West is so highly developed that, as Hilary Putnam has pointed out, we even leave the task of understanding some parts of our language to experts: it is because words like *electron* have precise meanings for physicists that I, who have no very good grasp of their meaning, can use them, and the same goes for the word *contract* and lawyers. These words, as my tool, only do their business for me because their meanings are sharpened by others.[44]

The literacy of the period immediately preceding the scientific revolution in Europe differed in at least one crucial respect from that of the High Middle Ages and of antiquity: it was beginning to be widespread. Through printing it had become possible for people other than clerics and the very rich to own books. There are many factors—some of which I have already mentioned—that made possible the breakdown of the cognitive authority of the Church in the Reformation, but for the purposes of a comparison with contemporary Africa, indeed with the contemporary developing world, printing, with the independence of mind that it breeds, is crucial.

We all know of the significance of printing in the spread of Bible-based Protestantism in the European Reformation, but the importance of widespread literacy for modern Africa was anticipated in nineteenth-century Asante. Some at the Asante court in the late nineteenth century were opposed to the transcription of their language, in part because they were able, in a nation without literacy, to maintain, as they thought, greater control of the flow of information. When they did want to send written messages, they used the literate Islamic scholars who were to be found in the major towns of the West African interior, relying on translation from Twi into Arabic or Hausa, and then back into the language of their correspondents. Now, only a hundred or so years later, a significant majority of the children of Kumasi can write— in English and (to a lesser extent) in Twi. And they can read books, from libraries, and newspapers and pamphlets, on the street, which effectively make it impossible for the authority of Asante tradition to remain unchallenged.

Let me say, finally, why I think that the gap between educated Africans and

Westerners may not be so wide for much longer, and why all of us will soon find it hard to know, from within, the nature of the traditional. The answer is simple enough: we now have a few generations of literate African intellectuals, and they have begun the process of examining our traditions. They are aided in this by the availability of Western traditions, their access to which, through writing, is no different from Westerners'. This process of analysis will produce new, unpredictable, fusions. Sometimes, something will have to give. What it will be, I cannot predict, though I have my suspicions, and you will be able to guess what they are if I say that it seems to me that the overwhelming political and economic domination of the Third World by the industrialized world will play its part.

The fact that our culture's future has the chance of being guided by a theoretical grasp of our situation is an extraordinary opportunity. In 1882 William Lecky, an English scholar, published a *History of the Rise and Influence of the Spirit of Rationalism in Europe*. Lecky wrote:

> If we ask why it is that the world has rejected what was once so universally and intensely believed, why a narrative of an old woman who had been seen riding on a broomstick, or who was proved to have transformed herself into a wolf, and to have devoured the flocks of her neighbours, is deemed so entirely incredible, most persons would probably be unable to give a very definite answer to the question. It is not always because we have examined the evidence and found it insufficient.[45]

When I first came across this passage it struck me at once as wonderfully apt to the situation of African intellectuals today. This paragraph records a sense that the intellectual secularization of Lecky's culture—the "growth of rationalism"—occurred without a proper examination of the evidence. I have enough faith in the life of reason to believe that Africans will have better prospects if we do not follow that example. And we have the great advantage of having before us the European and American—and the Asian and Latin American—experiments with modernity to ponder as we make our choices.

Why should the issues I have discussed be thought important? There are, for me, two reasons: a practical one (for us Africans), a moral one (for everybody). The moral one is simple: unless all of us understand each other, and understand each other as reasonable, we shall not treat each other with the proper respect. Concentrating on the noncognitive features of traditional religions not only misrepresents them but also leads to an underestimation of the role of reason in the life of traditional cultures.

The practical reason is this. Most Africans, now, whether converted to Islam or Christianity or not, still share the beliefs of their ancestors in an ontology of invisible beings. (This is, of course, true of many Europeans and Americans as well.) There is a story—probably apocryphal—of some missionaries in northern Nigeria who were worried about the level of infant mortality due to stomach infections transmitted in drinking water. They explained to "converts" at the mission that the deaths were due to tiny animals in the water, and that these animals would be killed if they only boiled the water before giving it to the children. Talk of invisible animals produced only a tolerant skepticism: the babies went on dying. Finally a visiting anthropologist suggested a remedy. There were, he said, evil spirits in the water; boil the water and you could see them going away, bubbling out to escape the heat. This time the message worked. These people were "converts"; for the missionaries' appeal to spirits was appeal to demons, to what the New Testament calls "principalities and powers." For the "converts," the Christian message was from the High God they had known existed (there is a king in every kingdom, then why not among the spirits?), and the injunction to abjure other spirits was a reflection only of the usual jealousy of the priests of one god for those of another.

It is this belief in the plurality of invisible spiritual forces that makes possible the—to Western eyes—extraordinary spectacle of a Catholic bishop praying at a Methodist wedding in tandem with traditional royal appeal to the ancestors. For most of the participants at the wedding, God can be addressed in different styles— Methodist, Catholic, Anglican, Moslem, traditional—and the ancestors can be addressed also. Details about the exact nature of the Eucharist, about any theological issues, are unimportant: that is a theoretical question, and theory is unimportant when the practical issue is getting God on your side. After all, who needs a theory about who it is that you are talking to, if you hear a voice speak?

These beliefs in invisible agents mean that most Africans cannot fully accept those scientific theories in the West that are inconsistent with it. I do not believe, despite what many appear to think, that this is a reason for shame or embarrassment. But it *is* something to think about. If modernization is conceived of, in part, as the acceptance of science, we have to decide whether we think the evidence obliges us to give up the invisible ontology. We can easily be misled here by the accommodation between science and religion that has occurred among educated people in the industrialized world, in general, and in the United States, in particular. For this has involved a considerable limitation of the domains in which it is permissible for intellectuals to invoke spiritual agency. The question how much of the world of the spirits we intellectuals must give up (or transform into something ceremonial without the old literal ontology) is one we must face: and I do not think the answer is obvious.

"Tout Africain qui voulait faire quelque chose de positif devait commencer par détruire toutes ces vieilles croyances qui consistent à creer le merveilleux là où il n'y a que phénomène natural: volcan, forêt vierge, foudre, soleil, etc."[46] says the narrator of Aké Loba's *Kocoumbo, l'etudiant noir*. But even if we agreed that all our old beliefs were superstitions, we should need principles to guide our choices of new ones. Further, there is evidence that the practical successes of technology, associated with the methods and motives of inquiry that I have suggested, are largely absent in traditional culture. The question whether we ought to adopt these methods is not a purely technical one. We cannot avoid the issue of whether it is possible to adopt adversarial, individualistic cognitive styles, and keep, as we might want to, accommodative, communitarian morals. Cultures and peoples have often not been capable of maintaining such double standards (and I use the term nonpejoratively, for perhaps we need different standards for different purposes), so that if we are going to try, we must face up to these difficulties. Scientific method may lead to progress in our understanding of the world, but you do not have to be a Thoreauvian to wonder if it has led only to progress in the pursuit of all our human purposes. In this area we can learn together with other cultures—including, for example, the Japanese culture, which has apparently managed a certain segregation of moral-political and cognitive spheres. In this respect, it seems to me obvious that the Ghanaian philosopher Kwasi Wiredu is right. We will only solve our problems if we see them as human problems arising out of a special situation, and we shall not solve them if we see them as African problems, generated by our being somehow unlike others.

SEVEN

The Postcolonial and
The Postmodern

You were called Bimbircokak
And all was well that way
You have become Victor-Emile-Louis-Henri-Joseph
Which
So far as I recall
Does not reflect your kinship with
Rockefeller.[1]

    YAMBO OUOLOGUEM

In 1987 the Center for African Art in New York organized a show entitled *Perspectives: Angles on African Art.*[2] The curator, Susan Vogel, had worked with a number of "cocurators," whom I list in order of their appearance in the table of contents: Ekpo Eyo, quondam director of the Department of Antiquities of the National Museum of Nigeria; William Rubin, director of painting and sculpture at the Museum of Modern Art and organizer of its controversial Primitivism exhibit; Romare Bearden, African-American painter; Ivan Karp, curator of African ethnology at the Smithsonian; Nancy Graves, European-American painter, sculptor, and filmmaker; James Baldwin, who surely needs no qualifying glosses; David Rockefeller, art collector and friend of the mighty; Lela Kouakou, Baule artist and diviner, from Ivory Coast (this a delicious juxtaposition, richest and poorest, side by side); Iba N'Diaye, Senegalese sculptor; and Robert Farris Thompson, Yale professor and African and African-American art historian. Vogel describes the process of selection in her introductory essay. The one woman and nine men were each offered a hundred-odd photographs of "African Art as varied in type and origin, and as high in quality, as we could manage" and asked to select ten for the show.[3] Or, I should say more exactly, that this is what was offered to eight of the men. For Vogel adds, "In the case of the Baule artist, a man familiar only with the art of his own people, only Baule objects were placed in the pool of photographs." At this point we are directed to a footnote to the essay, which reads:

> Showing him the same assortment of photos the others saw would have been interesting, but confusing in terms of the reactions we sought here. Field aesthetic studies, my own and others, have shown that African informants will criticize sculptures from other ethnic groups in terms of their own traditional criteria, often assuming that such works are simply inept carvings of their own aesthetic tradition.

I shall return to this irresistible footnote in a moment. But let me pause to quote further, this time from the words of David Rockefeller, who would surely never "criticize sculptures from other ethnic groups in terms of [his] own traditional criteria," discussing what the catalog calls a "Fante female figure":[4]

> I own somewhat similar things to this and I have always liked them. This is a rather more sophisticated version than the ones that I've seen, and I thought it was quite beautiful . . . the total composition has a very contemporary, very Western look to it. It's the kind of thing that goes very well with contemporary Western things. It would look good in a modern apartment or house.

We may suppose that David Rockefeller was delighted to discover that his final judgment was consistent with the intentions of the sculpture's creators. For a footnote to the earlier "Checklist" reveals that the Baltimore Museum of Art desires to "make public the fact that the authenticity of the Fante figure in its collection has been challenged." Indeed, work by Doran Ross suggests this object is almost certainly a modern piece introduced in my hometown of Kumasi by the workshop of a certain Francis Akwasi, which "specializes in carvings for the international market in the style of traditional sculpture. Many of its works are now in museums throughout the West, and were published as authentic by Cole and Ross"[5] (yes, the same Doran Ross) in their classic catalog *The Arts of Ghana*.

But then it is hard to be *sure* what would please a man who gives as his reason for picking another piece (this time a Senufo helmet mask), "I have to say I picked this because I own it. It was given to me by President Houphouet Boigny of Ivory Coast."[6] Or one who remarks, "concerning the market in African art":

> The best pieces are going for very high prices. Generally speaking, the less good pieces in terms of quality are not going up in price. And that's a fine reason for picking the good ones rather than the bad. They have a way of becoming more valuable.
>
> I like African art as objects I find would be appealing to use in a home or an office. . . . I don't think it goes with everything, necessarily—although the very best perhaps does. But I think it goes well with contemporary architecture.[7]

There is something breathtakingly unpretentious in Mr. Rockefeller's easy movement between considerations of finance, of aesthetics, and of decor. In these responses we have surely a microcosm of the site of the African in contemporary— which is, then, surely to say, postmodern—America.

I have given so much of David Rockefeller not to emphasize the familiar fact that questions of what we call "aesthetic" value are crucially bound up with market value; not even to draw attention to the fact that this is known by those who play the art market. Rather, I want to keep clearly before us the fact that David Rockefeller is permitted to say *anything at all* about the arts of Africa because he is a *buyer* and because he is at the *center,* while Lela Kouakou, who merely makes art and who dwells at the margins, is a poor African whose words count only as parts of the commodification[8]—both for those of us who constitute the museum public and for collectors, like Rockefeller—of Baule art.[9] I want to remind you, in short, of how important it is that African art is a *commodity*.

But the cocurator whose choice will set us on our way is James Baldwin—the only cocurator who picked a piece that was not in the mold of the Africa of the exhibition Primitivism, a sculpture that will be my touchstone, a piece labeled by the museum *Yoruba Man with a Bicycle*. Here is some of what Baldwin said about it:

> This is something. This has got to be contemporary. He's really going to town. It's very jaunty, very authoritative. His errand might prove to be impossible. He is challenging something—or something has challenged him. He's grounded in immediate reality by the bicycle. . . . He's apparently a very proud and silent man. He's dressed sort of polyglot. Nothing looks like it fits him too well.

Baldwin's reading of this piece is, of course and inevitably, "in terms of [his] own . . . criteria," a reaction contextualized only by the knowledge that bicycles are new in Africa and that this piece, anyway, does not look anything like the works he recalls seeing from his earliest childhood at the Schomburg museum in Harlem. And his response torpedoes Vogel's argument for her notion that the only "authentically traditional" African—the only one whose responses, as she says, could have been found a century ago—must be refused a choice among Africa's art cultures because he, unlike the rest of the cocurators, who are Americans and the European-educated Africans, will use his "own . . . criteria." This Baule diviner, this authentically African villager, the message is, does not know what *we*, authentic postmodernists, now know: that the first and last mistake is to judge the Other on one's own terms. And so, in the name of this, the relativist insight, we impose our judgment that Lela Kouakou may not judge sculpture from beyond the Baule culture zone because he will—like all the other African "informants" we have met in the field—read them as if they were meant to meet those Baule standards.

Worse than this, it is nonsense to explain Lela Kouakou's responses as deriving from an ignorance of other traditions—if indeed he is, as he is no doubt supposed to be, like most "traditional" artists today, if he is like, for example, Francis Akwasi of Kumasi. Kouakou may judge other artists by his own standards (what on earth else could he, could anyone, do, save make no judgment at all?), but to suppose that he is unaware that there are other standards within Africa (let alone without) is to ignore a piece of absolutely basic cultural knowledge, common to most precolonial as to most colonial and postcolonial cultures on the continent—the piece of cultural knowledge that explains why the people we now call "Baule" exist at all. To be Baule, for example, is, for a Baule, not to be a white person, not to be Senufo, not to be French.[10] The ethnic groups—Lele Kouakou's Baule "tribe," for example—within which all African aesthetic life apparently occurs, are (as I shall be arguing in Chapter 8) the products of colonial and postcolonial articulations. And someone who knows enough to make himself up as a Baule for the twentieth century surely knows that there are other kinds of art.

But Baldwin's *Yoruba Man with a Bicycle* does more than give the lie to Vogel's strange footnote; it provides us with an image of an object that can serve as a point of entry to my theme: a piece of contemporary African art that will allow us to explore the articulation of the postcolonial and the postmodern. *Yoruba Man with a Bicycle* is described as follows in the catalog:

Page 124
Man with a Bicycle

Yoruba, Nigeria 20th century
Wood and paint H. 35³/₄ in.
The Newark Museum

The influence of the Western world is revealed in the clothes and bicycle of this neo-traditional Yoruba sculpture which probably represents a merchant en route to market.[11]

And it is this word *neotraditional*—a word that is amost right—that provides, I think, the fundamental clue.

But I do not know how to explain this clue without saying first how I keep my bearings in the shark-infested waters around the semantic island of the postmodern. And since narratives, unlike metanarratives, are allowed to proliferate in these seas, I shall begin with a story about my friend the late Margaret Masterman. Sometime in the midsixties Margaret was asked to participate at a symposium, chaired by Karl Popper, at which Tom Kuhn was to read a paper and then she, J. M. W. Watkins, Stephen Toulmin, L. Pearce Williams, Imre Lakatos, and Paul Feyerabend would engage in discussion of Kuhn's work. Unfortunately for Margaret, she developed infective hepatitis in the period leading up to the symposium and she was unable, as a result, to prepare a paper. Fortunately for all of us, though, she *was* able to sit in her hospital bed—in Block 8, Norwich hospital, to whose staff the paper she finally did write is dedicated—and create a subject index to *The Structure of Scientific Revolutions*. In the course of working through the book with index cards, Margaret identified no "less than twenty-one senses, possibly more, not less" in which Kuhn uses the word *paradigm*. After her catalog of these twenty-one uses, she remarks laconically that "not all these senses of 'paradigm' are inconsistent with one another"; and she continues:

> Nevertheless, given the diversity, it is obviously reasonable to ask: "Is there anything in common between all these senses? Is there, philosophically speaking, anything definite or general about the notion of a paradigm which Kuhn is trying to make clear? Or is he just a historian-poet describing different happenings which have occurred in the history of science, and referring to them all by using the same word 'paradigm'?"[12]

The relevance of this tale hardly needs explication. And the task of chasing the word *postmodernism* through the pages of Lyotard and Jameson and Habermas, in and out of the *Village Voice* and the *T.L.S.* and even the *New York Times Book Review*, makes the task of pinning down Kuhn's *paradigm* look like work for a minute before breakfast.

Nevertheless, there *is*, I think, a story to tell about all these stories—or, of course, I should say, there are many, but this, for the moment, is mine—and, as I tell it, the Yoruba bicyclist will eventually come back into view.

Let me begin with the most-obvious and surely one of the most-often-remarked features of Jean-François Lyotard's account of postmodernity: the fact that it is a metanarrative of the end of metanarratives.[13] To theorize certain central features of contemporary culture as *post* anything, is, of course, inevitably to invoke a narrative, and, from the Enlightenment on, in Europe and European-derived cultures, that "after" has also meant "above and beyond" and to step forward (in time) has been ipso facto to *progress*.[14] Brian McHale announces in his recent *Postmodernist Fiction:*

> As for the prefix POST, here I want to emphasize the element of logical and historical *consequence* rather than sheer temporal *posteriority*. Postmodernism follows *from* modernism, in some sense, more than it follows *after* modernism. . . . Postmodernism is the posterity of modernism, that is tautological.[15]

My point, then, is not the boring logical point that Lyotard's view—in which, in the absence of "grand narratives of legitimation," we are left with only local legitimations, imminent in our own practices—might seem to presuppose a "grand narrative of legitimation" of its own, in which justice turns out to reside, unexcitingly, in the institutionalization of pluralism. It is rather that his analysis seems to feel the need to see the contemporary condition as over against an immediately anterior set of practices and as going beyond them. Lyotard's postmodernism—his theorization of contemporary life as postmodern—is *after* modernism because it rejects aspects of modernism. And in this repudiation of one's immediate predecessors (or, more especially, of their theories of themselves) it recapitulates a crucial gesture of the historic avant-garde: indeed, it recapitulates the crucial gesture of the modern "artist"; in that sense of modernity characteristic of sociological usage in which it denotes "an era that was ushered in via the Renaissance, rationalist philosophy, and the Enlightenment, on the one hand, and the transition from the absolutist state to bourgeois democracy, on the other";[16] in that sense of "artist" to be found in Trilling's account of Arnold's *Scholar Gypsy,* whose "existence is intended to disturb us and make us dissatisfied with our habitual life in culture."[17]

This straining for a contrast—a modernity or a modernism to be *against*—is extremely striking given the lack of any plausible account of what distinguishes the modern from the postmodern that is distinctively formal. In a recent essay, Fredric Jameson grants at one point, after reviewing recent French theorizings (Deleuze, Baudrillard, Debord) that it is difficult to distinguish formally the postmodern from high modernism:

> Indeed, one of the difficulties in specifying postmodernism lies in its symbiotic or parasitical relationship to [high modernism]. In effect with the canonization or a hitherto scandalous, ugly, dissonant, amoral, antisocial, bohemian high modernism offensive to the middle classes, its promotion to the very figure of high culture generally, and perhaps most importantly, its enshrinement in the academic institution, postmodernism emerges as a way of making creative space for artists now oppressed by those henceforth hegemonic categories of irony, complexity, ambiguity, dense temporality, and particularly, aesthetic and utopian monumentality.[18]

Jameson's argument in this essay is that we must characterize the distinction not in formal terms—in terms, say, of an "aesthetic of *textuality*," or of "the eclipse, finally, of all depth, especially historicity itself," or of "the 'death' of the subject," or "the *culture of the simulacrum*," or "the society of the spectacle"[19]—but in terms of "the social functionality of culture itself."

High modernism, whatever its overt political content, was oppositional and marginal within a middle-class Victorian or philistine or gilded age culture. Although postmodernism is equally offensive in all the respects enumerated (think of punk rock or pornography), it is no longer at all "oppositional" in that sense; indeed, it constitutes the very dominant or hegemonic aesthetic of consumer society itself and significantly serves the latter's commodity production as a virtual laboratory of new forms and fashions. The argument for a conception of post-modernism as a periodizing category is thus based on the presupposition that, even if *all* the formal features enumerated above were already present in the older high modernism, the very significance of those features changes when they become a cultural *dominant* with a precise socio-economic functionality.[20]

It is the "waning" of the "dialectical opposition" between high modernism and mass culture—the commodification and, if I may coin a barbarism, the deoppositionaliza-tion, of those cultural forms once constitutive of high modernism—that Jameson sees as key to understanding the postmodern condition.

There is no doubt much to be said for Jameson's theorizing of the postmodern. But I do not think we shall understand what is in common to all the various postmodernisms if we stick within Jameson's omnisubsumptive vision. The com-modification of a fiction, a stance, of oppositionality that is saleable precisely because its commodification guarantees for the consumer that it is no substantial threat was, indeed, central to the cultural role of "punk rock" in Europe and America. But what, more than a word and a conversation, makes Lyotard and Jameson competing theorists of the *same* postmodern?

I do not—this will come as no surprise—have a definition of the postmodern to put in the place of Jameson's or Lyotard's. But there is now a rough consensus about the structure of the modern-postmodern dichotomy in the many domains—from architecture to poetry to philosophy to rock to the movies—in which it has been invoked. In each of these domains there is an antecedent practice that laid claim to a certain exclusivity of insight and in each of them postmodernism is a name for the rejection of that claim to exclusivity, a rejection that is almost always more playful—though not necessarily less serious—than the practice it aims to replace. That this will not do as a *definition* of postmodernism follows from the fact that in each domain this rejection of exclusivity takes up a certain specific shape, one that reflects the specificities of its setting.

To understand the various postmodernisms this way is to leave open the question how their theories of contemporary social, cultural, and economic life relate to the actual practices that constitute that life; to leave open, then, the relations between postmodern*ism* and postmodern*ity*. Where the practice is theory—literary or philosophical—postmodernism as a *theory* of postmodernity can be adequate only if it reflects to some extent the realities of that practice, because the practice is itself fully theoretical. But when a postmodernism addresses, say, advertising or poetry, it may be adequate as an account of them even if it conflicts with their own narratives, their theories of themselves. For, unlike philosophy and literary theory, advertising and poetry are not largely *constituted* by their articulated theories of themselves.

It is an important question *why* this distancing of the ancestors should have become so central a feature of our cultural lives. And the answer, surely, has to do with the sense in which art is increasingly commodified. To sell oneself and one's products as art in the marketplace, it is important, above all, to clear a space in which one is distinguished from other producers and products—and one does this by the construction and the marking of differences.

It is this that accounts for a certain intensification of the long-standing individualism of post-Renaissance art production: in the age of mechanical reproduction, aesthetic individualism—the characterization of the artwork as belonging to the oeuvre of an individual—and the absorption of the artist's life into the conception of the work can be seen precisely as modes of identifying objects for the market. The sculptor of the bicycle, by contrast, will not be known by those who buy this object; his individual life will make no difference to its future history. (Indeed, he surely knows this, in the sense in which one knows anything whose negation one has never even considered.) Nevertheless, there is *some*thing about the object that serves to establish it for the market: the availability of Yoruba culture and of stories about Yoruba culture to surround the object and distinguish it from "folk art" from elsewhere. I shall return to this point.

Let me confirm this proposal by instances:

1. In philosophy, postmodernism is the rejection of the mainstream consensus from Descartes through Kant to logical positivism on foundationalism (there is one route to knowledge, which is exclusivism in epistemology) and of metaphysical realism (there is one truth, which is exclusivism in ontology), each underwritten by a unitary notion of reason; it thus celebrates such figures as Nietzsche (no metaphysical realist) and Dewey (no foundationalist). The modernity that is opposed here can thus be Cartesian (in France), Kantian (in Germany), and logical positivist (in America).

2. In architecture, postmodernism is the rejection of an exclusivism of function (as well as the embrace of a certain taste for pastiche). The modernity that is opposed here is the "monumentality," "elitism," and "authoritarianism" of the international style of Le Corbusier or Mies.[21]

3. In "literature," postmodernism reacts against the high seriousness of high modernism, which mobilized "difficulty" as a mode of privileging its own aesthetic sensibility and celebrated a complexity and irony appreciable only by a cultural elite. Modernity here is, say, and in no particular order, Proust, Eliot, Pound, Woolf.

4. In political theory, finally, postmodernism is the rejection of the monism of Big-M Marxist (though not of the newer little-m marxist) and liberal conceptions of justice, and their overthrow by a conception of politics as irreducibly plural, with every perspective essentially contestable from other perspectives. Modernity here is the great nineteenth-century political narratives, of Marx and Mill but includes, for example, such latecomers as John Rawls's reconstruction of *The Liberal Theory of Justice*.

These sketchy examples are meant to suggest how we might understand the family resemblance of the various postmodernisms as governed by a *loose* principle. They also suggest why it might be that the high theorists of postmodernism— Lyotard, Jameson, Habermas,[22] shall we say—can seem to be competing for the same territory: Lyotard's privileging of a certain philosophical antifoundationalism could surely be seen as underwriting (though not, I think, plausibly, as causing) each of these moves; Jameson's characterization of postmodernism as the logic of late capitalism—with the commodification of "cultures" as a central feature—might well account for many features of each of these transitions also; and Habermas's project is surely intended (though in the name of a most un-Lyotardian metanarrative) to provide a modus operandi in a world in which pluralism is, so to speak, a fact waiting for some institutions.

Postmodern culture is the culture in which all of the postmodernisms operate, sometimes in synergy, sometimes in competition. And because contemporary culture is, in certain senses to which I shall return, transnational, postmodern culture is global—though that does not by any means mean that it is the culture of every person in the world.

If postmodernism is the project of transcending some species of modernism—which is to say some relatively self-conscious self-privileging project of a privileged modernity—our *neotraditional* sculptor of the *Yoruba Man with a Bicycle* is presumably to be understood, by contrast, as premodern, that is, traditional. (I am supposing, then, that being neotraditional is a way of being traditional; what work the "neo" does is matter for a later moment). And the sociological and anthropological narratives of tradition through which he or she came to be so theorized is dominated, of course, by Weber.

Weber's characterization of traditional (and charismatic) authority *in opposition* to rational authority is in keeping with his general characterization of modernity as the rationalization of the world, and he insisted on the significance of this characteristically Western process for the rest of humankind. The introduction to *The Protestant Ethic* begins:

> A product of modern European civilization, studying any problem of universal history, is bound to ask himself to what combination of circumstances the fact should be attributed that in Western civilization, and in Western civilization only, cultural phenomena have appeared which (as we like to think) lie in a line of development having universal significance and value.[23]

There is certainly no doubt that Western modernity now has a universal *geographical* significance. The Yoruba bicyclist—like Sting and his Amerindian chieftains of the Amazon rain forest or Paul Simon and the Mbaqanga musicians of *Graceland*—is testimony to that. But, if I may borrow someone else's borrowing, the fact is that the Empire of Signs strikes back. Weber's "as we like to think" reflects his doubts about whether the Western imperium over the world was as clearly of universal *value* as it was certainly of universal *significance,* and postmodernism surely fully endorses his resistance to this claim. The bicycle enters our museums to be valued by us (David Rockefeller tells us *how* it is to be valued). But just as the *presence* of the object reminds us of this fact, its *content* reminds us that the trade is two-way.

I want to argue that to understand our—our human—modernity we must first understand why the rationalization of the world can no longer be seen as the tendency either of the West or of history; why, simply put, the modernist characterization of modernity must be challenged. To understand our world is to reject Weber's claim for the rationality of what he called rationalization and his projection of its inevitability; it is, then, to have a radically post-Weberian conception of modernity.

We can begin with a pair of familiar and helpful caricatures: Thomas Stearns Eliot is against the soullessness and the secularization of modern society, the reach of Enlightenment rationalism into the whole world. He shares Weber's account of modernity and more straightforwardly deplores it. Le Corbusier is in favor of rationalization—a house is a "machine for living in"—but he, too, shares Weber's vision of modernity. And, of course, the great rationalists—the believers in a transhistorical reason triumphing in the world—from Kant on are the source of Weber's Kantian vision. Modernism in literature and architecture and philosophy (the account of modernity that, on my model, *post*modernism in these domains seeks to subvert) may be for reason or against it: but in each domain rationalization—the pervasion of reason—is seen as the distinctive dynamic of contemporary history.

But the beginning of postmodern wisdom is to ask whether Weberian rationalization is in fact what has happened. For Weber, charismatic authority—the authority of Stalin, Hitler, Mao, Guevara, Nkrumah—is antirational, yet modernity has been dominated by just such charisma. Secularization seems hardly to be proceeding: religions grow in all parts of the world; more than 90 percent of North Americans still avow some sort of theism; what we call "fundamentalism" is as alive in the West as it is in Africa and the Middle and Far East; Jimmy Swaggart and Billy Graham have business in Louisiana and California as well as in Costa Rica and Ghana.

What we can see in all these cases, I think, is not the triumph of Enlightenment capital-R Reason—which would have entailed exactly the end of charisma and the universalization of the secular—not even the penetration of a narrower instrumental reason into all spheres of life, but what Weber mistook for that: namely, the incorporation of all areas of the world and all areas of even formerly "private" life into the money economy. Modernity has turned every element of the real into a sign, and the sign reads "for sale"; this is true even in domains like religion where instrumental reason would recognize that the market has at best an ambiguous place.

If Weberian talk of the triumph of instrumental reason can now be seen to be a mistake, what Weber thought of as the disenchantment of the world—that is, the penetration of a scientific vision of things—describes at most the tiny, and in the United States quite marginal, world of the higher academy and a few islands of its influence. The world of the intellectual *is*, I think, largely disenchanted (even theistic academics largely do not believe in ghosts and ancestor spirits), and fewer people (though still very many) suppose the world to be populated by the multitudes of spirits of earlier religion. Still, what we have seen in recent times in the United States is not secularization—the end of religions—but their commodification; with that commodification, religions have reached further and grown—their markets have expanded—rather than dying away.

Postmodernism can be seen, then, as a new way of understanding the multiplication of distinctions that flows from the need to clear oneself a space; the need that drives the underlying dynamic of cultural modernity. Modernism saw the economization of the world as the triumph of reason; postmodernism rejects that claim, allowing in the realm of theory the same multiplication of distinctions we see in the cultures it seeks to understand.

I anticipate that objection that the Weber I have been opposing is something of a caricature. And I would not be unhappy to admit that there is some truth in this. Weber foresaw, for example, that the rationalization of the world would continue to be resisted, and his view that each case of charisma needed to be "routinized" was not meant to rule out the appearance of new charismatic leaders in our time as in earlier ones: our politics of charisma would, perhaps, not have suprised him.[24] Certainly, too, his conception of reason involved far more than instrumental calculation. Since much of what I have noticed here would have been anticipated by him, it may be as well to see this as a rejection of a narrow (if familiar) misreading of Weber than an argument against what is best in the complex and shifting views of Weber himself.

But I think we could also construe this misreading—which we find, perhaps, in Talcott Parsons—as in part a consequence of a problem with Weber's own work. For part of the difficulty with Weber's work is that, despite the wealth of historical detail in his studies of religion, law, and economics, he often mobilizes theoretical terms that are of a very high level of abstraction. As a result, it is not always clear that there really are significant commonalities among the various social phenomena he assimilates under such general concepts as "rationalization" or "charisma." (This is one of the general problems posed by Weber's famous reliance on "ideal types.") Reinhard Bendix, one of Weber's most important and sympathetic interpreters, remarks at one point in his discussion of one of Weber's theoretical distinctions (the distinction, as it happens, between patrimonialism and feudalism) that "this distinction is clear only so long as it is formulated in abstract terms."[25] In reading Weber it is a feeling that one has over and over again. The problem is exemplified in Weber's discussion of "charisma" in *The Theory of Social and Economic Organization:*

> The term "charisma" will be applied to a certain quality of an individual personality by virtue of which he is set apart from ordinary men and treated as endowed with supernatural, superhuman, or at least specifically exceptional powers or qualities. These are . . . regarded as of divine origin or examplary, and on the basis of them the individual concerned is treated as a leader.[26]

Notice how charisma is here defined disjunctively as involving *either* magical ("supernatural, superhuman," "of divine origin") capacities, on the one hand, *or* merely "exceptional" or "exemplary" qualities on the other. The first disjunct in each case happily covers the many cases of priestly and prophetic leadership that Weber discusses, for example, in his study *Ancient Judaism.* But it is the latter, presumably, that we should apply in seeking to understand the political role of Hitler, Stalin, or Mussolini, who though no doubt "exceptional" and "exemplary" were not regarded as having "supernatural" powers "of divine origin." The point is that much of what Weber has to say in his general discussion of charisma in *The Theory of Social and Economic Organization* and in the account of "domination" in *Economy and Society* requires that we take its magical aspect seriously. When, however, we do take it seriously, we find his theory fails to apply to the instances of charisma that fall under the second disjunct of his definition. In short, Weber's account of charisma assimilates too closely phenomena—such as the leadership of Stalin, at one end of the spectrum, and of King David or the emperor Charlemagne, at the other—in which magico-religious ideas seem, to put it mildly, to play remarkably different roles. If we follow out the logic of this conclusion by redefining Weberian charisma in such a way as to insist on its magical component, it will follow, by definition, that the disenchantment of the world—the decline of magic—leads to the end of charisma. But we shall then have to ask ourselves how correct it is to claim, with Weber, that magical views increasingly disappear with modernity. And if he is right in this, we shall also have to give up the claim that Weber's sociology of politics—in which charisma plays a central conceptual role—illuminates the characteristic political developments of modernity.

There is a similar set of difficulties with Weber's account of rationalization. In *The Protestant Ethic and the Spirit of Capitalism,*[27] Weber wrote: "If this essay makes any contribution at all, may it be to bring out the complexity of the only superficially simple concept of the rational." But we may be tempted to ask whether our understanding of the genuine complexities of the historical developments of the last few centuries of social, religious, economic, and political history in Western Europe is truly deepened by making use of a concept of rationalization that brings together a supposed increase in means-end calculation (instrumental rationality); a decline in appeal to "mysterious, incalculable forces" and a correlative increasing confidence in calculation (disenchantment or intellectualization);[28] and the growth of "value rationality," which means something like an increasing focus on maximizing a narrow range of ultimate goals.[29] Here, seeking to operate at this high level of generality, assimilating under one concept so many, in my view, distinct and independently intelligible processes, Weber's detailed and subtle appreciation of the dynamics of many social processes is obscured by his theoretical apparatus; it is, I think, hardly surprising that those who have been guided by his theoretical writings have ascribed to him a cruder picture than is displayed in his historical work.

I have been exploring how modernity looks from the perspective of the Euro-American intellectual. But how does it look from the postcolonial spaces inhabited by the *Yoruba Man with a Bicycle?* I shall speak about Africa, with confidence *both* that some of what I have to say will work elsewhere in the so-called Third World *and* that, in some places, it will certainly not. And I shall speak first about the producers of these so-called neotraditional artworks and then about the case of the African novel, because I believe that to focus exclusively on the novel (as theorists of contemporary African cultures have been inclined to do) is to distort the cultural situation and the significance within it of postcoloniality.

I do not know when the *Yoruba Man with a Bicycle* was made or by whom; African art has, until recently, been collected as the property of "ethnic" groups, not of individuals and workshops, so it is not unusual that not one of the pieces in the Perspectives show was identified in the "Checklist" by the name of an individual artist, even though many of them are twentieth-century; (and no one will have been surprised, by contrast, that most of them *are* kindly labeled with the name of the people who own the largely private collections where they now live). As a result I cannot say if the piece is literally postcolonial, produced after Nigerian independence in 1960. But the piece belongs to a genre that has certainly been produced since then: the genre that is here called *neotraditional*. And, simply put, what is distinctive about this genre is that it is produced for the West.

I should qualify. Of course, many of the buyers of first instance live in Africa, many of them are juridically citizens of African states. But African bourgeois consumers of neotraditional art are educated in the Western style, and, if they want African art, they would often rather have a "genuinely" traditional piece—by which I mean a piece that they believe to be made precolonially, or at least in a style and by methods that were already established precolonially. And these buyers are a minority. Most of this art, which is *traditional* because it uses actually or supposedly precolonial techniques, but is *neo*—this, for what it is worth, is the explanation I promised earlier—because it has elements that are recognizably from the colonial or postcolonial in reference, has been made for Western tourists and other collectors.

The incorporation of these works in the West's world of museum culture and its art market has almost nothing, of course, to do with postmodernism. By and large, the ideology through which they are incorporated is modernist: it is the ideology that brought something called "Bali" to Artaud, something called "Africa" to Picasso, and something called "Japan" to Barthes. (This incorporation as an official Other was criticized, of course, from its beginnings: Oscar Wilde once remarked that "the whole of Japan is a pure invention. There is no such country, no such people.")[30] What *is* postmodernist is Vogel's muddled conviction that African art should not be judged "in terms of [someone else's] traditional criteria." For modernism, primitive art was to be judged by putatively *universal* aesthetic criteria, and by these standards it was finally found possible to value it. The sculptors and painters who found it possible were largely seeking an Archimedean point outside their own cultures for a critique of a Weberian modernity. For *post*moderns, by contrast, these works, however they are to be understood, cannot be seen as legitimated by culture- and history-transcending standards.

What is useful in the *neotraditional* object as a model—despite its marginality in most African lives—is that its incorporation in the museum world (while many objects made by the same hands—stools, for example—live peacefully in non-bourgeois homes) reminds one that in Africa, by contrast, the distinction between high culture and mass culture, insofar as it makes sense at all, corresponds by and large to the distinction between those with and those without Western-style formal education as cultural consumers.

The fact that the distinction is to be made this way—in most of sub-Saharan Africa excluding the Republic of South Africa—means that the opposition between high culture and mass culture is available only in domains where there is a significant body of Western formal training, and this excludes (in most places) the plastic arts and music. There are distinctions of genre and audience in African musics, and for various cultural purposes there is something that we call "traditional" music that we still practice and value. But village and urban dwellers alike, bourgeois and nonbourgeois, listen, through discs and, more importantly, on the radio, to reggae, to Michael Jackson, and to King Sonny Adé.

And this means that by and large the domain in which it makes most sense is the one domain where that distinction is powerful and pervasive—namely, in African writing in Western languages. So that it is here that we find, I think, a place for consideration of the question of the *post*colonality of contemporary African culture.

Postcoloniality is the condition of what we might ungenerously call a comprador intelligentsia: of a relatively small, Western-style, Western-trained, group of writers and thinkers who mediate the trade in cultural commodities of world capitalism at the periphery. In the West they are known through the Africa they offer; their compatriots know them both through the West they present to Africa and through an Africa they have invented for the world, for each other, and for Africa.

All aspects of contemporary African cultural life—including music and some sculpture and painting, even some writings with which the West is largely not familiar—have been influenced, often powerfully, by the transition of African societies *through* colonialism, but they are not all in the relevant sense *post*colonial. For the *post* in postcolonial, like the *post* in postmodern is the *post* of the space-clearing gesture I characterized earlier: and many areas of contemporary African cultural life—what has come to be theorized as popular culture, in particular—are not in this way concerned with transcending, with going beyond, coloniality. Indeed, it might be said to be a mark of popular culture that its borrowings from international cultural forms are remarkably insensitive to—not so much dismissive of as blind to— the issue of neocolonialism or "cultural imperialism." This does not mean that theories of postmodernism are irrelevant to these forms of culture: for the internationalization of the market and the commodification of artworks are both central to them. But it *does* mean that these artworks are not understood by their producers or their consumers in terms of a postmodern*ism:* there is no antecedent practice whose claim to exclusivity of vision is rejected through these artworks. What is called "syncretism" here is made possible by the international exchange of commodities, but is not a consequence of a space-clearing gesture.

Postcolonial intellectuals in Africa, by contrast, are almost entirely dependent for their support on two institutions: the African university—an institution whose intellectual life is overwhelmingly constituted as Western—and the Euro-American publisher and reader. (Even when these writers seek to escape the West—as Ngugi wa Thiong'o did in attempting to construct a Kikuyu peasant drama—their theories of their situation are irreducibly informed by their Euro-American formation. Ngugi's conception of the writer's potential in politics is essentially that of the avant-garde, of Left modernism.)

Now this double dependence on the university and the European publisher means that the first generation of modern African novels—the generation of Achebe's *Things Fall Apart* and Laye's *L'Enfant noir*—were written in the context of notions of politics and culture dominant in the French and British university and publishing worlds in the fifties and sixties. This does not mean that they were like novels written in Western Europe at that time: for part of what was held to be obvious both by these writers and by the high culture of Europe of the day was that new literatures in new nations should be anticolonial and nationalist. These early novels seem to belong to the world of eighteenth- and nineteenth-century literary nationalism; they are theorized as the imaginative recreation of a common cultural past that is crafted into a shared tradition by the writer; they are in the tradition of Scott, whose *Minstrelsy of the Scottish Border* was intended, as he said in the preface, to "contribute somewhat to the history of my native country; the peculiar features of whose manners and character are daily melting and dissolving into those of her sister and ally." The novels of this first stage are thus realist legitimations of nationalism: they authorize a "return to traditions" while at the same time recognizing the demands of a Weberian rationalized modernity.

From the later sixties on, these celebratory novels of the first stage become rarer: Achebe, for example, moves from the creation of a usable past in *Things Fall Apart* to a cynical indictment of politics in the modern sphere in *A Man of the People*. But I should like to focus on a francophone novel of the later sixties, a novel that thematizes in an extremely powerful way many of the questions I have been asking about art and modernity: I mean, of course, Yambo Ouologuem's *Le Devoir de Violence*. This novel, like many of this second stage, represents a challenge to the novels of this first stage: it identifies the realist novel as part of the tactic of nationalist legitimation and so it is (if I may begin a catalog of its ways-of-being-*post*-this-and-that) *postrealist*.

Now postmodernism is, of course, postrealist also. But Ouologuem's postrealism is surely motivated quite differently from that of such postmodern writers as, say, Pynchon. Realism naturalizes: the originary "African novel" of Chinua Achebe (*Things Fall Apart*) and of Camara Laye (*L'Enfant noir*) is "realist." So Ouologuem is against it, rejects—indeed, assaults—the conventions of realism. He seeks to delegitimate the forms of the realist African novel, in part, surely, because what it sought to naturalize was a nationalism that, by 1968, had plainly failed. The national bourgeoisie that took on the baton of rationalization, industrialization, bureaucratization in the name of nationalism, turned out to be a kleptocracy. Their enthusiasm for nativism was a rationalization of their urge to keep the national bourgeoisies of other nations—and particularly the powerful industrialized nations—out of their way. As Jonathan Ngaté has observed, *"Le Devoir de Violence . . . deal[s] with a world in which the efficacy* of the call to the Ancestors as well as the Ancestors themselves is seriously called into question."[31] That the novel is in this way postrealist allows its author to borrow, when he needs them, the techniques of modernism, which, as we learned from Fred Jameson, are often also the techniques of postmodernism. (It is helpful to remember at this point how Yambo Ouologuem is described on the back of the Éditions Du Seuil first edition: "Né en 1940 au Mali. Admissible à l'École normale supérieure. Licencié ès Lettres. Licencié en Philosophie. Diplômé d'études supérieures d'Anglais. Prépare une thèse de doctorat de Sociologie." Borrowing from European modernism is hardly going to be difficult for someone so qualified, to be a Normalien is indeed, in Christopher Miller's charming formulation, "roughly equivalent to being baptized by Bossuet.")[32]

Christopher Miller's discussion—in *Blank Darkness*—of *Le devoir de violence* focuses usefully on theoretical questions of intertextuality raised by the novel's persistent massaging of one text after another into the surface of its own body. The book contains, for example, a translation of a passage from Graham Greene's 1934 novel *It's a Battlefield* (translated and improved, according to some readers!) and borrowings from Maupassant's *Boule de suif* (hardly an unfamiliar work for francophone readers; if this latter is a theft, it is the adventurous theft of the kleptomaniac, who dares us to catch him at it).

And the book's first sentence artfully establishes the oral mode—by then an inevitable convention of African narration—with words that Ngaté rightly describes as having the "concision and the striking beauty and power of a proverb,"[33] and mocks us in this moment because the sentence echoes the beginning of André Schwartz-Bart's decidedly un-African 1959 holocaust novel *Le Dernier des justes,* an echo that more substantial later borrowings confirm.[34]

Our <u>eyes</u> drink the flash of the sun, and, conquered, surprise themselves by weeping. Maschallah! oua bismillah! . . . An account of the bloody adventure of the niggertrash— dishonor to the men of nothing—<u>could</u> <u>easily begin in the</u> first half of this <u>century; but the true history of</u> the Blacks <u>begins</u> very much <u>earlier,</u> with the Saifs, in the year 1202 of our era, in the African kingdom of Nakem. . . .[35]

<u>Our eyes</u> receive the light of dead stars. A biography of my friend Ernie <u>could</u> <u>easily begin in the</u> second quarter of the 20th <u>century; but the true history of</u> Ernie Lévy <u>begins</u> much <u>earlier,</u> in the old anglican city of York. More precisely: on the 11 March 1185.[36]

The reader who is properly prepared will expect an African holocaust, and these echoes are surely meant to render ironic the status of the rulers of Nakem as descendants of Abraham El Héït, "le Juif noir."[37]

The book begins, then, with a sick joke at the unwary reader's expense against nativism: and the assault on realism is—here is my second signpost—postnativist; this book is a murderous antidote to a nostalgia for *Roots.* As Wole Soyinka has said in a justly well-respected reading, "the Bible, the Koran, the historic solemnity of the griot are reduced to the histrionics of wanton boys masquerading as humans."[38] It is tempting to read the attack on history here as a repudiation not of roots but of Islam, as Soyinka does when he goes on to say:

A culture which has claimed indigenous antiquity in such parts of Africa as have submitted to its undeniable attractions is confidently proven to be imperialist; worse, it is demonstrated to be essentially hostile to the indigenous culture. . . . Ouologuem pronounces the Moslem incursion into black Africa to be corrupt, vicious, decadent, elitist and insensitive. At the least such a work functions as a wide swab in the deck-clearing operation for the commencement of racial retrieval.[39]

But it seems to me much clearer to read the repudiation as a repudiation of national history; to see the text as postcolonially postnationalist as well as anti- (and thus, of course, post-) nativist. (Indeed, Soyinka's reading here seems to be driven by his own equally representative tendency—which I discussed in Chapter 4—to read Africa as race and place into everything.) Raymond Spartacus Kassoumi—who, if anyone, is the hero of this novel—is, after all, a son of the soil, but his political prospects by the end of the narrative are less than uplifting. More than this, the novel explicitly thematizes, in the anthropologist Shrobenius—an obvious echo of the name of the

German Africanist Frobenius, whose work is cited by Senghor—the mechanism by which the new elite has come to invent its traditions through the "science" of ethnography:

> Saif made up stories and the interpreter translated, Madoubo repeated in French, refining on the subtleties to the delight of Shrobenius, that human crayfish afflicted with a groping mania for resuscitating an African universe—cultural autonomy, he called it, which had lost all living reality; . . . he was determined to find metaphysical meaning in everything . . . African life, he held, was pure art. . . .[40]

At the start we have been told that "there are few written accounts and the versions of the elders diverge from those of the griots, which differ from those of the chroniclers."[41] Now we are warned off the supposedly scientific discourse of the ethnographers.[42]

Because this is a novel that seeks to delegitimate not only the form of realism but the content of nationalism, it will to that extent seem to us misleadingly to be postmodern. *Mis*leadingly, because what we have here is not postmodern*ism* but postmoderni*zation;* not an aesthetics but a politics, in the most literal sense of the term. After colonialism, the modernizers said, comes rationality; that is the possibility the novel rules out. Ouologuem's novel is typical of this second stage in that it is not written by someone who is comfortable with and accepted by the new elite, the national bourgeoisie. Far from being a celebration of the nation, then, the novels of the second stage—the postcolonial stage—are novels of delegitimation: rejecting the Western imperium, it is true, but also rejecting the nationalist project of the postcolonial national bourgeoisie. And, so it seems to me, the basis for that project of delegitimation is very much not the postmodernist one: rather, it is grounded in an appeal to an ethical universal; indeed it is based, as intellectual responses to oppression in Africa largely are based, in an appeal to a certain simple respect for human suffering, a fundamental revolt against the endless misery of the last thirty years. Ouologuem is hardly likely to make common cause with a relativism that might allow that the horrifying new-old Africa of exploitation is to be understood—legitimated—in its own local terms.

Africa's postcolonial novelists—novelists anxious to escape neocolonialism—are no longer committed to the nation, and in this they will seem, as I have suggested, misleadingly postmodern. But what they have chosen instead of the nation is not an older traditionalism but Africa—the continent and its people. This is clear enough, I think, in *Le Devoir de violence,* at the end of which Ouologuem writes:

> Often, it is true, the soul desires to dream the echo of happiness, an echo that has no past. But projected into the world, one cannot help recalling that Saïf, mourned three million times, is forever reborn to history beneath the hot ashes of more than thirty African republics.[43]

If we are to identify with anyone, *in fine,* it is with "la négraille"—the niggertrash, who have no nationality. For these purposes one republic is as good—which is to say as bad—as any other. If this postulation of oneself as African—and neither as of this or that allegedly precolonial ethnicity nor of the new nation-states—is implicit in *Le Devoir de violence,* in the important novels of V. Y. Mudimbe, *Entre les Eaux, Le Bel immonde*—recently made available in English as *Before the Birth of the Moon*—

and *L'Écart,* this postcolonial recourse to Africa is to be found nearer the surface and over and over again.[44]

There is a moment in *L'Écart,* for example, when the protagonist, whose journal the book is, recalls a conversation with the French girlfriend of his student days—the young woman on whom he reflects constantly as he becomes involved with an African woman.

> "You can't know, Isabelle, how demanding Africa is."
> "It's important for you, isn't it?"
> "To tell you the truth, I don't know . . . I really don't . . . I wonder if I'm not usually just playing around with it."
> "Nara . . . I don't understand. For me, the important thing is to be myself. Being european isn't a flag to wave."
> "You've never been wounded like . . ."
> "Your dramatizing, Nara. You carry your african-ness like a martyr. . . . That makes one wonder. . . . I'd be treating you with contempt if I played along with you."
> "The difference is that Europe is above all else an idea, a juridical institution . . . while Africa . . ."
> "Yes? . . ."
> "Africa is perhaps mostly a body, a multiple existence. . . . I'm not expressing myself very well."[45]

This exchange seems to me to capture the essential ambiguity of the postcolonial African intellectual's relation to Africa. But let me pursue Africa, finally, in Mudimbe's first novel, *Entre les eaux,* a novel that thematizes the question most explicitly.

In *Entre les eaux*—a first-person narrative—our protagonist is an African Jesuit, Pierre Landu, who has a "doctorat ne théologie et [une] licence en droit canon"[46] acquired as a student in Rome. Landu is caught between his devotion to the church and, as one would say in more protestant language, to Christ; the latter leads him to repudiate the official Roman Catholic hierarchy of his homeland and join with a group of Marxist guerrillas, intent on removing the corrupt postindependence state. When he first tells his immediate superior in the hierarchy, Father Howard, who is white, of his intentions, the latter responds immediately and remorselessly that this will be treason.

> "You are going to commit treason," the father superior said to me when I informed him of my plans.
> "Against whom?"
> "Against Christ."
> "Father, isn't it rather the West that I'm betraying. Is it still treason? Don't I have the right to dissociate myself from this christianity that has betrayed the Gospel?"
> "You are a priest, Pierre."
> "Excuse me, Father, I'm a black priest."[47]

It is important, I think, not to see the blackness here as a matter of race. It is rather the sign of Africanity. To be a black priest is to be a priest who is also an African and thus committed, nolens-volens, to an engagement with African suffering. This demand that Africa makes has nothing to do with a sympathy for African cultures and traditions; reflecting—a little later—on Father Howard's alienating response, Landu makes this plain.

> Father Howard is also a priest like me. That's the tie that binds us. Is it the only one?
> No. There's our shared tastes.
> Classical music. Vivaldi. Mozart. Bach. . . .
> And then there was our reading. The books, we used to pass each other. Our shared memories of Rome. Our impassioned discussions on the role of the priest, and on literature and on the mystery novels that we each devoured. I am closer to Father Howard than I am to my compatriots, even the priests.
> Only one thing separates us: the color of our skins.[48]

In the name of this "couleur de la peau," which is precisely the *sign* of a solidarity with Africa, Landu reaches from Roman Catholicism to Marxism, seeking to gather together the popular revolutionary energy of the latter and the ethical—and religious—vision of the former; a project he considers in a later passage, where he recalls a long-ago conversation with Monseigneur Sanguinetti in Rome. "The Church and Africa," the Monseigneur tells him, "are counting on you."[49] Landu asks in the present:

> Could the church really still count on me? I would have wished it and I wish it now. The main thing meanwhile is that Christ counts on me. But Africa? Which Africa was Sanguinetti speaking of? That of my black confrères who have stayed on the straight and narrow, or that of my parents whom I have already betrayed? Or perhaps he was even speaking of the Africa that we defend in this camp?[50]

Whenever Landu is facing a crucial decision, it is framed for him as a question about the meaning of Africa.

After he is accused of another betrayal—this time by the rebels, who have intercepted a letter to his bishop (a letter in which he appeals to him to make common cause with the rebels, to recover them for Christ)—Landu is condemned to death. As he awaits execution, he remembers something an uncle had said to him a decade earlier about "the ancestors."

> "You'll be missed by them . . . ," my uncle had said to me, ten years ago. I had refused to be initiated. What did he mean? It is I who miss them. Will that be their curse? The formula invaded me, at first unobtrusively, but then it dazzled me, stopping me from thinking: "Wait till the ancestors come down. Your head will burn, your throat will burst, your stomach will open and your feet will shatter. Wait till the ancestors come down. . . ." They had come down. And I had only the desiccation of a rationalized Faith to defend myself against Africa.[51]

The vision of modernity in this passage is not, I think, Weberian. In being postcolonial, Pierre Landu is against the rationalizing thrust of Western modernity (that modernity here, in this African setting, is represented by Catholicism confirms how little modernity has ultimately to do with secularization). And even here, when he believes he is facing his own death, the question "What does it mean to be an African?" is at the center of his mind.

A raid on the camp by government forces saves Pierre Landu from execution; the intervention of a bishop and a brother powerfully connected within the modern state saves him from the fate of a captured rebel. He retreats from the world to take up the life of a monastic with a new name—no longer Peter-on-whom-I-will-build-my-church but Mathieu-Marie de L'Incarnation—in a different, more contemplative order. As we leave him his last words, the last of the novel, are "l'humilité de ma bassesse, quelle gloire pour l'homme!"[52] Neither Marx nor Saint Thomas, the novel suggests—neither of the two great political energies of the West in Africa—offers a way forward. But this retreat to the otherworldly cannot be a political solution. Postcoloniality has, also, I think, become a condition of pessimism.

Postrealist writing; postnativist politics; a *transnational* rather than a *national* solidarity. And pessimism: a kind of *post*optimism to balance the earlier enthusiasm for *The Suns of Independence*. Postcoloniality is *after* all this: and its *post*, like postmodernism's, is also a *post* that challenges earlier legitimating narratives. And it challenges them in the name of the suffering victims of "more than thirty republics." But it challenges them in the name of the ethical universal; in the name of *humanism*, "le gloire pour l'homme." And on that ground it is not an ally for Western postmodernism but an agonist, from which I believe postmodernism may have something to learn.

For what I am calling humanism can be provisional, historically contingent, antiessentialist (in other words, postmodern), and still be demanding. We can surely maintain a powerful engagement with the concern to avoid cruelty and pain while nevertheless recognizing the contingency of that concern.[53] Maybe, then, we can recover within postmodernism the postcolonial writers' humanism—the concern for human suffering, for the victims of the postcolonial state (a concern we find everywhere: in Mudimbe, as we have seen; in Soyinka's *A Play of Giants;* in Achebe, Farah, Gordimer, Labou Tansi—the list is difficult to complete)—while still rejecting the master narratives of modernism. This human impulse—an impulse that transcends obligations to churches and to nations—I propose we learn from Mudimbe's Landu.

But there is also something to reject in the postcolonial adherence to Africa of Nara, the earlier protagonist of Mudimbe's *L'Écart:* the sort of Manicheanism that makes Africa *"a body"* (nature) against Europe's juridical reality (culture) and then fails to acknowledge—even as he says it—the full significance of the fact that Africa is also *"a multiple existence." Entre les eaux* provides a powerful postcolonial critique of this binarism: we can read it as arguing that if you postulate an either-or choice between Africa and the West, there is no place for you in the real world of politics, and your home must be the otherworldly, the monastic retreat.

If there is a lesson in the broad shape of this circulation of cultures, it is surely that we are all already contaminated by each other, that there is no longer a fully autochthonous *echt*-African culture awaiting salvage by our artists (just as there is, of course, no American culture without African roots). And there is a clear sense in some postcolonial writing that the postulation of a unitary Africa over against a monolithic West—the binarism of Self and Other—is the last of the shibboleths of the modernizers that we must learn to live without.

Already in *Le Devoir de violence,* in Ouologuem's withering critique of "Shrobéniusologie," there were the beginnings of this postcolonial critique of what we might call "alteritism," the construction and celebration of oneself as Other. Ouologuem writes, ". . . henceforth Negro art was baptized 'aesthetic' and hawked in the imaginary universe of 'vitalizing exchanges.' "[54] Then, after describing the phantasmic elaboration of some interpretative mumbo jumbo "invented by Saïf," he announces that ". . . Negro art found its patent of nobility in the folklore of mercantile intellectualism, oye, oye, oye . . ."[55] Shrobenius, the anthropologist, as apologist for "his" people; a European audience that laps up this exoticized other; African traders and producers of African art, who understand the necessity to maintain the "mysteries" that construct their product as "exotic"; traditional and contemporary elites who require a sentimentalized past to authorize their present power: all are exposed in their complex and multiple mutual complicities.

> "Witness the splendor of its art—the true face of Africa is the grandiose empires of the Middle Ages, a society marked by wisdom, beauty, prosperity, order, nonviolence, and humanism, and it is here that we must seek the true cradle of Egyptian civilisation.
>
> Thus drooling, Shrobenius derived a twofold benefit on his return home: on the one hand, he mystified the people of his own country who in their enthusiasm raised him to a lofty Sorbonnical chair, while on the other hand he exploited the sentimentality of the coons, only too pleased to hear from the mouth of a white man that Africa was 'the womb of the world and the cradle of civilization.'
>
> In consequence the niggertrash donated masks and art treasures by the ton to the acolytes of 'Shrobeniusology.'[56]

A little later, Ouologuem articulates more precisely the interconnections of Africanist mystifications with tourism, and the production, packaging, and marketing of African artworks.

> An Africanist school harnessed to the vapors of magico-religious, cosmological, and mythical symbolism had been born: with the result that for three years men flocked to Nakem—and what men!—middlemen, adventurers, apprentice bankers, politicians, salesmen, conspirators—supposedly 'scientists,' but in reality enslaved sentries mounting guard before the 'Shrobeniusological' monument of Negro pseudosymbolism.
>
> Already it had become more than difficult to procure old masks, for Shrobenius and the missionaries had had the good fortune to snap them all up. And so Saif— and the practice is still current—had slapdash copies buried by the hundredweight, or sunk into ponds, lakes, marshes, and mud holes, to be exhumed later on and sold at exorbitant prices to unsuspecting curio hunters. These three-year-old masks were said to be charged with the weight of four centuries of civilization.[57]

Ouologuem here forcefully exposes the connections we saw earlier in some of David Rockefeller's insights into the international system of art exchange, the international art world: we see the way in which an ideology of disinterested aesthetic value—the "baptism" of "Negro art" as "aesthetic"—meshes with the international commodification of African expressive culture, a commodification that requires, by the logic of the space-clearing gesture, the manufacture of Otherness. (It is a significant bonus that it also harmonizes with the interior decor of modern apartments.)

Shrobenius, "ce marchand-confectionneur d'idéologie," the ethnographer allied with Saif—image of the "traditional" African ruling caste—has invented an Africa that is a body over against Europe, the juridical institution, and Ouologuem is urging us vigorously to refuse to be thus Other.

Sara Suleri has written recently, in *Meatless Days*, of being treated as an "Otherness-machine"—and of being heartily sick of it.[58] If there is no way out for the post-colonial intellectual in Mudimbe's novels, it is, I suspect, because *as* intellectuals—a category instituted in black Africa by colonialism—we are always at risk of becoming Otherness-machines. It risks becoming our prinicpal role. Our only distinction in the world of texts to which we are latecomers is that we can mediate it to our fellows. This is especially true when postcolonial meets postmodern, for what the postmodern reader seems to demand of its Africa is all too close to what modernism—as documented in William Rubin's Primitivism exhibit of 1985—demanded of it. The role that Africa, like the rest of the Third World, plays for Euro-American post-modernism—like its better-documented significance for modernist art—must be distinguished from the role postmodernism might play in the Third World. What that might be it is, I think, too early to tell. And what happens will happen not because we pronounce upon the matter in theory but out of the changing everyday practices of African cultural life.

For all the while, in Africa's cultures, there are those who will not see themselves as Other. Despite the overwhelming reality of economic decline; despite unimaginable poverty; despite wars, malnutrition, disease, and political instability, African cultural productivity grows apace: popular literatures, oral narrative and poetry, dance, drama, music, and visual art all thrive. The contemporary cultural production of many African societies—and the many traditions whose evidences so vigorously remain—is an antidote to the dark vision of the postcolonial novelist.

And I am grateful to James Baldwin for his introduction to the *Yoruba Man with a Bicycle*—a figure who is, as Baldwin so rightly saw, polyglot, speaking Yoruba and English, probably some Hausa and a little French for his trips to Cotonou or Cameroon; someone whose "clothes do not fit him too well." He and the other men and women among whom he mostly lives suggest to me that the place to look for hope is not just to the postcolonial novel—which has struggled to achieve the insights of a Ouologuem or Mudimbe—but to the all-consuming vision of this less-anxious creativity. It matters little who it was made *for;* what we should learn from is the imagination that produced it. The *Man with a Bicycle* is produced by someone who does not care that the bicycle is the white man's invention—it is not there to be Other to the Yoruba Self; it is there because someone cared for its solidity; it is there because it will take us further than our feet will take us; it is there because machines are now as African as novelists—and as fabricated as the kingdom of Nakem.[59]

EIGHT

Altered States

Aban eεgu a, εfiri yam.
If the state is going to fall, it is from the belly.[1]

W hen I was a child in Asante, there were, I suppose, only about a million of us and there would soon be 10 million Ghanaians, but we knew that Kumasi, the country's second-largest city (built, my father said, like Rome, like so many great cities, on seven hills) had a longer and nobler history than the capital, Accra. Kumasi was a proud, bustling, busy place, a city of gorgeous parks and flowered roundabouts; people all along the west coast knew it as the capital of our famous kingdom, as the "garden city of West Africa." I grew up knowing that I lived in Asante and that the Asantehene was our king. I also grew up singing enthusiastically the Ghanaian national anthem—"Lift High the Flag of Ghana"—and knowing that Nkrumah was, first, our prime minister, then, our president. It did not occur to me as a child that the "we," of which this "our" was the adjective, was fluid, ambiguous, obscure.

I knew my father was, and cared that he was, an Asante man, and that he was, and cared that he was, a Ghanaian nationalist: proud of his role in the struggle for our independence from Britain; committed, nevertheless, to our learning English, not as the tongue of the colonizer but as the unifying language of our new and polyglot nation. It did not occur to me—it never occurred to him—that these identities might be in conflict: though it occurred to others (many of them journalists from Europe and North America) to say that of him when he joined the opposition to his old friend Nkrumah and entered Ghana's first independent parliament in the United party, with J. B. Danquah and Kofi Busia; and it occurred to many in Asante when he did not join Busia's Progress party, as it, in turn, came to power, a coup and a couple of constitutions later, when I was in my teens. I grew up knowing that we were Ghanaian nationalists and that we were Asante.

I grew up also believing in constitutional democracy, or to speak more precisely, believing that what these words stood for was important. When my father and his friends were locked up by Kwame Nkrumah in the early sixties, I was too young to think of it as anything more than a family tragedy. By the time they came out, I knew that the abolition of the legal opposition in 1960 had been a blow against democracy, that it had led naturally to imprisoning those who disagreed with our president and what my father called the "gaping sycophants" who surrounded him, that all this evil began when multiparty electoral democracy ended. Of course, I also knew that we owed respect to the chiefs of Asante (indeed, of other regions of Ghana), that their role in controlling the allocation of land, and in the settlement of family disputes, was an essential part of life. I grew up knowing we were democrats and that we respected chieftaincy.

And by the time I was old enough to be *for* democracy, I knew we were also *for* development and modernization; that this meant roads and hospitals and schools (as opposed to paths through the bush, and juju and ignorance); cities (as opposed to the idiocy of rural life); money and wages (as opposed to barter and domestic production). None of which, of course, did we take to rule out the proper pouring of libation to the ancestors, or the complex multilayered practices of the Asante funeral. If you had to wear a white coat to be a doctor, you did not have to give up *ntoma,* the togalike cloth my father wore almost always, in the world outside the hospital. In a slogan: I grew up believing in development *and* in preserving the best of our cultural heritage.

I doubt that these experiences were unusual in the (admittedly itself somewhat unusual) situation of a young person growing up around independence in sub-Saharan Africa in the household of professional people.[2] Yet it is natural enough for someone looking from Europe or North America at the political history of sub-Saharan African states since independence to see this cluster of beliefs and commitments as inconsistent. Perhaps it might be possible to hold together ethnoregional and national allegiances (African-American, southern in the United States; Welsh or northern in Britain; perhaps more controversially, Québecois in Canada); perhaps it may even be possible (with enough constitutional theory to paper over the problems) to combine social deference for a hereditary aristocracy with a form of democracy, as in Britain; perhaps postmodernism in the domain of expressive culture gives us reason for skepticism about modernization and development conceived of as inconsistent with older folkways. But few in the industrialized West, I think, have been able to proceed as blithely as we did in ignoring what must be admitted at least to be tensions here, even if they do not amount to outright contradictions.

Of course, Ghana and I have grown uneasy with all of these childhood faiths. Yet, looking back now, I can discern a pattern to these paired adherences, yoked so uneasily together—Ghana, Asante; development, heritage; democracy, chieftaincy— and it is a pattern that makes a sort of sense. For, though we would not have put it this way when I was growing up, I think that we can say that in each case, the first member of the pair was something we took to belong to the sphere of the state, the business of the government in the capital, Accra, while the second belonged to a sphere that we could call society.

But this way of thinking leaves too much obscure. In Western political theory, the state is naturally characterized in terms that it is usual to trace back, once more, to Weber: where there is a state the government claims supreme authority over a territorial domain and the right to back up that authority with coercive force. Taxes and conscription are not voluntary; the criminal law is not an optional code. Imprisonment, the lash, the gallows, stand behind state power. The sphere of society, by contrast, though equally demanding, is bound together by ethical conviction, ties of affection, shared worlds of meaning. Correlative—but, alas for theoretical convenience, only roughly correlative—with these distinctions between state and society are others: between law and custom, private and public life, the obligations of citizenship and the more elective world of communal reciprocity. Perhaps, in our theories, we imagine a state in which only the government regularly coerces—and only in matters of public concern; where personal affection and region and ethnicity play no role in the assignment and execution of state offices; where, in a formula, careers are open to talent. But there is a common currency of state and society, thus conceived, and it is the economy. Whatever the extent of state involvement in the economy (and the collapse of the Soviet empire and its model of the state-managed economy should not lead us to lose sight of the centrality of the state in all functioning economies in the modern world), there will always be enough economically at stake in the operations of the modern state for our social impulses—the call of society—to enter inextricably into the operations of government. Social relations, family relations, cannot always be bought and sold, but even in the most intimate of domestic relationships money has its uses, and in the sphere of the state, social relations— family, ethnicity, regional allegiances, clubs, societies, and associations—provide the materials of alliances.

In the United States (as in Europe) this is an all-too-familiar fact: economic interests, ethnic affiliations, regional alliances, struggle together to shape the operations of the state. In Europe and North America, with powerfully important exceptions (in Ireland and the Basque country, in "Soviet" Lithuania or in Puerto Rico), there is an overwhelming consensus that the claims of the state to the monopoly of coercion are legitimate, and they are, as a result, largely effective. Even where some of the state's specific injunctions do not have that ethical consensus behind them, this fact does not, by and large, threaten its other claims. Recall that in many American cities and states, one of the largest industries is the drug industry, every step of which, from production to distribution to consumption, is illegal. Like the so-called parallel economies of Africa, it involves state functionaries, including police officers; entails bribery and corruption of officials; mobilizes ethnic and family loyalties; and depends on the existence of subcultures whose norms simply do not fit with the legal norms enunciated in law and the pronouncements of officials. Still the majority of Americans who use and trade drugs—and thus question a central norm of the American government—do not go on to question their allegiance to the United States.

But in Ghana (as in the rest of sub-Saharan Africa) something else is going on. In Ghana, for a short period before and after independence, it may well have been true that many urban literate citizens (and some others) shared a similar allegiance to the Ghanaian state. In the high days of postindependence nationalism, many of us shared a sense of the meaning of Ghana because it was clear what it was that we were *against*—namely, British imperialism. But even then Asante had, in the minds of many, legitimate claims—at least in some domains—to obedience. And a formalistic distinction between law (enforceable, in theory, by the police power of the state) and custom (no longer entitled to coerce in spheres where the law held technical sovereignty) would help to explain nothing about how it looked to *us* at all.

Nor, for that matter, could we have made much use of a distinction between an ethnic private and a national public life. Public life in Ghana has consistently involved the ceremonial of chieftaincy; and, conversely, chiefs and heads of families, whose conceptions of obligation do not belong to the modern state, continue to claim real legitimacy and exercise substantial power in matters of marriage, inheritance, and upbringing, and through all these, of wealth.

Yet, for a time, as I say—while we were enthusiastic for national independence and Nkrumah created the first (and last) mass party in Ghana, the CPP, which involved organizations of market women and first-generation-literate "veranda boys," products of the expanding system of primary and secondary education—all these complications failed to diminish our enthusiasm. But the "we" here was, in fact, rather limited. Nkrumah's electoral support in the 1957 preindependence elections in Ghana was a 57 percent majority of half of the population registered to vote, and amounted perhaps to 18 percent of the adult population.[3] Our vision of Nkrumah is in part one of those typical illusions of modernity: Osagyefo Dr. Kwame Nkrumah, the "Redeemer," the organizer of rallies, the charismatic public speaker, the international statesman—even Nkrumah the blind tyrant—was a creature of the modern media and all these roles fit easily into our narratives; we did not see the millions (especially away from the coast) for whom he was almost as mysterious as the colonial governor who had preceded him. (I can still vividly recall the retired watchman, who had been long in service to colonial masters, who visited us annually at Christmas through much of my childhood to inquire after a calendar with photographs of the British queen. In his opinion, it was clear, independence had been a mistake.) By 1966, when the first of our many postindependence coups exiled Nkrumah, the real, if limited, enthusiasm there once had been had largely evaporated and the complications began to take up our attention. When Jerry Rawlings came to power in a coup after our third civilian constitution (itself his own creation) in 1981, his nationalist rhetoric and the resurrection of Nkrumahism generated enthusiasm mostly among students, who had not seen all this before. Cynicism about the state and its rhetoric was the order of the day. It is instructive to reflect on the processes of this disillusion.

But first we should recognize how surprising it is that there was a moment of "nationalism" at all. The state that inherited Ghana from the British was like most of the twoscore-odd sub-Saharan states of postcolonial Africa. It had a rather wide range of cultures and languages within its borders (despite the fact that much of modern Ghana was at one time or another within the hegemonic sphere of the Asante empire). There was, for example, the relatively centralized bureaucratic Asante state itself, along with various other Akan states of lesser size and power (with, in the case of Akuapem, a significant Guan-speaking subordinate ethnicity); there were the much less centralized Ewe-speaking peoples of the southeast, whose dialects were not always easily mutually intelligible and whose separation from their fellow Ewe speakers in Togo was an artifact of the division of Germany's colonial possessions at the end of the First World War; there were the significantly urbanized Ga-Adangbe who dominate the region of the capital; there were miscellaneous small chieftaincies and acephalous societies in what we in Kumasi called "the North."

In a few cases elsewhere in black Africa—Somalia, Lesotho, Swaziland—the new national states corresponded to precolonial societies with a single language; in the case of the latter two, the modern nation-state derived from a precolonial monarchy.[4] In most places, however, the new states brought together peoples who spoke different languages, had different religious traditions and notions of property, and were politically (and, in particular, hierarchically) integrated to different—often radically different—degrees. By the end of European decolonization—when more than 80 percent of black Africa's population was in the ten largest sub-Saharan Africa countries and 2 percent was in the smallest ten—even the states with the smallest populations were by and large not ethnically homogeneous.

Ghana also had a diverse ecology, ranging from coastal savannah (economically integrated into the world economy by four centuries of sea trade), through a forest belt (relatively rich from nearly a century of cocoa production), to the savannah and semiarid tropics of the northern and upper regions stretching on to Upper Volta (now Burkina Faso) and the southern fringes of the Sahara. Here, too, it was like many of the anglophone and francophone states of the West African littoral, and many of the states of East Africa—Kenya, Uganda, Malawi—are similarly economically and ecologically diverse.

Out of all these diverse cultures, economies, and ecologies, four European states—Britain, France, Portugal, and Belgium—constructed the national geography of contemporary Africa. (Spain never mattered much; Germany lost its African possessions after the First World War; after the Second World War, Italy ceased to be a player.) In Ghana, as in almost all others, the colonial language remained the language of government after independence, for the obvious reason that the choice of any other indigenous language would have favored a single linguistic group. (Even largely monolingual Somalia, as I pointed out in Chapter 1, took a while to get around to using Somali.)

If the history of metropolitan Europe in the last century and a half has been a struggle to establish statehood for nationalities, Europe left Africa at independence with states looking for nations. Once the moment of cohesion against the British was over (a moment whose meaning was greatest for those of us—often in the cities—who had had most experience of the colonizers), the symbolic register of national unity was faced with the reality of our differences.

How was Nkrumah's nationalism able to ignore the fact of our diversity? Partly, I think, because at the level of symbolism it was rather oddly unconnected with the Ghanaian state. Nkrumah's nationalist enthusiasms were, famously, Pan-Africanist. In Chapter 1 I quoted a speech Nkrumah made in Liberia in 1952: "Africa for the Africans! . . . We want to be able to govern ourselves in this country of ours without outside interference.⁵ It was natural for him to speak of "our" country anywhere in (black) Africa. At the level of generality at which Africans are opposed to Europeans, it is easy to persuade us that we have similarities: most of "us" are black, most of "them" white; we are ex-subjects, they are ex-masters; we are or were recently "traditional," they are "modern"; we are "communitarian," they are "individualistic"; and so on. That these observations are, by and large, neither very true nor very clear does not stop them from being mobilized to differentiate, in part because, in the end, "they" are mostly quite rich and "we" are mostly very poor. Only in the richest of sub-Saharan black African countries has the average annual per capita GNP exceeded a thousand dollars (Gabon, with its small population, its oil, and its rich mineral reserves heading the list at about three thousand dollars in 1988). More characteristic are the per capita GNPs of a few hundred dollars in Senegal, Ghana, Kenya, and Zambia.

It was an important part of Nkrumah's appeal, therefore, that he was central to the foundation of the Organization of African Unity, that he represented Africa in the nonaligned movement and at the UN, that he was consistently and publicly preoccupied with the complete liberation of Africa from colonial rule. Being proud to be Ghanaian, for many of us, was tied up with what Nkrumah was doing not for Ghana but for Africa. And so it is not so surprising that as decolonization continued and Ghana, impoverished in part by Nkrumah's international adventures, became less of a figure on the African scene, the post-Nkrumah state was able to appeal less and less successfully to this nationalist register.

Like the inheritors of the postcolonial state who followed him in other parts of Africa, Nkrumah had extensive ambitions for that state; they were shaped, in part, by Ghana's specific experience with colonialism. And while Ghana's cultural plurality was typical of the new states, the form of colonialism it had known was not found everywhere.

Samir Amin, a leading African political economist and director of the Third World Forum in Dakar, Senegal, has usefully classified sub-Saharan Africa's colonial experiences as falling under three broad headings. Countries like Ghana belong to the ''Africa of the colonial trade economy,'' where the slave trade had been at the heart of initial integration into the world economy, known mineral reserves were not substantial during the colonial era, and tropical agricultural products— cocoa, palm oil, coffee—were the basis of an export-oriented agricultural economy. Nigeria, with perhaps a quarter of the population of black Africa, is the most important such state. In francophone central Africa—Gabon, the Central African Republic, Congo, and Zaire—is ''Africa of the concession-owning companies,'' the creation of France and Belgium. Here low populations and a difficult climate and ecology made the tropical agriculture of West Africa a dubious proposition: concessionary companies dealing in timber, rubber, and ivory practiced a brutal form of exploitation, investing as little as possible and creating, as a result, no local surpluses and offering little in the way of Western education. (At independence in 1960 there were only three Africans among the top 4,700 civil servants in Zaire.)[6] The final colonial sphere was ''Africa of the labor reserves''—including the settler plantation economies of German Tanganyika, Kenya, and Rhodesia, and the whole of Africa south of Zaire, where the colonial economy was dominated by mining. In these areas societies were radically disrupted by the institution of new, massive, and not-always-voluntary migration to the mines and plantations.[7]

In the Africa of the colonial trade economy, the development of tropical agricultural cash crops as the heart of the economy—in our case it was cocoa that mattered—made the financing of government a matter of appropriating the agricultural surplus. Influenced as he was by notions of planning that were as likely to be advocated in those days by liberal as by socialist development economists, Nkrumah used the machinery of a national Cocoa Marketing Board (originally a colonial contrivance), with a legal purchasing and trading monopoly and a large agricultural extension division, to supervise the state's extraction of money from the cocoa economy. Production was not nationalized; marketing (and thus access to the foreign exchange value of the commmodity) was. In theory the surplus generated by this monopsony was to be used to finance development; in practice it went to the cities. As the predominant source of money profits in our economy, the Cocoa Marketing Board and the state that "owned" it—which is to say all the politicians and bureaucrats who had some sort of leverage—were prime sites for enrichment. In other systems of political economy, different methods of financing the state suggested themselves, often to much the same effect.

But despite the variations in the political economy of empire, the colonial systems had shared a fundamental set of structuring assumptions: in each sphere the dominant economic concern was at the center of metropolitan attention, and all colonies were supposed to be economically self-financing until after the Second World War; this included the financing of their own administration. As a result, once roughly half of the colonial government revenues had been spent on paying for expatriate bureaucrats and another sixth had been spent on servicing loans raised for capital expenditures, many of which were in the interest of control rather than development, there was little left for the cultivation—through education, health, and social services—of human capital. Outside the maintenance of an economic and political order within which tropical agriculture or labor reserves or concessions could develop, colonial management had very limited interests. "The formal agencies transferred to African hands were . . . alien in derivation, functionally conceived, bureaucratically designed, authoritarian in nature and primarily concerned with issues of domination rather than legitimacy," as a recent study observes.[8] The colonial states were made for raising— not spending—government revenues. By 1960 only one in six adults in Africa was literate, and in Belgian and Portuguese possessions there were hardly any university graduates at all.

In view of the limited aims of colonial governance, it is perhaps unsurprising how few were the foreign administrators, the colonialists, who were required to maintain the short-lived colonial hegemony. Just as the British had "ruled" the Indian subcontinent through an Indian Civil Service with under a thousand British members, so the British and French and Portuguese colonial civil services were massively outnumbered by the populations supposedly in their charge. The armies and police forces that kept the colonial peace were officered by Europeans but manned by African subjects.

The apparent ease of colonial administration generated in the inheritors of the postcolonial nation the illusion that control of the state would allow them to pursue as easily their much more ambitious objectives. "Seek ye first the political kingdom," Nkrumah famously urged. But that kingdom was designed to manage limited goals. Once it was turned to the tasks of massive developments in infrastructure—to the building of roads and dams, schools and government offices—and to universal primary education and the enormous expansion of health and agricultural extension services, it proved unequal to the task. When the postcolonial rulers inherited the apparatus of the colonial state, they inherited the reins of power; few noticed, at first, that they were not attached to a bit.

One reason, of course, was that planning and directing an economy requires not only will but knowledge. And economic planning in sub-Saharan Africa has had to rely on very modest statistical bases. But a second crucial reason was exactly the ethnoregional loyalties with which I began.

These were often not especially old, it is important to note, being the product, often—in ways I have discussed and will take up again finally in Chapter 9—of responses to colonial and postcolonial experiences. When people from related cultures speaking similar languages arrived in the colonial towns and cities; when they listened to programs on the radio, transmitted in a dialect related to their own; when they realized that there were other parts of their countries where people had different practices, an old and vague body of shared cultural practice was often transformed into a new campaigning ethnicity. In many places, then, newly organized ethnoregional identities are extremely powerful. Here, however, was another point where differences in colonial experience mattered. For British and French colonial administrations were guided by very different theories of empire, and while ethnoregional affiliations are central across the anglophone-francophone divide, one result of these different theories has been a difference not so much in the importance of ethnicity—it is crucial everywhere—as in the role it plays in the postcolonial state.

British indirect rule maintained "native administrations," attempting to regulate the colonial states' limited interests in taxes and order by using the structures of existing precolonial states. So far as was possible, attempts were made, with the aid of official colonial anthropologists, to understand what came to be called "customary law" and to allow traditional elites to enforce those customs—in marriage and land rights, for example—that were (roughly) consistent with British mores. Buganda—the kingdom at the heart of modern Uganda that gave the new republic its capital—and the northern Moslem states of Nigeria were like Asante in fitting with the monarchical vision of the Indian civil servants from among whom were recruited the colonial officers who invented British colonial policy in Africa. (Where there were no traditional rulers to support, as in eastern Nigeria among the Igbo-speaking peoples, the colonial authorities sought to invent a form of "chieftaincy.")

The result of this policy, of course, was that, especially in places—like Asante, in Ghana, Buganda in Uganda, or in the Islamic states of northern Nigeria—where there were strong precolonial state structures on which to build, many local elites were not at all happy at independence to defer to the centralizing impulses of the independent states. This process helped produce in Nigeria, for example, the strong centripetal forces that gave rise to the Nigerian civil war of the late sixties. What began as a pogrom against Igbo traders in northern Nigeria led first to Igbo secession and then to a civil war in which Yoruba people aligned with the North to "save the union."

In Ghana, too, when we have had civilian elections in the period since Nkrumah, parties have usually come with "tribal" labels; labels whose force has little to do with the announced intentions of their leaders. Certainly, the Asante kingdom in which I grew up was a source of resistance to Nkrumah's vision of the nation. The party that came to focus parliamentary opposition to Nkrumah in the late fifties, in the first years after independence, was the United party, whose founders and electoral support were solidly in Asante. Because of the association of Nkrumah's opposition with Asante, in particular, and the wider sphere of Akan societies in general, Busia's Progress Party in the 1969 elections was seen as Asante; the opposition to Busia, Gbedemah's National Alliance of Liberals, was Ewe (at least, in Asante eyes) because Gbedemah was. Even the tiny United Nationalist party my father founded for the second republic, known by its Akan slogan "Abaa basε," came to be identified with Ga people and the capital. Traveling on public transport in Akan areas of Ghana, in the eighties, one heard (if one understood Twi, the language of most of Ghana's Akan peoples)[9] the present government of Jerry Rawlings, whose mother was Ewe, discussed as an instrument of Ewe domination (an accusation that seems only marginally more reasonable than the allegation that he represents the domination of Scotland, through his father).

The French colonial project, by contrast with the British, entailed the evolution of francophone Africans; its aim was to produce a more homogeneous francophone elite. Schools did not teach in "native" languages, and the French did not assign substantial powers to revamped precolonial administrations. You might suppose, therefore, that the French project of creating a class of black "evolués" had laid firmer foundations for the postcolonial state. To the extent that precolonial political relations were successfully extirpated, they could not be the basis of resistance to the penetration of state power.

And it is certainly true that some of the states of the old French African Empire—in particular, Senegal and Ivory Coast in the West, and Cameroon and Gabon further east—have been relatively stable. But this has not, in my view, been the result of the eradication of ethnicity. The majority of French colonies have chosen to stay connected to France, and all but Guinée (which hardly has had a record of stable progress) have accepted varying degrees of "neocolonial" supervision by the metropole. No military coups have been possible in Ivory Coast, for example, because the defense of the state apparatus is in the hand of French troops stationed there (while reinforcements can be flown in from elsewhere); in Gabon, the French actually removed some soldiers who had the temerity to attempt to install themselves by way of a coup. And while Dahomey (later Benin) had an average of about one coup per year in its first decade of independence, they involved the circulation of power among a small group, usually with the tacit consent of the Quai d'Orsay. (That the French have recently officially withdrawn from this commitment poses problems for a number of states.) The CFA franc, used throughout almost all the former French colonies in West and central Africa, is maintained convertible by France, and this also limits the autonomy of the states, ruling out the sort of massive inflations caused by the printing of money that we witnessed in Ghana in the midseventies under General Acheampong, and thus also helps to maintain political stability.

But the fact is that despite these legacies of the difference between British and French approaches to colonial policy and the politics of decolonization, figures such as Félix Houphouët-Boigny, Ivory Coast's leader since independence, have had to play a complex ethnoregional balancing game in managing the forces that keep them in power. The reason is simple: because, as I have suggested, ethnicities can be new as well as old, merely removing old political institutions—chieftaincy is largely ceremonial in Ivory Coast—has not wiped out the power of cultural commonalities. (This idea should hardly surprise Americans: African-Americans have a politicized ethnicity without any traditional systems of rule.) President Houphouët-Boigny of Ivory Coast hails from a small town in the Baoule region of southeastern Ivory Coast (home, too, you will recall to Lela Kouakou). In the precolonial era the Baoule were a relatively decentralized group speaking an Akan language, held together by complex affiliations of trade and marriage—certainly not a great kingdom like their Akan neighbors in the Asante state to their east. But because the president is Baoule, and because migrants to Abidjan, the capital, discover the significance of the cultures they bring with them as modes of association in urban life, being Baoule (and, equally importantly, not being Baoule) in a capital where the president *is* Baoule comes to have profound significance. Furthermore, the president, in building his support in regions other than his own, has practiced a careful policy of including representatives of all the country's regions in his party—the Parti Democratique de la Côte d'Ivoire—and in his cabinet.

In the lusophone states of Angola and Mozambique, which achieved independence through long colonial wars in which the resistance was dominated by Marxists, their Marxism—whatever it amounted to—led the United States (acting often in concert with South Africa) and the Soviet Union (acting sometimes through Cuba) to play out their mutual antagonisms with African lives. In each of these countries a major preoccupation of the central government is an opposition that is, in large part, and at least in military terms, the creation—if not the creature—of South Africa and the United States. But here, too, ethnoregional affiliations have played a substantial role in shaping these civil wars; the National Union for the Total Independence of Angola (UNITA), the South African–backed resistance to the government of Angola, for example, is strongest among some southern ethnic groups.

In all their extremely varied circumstances, those who seek to control the institutions of the African state have to mobilize the standard repertory of the resources of statecraft. They can use the symbolism through which Nkrumah captured the attention of so many; they may offer material rewards and the Hobbesian virtues of security; and (when the carrot fails) they can use the coercive stick.

Deteriorating terms of trade, the oil shocks of the seventies, droughts, and a good deal of mismanagement—some of it careless, some well intentioned, much venally oblivious to the common good—have meant that the states of sub-Saharan Africa have few resources to buy loyalty and few achievements since independence to earn it in symbolic coin. As for coercion, this, too, requires resources for surveillance and enforcement. To the extent that African states have continued to be able to offer both carrot and stick, it has often been because the international community has provided (admittedly limited) financial and military support to regimes, in large part because national governments and multilateral donors have only recently tried to help the citizens of African states without supporting their governments. As a result of notions of international legality, and the widespread acceptance (at least in theory) of the idea that relations between states should respect principles of noninterference in each others' internal affairs, state elites in Africa have been able to resist, in the name of legality, attempts to keep their hands out of the aid pot. But increasingly, under the coordinated instrumentalities of the IMF and the World Bank, programs of so-called structural adjustment have forced elites to accept reduced involvement in the economy as the price of the financial (and technical) resources of international capital.[10] The price of shoring up the state is a frank acknowledgement of its limits: a reining in of the symbolic, material, and coercive resources of the state.

Because of the role of the state in mediating between citizens in different countries, there is an obvious role for even the weakened states of contemporary Africa in facilitating the integration of African economies. This is a goal toward which a proliferation of regional organizations is allegedly aimed: the Economic Community of West African states (ECOWAS); the francophone Communauté Economique de l'Afrique de l'Ouest (CEAO); the South African Development Coordination Conference (SADCC); and l'Organisation pour la Mise en Valeur du Fleuve Sénégal (OMVS). These and a host of other organizations—under the broad umbrella of the OAU—have sought such grand goals as free movement of labor (ECOWAS) and the lifting of trade barriers (CEAO), and they have done so, on the whole, without much success. (SADCC has set itself more modest goals and has modestly achieved some of them, united, in part, so far, by their common enmity to and dependence on the apartheid state.)

These international organizations demonstrate the problem—which we also see in the European community, and which Americans should remember from their Civil War—that the integration of states often poses a threat to those states' elites.[11] In fact, far from wanting to facilitate intraregional trade, many African state elites have depended on the existence of barriers to trade and finance as a mechanism for making money, continuing in the long tradition of African rulers who have lived off taxes on trade. One of the most successful patterns of trade in southeastern Ghana in the seventies was the smuggling of cocoa (eventually a majority of the eastern region's production!) into the neighboring Republic of Togo, a mechanism that circumvented the state's attempt to profit both from the difference between the prices it offered to farmers and the world market price and from artificial exchange rates and control of access to foreign exchange. And, conversely, one of the most valued commodities in Ghana at many periods since independence has been the import license, which, given artificial exchange rates and limited foreign exchange, was often more like a license to print money.

And what of the Hobbesian currency of order? In the midseventies, as the Ghanaian state began its precipitous decline, I was teaching in Ghana. As it happens, one of my tasks at the university was to teach political philosophy, and, in particular, the *Leviathan*. For a Hobbesian, I suppose, the withdrawal of the Ghanaian state, in the face of its incapacity to raise the income to carry out its tasks, should have led to disaster. Yet, despite the extent to which the government was not in control, Ghanaian life was not a brutish war of all against all. Life went on. Not only did people not "get away with murder," even though the police would usually not have been in a position to do anything about it if they did, but people made deals, bought and sold goods, owned houses, married, raised families.

If anything could be said about the role of state officials (including the army and the police), it was that by and large their intervention was as likely to get in the way of these arrangements as to aid them, as likely to be feared and resented as welcomed. For many Ghanaians, and especially those in the culturally more homogeneous world of rural farming people—a world where one language, a mother tongue other than English, the language of our colonizers and the government that succeeded them, was sovereign—what mattered was the regulation of life through the shared and intelligible norms that grew out of the responses of precolonial cultures to their engagement with European imperialism. Disputes in urban as well as in rural areas were likely to end up in arbitration, between heads of families, or in the courts of "traditional" chiefs and queen mothers, in procedures that people felt they could understand and, at least to some extent, manage: once the lawyers and the magistrates and the judges of the colonial (and, now, with little change, the postcolonial) legal system came into play, most people knew that what happened was likely to pass beyond their comprehension and control.[12]

In these circumstances, an argument for the state as the provider of security would rightly have been laughed to scorn. Only in a few extreme situations—among them Uganda, since the depredations of Idi Amin—have things reached a point of Hobbesian crisis. Even in Nigeria, where urban armed robbery and banditry on the highways have become accepted inconveniences, citizens are unlikely to see the state as a solution, since (rightly or wrongly) they seem to suspect that the rulers have allies (or surrogates) through whom they profit from these offenses against order.

Yet despite all their limitations, African states persist, and, so it seems to me, in Ghana, as in a number of other places, the decline has been halted. I am not in a position to judge how much of this can be credited to the policies of structural adjustment whose strictly economic effects have been a good deal less positive than the World Bank has sometimes claimed. But in trying to make sense of what has happened with the return of the state in Ghana, I think it is useful to point to the way in which the government has become a facilitator, rather than a director, mobilizing and enabling social allegiances that are largely autonomous. And it is important to be clear that I am not speaking only of the mobilization of ethnoregional (or "tribal") allegiances.

To explain what I mean, it will help to return to Kumasi.

One of the most important organizations in my grandfather's life was the Asante Kotoko society, a modern Asante organization that engaged in various, often charitable, activities. Equally important, I suspect, was the Masonic lodge of which he was master (the picture of him that hangs in my parents' home shows him in his Masonic outfit). All over Africa in the colonial period, new social organizations developed, drawing sometimes, like the Masons, on imported European models, sometimes building on traditional secret societies, guilds, and cults. When people moved to towns, they often formed hometown societies (*associations des originaires*)—like the Umuofia Progressive Union in Chinua Achebe's *No Longer at Ease;* among the most important other forms of organization were many centered on Christian churches and Islamic mosques.[13]

It became clear in the seventies, and increasingly in the eighties, that organizations in Kumasi like the Methodist church (to which my father belonged) and smaller churches (such as my mother's) were becoming more and more central in organizing the financing, building, staffing, and equipping of schools; in supporting the city hospital; and working, often in combination with each other and with the leaders of the Moslem community and the Catholic archbishop, to maintain orphanages and homes for the mentally ill and old people without families to care for them. (Indeed, when he stopped working within state politics in the mideighties, it was to his church and its institutional politics that my father, like many others, turned his attention.)

It was not that churches and mosques had not done these things earlier: much of the best secondary schooling in Ghana has been in church schools since my father was a boy, and mission hospitals are a familiar feature of the African landscape. Moslems are obliged as a matter of religious duty to support the poor. What was significant about these changes in the last decade and a half was that they involved explicit recognition that these organizations (and other groups, such as the Rotary Club) were taking over functions formerly reserved to government, and that they were doing so in circumstances where state officials were only too keen to have their aid.

But it has not only been the churches. Chiefs and elders have organized the maintenance of "public" roads; business organizations and other private groups have provided food for "state" schools; citizens groups have bought and imported medical equipment for "government" hospitals. Along with new but ethnically based clubs, universalist religious organizations and transplanted societies like the Masons, the institutions of chieftaincy, in Asante and elsewhere, also began increasingly to carry out what were formerly government functions: mediating between labor and management in industrial disputes, for example.

So that one might say in a general way that allegiances whose salience depends on the ways in which all the various forms of association have economic, affectional, and symbolic rewards—rewards, now often substantially exceeding those formerly available to the state—came to be used to carry out what were formerly state functions, *and that the state acquiesced in this*. The significance of the withdrawal of the state goes beyond official announcements in the capital; local bureaucrats in towns and villages increasingly rely on nonstate associations to carry out their functions. The management of "government" old-people's homes and orphanages in Kumasi depends crucially on "private" support, on the cooperation of chiefs, business people, and community leaders in mobilizing and providing support.

To the extent that the government provides some technical assistance and serves a coordinating function in this process, we can speak, as I said, of the state adopting a role now not as *directing* but as *facilitating* certain functions; this is surely to be welcomed to the extent that it increases the control of citizens over their own lives.[14] As I have suggested, it has always been true that in large parts of Africa, "tribalism"—what, in Ivory Coast, is half humorously called geopolitics, the politics of geographical regions, the mobilization and management of ethnic balancing—far from being an obstacle to governance, is what makes possible any government at all. And we can see this new role as facilitator—acknowledging the associations of society rather than trying to dominate to ignore or to eradicate them— as an extension of this established pattern.

While it has occurred at different rates and with different effects, the proliferation of nonstate organizations is, if anything is, a universal phenomenon in postcolonial Africa. And it is important to be clear that the ethnoregional and religious associations that I have been focusing on are only first among many. Sports clubs, market-women's groups, professional organizations, trade unions, and farming cooperatives; all provide the multifarious rewards of association. In many of these organizations—whether it be a sports club or a choir or an *association des originaires* or the Asante Kotoko Society—there is a remarkable degree of formality: elections, rules of procedure (in the anglophone world, sometimes even Robert's Rules), and a considerable concern with the responsibility of leaders—those who manage the organization's day-to-day life and, in particular, its finances; a concern with constitutions and procedure is a key feature of churches in Ghana and elsewhere, and where the Catholic church sets antidemocratic procedures for the church itself, it cannot stop the development of lay associations—a proliferation of what we might call paraecclesial organizations—in which the very same phenomena occur. Women's "auxiliaries"—whether they be auxiliary to church or union organizations —allow women, who have, by and large, been much worse treated (and a good deal worse represented) in the postcolonial state, access to the practice of something like democratic participation. This is not an exclusively urban phenomenon, either. Clubs, associations, and cooperatives abound in the rural sector.

These organizations and their experiences with autonomous and relatively democratic organization are, I believe, of tremendous significance for the development of public life in Africa, and for the simplest of reasons: they give people a chance to practice participatory modes of organizing communal life; they offer the experience of autonomy. As a result it will become increasingly difficult for weak states to maintain legitimacy without offering such forms of democratic participation. In 1989 and 1990 there were riots in Ivory Coast and in Kenya (two of the stablest and economically strongest African states), in each case plausibly connected with a sense that the president, in particular, and the elite, more generally, were not responsive to the concerns of his people. We have seen in Eastern Europe how the removal of the army as a mechanism of control leads to resistance to apparently well-established authoritarian states with elaborate security apparatuses and even the appearance of some degree of legitimacy. Many African states have none of these to fall back on.

Democracy in this context is not simply a matter of parliaments and elections— though these would be welcomed by some, though not always the most thoughtful, in every state in Africa—but entails the development of mechanisms by which the rulers can be restrained by the ruled. And in Africa, without such a compact, citizens have few reasons to acquiesce to the wishes (or the whims) of those who claim to rule. Paradoxically, so it seems to me, it is the state that needs democracy, more than the citizen.

But while it is easy to remark the inadequacy of the nation-state model in face of the complex institutions and allegiances through which civil society may be organized, it may be too soon to pronounce on the outcome. Clearly, if the state is ever to reverse recent history and expand the role it plays in the lives of its subjects, it will have to learn something about the surprising persistence of these "premodern" affiliations, the cultural and political fretwork of relations through which our very identity is conferred.

When I was about eight, I fell very ill. Toward the end of my couple of months in bed in the local hospital, the English queen paid her first postindependence visit to Ghana. She and her husband and the president of Ghana, Osagyefo Dr. Kwame Nkrumah, duly arrived in Kumasi and made their way through the hospital, passing, as they did so, by my bed. The queen, whose mastery of small talk is proverbial, asked me how I was, and I, in a literal fever of excitement at meeting my mother's queen and my father's president all on the same day, mumbled with equal, but perhaps more excusable, fatuousness, that I was quite well. Throughout all this, the president, who had only recently locked up my father, stared at the ceiling tapping his foot (making, as it turned out, a mental note to return my doctor to what was then still Rhodesia). When they had passed through, I went, against the orders of my doctor and to the consternation of the nurses, to the window and looked out in time to see an extraordinary sight: the duke of Edinburgh and the president of Ghana trying, halfheartedly, to pull an ancient Asante sword out of the ground in which it was embedded. The sword, tradition had it, was put there by Okomfo Anokye, the great priest of Asante, who with the first great king, Osei Tutu, had founded the kingdom two and a half centuries earlier. Not long after independence, the colonial "Central Hospital," where I was, had been renamed Okomfo Anokye Hospital. Tradition also said that the great priest had declared that, with all the spells he had spoken, if the sword were ever to be pulled out of the ground, the Asante nation would fall apart into the many units from which he and Osei Tutu had forged it.

It seemed to me, from way up above the crowd of dignitaries, that Nkrumah's tug on the sword was even more halfhearted than the duke's. No Ghanaian ruler could even jestingly simulate an assault on Asante unity here in the heartland. Now, long after Nkrumah has gone to his ancestors, Asante, of course, remains; refashioned, perhaps, but strangely obdurate. The sword, they tell me, has disappeared.

NINE

African Identities

It is, of course true that the African identity is still in the making. There isn't a final identity that is African. But, at the same time, there *is* an identity coming into existence. And it has a certain context and a certain meaning. Because if somebody meets me, say, in a shop in Cambridge, he says "Are you from Africa?" Which means that Africa means something to some people. Each of these tags has a meaning, and a penalty and a responsibility.[1]

CHINUA ACHEBE

The cultural life of most of black Africa remained largely unaffected by European ideas until the last years of the nineteenth century, and most cultures began our own century with ways of life formed very little by direct contact with Europe. Direct trade with Europeans—and especially the slave trade—had structured the economies of many of the states of the West African coast and its hinterland from the mid-seventeenth century onward, replacing the extensive gold trade that had existed at least since the Carthaginian empire in the second century B.C.E. By the early nineteenth century, as the slave trade went into decline, palm nut and groundnut oils had become major exports to Europe, and these were followed later by cocoa and coffee. But the direct colonization of the region began in earnest only in the later nineteenth century, and European administration of the whole of West Africa was only accomplished—after much resistance—when the Sokoto caliphate was conquered in 1903.

On the Indian ocean, the eastward trade, which sent gold and slaves to Arabia, and exchanged spices, incense, ivory, coconut oil, timber, grain, and pig iron for Indian silk and fine textiles, and pottery and porcelain from Persia and China, had dominated the economies of the East African littoral until the coming of the Portuguese disrupted the trade in the late fifteenth century. From then on European trade became increasingly predominant, but in the mid-nineteenth century the major economic force in the region was the Arab Omanis, who had captured Mombasa from the Portuguese more than a century earlier. Using slave labor from the African mainland, the Omanis developed the profitable clove trade of Zanzibar, making it, by the 1860s, the world's major producer. But in most of East Africa, as in the West, extended direct contact with Europeans was a late-nineteenth-century phenomenon, and colonization occurred essentially only after 1885.

In the south of the continent, in the areas where Bantu-speaking people predominate, few cultures had had any contact with Europeans before 1900. By the end of the century the region had adopted many new crops for the world economy; imports of firearms, manufactured in the newly industrialized West, had created a new political order, based often on force; and European missionaries and explorers—of whom David Livingstone was, for Westerners, the epitome—had traveled almost everywhere in the region. The administration of southern Africa from Europe was established in law only by the ending, in 1902, of the Boer War.

Not surprisingly, then, European cultural influence in Africa before the twentieth century was extremely limited. Deliberate attempts at change (through missionary activity or the establishment of Western schools) and unintended influence (through contact with explorers and colonizers in the interior, and trading posts on the coasts) produced small enclaves of Europeanized Africans. But the major cultural impact of Europe is largely a product of the period since the First World War.

To understand the variety of Africa's contemporary cultures, therefore, we need, first, to recall the variety of the precolonial cultures. Differences in colonial experience have also played their part in shaping the continent's diversities, but even identical colonial policies identically implemented working on the very different cultural materials would surely have produced widely varying results.

No doubt we can find generalizations at a certain abstract level, which hold true of most of black Africa before European conquest. It is a familiar idea in African historigography that Africa was the last continent in the old world with an "uncaptured" peasantry, largely able to use land without the supervision of feudal overlords and able, if they chose, to market their products through a complex system of trading networks.[2] While European ruling classes were living off the surplus of peasants and the newly developing industrial working class, African rulers were essentially living off taxes on trade. But if we could have traveled through Africa's many cultures in those years—from the small groups of Bushman hunter-gatherers, with their stone-age materials, to the Hausa kingdoms, rich in worked metal—we should have felt in every place profoundly different impulses, ideas, and forms of life. To speak of an African identity in the nineteenth century—if an identity is a coalescence of mutually responsive (if sometimes conflicting) modes of conduct, habits of thought, and patterns of evaluation; in short, a coherent kind of human social psychology—would have been "to give to aery nothing a local habitation and a name."

Yet there is no doubt that now, a century later, an African identity is coming into being. I have argued throughout these essays that this identity is a new thing; that it is the product of a history, some of whose moments I have sketched; and that the bases through which so far it has largely been theorized—race, a common historical experience, a shared metaphysics—presuppose falsehoods too serious for us to ignore.

Every human identity is constructed, historical; every one has its share of false presuppositions, of the errors and inaccuracies that courtesy calls "myth," religion "heresy," and science "magic." Invented histories, invented biologies, invented cultural affinities come with every identity; each is a kind of role that has to be scripted, structured by conventions of narrative to which the world never quite manages to conform.

Often those who say this—who deny the biological reality of races or the literal truth of our national fictions—are treated by nationalists and "race men" as if they are proposing genocide or the destruction of nations, as if in saying that there is literally no Negro race one was obliterating all those who claim to be Negroes, in doubting the story of Okomfo Anokye one is repudiating the Asante nation. This is an unhelpful hyperbole, but it is certainly true that there must be contexts in which a statement of these truths is politically inopportune. I am enough of a scholar to feel drawn to truth telling, *ruat caelum;* enough of a political animal to recognize that there are places where the truth does more harm than good.

But, so far as I can see, we do not have to choose between these impulses: there is no reason to believe that racism is always—or even usually—advanced by denying the existence of races; and, though there is some reason to suspect that those who resist legal remedies for the history of racism might use the nonexistence of races to argue in the United States, for example, against affirmative action, that strategy is, as a matter of logic, easily opposed. For, as Tvetzan Todorov reminds us, the existence of racism does not require the existence of races. And, we can add, nations are real enough, however invented their traditions.[3]

To raise the issue of whether these truths are truths to be uttered is to be forced, however, to face squarely the real political question: the question, itself, as old as political philosophy, of when we should endorse the ennobling lie. In the real world of practical politics, of everyday alliances and popular mobilizations, a rejection of races and nations in theory can be part of a program for coherent political practice, only if we can show more than that the black race—or the Shona tribe or any of the other modes of self-invention that Africa has inherited—fit the common pattern of relying on less than the literal truth. We would need to show not that race and national history are falsehoods but they are useless falsehoods at best or—at worst—dangerous ones: that another set of stories will build us identities through which we can make more productive alliances.

The problem, of course, is that group identity seems to work only—or, at least, to work best—when it is seen by its members as natural, as "real." Pan-Africanism, black solidarity, can be an important force with real political benefits, but it doesn't work without its attendant mystifications. (Nor, to turn to the other obvious exemplum, is feminism without its occasional risks and mystifications either.) Recognizing the constructedness of the history of identities has seemed to many incompatible with taking these new identities with the seriousness they have for those who invent—or, as they would no doubt rather say, discover—and possess them.[4] In sum, the demands of agency seem always—in the real world of politics—to *entail a misrecognition of its genesis;* you cannot build alliances without mystifications and mythologies. And this chapter is an exploration of ways in which Pan-African solidarity can be appropriated by those of us whose positions as intellectuals—as searchers after truth—make it impossible for us to live through the falsehoods of race and tribe and nation, whose understanding of history makes us skeptical that nationalism and racial solidarity can do the good that they can do without the attendant evils of racism—and other particularisms; without the warring of nations.

Where are we to start? I have argued often in these pages against the forms of racism implicit in much talk of Pan-Africanism. (And in other places, especially in "Racisms" and "Racism and Moral Pollution," I have offered further arguments against these racist presuppositions.)

But these objections to a biologically rooted conception of race may still seem all too theoretical: if Africans can get together around the idea of the Black Person, if they can create through this notion productive alliances with African-Americans and people of African descent in Europe and the Caribbean, surely these theoretical objections should pale in the light of the practical value of these alliances. But there is every reason to doubt that they can. Within Africa—in the OAU, in the Sudan, in Mauritania[5]—racialization has produced arbitrary boundaries and exacerbated tensions; in the diaspora alliances with other peoples of color, qua victims of racism—people of south Asian descent in England, Hispanics in the United States, "Arabs" in France, Turks in Germany—have proved essential.

In short, I think it is clear enough that a biologically rooted conception of race is both dangerous in practice and misleading in theory: African unity, African identity, need securer foundations than race.

The passage from Achebe with which I began this chapter continues in these words: "All these tags, unfortunately for the black man, are tags of disability." But it seems to me that they are not so much labels of disability as disabling labels; which is, in essence, my complaint against Africa as a racial mythology—the Africa of Crummell and Du Bois (from the New World) and of the *bolekaja* critics (from the Old); against Africa as a shared metaphysics—the Africa of Soyinka; against Africa as a fancied past of shared glories—the Africa of Diop and the "Egyptianists."

Each of these complaints can be summarized in a paragraph.

"Race" disables us because it proposes as a basis for common action the illusion that black (and white and yellow) people are fundamentally allied by nature and, thus, without effort; it leaves us unprepared, therefore, to handle the "intraracial" conflicts that arise from the very different situations of black (and white and yellow) people in different parts of the economy and of the world.

The African metaphysics of Soyinka disables because it founds our unity in gods who have not served us well in our dealings with the world—Soyinka never defends the "African World" against Wiredu's charge that since people die daily in Ghana because they prefer traditional herbal remedies to Western medicines, "any inclination to glorify the unanalytical [i.e. the traditional] cast of mind is not just retrograde; it is tragic." Soyinka has proved the Yoruba pantheon a powerful literary resource, but he cannot explain why Christianity and Islam have so widely displaced the old gods, or why an image of the West has so powerful a hold on the contemporary Yoruba imagination; nor can his mythmaking offer us the resources for creating economies and polities adequate to our various places in the world.

And the Egyptianists—like all who have chosen to root Africa's modern identity in an imaginary history—require us to see the past as the moment of wholeness and unity; tie us to the values and beliefs of the past; and thus divert us (this critique is as old as Césaire's appraisal of Tempels) from the problems of the present and the hopes of the future.

If an African identity is to empower us, so it seems to me, what is required is not so much that we throw out falsehood but that we acknowledge first of all that race and history and metaphysics do not enforce an identity: that we can choose, within broad limits set by ecological, political, and economic realities what it will mean to be African in the coming years.

I do not want to be misunderstood. We are Africans already. And we can give numerous examples from multiple domains of what our being African means. We have, for example, in the OAU and the African Development Bank, and in such regional organizations as SADDC and ECOWAS, as well as in the African caucuses of the agencies of the UN and the World Bank, African institutions. At the Olympics and the Commonwealth games, athletes from African countries are seen as Africans by the world—and, perhaps, more importantly, by each other. Being African already has "a certain context and a certain meaning."

But, as Achebe suggests, that meaning is not always one we can be happy with, and that identity is one we must continue to reshape. And in thinking about how we are to reshape it, we would do well to remember that the African identity is, for its bearers, only one among many. Like all identities, institutionalized before anyone has permanently fixed a single meaning for them—like the German identity at the beginning of this century, or the American in the latter eighteenth century, or the Indian identity at independence so few years ago—being African is, for its bearers, one among other salient modes of being, all of which have to be constantly fought for and rethought. And indeed, in Africa, it is another of these identities that provides one of the most useful models for such rethinking; it is a model that draws on other identities central to contemporary life in the subcontinent, namely, the constantly shifting redefinition of "tribal" identities to meet the economic and political exigencies of the modern world.

Once more, let me quote Achebe:

> The duration of awareness, of consciousness of an identity, has really very little to do with how deep it is. You can suddenly become aware of an identity which you have been suffering from for a long time without knowing. For instance, take the Igbo people. In my area, historically, they did not see themselves as Igbo. They saw themselves as people from this village or that village. In fact in some place "Igbo" was a word of abuse; they were the "other" people, down in the bush. And yet, after the experience of the Biafran War, during a period of two years, it became a very powerful consciousness. But it was *real* all the time. They all spoke the same language, called "Igbo," even though they were not using that identity in any way. But the moment came when this identity became very very powerful . . . and over a very short period.

A short period it was, and also a tragic one. The Nigerian civil war defined an Igbo identity: it did so in complex ways, which grew out of the development of a common Igbo identity in colonial Nigeria, an identity that created the Igbo traders in the cities of northern Nigeria as an identifiable object of assault in the period that led up to the invention of Biafra.

Recognizing Igbo identity as a new thing is not a way of privileging other Nigerian identities: each of the three central ethnic identities of modern political life—Hausa-Fulani, Yoruba, Igbo—is a product of the rough-and-tumble of the transition through colonial to postcolonial status. David Laitin has pointed out that "the idea that there was a single Hausa-Fulani tribe . . . was largely a political claim of the NPC [Northern Peoples' Congress] in their battle against the South," while "many elders intimately involved in rural Yoruba society today recall that, as late as the 1930s, 'Yoruba' was not a common form of political identification."[6]

Nnamdi Azikiwe—one of the key figures in the construction of Nigerian nationalism—was extremely popular (as Laitin also points out) in Yoruba Lagos, where "he
edited his nationalist newspaper, the *West African Pilot*. It was only subsequent
events that led him to be defined in Nigeria as an *Igbo* leader."[7] Yet Nigerian
politics—and the more everyday economy of ordinary personal relations—is oriented
along such axes, and only very occasionally does the fact float into view that even
these three problematic identities account for at most seven out of ten Nigerians.

And the story is repeated, even in places where it was not drawn in lines of blood.
As Johannes Fabian has observed, the powerful Lingala and Swahili-speaking
identities of modern Zaire exist "because spheres of political and economic interest
were established before the Belgians took full control, and continued to inform
relations between regions under colonial rule."[8] Modern Ghana witnesses the
development of an Akan identity, as speakers of the three major regional dialects of
Twi—Asante, Fante, Akuapem—organize themselves into a corporation against an
(equally novel) Ewe unity.[9]

When it is not the "tribe" that is invested with new uses and meanings, it is
religion. Yet the idea that Nigeria is composed of a Muslim North, a Christian South,
and a mosaic of "pagan" holdovers is as inaccurate as the picture of three historic
tribal identities. Two out of every five southern Yoruba people are Muslim, and, as
Laitin, tell us:

> Many northern groups, especially in what are today Benue, Plateau, Gongola, and
> Kwara states, are largely Christian. When the leaders of Biafra tried to convince the
> world that they were oppressed by northern Muslims, ignorant foreigners (includ-
> ing the pope) believed them. But the Nigerian army . . . was led by a northern
> Christian.[10]

It is as useless here, as in the case of race, to point out in each case that the tribe or the
religion is, like all social identities, based on an idealizing fiction, for life in Nigeria
or in Zaire has come to be lived through that idealization: the Igbo identity is real
because Nigerians believe in it, the Shona identity because Zimbabweans have given
it meaning. The rhetoric of a Muslim North and a Christian South structured political
discussions in the period before Nigerian independence. But it was equally important
in the debates about instituting a Muslim Court of Appeals in the Draft Constitution of
1976, and it could be found, for example, in many an article in the Nigerian press as
electoral registration for a new civilian era began in July 1989.

There are, I think three crucial lessons to be learned from these cases. First, that
identities are complex and multiple and grow out of a history of changing responses to
economic, political, and cultural forces, almost always in opposition to other
identities. Second, that they flourish despite what I earlier called our "misrecognition" of their origins; despite, that is, their roots in myths and in lies. And third, that
there is, in consequence, no large place for reason in the construction—as opposed to
the study and the management—of identities. One temptation, then, for those who
see the centrality of these fictions in our lives, is to leave reason behind: to celebrate
and endorse those identities that seem at the moment to offer the best hope of
advancing our other goals, and to keep silence about the lies and the myths. But, as I
said earlier, intellectuals do not easily neglect the truth, and, all things considered,

our societies profit, in my view, from the institutionalization of this imperative in the academy. So it is important for us to continue trying to tell our truths. But the facts I have been rehearsing should imbue us all with a strong sense of the marginality of such work to the central issue of the resistance to racism and ethnic violence—and to sexism, and to the other structures of difference that shape the world of power; they should force upon us the clear realization that the real battle is not being fought in the academy. Every time I read another report in the newspapers of an African disaster— a famine in Ethiopia, a war in Namibia, ethnic conflict in Burundi—I wonder how much good it does to correct the theories with which these evils are bound up; the solution is food, or mediation, or some other more material, more practical step. And yet, as I have tried to argue in this book, the shape of modern Africa (the shape of our world) is in large part the product, often the unintended and unanticipated product, of theories; even the most vulgar of Marxists will have to admit that economic interests operate *through* ideologies. We cannot change the world simply by evidence and reasoning, but we surely cannot change it without them either.

What we in the academy *can* contribute—even if only slowly and marginally—is a disruption of the discourse of "racial" and "tribal" differences. For, in my perfectly unoriginal opinion, the inscription of difference in Africa today plays into the hands of the very exploiters whose shackles we are trying to escape. "Race" in Europe and "tribe" in Africa are central to the way in which the objective interests of the worst-off are distorted. The analogous point for African-Americans was recognized long ago by Du Bois.[11] Du Bois argued in *Black Reconstruction* that racist ideology had essentially blocked the formation of a significant labor movement in the U.S., for such a movement would have required the collaboration of the 9 million ex-slave and white peasant workers of the South.[12] It is, in other words, because the categories of difference often cut across our economic interests that they operate to blind us to them. What binds the middle-class African-American to his dark-skinned fellow citizens downtown is not economic interest but racism and the cultural products of resistance to it that are shared across (most of) African-American culture.

It seems to me that we learn from this case what John Thompson has argued recently, in a powerful but appreciative critique of Pierre Bourdieu: namely, that it may be a mistake to think that social reproduction—the processes by which societies maintain themselves over time—presupposes "some sort of consensus with regard to dominant values or norms." Rather, the stability of today's industrialized society may require "a pervasive *fragmentation* of the social order and a proliferation of divisions between its members." For it is precisely this fragmentation that prevents oppositional attitudes from generating "a coherent alternative view which would provide a basis for political action."

> Divisions are ramified along the lines of gender, race, qualifications and so on, forming barriers which obstruct the development of movements which could threaten the *status quo*. The reproduction of the social order may depend less upon a consensus with regard to dominant values or norms than upon a *lack of consensus* at the very point where oppositional attitudes could be translated into political action.[13]

Thompson allows us to see that within contemporary industrial societies an identification of oneself as an African, above all else, allows the fact that one is, say, not an

Asian, to be used against one; in this setting—as we see in South Africa—a racialized conception of one's identity is retrogressive. To argue this way is to presuppose that the political meanings of identities are historically and geographically relative. So it is quite consistent with this claim to hold, as I do, that in constructing alliances *across* states—and especially in the Third World—a Pan-African identity, which allows African-Americans, Afro-Caribbeans, and Afro-Latins to ally with continental Africans, drawing on the cultural resources of the black Atlantic world, may serve useful purposes. Resistance to a self-isolating black nationalism *within* England or France or the United States is thus theoretically consistent with Pan-Africanism as an international project.

Because the value of identities is thus relative, we must argue for and against them case by case. And given the current situation in Africa, I think it remains clear that another Pan-Africanism—the project of a continental fraternity and sorority, *not* the project of a racialized Negro nationalism—however false or muddled its theoretical roots, can be a progressive force. It is as fellow Africans that Ghanaian diplomats (my father among them) interceded between the warring nationalist parties in Rhodesia under UDI; as fellow Africans that OAU teams can mediate regional conflicts; as fellow Africans that the human rights assessors organized under the Banjul Declaration can intercede for citizens of African states against the excesses of our governments. If there is, as I have suggested, hope, too, for the Pan-Africanism of an African diaspora once it, too, is released from bondage to racial ideologies (alongside the many bases of alliance available to Africa's peoples in their political and cultural struggles), it is crucial that we recognize the independence, once "Negro" nationalism is gone, of the Pan-Africanism of the diaspora and the Pan-Africanism of the continent. It is, I believe, in the exploration of these issues, these possibilities, that the future of an intellectually reinvigorated Pan-Africanism lies.

Finally, I would like to suggest that it is really unsurprising that a continental identity is coming into cultural and institutional reality through regional and subregional organizations. We share a continent and its ecological problems; we share a relation of dependency to the world economy; we share the problem of racism in the way the industrialized world thinks of us (and let me include here, explicitly, both "Negro" Africa and the "Maghrib"); we share the possibilities of the development of regional markets and local circuits of production; and our intellectuals participate, through the shared contingencies of our various histories, in a common discourse whose outlines I have tried to limn in this book.

"Ɔdenkyɛm nwu nsuo-ase mma yɛmmefrɛ kwakuo sɛ ɔbeyɛ no ayie," goes an Akan proverb. "The crocodile does not die under the water so that we can call the monkey to celebrate its funeral." Each of us, the proverb can be used to say, belongs to a group with its own customs. To accept that Africa can be in these ways a usable identity is not to forget that all of us belong to multifarious communities with their local customs; it is not to dream of a single African state and to forget the complexly different trajectories of the continent's so many languages and cultures. "African solidarity" can surely be a vital and enabling rallying cry; but in this world of genders, ethnicities, and classes, of families, religions, and nations, it is as well to remember that there are times when Africa is not the banner we need.

EPILOGUE:

In My Father's House

Abusua dɔ funu.
The matriclan loves a corpse.
 AKAN PROVERB

My father died, as I say, while I was trying to finish this book. His funeral was an occasion for strengthening and reaffirming the ties that bind me to Ghana and "my father's house" and, at the same time, for straining my allegiances to my king and my father's matriclan—perhaps, even tearing them beyond repair. When I last saw him alive, my father asked me to help him draft a codicil to his will describing his wishes for his funeral. I did not realize then that in recording these requests on his deathbed and giving them legal force, he was leaving us, his children, an almost impossible mission. For in our efforts to conduct the funeral in accordance with my father's desires—expressed in that codicil—we had to challenge, first, the authority of the matriclan, the *abusua*, of which my father was erstwhile head and, in the end, the will of the king of Ashanti, my uncle.

And in the midst of it—when partisans of our side were beaten up in my father's church, when sheep were slaughtered to cast powerful spells against us, when our household was convinced that the food my aunt sent me was poisoned—it seemed that every attempt to understand what was happening took me further back into family history and the history of Asante; further away from abstractions ("tradition" and "modernity," "state" and "society," "matriclan" and "patriclan"); further into what would probably seem to a European or American an almost fairytale world of witchcraft and wicked aunts and wise old women and men.

Often, in the ensuing struggles, I found myself remembering my father's parting words, years ago, when I was a student leaving home for Cambridge—I would not see him again for six months or more. I kissed him in farewell, and, as I stood waiting by the bed for his final benediction, he peered at me over his newspaper, his glasses balanced on the tip of his nose, and pronounced: "Do not disgrace the family name." Then he returned to his reading.

I confess that I was surprised by this injunction: so much an echo of a high Victorian paterfamilias (or perhaps of the Roman originals that my father knew from his colonial education in the classics). But mostly I wondered what he meant. Did he mean my mother's family (whose tradition of university scholarship he had always urged me to emulate), a family whose name I did not bear? Did he mean his own *abusua* (not, by tradition, my family at all) from which he had named me Anthony Akroma-Ampim? Did he mean his legal name, Appiah, the name invented for him when the British colonial authorities decided (after their own customs) that we must have "family" names and that the "family" name should be the name of your father? When your father's family tradition casts you into your matriclan and your mother's claims you for your father, such doubts are, I suppose, natural enough.

Pops, by contrast, was afflicted by no such uncertainties. He was the head of his matriclan, his *abusua,* the matriclan of Akroma-Ampim, for whom, as I say, I am named. In the autobiography that was his final gift to us, he wrote:

> My matrilineal ancestors were among the very early Akans of the great Ekuona (Bush Cow) clan which originally settled at Asokore, some twenty-six miles from Kumasi, long before Ashanti was created a nation by the great warrior-King, Osei Tutu and his great Priest Okomfo Anokye. In the course of time, some of my ancestors moved to Fomena and Adanse, where other members of the clan had settled earlier. Of the long line of ancestors, Akroma-Ampim ("the hawk is never impeded in its flight") and his sister Nana Amofa later joined this migration to Fomena and established the family reputation and themselves at Mfumenam in Adanse sometime well before the beginning of the nineteenth century. . . .
> Being a great warrior, Akroma-Ampim had acquired a thousand personal "slaves" as his reward for his valor in various wars. These were all men captured in battle and therefore a great asset to a warrior-adventurer. My ancestor settled these men at Mfumenam, a forest-belt on the Adanse side of the Offin River. Daily, he watched the vast unoccupied forest land on the other side of the great river, until his adventurous spirit decided him to cross over with his sister and men and to occupy it all. . . . All precautions against any eventuality having been taken, he and his brave band of one thousand set out to the new lands with his famous war fetish *Anhwere* and *Tano Kofi* being carried before him. . . . Satisfied with what he had acquired, he set out the boundaries and placed his war fetish *Tano Kofi* on the western end of the boundary. . . . This settlement was named "Nyaduom" or the place of the garden eggs.[1]

But if he was clear that this was his family, he was clear, too, that we were his family, also. In a notebook that we found after he died, he had written a message to us, his children, telling us about the history of his *abusua,* of our mother's family, and of his father, of his hopes for us. And the tenderness of his tone was all the more striking since he wrote of his own father:

> I did not have the good fortune to know him as intimately as you have known me and this for two reasons; he was reserved and what's more, it was not then the custom here for a father to get too acquainted with his children for fear of breeding contempt.

In his autobiography, he also told us how he was acknowledged head of his *abusua* after the funeral of his predecessor (the man for whom I am also named, Yao Antory, corrupted later to Yao Antony, anglicized on my British baptismal record to Anthony—dubbed the "Merchant Prince," a businessman who, though nonliterate, managed a vast empire).

> The next day's ceremonies started at about 6 AM. Leading us—the elders, my sister, and I—was a man carrying the sacrificial lamb and a bottle of schnapps. A

few yards only to the broad river, I saw a huge crocodile, mouth fully open, dancing in circles in the middle of the river. . . . The libation with schnapps over, the oldest among the elders and I, holding two legs each, flung the sheep into the river, to be grabbed, happily for me, by the dancing crocodile. After three dives followed by a circular dance, the crocodile vanished, holding the sheep between its mighty jaws. Firing of musketry began, amid the singing of war songs, as we made the journey back home. I had been proved to be the rightful and true successor to my recently-deceased grand-uncle, in the long line to Akroma-Ampim. Now, every word of mine was an edict—never to be challenged so long as I breathed the breath of life.[2]

My father refound his family at the funeral of his great-uncle: at his funeral I learned more about that family and discovered the ways in which it was and was not mine.

In the codicil to his will, my father instructed his church and "my beloved wife, Peggy" to carry out all the rites in association with his funeral. Not much to notice in that, you might think, but, given the centrality of the *abusua* in Asante (a centrality so clearly displayed in my father's account of his origins) it is not surprising that by Asante custom the funeral is their business. In practice, this usually means the business of one's brothers and sisters (or the children of one's mother's sisters) along with one's mother and her sisters and brothers, if they are living. Since you belong to your mother's *abusua,* the widow and children belong to a different family from their husband and father. Of course, the widow and children of a dead man are part of the furniture of an Asante funeral. But they do not control it.

Naturally, in these circumstances, the codicil did not please the *abusua.* In particular, it displeased my father's sister, my aunt Victoria, and she and her brother Jojo were determined to wrest control of the funeral away from the church, the wife, and the children. Their displeasure was compounded by the inescapable publicity of my father's deathbed repudiation of them. For the funeral, as the leave-taking of a Ghanaian statesman, a brother-in-law of the king, a leading lawyer, a member of an important *abusua* was, inevitably, a public event. Through a long career in public life, Papa (or Paa) Joe, as he was known, was a well-known figure in Ghana. His gusts of eloquence in parliament, at public rallies, when he preached at church; his cantankerous resistance to government policies he disapproved of; his mischievous anecdotes: a hundred tales in a thousand mouths would surround his coffin. The services were an occasion for the cameras of national television; for articles in the Ghanaian newspapers that told familiar stories demonstrating his reputation for incorruptibility; for tales of the corruption he had rooted out, the legendary bribes he had scorned. There were long obituaries in the national and international press; later there were editorials about the funeral. Removing the *abusua* from normal control inevitably entailed an element of public disgrace.

Speculation about my father's motives in excluding his *abusua* from his obsequies was bound to run rampant. I speculated also, since he never explained his decision directly to me. Still, I knew, along with almost everybody in Kumasi, that he had had a dispute with my aunt over properties left to them and their sister Mabel in the will of my great-great-uncle, Yao Antony. We all also knew that my aunt had refused to come and make peace with her brother even on his deathbed.

My father felt strongly about his burial rites. In his autobiography, he wrote:

> The exhibition of dead bodies to all and sundry prior to burial and subsequent unnecessary and elaborate funeral celebrations have always distressed me; therefor, I solemnly request that these abominable trappings be avoided at my passing away. I wish my family and friends to remember me as I was before my demise and to clothe themselves in white instead of the traditional black and dark browns that portray man's inevitable transition as a gloomy specter.[3]

Despite my father's codicil, neither my mother nor the church sought at first to exclude the *abusua* from the funeral arrangements. Rather, we hoped to include them in a public display of solidarity around the coffin. In retrospect, it seems altogether natural that our overtures to them were rebuffed. Whatever dates we suggested, for example, the *abusua* proposed others. The issue was not convenience but control.

Within a week of daddy's death, the world around us, it seemed, took sides. On the one hand, there were the church and its leaders, the Reverend Dr. Asante-Antwi, district chairman, and the Reverend Dr. Asante, pastor of the Wesley Methodist Church; and my sisters and myself. (So far as was possible, we kept my mother out of the dispute.) Since the church was professionally preoccupied with healing breaches, and I was my mother's eldest child and only son, the leadership of "our" side—insofar as it involved confrontation—devolved upon me. (Never confuse a martilineal society with a society where women are in public control.)

Leading the opposing "side" was my father's sister, Victoria, whose husband is the Asantehene, our king. She is, perhaps, the most powerful person in the kingdom. (Never assume that individual women cannot gain power under patriarchy.) By the time we began to make arrangements, Auntie Vic had begun to mobilize the considerable power of the throne (or the "stool," as we say in Asante) in an attempt to wrest control of the funeral from us.

The immediate locus of debate seems trivial. We settled on Thursday, 26 July 1990, as the day for my father's burial, which was already eighteen days after his death. That meant Wednesday night would be the wake; Friday would be a day of rest; Saturday the *ayie,* the traditional Asante funeral; and Sunday the thanksgiving service. We were keen to get the funeral over with, in part because it seemed the longer we waited the more likely it was that the church would be forced to give in and let the *abusua* take over; in part, for sundry practical considerations; in part, for the normal reason that contemplating the funeral would continue, until it was over, to be a source of strain and distress. We had explained our reasons to the *abusua* on several occasions in several forums, and they seemed to have acquiesced. Then, the week before the burial was due, a message came summoning my sisters and me to a meeting at 11:00 A.M. in the palace of the king of Asante—the Asantehene—in his capital, our hometown, Kumasi.

The summons was not altogether surprising. We had begun to hear rumors that the Asantehene was objecting to the dates we had suggested because he was planning to celebrate the anniversary of his accession to the stool on Friday, 27 July, which would place it on the very next day after the burial.

Even if, as we suspected, the event had been created as a pretext, we had to take the matter seriously, because we knew the church would. We obeyed Nana's summons.[4]

We were accompanied to the palace by our father's best friend, Uncle T.D., a journalist, who had been with my father when he died. After being kept waiting for an interval (no doubt to establish who was in charge), we were summoned along with the church committee into the huge sitting room of the palace; it is enormous, with its two sitting areas, each centered on a giant Oriental rug and surrounded by expensive, mock-antique furniture that looks as though it came from Harrods in London (probably because it did). My uncle, Otumfuo Nana Opoku Ware the Second, Asantehene, was already seated across the room.

He was surrounded by the largest collection of courtiers I had ever seen in the palace. Seated in two ranks on his right were five or six linguists, led by Baffuor Akoto, who had been senior linguist for the last king. The Sanahene, chief of the treasury, and his colleague the Banahene were also present, and there were others I recognized but whose names I did not know. Behind the Asantehene and seated to his right was the Juabenhene, whose stool is the "uncle" of the Golden Stool. Nana Juabenhene was a schoolmate of mine in primary school and went on to study engineering at the Kumasi University of Science and Technology. Though, like me, he is in his midthirties, the seniority of his stool and its relation to the Asantehene mean that he is a very important chief. There were other chiefs around, including Nana Tafohene, chief of a town on the outskirts of Kumasi, a lawyer dressed in a formal suit that he had presumably been wearing in court that morning. To the left of the king (who had himself studied law in England), and a few feet away, sat my aunt, also on a thronelike chair. As we were about to begin, Uncle George, head of my grandfather's *abusua,* a son of the last king and henchman of my aunt's, arrived through the French windows to our right and sat down on a chair beside her.

On the sofas and chairs at right angles to them and to the king, facing the serried ranks of linguists and other courtiers, were the members of the church's funeral committee and the Reverends Asante-Antwi and Asante.

We came resolved not to let the church be pressured into changing what we had agreed. Naturally, we had no intention of being pressured ourselves. But this gathering of notables was impressive and designed to intimidate. According to custom, each time my uncle, the king, spoke, his senior linguist would address us with the formal version of his remarks in his beautiful courtly Twi. And as he spoke, the others would utter various words and noises to stress the key points: *"Ampa"* (That's true), three or four of them would say; or *"Hwiem!"*—a kind of auditory punctuation, an exclamation point, at the end of a significant utterance. (If you wanted to know where the tradition of the African-American church with its cries of "Testify!" comes from, you could start by looking here.)

Baffuor Akoto had clearly been prepared by the Asantehene for what he had to say. He explained to us, as we expected, the problem about the conflict with the anniversary. Nana obviously wanted to come to as many of the ceremonies in association with his brother-in-law's deaths as he could. But he could not come in the white cloth of celebration to a burial service, and he could hardly come in the cloth of mourning to celebrate his two decades on the stool. The timing was in the hands of the church. Nana did not ask us to change anything. He had called us only to let us know of this problem.

It was striking to me how, even in this display of power, Asante kingship operates nowadays (as, perhaps, it has always operated) by a kind of euphemism. There were no orders here; there was no acknowledgment of conflict. Nana would come to as much as he could of the funeral, we were told. Obviously, if we moved it, he could come to all of it. But the decision was up to us.

The church people tried to explain the reasoning behind the choice of dates, and they were interrupted from time to time by my aunt; she was rather less euphemistic in her demands. Why were they not willing to do this little thing for Nana?

The members of the church committee responded politely but with diminishing firmness to all the questions put to them; at a certain point, it seemed that they might be beginning to waver. We faced the prospect of a funeral delayed for weeks by my aunt, while she made efforts to undo the effects of my father's codicil.

As this spectacle continued, my sisters and I grew angry. Their murmuring in my ear became increasingly urgent. Finally, when indignation had turned into the unfamiliar emotion of rage, when the blood was pounding through my head, I could not take any more. This wrangling over my father's corpse (as it struck me) by people who had ignored his suffering when he was living, apparently without any concern for those of us who had loved and cared for him, was more than I could bear. If I believed in possession, I would say that I was possessed. Despite years of training in deference to Asante kingship and its institutions, I could not restrain myself. I stood up, the violence of my movement interrupting, I think, poor old Baffuor Akoto (a longtime friend and political ally of my father's), and I walked to the edge of the rug nearest the door, with my sisters gathered around me, before I spoke.

"Everybody here knows what is going on and my sisters and I are not going to sit here and let it happen. That woman," I said pointing at my aunt, "and that man," pointing now at her cohort Uncle George, "are trying to use Nana to get their way; to force the church to do what *they* want." We were not going to be party to such an abuse of the stool; we were leaving. By now my sisters were all in tears, shouting too at them, "Why are you doing this to us?"

Pandemonium broke out. Never, they told us later, in the history of the court had anyone walked out on the king. As we hurried out to our car, crowds of agitated courtiers streamed after us, preceded by Uncle T.D. "You can't go," he said. "You can't leave like this." My childhood friend, the Juabenhene, joined him. "You must come back. You owe it to Nana." I told him that I had indeed been brought up to respect the stool and its occupant; that I was still trying to do so, but that the stool was being "spoiled" by my aunt; and that after what I had seen today, it was hard for me to hold Nana himself in respect. Nana Juabenhene was sympathetic. "But," he insisted, "you cannot leave like this. You must return."

After a few minutes that passed like hours, we had recovered enough to reenter the palace. "Don't worry," Uncle T.D. said. "What you did will have helped. Now everyone will know how strongly you feel. But you must go back now and finish this."

When we entered and everyone was settled, Nana Tafohene rose on our right. He addressed Baffuor Akoto, as chief linguist, seeking pardon from Nana for the disgraceful exhibition that had just occurred. At the height of Nana Tafohene's peroration he remarked on my trespass: "Of course, we should beat him with rods of iron until he bleeds. But then,'' he added after a masterful pause, ''he is our child, and we would only have to tend his wounds.''

Then all of the church committee and the *abusua* (even my aunt) rose and begged on my behalf for forgiveness, bending the right knee, with a hand on it, and saying the traditional formula of apology: *"Dibim."* I joined in, clumsily, at the urging of Uncle T.D. Has I disgraced the family name after all?

Nana spoke. ''We have locked what happened here in a box and thrown away the key,'' he said. And he meant: the matter is closed.

He couldn't have been more wrong.

As we filed out into the sunlight and into our car, trying to calm down, preparing to leave, one of the palace servants slipped over to the car where we were seated. ''Wayε *adee,*'' he said, smiling and grabbing my hand—''You have done something,'' which is the Akan way of saying ''Well done.'' He was not expressing hostility to the king: he was telling us that he, and many others around the palace, thought it was time someone told the king's wife to stop abusing Nana's power. He was speaking out of concern for the king and respect for the stool—and, perhaps, out of love for my father.

Within a few hours, people came to the house from all over town to ask for our version of what happened, and to say to me, ''Wayε *adee.*'' Some in the family suggested I would now be the obvious choice for a stool—chieftaincy—at the ancestral village of Nyaduom. (The fact that I did not belong to their *abusua* was brushed aside. It was as if for them I had become truly an Asante in the act of opposing Asante tradition.) They were claiming me back, claiming back the child they had known as one of their own. Curiously, to many, defiance at court made me something of a hero.

It was clear that many people wanted us to know that they disapproved of my aunt's campaign; they came with stories of how she had influenced Nana to make bad decisions in chieftaincy disputes; they implied that his decisions could be bought by paying off his wife. These were accusations I had never heard before; before, I had been one of her favorite nephews, her favorite brother's only son. Now that we were on opposite sides, I could hear these stories. True or not, they revealed a degree of hostility to my aunt and contempt for the king of which I had been totally unaware. Someone even said: ''She better get out of town fast when Nana goes,'' thus both breaking the taboo against mentioning the Asantehene's death and uttering threats against his wife at the same time.

But even I knew how difficult it was to lock things in a box in Asante. I got used to it a long time ago. I remember, about fifteen years ago, when I was staying in Kumasi with an English friend from college. I was teaching in those days at the University of Ghana and my father was a minister in the government, working in ''the Castle,'' the center of government in the old Dutch slaving castle of Christiansborg in Accra. My friend James and I were alone in Kumasi for the weekend—alone, that is, except for the driver and the cook and our steward—because both my parents were away. He asked to be taken out to the discos of Kumasi. ''Fine,'' I said, ''let Boakye, our driver, take you. He'll enjoy it.''

At dawn the next morning my father, then a minister in the government, called from his office in the capital. Word had reached him that our car had been seen in a "strange" part of town last night. What had we been doing? My father reminded me that our car would be recognized anywhere it went, asked that I should bear that in mind in deciding where to send the driver, and went back to his investigations of the financial dealing of another crooked multinational.

At breakfast I told James about the early morning call. Where had he been? He didn't know exactly, but the women had been very friendly. And from then on he took himself about in a taxi. The family name would not be disgraced.

The *abusua* did not limit itself to appeals to earthly powers. At the height of the tensions, my kinsman Kwaku came from the family house to tell us that a sheep had been slaughtered and buried there, in the main courtyard, and spells cast against us after the sacrifice. We met with Kwaku and worried members of our household on the landing, whispering: so as not to disturb my mother upstairs; so as not to be heard by the crowd of mourners gathered in the hall and the dining room downstairs. Kwaku had gone at once to find a malam, a Moslem medicine man, who could produce some countermedicine. A white chicken and some doves would be sacrificed. The consensus was with Kwaku; some sort of countersacrifice was obviously necessary. I arranged for it.

It was a form of remedy with which my father was highly experienced from his earliest childhood in Adum, "the hub and heart of Kumasi, even Ashanti."

> We, the true youth of Adum, spent most of our time learning to fight in anticipation of frequent raids that we made on the citizens of other areas of Kumasi who we felt were collaborators of the British usurpers in our midsts. In order to ensure victory at all times, our leaders provided us with juju, which we rubbed into our shaven heads and bodies and was meant to break or deflect bottles or other missiles thrown at us by the enemy. For this and other purposes, no chicken was really safe at night.[5]

That I myself do not believe in magic was oddly beside the point. It was my responsibility to respond to the spiritual menace, as the local head of our *abusua*, the only (and thus, I suppose, the senior) male. So what if members of "our" side were beaten up in the street by loyalists of the other "side"; at least the juju was checked by counterjuju.

Meanwhile, even more disquieting stories began to circulate: the Uncle Jojo was arranging a crowd of the notoriously tough men of Adum to "kidnap" the corpse when it arrived and take it off.

There was also talk of threats to the business interests of members of the funeral committee, to the priests, to the district chairman; on the Sunday before the burial was due to take place, we were informed that someone had entered the vestry of the Wesley Methodist Church and tried to beat up one of the priests. They wavered; their business was healing breaches, not engaging in hostilities. They urge me to have *abotare*, a Twi virtue, usually translated as "patience." It was a word that came up often in the ensuing days. My sisters and I agreed that if there was one word we would like expunged from the language, this was it. In the name of *abotare*, people were willing to wait and listen while the *abusua*, in general, and Uncle Jojo, in particular, took advantage over and over again of our desire to meet them halfway. It was, in part, in the name of *abotare* that my aunt's abuses of the stool were tolerated: in time, everyone thinks, this too will pass. To urge *abotare,* so it seems to me, is to do what Moslem peasants mean when they say "if Allah wills": it is to leave in the lap of the gods what could be in the sphere of human action. But sometimes, I think, what they really meant was not "have patience" but "keep looking for compromise." We wanted to bury our father on his terms (or, at any rate, on ours): they wanted to keep the peace. We wanted what we thought was fair and just; they wanted a solution that would allow them to live together in peace. This is an old confrontation, between "abstract rights" and "social community," an opposition much beloved of those legal anthropologists who urge us to see "African values of community" expressed in our procedures of arbitration and our hostility to the colonial legal system. Yet, if I ask myself where my own concern for abstract rights came from, my own passion for fairness, I think I must answer that I got it not from my British schooling but from my father's example. And, often, so it seems to me, as in this case, those who urge compromise as an African virtue are only supporting a compromise with the status quo, a concession to those with money and power, and a little bit of concern for abstract rights might reflect not a colonized mind but an urge to take sides against the mighty, and "speak the truth to power."

I had broken with my king, with my father's *abusua*. I had crossed my father's sister, a powerful woman in her own right. This was not to be done lightly. When food from the palace was conveyed to our house, we were told it was most likely poisoned (by means of witchcraft, of course). Auntie Vic made her weight felt around town, driven around in one of her fleet of Mercedes-Benzes, cultivating a faintly plutocratic aura. The displeasure of the *abusua* was not something to be lightly incurred, either. My cousin Nana Ama, whom I had always thought of as good-hearted and put-upon, revealed the depth of feeling in the *abusua* when she warned us coldly to consider the future welfare of our mother. "Be careful," she said to my sisters and I. "You do not live here. We are here with your mother." When my sisters challenged her to say directly if she was threatening my mother—asked her if she remembered how my mother had watched over her education—she shouted defensively that she had "said what she had said."

On the day that we retrieved my father's remains in Accra and brought him back in a military plane, the lead editorial in the *Ghanaian Times* was entitled "Paa Joe's Lesson"; explicitly, it took our side against the *abusua*. The man's wishes should be respected, it insisted. Powerful enemies we had, but it was also clear that we had popular sentiment on our side.

Flying over southern Ghana toward Kumasi, a trip I had not taken by air for nearly two decades, we could see the red laterite roads snaking through the forests to the villages and towns of Akwapim and Asante. When our city came into view I could see how much it had grown in the last years, gathering around it a girdle of new housing stretching out into what had once been farms in the forest. As we came down the runway we saw the hundreds of people gathered at the airport in red and black cloths; the priests in their robes; the hearse waiting on the tarmac for the coffin. Most of our party descended from the rear door of the aircraft, but a few of us gathered at the front, by the cargo door: I leapt down the few feet to the tarmac, the black cloth I was wearing trailing behind me, and waited to lift down the coffin. We had done it. We had brought Pops home. As the wails of the mourners rose and fell, Uncle George, head of my grandfather's *abusua,* stepped forward to pour libations. (Uncle Jojo hovered nearby, plainly keen to exercise his prerogatives as self-appointed heir-presumptive to the headship of the *abusua* but aware, too, that his participation at this moment would be unwelcome. Not that he had been idle: we discovered later that he had spent the time we were in Accra trying to find a lawyer who would file an injunction to stop the burial. Because the bar was involved in the funeral arrangements—the president of the national bar, the chairman of the Asante bar, and other senior lawyers were to carry his coffin from the church—every lawyer in Kumasi knew what was going on, and, amazingly enough, Jojo couldn't find a single lawyer who would file the papers.)

Home is a house my parents built just before independence. Downstairs two doors come off the front veranda: one to the house, one to my father's legal office. As children we would go to school in the mornings past the many people who gathered from early in the morning on that veranda to see him. Many of them were very poor, and they brought chickens or yams or tomatoes in lieu of money, because they knew my father never insisted on being paid. Sometimes, the people who came were not clients but constituents, who had walked miles from Lake Bosomtwi to catch a "mammy-wagon" to town, to ask for his help in dealing with the government; sometimes they were not constituents but people from Nyaduom, seeking a decision about land rights or help in getting a road through, so that they could take out their crops in trucks and not in headloads.

My father's coffin traveled in under the tree that my English grandmother had planted the first time she visited that house (a tree where, as a child, I had pretended to be Tarzan, swinging from the branches, oblivious of the cultural politics of my play) and up onto this veranda, passing by the office where he had been Mr. Joe Appiah, barrister and solicitor of the Supreme Court of Ghana in his Ekuona chambers; the Honorable Member of Parliament for Atwima-Amansie, known as the Leopard, Ɔsebɔ, for his fearless opposition to the government; Ɔpanin Kwabena Gyamfi, heir to Akroma-Ampim, elder and hereditary owner of Nyaduom. When he entered into the house he was once more my mother's Joe, and our papa.

There was loud drumming and louder weeping as the body was delivered into the house on the shoulders of a half dozen young men, with cloths tied around their waists, some from my stepgrandmother's house, some simply neighbors on the street. I wrapped my cloth around my waist and joined them. In the dining room a platform had been raised, surrounded by flowers, and there we placed him, the coffin covered in his finest *kente,* and opened the small window above his head, so that we could see his face.

A year and a half after he fell ill in Norway, nearly a year after he returned to Accra, our father, heir to Akroma-Ampim and Yao Antony, Ɔpanin Kwabena Gyamfi—alias Ɔsebɔ, the Leopard; Papa Joe; Pops—was home for the last time.

By 10:00 A.M. of the day of the funeral, the church was full, and the Asantehene and his queen mother were seated in the royal seats, my Aunt Victoria between them. (Somebody told us later that during the service at one moment, when my aunt started weeping, the queen mother turned to her and asked, "Why are you crying? Has somebody you know died?" It was a royal rebuke to my aunt for her attempts to block the funeral.) The stalls we had set aside for VIPs were empty save for the president of the Ghana Academy of Arts and Sciences, Dr. Evans-Amfom, a family friend since his days as vice-chancellor of Kumasi's university. As the strains of the first hymn came to a close there was a good deal of noise outside, including sirens and the sounds of a cheering crowd. An official-looking person walked over from the side door to Rev. Asante and they whispered for a moment. At the end of the verse he spoke: "Would you please all rise," he said "to welcome the head of state and chairman of the PNDC, Flight-Lieutenant Jerry Rawlings and his party."

It was an electric moment, for security considerations meant that almost no one had been told he was coming. The head of state entered, dressed in a civilian suit, open at the neck, accompanied by a civilian member of the PNDC—an old friend with whom I had taught at the University of Ghana, over a decade ago—and some uniformed companions. Now I knew that people would feel we had done our father the honor he deserved of us; that at least we had honored *his* name.

Throughout the service, lawyers in their court robes stood guard at the head and foot of the coffin, taking five-minute turns to honor their colleague. If I turned to my left and scanned to the right, I could see the *abusua*, first; then the royal party; then the priests of the various denominations; then, behind the head of the chairman of the PNDC on the wall, the plaque in memory of my father's father, who had also served this church. Further to the right were the serried ranks of the legal profession in their robes. On my immediate left was Uncle T.D.; behind me my sisters, my Nigerian in-laws and friends, my friends from America. And to my right, somber and dignified in her black cloth and black scarf, was my mother. All the identities my father cared for were embodied about us: lawyer, Asante man, Ghanaian, African, internationalist; statesman and churchman; family man, father, and head of his *abusua;* friend; husband. Only something so particular as a single life—as my father's life, encapsulated in the complex pattern of social and personal relations around his coffin—could capture the multiplicity of our lives in a postcolonial world.

"I had to play the man and restrain any tears as best I could," my father wrote about Yao Antony's funeral. "It was not the done thing for the head of a family or a leader of men to shed tears publicly."[6] I did not manage this Asante restraint as well.

Outside, the people, thousands upon thousands who had shouted, "Pops, O, Pops," the watchword of my father's friends when we arrived, turned to shouting "J.J., J.J." (Rawlings's initials) as his cortege swept away. Somehow we were hurried through the crowds (many among them dressed in the black-and-white cloth we had asked for—celebrating his life, mourning his passing; many in ordinary brown and red and cloths of mourning) toward the central police station, where our car was parked. And then we followed the hearse, led by police motocycles that cleared the way. We passed the law courts, where my father had argued so many cases, down along the main street of Kumasi, Kingsway, alongside Adum, where he was born, a curious crowd lining our way; we traveled through the Kejetia roundabouts, with the huge central sculpture—worker, soldier, and farmer, symbolizing our nation—along by the lorry park from which thousands of people travel daily out from Kumasi in every direction of the compass; we drove by our house and past the houses of a dozen of my father's colleagues and friends. We passed the Methodist Wesley College, where he had worked with the missionaries as a boy; we entered Tafo, domain of the Tafohene, and the city cemetery where my father, like his father before him, was to be buried. And as we settled in by the graveside, and the coffin was placed in the ground, Jerry Rawlings joined us. His remarks at the graveside were terse but pointed. If we truly wish to honor the memory of a great man, he said, we will not disturb his widow and children over questions of property.

In effect, his mere presence at the funeral, which he would not ordinarily have attended, was a rebuke to the Asantehene and his wife: that the words he spoke at the graveside were addressed to the heart of the dispute between my father and his sister only made this explicit. In the normal business of Ghana, the head of state and the king circle warily about each other, each aware of the symbolic and material resources at the other's disposal. To come to the Asantehene's capital to deliver this rebuke, Jerry Rawlings had to have a point to make. In the context of public knowledge, the main political effects of his presence were three: first, to claim affinity with a politician of the independence generation; second, to underline recent government decrees expanding the property rights of widows; third, to imply an awareness of the manipulations of the stool for private ends. The knowledge that he might have come for private reasons—out of personal respect, as someone told me later, for my father—did nothing to undermine these public messages.

"*Wowu na w'ayie bɛba a, wohwɛ wo yareda hɔ mu,*" our proverb says. "If you die and your funeral is coming, you foresee it from your sickbed." I do not know how much my father would have foreseen, whether he knew his funeral would provide the occasion for conflict between monarch and head of state, between Asante and Ghana. To most of my kinsmen, to be sure, his thoughts on the matter are hardly hypothetical; for them, he was a witness to the ceremonies. Some of them tell me that he would have been pleased.

My father's successor as head of the *abusua* will be named in time (the succession is still in dispute as I write), the latest in Akroma-Ampim's long line. Perhaps, if matters are properly arranged, another crocodile will seize another sheep, signaling acceptance of the choice by the powers and principalities of the spirit world. The lineage will continue.

Another proverb says: *Abusua te sɛ kwaeɛ, wowɔ akyiri a ɛyɛ kusuu, wopini ho a, na wohunu sɛ dua koro biara wɔ ne siberɛ.* "The matriclan is like the forest; if you are outside it is dense, if you are inside you see that each tree has its own position." So it now seems to me. Perhaps I have not yet disgraced my families and their names. But as long as I live I know that I will not be out of these woods.

Notes

The Invention of Africa

1. Kwame Nkrumah, *Autobiography of Kwame Nkrumah,* 153; reporting a speech made in Liberia in 1952.

2. Alexander Crummell, "The English Language in Liberia."

3. See David Laitin, *Politics, Language, and Thought;* and "Linguistic Dissociation: A Strategy for Africa."

4. Though this does *not* necessarily exclude North Africans, for there is a large literature—to which I shall refer in Chapter 5—that argues that the Egyptians are of Negro ancestry; see, for example, Chiekh Anta Kiop's *The African Origin of Civilization: Myth or Reality.*

5. Wole Soyinka, *Death and the King's Horseman,* author's note.

6. The formal colonial era was over by the time I went to primary school. But the transition to postcolonial attitudes did not disappear in the instant the Union Jack was taken down on government house. I believe, however, that there are differences between the generation that inherited the colonial state and the present generation of Western-educated Africans and that—at least in Ghana and Nigeria—these differences are the result of changes that began in the sixties. Antiwhite racism seems to me commoner among people with university educations in these countries now—though it is emphatically still a minority view—than it was when I was a child. Central to these changes are at least two facts: first, the worldwide exposure of American racism as the result of the coverage of the civil rights movement in the United States, which led to an increasingly broadly based identification of Africans with African-American political aspirations; second, the growing belief that the West's refusal to take action on South Africa, as well as its extraordinary reluctance to act against the Rhodesian minority government, grew out of an entrenched antiblack racism. Most people outside Africa are probably unaware of the intense interest in southern Africa that exists among a very wide class of ordinary Africans in other parts of the continent.

7. The position of Césaire—born in 1913 in Martinique—on this question changed substantially in later years. But in the period around the Second World War—the period that formed the intellectual culture of the period of decolonization—there is no doubt of the racial basis of his theories: A. James Arnold in his interesting discussion of this issue in *Modernism and Négritude* quotes a passage from *Tropiques,* no. 5 (April 1942): "There flows in our veins a *blood* that requires of us a unique attitude towards life . . . we must respond . . . to the special dynamics of our complex biological reality" (38, italics in original). Blood here is synecdoche, not metaphor.

8. Alexander Crummell "The Relations and Duties of Free Colored Men in America to Africa," a letter to Mr. Charles B. Dunbar, M.D., 1 September 1860, which originally appeared in *The Future of Africa.* (Citations are from H. Brotz ed., *Negro Social and Political Thought.* Brotz's book would by itself be sufficient to refute the extraordinary claim made by

Joyce Joyce in her essay "Who the Cap Fit" that "most Black people have always known[:] that the division of mankind into races is a biologically unsound contrivance" [377].)

9. Robert K. July, *The Origins of Modern African Thought*, 108.

10. Brotz, *Negro Social and Political Thought*, 181, 184.

11. Neptune—who is angry with Ulysses for blinding Polyphemus and plays a hefty role in keeping him on his wanderings—is busy enjoying an Ethiopian hecatomb in his honor at the start of the *Odyssey*, when Minerva intercedes with Zeus for Ulysses. See Frank Snowden's *Blacks in Antiquity* and Martin Bernal's *Black Athena*, vol. 1, for a full discussion of these issues.

12. The philosophical controversy arises because talk of moral *knowledge* seems to presuppose a notion of moral *truth:* and that is an idea that many moral philosophers (among them most relativists, for example) find troublesome. See Chapter 5 of my *Necessary Questions*, especially pp. 121–24.

13. Cited in Brotz, *Negro Social and Political Thought*, 185.

14. Ibid., 175.

15. Ibid., 180.

16. "The Race Problem in America," in Brotz, *Negro Social and Political Thought*, 184.

17. Brotz, *Negro Social and Political Thought*, 197.

18. Nkrumah, *Autobiography of Kwame Nkrumah*, 152–53.

19. Wilson Moses, *The Golden Age of Black Nationalism*, 25.

20. Ibid., 61.

21. See Lewis's biographical note to E. W. Blyden's *Christianity, Islam and the Negro Race*, ix.

22. Blyden, *Christianity, Islam and the Negro Race*, 94; from an address to the American Colonization Society given in 1883.

23. Ibid., 124.

24. Ibid., 212; from a lecture at Sierra Leone, April 1884, on "Sierra Leone and Liberia."

25. The first two allegations are on p. 6, the next on pp. 58–59, and the last on p. 176 of Blyden's *Christianity, Islam and the Negro Race*.

26. Ibid., 58.

27. Johannes Fabian has recently argued (in *Time and the Other*) that seeing Africa as a reflection of the European past is fundamentally a device of "temporal othering"; a way of establishing and maintaining cultural distance.

28. Blyden, *Christianity, Islam and the Negro Race*, 17.

29. See the article on *Guinée*. (The translations from the *Encyclopédie* are my own.)

30. This is from Jaucourt's famous diatribe against the slave trade, in the article "Traite des Nègres."

31. This quotation and the last are from Brotz, *Negro Social and Political Thought*, 174.

32. Blyden, *Christianity, Islam and the Negro Race*, 115; address to the American Colonization Society, 1880.

33. Crummell, *The Future of Africa*, 305; cited by Blyden in *Christianity, Islam and the Negro Race*, 175.

34. This impression has persisted: see, for example, John S. Mbiti's influential *African Religions and Philosophy*.

35. See also my "Old Gods, New Worlds: Some Recent Work in the Philosophy of African Traditional Religion."

36. Gerald Moore and Ulli Beier, eds., *Modern African Poetry*, 59.

37. This expression seems to originate with Blyden, in a speech in Freetown, Sierra Leone, in 1893, and was used by a number of Pan-Africanists—including Sylvester Williams,

who convened the 1900 Pan-African Congress—from then on. (The speech is reprinted as "Study and Race" in *Black Spokesman: Selected Published Writings of Edward Wilmot Blyden.*)

38. See E. E. Evans-Pritchard, *Witchcraft, Oracles and Magic among the Azande.*

39. Blyden, *Christianity, Islam and the Negro Race,* 272–73; this passage shows how people can face the truth when they need to: Blyden's argument here requires that blacks in Christian lands should be unrepresentative, and so he is able to challenge the very idea of a representative Negro. Blyden was, in any case, generally more of an environmental—and less of a hereditary—determinist than Crummell; he is consistent in insisting on the variety of character created by the variety of Africa's ecology.

40. Wener Sollors, *Beyond Ethnicity,* 7.

Illusions of Race

1. W. E. B. Du Bois, "The Conservation of Races," 76.

2. W. E. B. Du Bois, *Dusk of Dawn: An Essay Toward an Autobiography of a Race Concept.*

3. Du Bois, "The Conservation of Races," 73–74.

4. Ibid., 75.

5. Ibid., 75–76.

6. Ibid., 76.

7. Ibid., 77.

8. Ibid., 78.

9. Ibid., 78–79. This talk of racial absorption, and similar talk of racial extinction, reflects the idea that African-Americans might disappear because their genetic heritage would be diluted by the white one. This idea might be thought to be absurd on any view that believes in a racial essence: either a person has it or they don't. But to think this way is to conceive of racial essences as being like genes, and Mendelian genetics was not yet "rediscovered" when Du Bois wrote this piece. What Du Bois is probably thinking of is the fact "passing for white"; on views of inheritance as the blending of parental "blood," it might be thought that the more it is the case that black "blood" is diluted, the more likely that every person of African descent in America could pass for white. And that *would* be a kind of extinction of the socially recognized Negro. It is an interesting question why those who discussed this question assumed that it would not be the extinction of the white also, and the creation of a "hybridized" human race. But, as I say, such speculation is ruled out by the coming of Mendelian genetics.

10. Ibid., 85.

11. Jean-Paul Sartre, "Orphée Noir," in *Anthologie de la Nouvelle Poésie Nègre et Malagache de Langue Francaise,* ed. L. S. Senghor, xiv. Sartre in this passage explicitly argues that this antiracist racism is a path to the "final unity . . . the abolition of differences of race."

12. Shared traditions do not help: the traditions of African-Americans that are African-derived are derived from *specific* African cultures, and are thus not a common black possession; and the American-ness of African-Americans has to do with traditions developed in the New World in interaction with the cultures brought by other Americans from Europe and Asia.

13. Even dual-descent systems, in which ancestry can be traced through both sexes, tend to follow one branch backward in each generation.

14. This way of thinking about the distance between social and biological ancestry I owe to R. B. Le Page and A. Tabouret-Keller's *Acts of Identity,* chap. 6. I am very grateful to Professor Le Page for allowing me to see a typescript many years ago.

15. It might be suggested in Du Bois's defense that he meant by two people sharing a common history only that two people at the present who are of the same race have common ancestry—the historical relationship between them being that each of them can trace their ancestry back to members of the same past group of people. But then this would clearly not be a sociohistorical conception of race but, once more, the biological one.

16. There is a different sense in which the discipline of history is always a matter of making as well as finding: all telling of the past is controlled by narrative conventions. Neither this point nor the one I make in the text here entails either that there are no facts about the past or that historical narratives are fictions, in the sense that we cannot make valid judgments of their truth and falsity.

17. Du Bois, "The Conservation of Races," 75.

18. This seems to me the very notion that the biologists have ended up with: that of a population, which is a group of people (or, more generally, organisms) occupying a common region (or, more generally, an environmental niche), along with people in other regions who are largely descended from people of the same region. See M. Nei and A. K. Roychoudhury, "Genetic Relationship and Evolution of Human Races"; for useful background see also M. Nei and A. K. Roychoudhury, "Gene Differences between Caucasian, Negro and Japanese Populations."

19. Du Bois, "The Conservation of Races," 75.

20. This claim was prompted by G. Spiller, ed., *Papers in Inter-Racial Problems Communicated to the First Universal Races Congress Held at the University of London, July 26–29, 1911.*

21. W. E. B. Du Bois, "Races," 13.

22. M. Nei and A. K. Roychoudhury, "Genetic Relationship and Evolution of Human Races," 4.

23. I call a characteristic of an organism genetically *determined* if, roughly, the organism has a certain genetic constitution whose possession entails, within the normal range of the environments it inhabits, and in the course of an uninterrupted normal development, the possession of that characteristic. "Normal" and "interrupted" are concepts that need detailed explication, of course, but the general idea is enough for our purposes here.

24. Strictly we should say that the character of an organism is fixed by genes, along with sequences of nucleic acid in the cytoplasm and some other features of the cytoplasm of the ovum. But the differential influences of these latter sources of human characteristics are largely swamped by the nucleic DNA; they are substantially similar in almost all people. It is these facts that account, I think, for their not being generally mentioned.

25. It follows, from these definitions, of course, that where a locus is monomorphic the expected homozygosity is going to be one.

26. These figures come from Nei and Roychoudhury, "Genetic Relationship and Evolution of Human Races." I have used the figures derived from looking at proteins, not blood groups, since they claim these are likely to be more reliable. I have chosen a measure of "racial" biological difference that makes it look spectacularly small, but I would not wish to imply that it is not the case, as these authors say, that "genetic differentiation is real and generally statistically highly significant" (41). I *would* dispute their claim that their work shows there is a biological basis for the classification of human races: what it shows is that human populations differ in their distributions of genes. That *is* a biological fact. The objection to using this fact as a basis of a system of classification is that far too many people don't fit into just one category that can be so defined.

I should add that these are only illustrative figures. One way, which I would recommend, to get a sense of the current total picture, if you aren't familiar with this literature, is to read the two articles by these authors in the bibliography, in the order of publication. For purposes of cross-reference I should point out that the "average heterozygosity" they refer to is just 1 minus the average homozygosity, which I explain above.

27. Nei and Roychoudhury, "Genetic Relationship and Evolution of Human Races," 44.

28. See John Maynard-Smith, *The Theory of Evolution*, 212–14. The European crow is a similar reminder of the relative arbitrariness of some species boundaries: there is interbreeding of neighboring populations but reproductive isolation of the birds of the eastern and western limits.

29. See Jonathan Westphall's *Colour: Some Philosophical Problems from Wittgenstein*.

30. Heisenberg's *Philosophic Problems of Nuclear Science* (1952), as cited in Robin Horton's paper "Paradox and Explanation: A Reply to Mr. Skorupski," 243.

31. In particular sociocultural setting supposedly "racial" characteristics may be highly predictive, of course, of social or cultural traits. African-Americans are much more likely to be poor, for example, than Americans taken at random; they are thus more likely to be poorly educated. Even here, though, just a small piece of sociocultural information can change the picture. First-generation Afro-Caribbean immigrants, for example, look very different statistically from other African-Americans.

32. Nei and Roychoudhury, "Genetic Relationship and Evolution of Human Races," 40.

33. Du Bois, "Races," 14.

34. Du Bois, *Dusk of Dawn*, 137.

35. Ibid., 137–38.

36. Ibid., 153.

37. Ibid., 116–17.

38. See the epigraph to Chapter 4.

39. For further thoughts along these lines see my "But Would That Still Be Me? Notes on Gender, 'Race,' Ethnicity as Sources of Identity."

40. Kallen no doubt acquired some of his ideas from the same Harvard courses as Du Bois, and he plainly identified with the struggles of blacks against racial intolerance, on one occasion refusing to attend a Rhodes scholars' dinner at Oxford from which Alain Locke, as a black man, was excluded.

41. Horace M. Kallen, "The Ethics of Zionism," 62.

42. Ibid.

43. Ibid., 69. Kallen also endorses various more specific racialist doctrines —notably a view of intermarriage as leading to sterility—that Afro-Americans were less likely to endorse. "That the Jew merits and must have his self-hood, must retain his individuality, is beyond question. He has the fundamental biological endowment and the transcendent efficiency of moral function which are the ethical conditions of such self-maintenance. . . . It is the Jew that dominates in the child of a mixed marriage, and after a few generations, if sterility does not supervene, as it usually does, what is not Jewish dies out or is transmuted" (70). But notice that this view, mutatis mutandis, would be consistent with the American practice, endorsed by Du Bois, of treating people with *any* identifiable African ancestry as "black."

44. Ibid., 71.

45. Ibid., 70.

46. I am very grateful to Jeff Vogel for drawing Kallen's article to my attention, and for what I have learned from discussions of this issue with him.

47. Nkrumah, *Autobiography of Kwame Nkrumah*, pp. 166–71; this is the July 1953 motion that Nkrumah called the "Motion of Destiny."

48. Nei and Roychoudhury, "Genetic Relationship and Evolution of Human Races," 4.

Topologies of Nativism

1. "Beyond the refusal of all exterior domination is the urge to reconnect in a deep way with Africa's cultural heritage, which has been for too long misunderstood and rejected. Far from being a superficial or folkloric attempt to bring back to life some of the traditions or practices of our ancestors, it is a matter of constructing a new African society, whose identity is not conferred from outside." Cited by Valentin Mudimbe in "African Gnosis. Philosophy and the Order of Knowledge: An Introduction," 164.

2. This is cited in Sollors's *Beyond Ethnicity* (57), which gives a lucid discussion of the role of notions of descent in the understanding of ethnicity in America; see my discussion of Sollors in "Are We Ethnic? The Theory and Practice of American Pluralism." My discussion here is much indebted to Sollors's work.

3. See Hugh B. MacDougall's *Racial Myth in English History: Trojans, Teutons, and Anglo-Saxons.* The discussion of these paragraphs is based on MacDougall's account.

4. See Reginald Horsman's *Race and Manifest Destiny: The Origins of American Racial Anglo-Saxonism.* My discussion of Jefferson is based on Horsman's account, from which these citations come; see 19, 101, 108.

5. See Hans Kohn, *The Idea of Nationalism,* 431–32, which includes the reference to Herder's *On the New German Literature: Fragments.*

6. Alexander Crummell, "The Race Problem in America," in Brotz, *Negro Social and Political Thought,* 184.

7. Hippolyte A. Taine, *History of English Literature,* 1.

8. Ibid., 17.

9. Ibid., 37.

10. Ibid., 39.

11. David Hume, *Of National Characters* (1748), 521–22 n. [M].

12. See Henry Louis Gates's preface to *Black Literature and Literary Theory.*

13. Cited in John Guillory, "Canonical and Non-Canonical: A Critique of the Current Debate." This essay will surely come to be seen as a definitive analysis.

14. "'The teaching of literature' is for me almost tautological. Literature is what is taught, that is all. It's an object of teaching." Roland Barthes, "Reflections sur un manuel," 170.

15. Chinweizu, Onwuchekwa Jemie, and Ihechukwu Madubuike, *Toward the Decolonization of African Literature,* xiv, text and footnote.

16. Ibid., 89.

17. Ibid., 151.

18. Ibid., 147.

19. Ibid., 4.

20. Eliot is cited on p. 106. When Chinweizu et al. assert, typically, that "there was in pre-colonial Africa an abundance of oral narratives which are in no way inferior to European novels" (27), they presuppose the universalist view that there is some (universal) value-metric by which the relative excellence of the two can be gauged.

21. Renan's influential essay "Qu'est-ce qu'une nation" is the locus classicus of attempts to define nationality through a "common memory." For recent work on the invention of traditions see Eric Hobsbawm and Terence Ranger, eds., *The Invention of Tradition.*

22. Michel de Certeau, *Heterologies: Discourse on the Other,* 32.

23. "The sources of each of these tendencies can be discerned from the Renaissance, but it was in the eighteenth and nineteenth centuries that they came through most powerfully, until they became, in the twentieth century, in effect received assumptions." Raymond Williams,

Marxism and Literature, 47. See also Louis Montrose, "Of Gentlemen and Shepherds: The Politics of Elizabethan Pastoral Form," and Michel Beaujour, "Genus Universum."

24. Ernesto Laclau and Chantal Mouffe write: "Only if it is accepted that the subject positions cannot be led back to a positive and unitary founding principle—only then can pluralism be considered radical. Pluralism is *radical* only to the extent that each term of this plurality of identities finds within itself the principle of its own validity, without this having to be sought in a transcendent or underlying positive ground for the hierarchy of meaning of them all and the source and guarantee of their legitimacy." *Hegemony and Socialist Strategy,* 167.

25. William Carlos Williams, *In the American Grain,* 226.

26. For Pêcheux the more radical move is toward what he terms dis-identification, in which we are no longer invested in the specific institutional determinations of the West. Michel Pêcheux, *Language, Semantics and Ideology,* 156–59.

27. Frantz Fanon, *The Wretched of the Earth,* 221.

28. Ibid., 223–24.

29. Ibid., 226. For Ngugi, the cause of cultural nationalism has lead him to write in Gikuyu, eschewing the languages of Europe. In fact, he insists of his europhone compeers that "despite any claims to the contrary, what they have produced is not African literature," and he consigns the work of Achebe, Soyinka, Sembene, and others to a mere hybrid aberrancy that "can only be termed Afro-European literature" (Ngugi wa Thiong'o, "The Language of African Literature," p. 125). So it is interesting to note that, despite his *linguistic* nativism, he does not eschew innovations rooted in Western expressive media. Recently he explained some of the effects he achieved in his latest Gikuyu novel, *Matigari ma Njirugi,* by the happy fact of his being "influenced by film technique. . . . I write as if each scene is captured in a frame, so the whole novel is a series of camera shots." "Interview with Ngugi wa Thiong'o by Hansel Nolumbe Eyoh," 166.

30. Terence Ranger, "Invention of Tradition in Colonial Africa," in Hobsbawm and Ranger, *The Invention of Tradition,* 212.

31. Ibid.

32. Ibid., 262. Al-Amin M. Mazrui has argued, to the point, that "empirical observations have tended to suggest a shift towards increasing ethnic consciousness, despite the reverse trend towards decreasing ethnic behavior. Losing sight of such observations necessarily culminates in the distortion of the nature of tribal identity and in the mystification of cultural revival as an aid to tribal identity. In fact, this tendency to mystify tribal identity is precisely the factor which has made imperialist countries realise that there is no conflict of interest in their sponsoring all sorts of parochial tribal cultural festivals in the guise of reviving African cultural heritage, while attempting to infuse our societies with a 'new' cultural ethos that will be conducive to further consolidation of neocolonial capitalism in Africa." Al-Amin M. Mazrui, "Ideology or Pedagogy: The Linguistic Indigenisation of African Literature," 67.

33. Johannes Fabian, *Language and Colonial Power,* 42–43. The dominance of Swahili in many areas is, itself, a colonial product (see p. 6).

34. Fanon, *The Wretched of the Earth,* 212.

35. Christopher Miller, "Theories of Africans: The Question of Literary Anthropology."

36. Paul de Man, "The Resistance to Theory," 14.

37. Paul de Man, *Allegories of Reading,* 16–17.

38. Denis Kambouchner, "The Theory of Accidents," 149.

39. Ibid., 150.

40. It is important to be clear that Chase's claim for dependency is a complex one; de Man, she argues, is in part engaged in a *critique* of romantic ideology; see her "Translating

Romanticism: Literary Theory as the Criticism of Aesthetics in the Work of Paul de Man" for an elaboration of this point.

41. Miller, "Theories of Africans," 281.

42. See my "Strictures on Structures: On Structuralism and African Fiction."

43. Marilyn Butler, "Against Tradition: The Case for a Particularized Historical Method."

44. For an illuminating discussion of the charges that Ouologuem was guilty of "plagiarism" of Greene's work, see Christopher Miller's *Blank Darkness: Africanist Discourse in French*, 219–28.

45. Chinua Achebe, Interview (Anthony Appiah, John Ryle, and D. A. N. Jones), 26 February 1982.

46. Okot p'Bitek, *Song of Lawino and Song of Ocol*, 43–44.

47. Gerald Moore, *Twelve African Writers*, 124–25.

48. See G. D. Killam, ed., *African Writers and Writing*, 3.

49. Significantly, when, in my own undergraduate days there, Cambridge University appointed Wole Soyinka as a lecturer, it was through the department of anthropology.

50. Immanuel Wallerstein, *Historical Capitalism*, 88.

51. I would contrast this to serious attempts to use notions borrowed from *Ifa* divination, for example, in a situated way for literary theory, as Henry Louis Gates has done in his *Signifying Monkey*. But there we have moved far beyond the mere insertion of the occasional metaphor. What I am objecting to is nativist icing, not an African cake.

52. Achebe, Interview. This passage, which comes from my original transcription, was edited out of the version published in the *T.L.S.*

53. Soyinka, of course, uses the expression "social vision" to other more complex purposes in Wole Soyinka, *Myth, Literature and the African World*. For further discussion of these issues see Chapter 4.

54. "Tout le long du jour" is from *Chants d'ombre*.

The Myth of an African World

1. Achebe, Interview.

2. Ibid.

3. Wole Soyinka, *Death and the King's Horseman*, 49.

4. Ibid., 11.

5. Lionel Trilling, *Sincerity and Authenticity*, 6.

6. Ibid., 97.

7. Stephen Greenblatt, *Renaissance Self-fashioning*, 256.

8. I have tried to say more about the issues of agency that Greenblatt's work raises in "Tolerable Falsehoods: Agency and the Interests of Theory."

9. Lionel Trilling, *The Opposing Self*, xii–xiv.

10. Ngugi wa Thiong'o, *Homecoming*, 39.

11. Soyinka, *Death and the King's Horseman*, author's note.

12. Ibid., 62.

13. Ibid., 28.

14. Ibid., 40.

15. Ibid., 65.

16. Soyinka, *Myth, Literature and the African World*, 50.

17. Ibid., xii.

18. Ibid., 97.

19. Ibid., 14; italics mine.

20. Ibid., 97.

21. My discussion of *Death and the King's Horseman* is much influenced by Soyinka's production at Lincoln Center in early 1987.

Ethnophilosophy and Its Critics

1. Paulin Hountondji, *African Philosophy: Myth and Realiity,* 33.

2. Though, to repeat a point I made in the first essay, the situation of the intellectuals is of the first importance for Africans quite generally.

3. I should not want to be thought to be supposing that the gap between French and German philosophical traditions is negligible, either: Jürgen Habermas's *The Philosophical Discourse of Modernity: Twelve Lectures,* for example, is often sublimely uncomprehending of the work of such leading French philosophes as Derrida, Lyotard, and Foucault. See John Rajchman's ''Habermas's Complaint.''

4. Bernard Williams, *Ethics and the Limits of Philosophy,* 6.

5. Hountondji, *African Philosophy: Myth and Reality,* 66.

6. Kwasi Wiredu, *Philosophy and an African Culture,* xi.

7. Aimé Césaire, *Cahier d'un retour au pays natal,* 117. I should note that Césaire's expression of this sentiment probably deserves an ironical reading.

8. Richard Wright, ed., *African Philosophy: An Introduction,* 26–27.

9. Many of the references in the thorough bibliography of Richard Wright's collection are to anthropological reports of the concepts and beliefs of the folk philosophies of various groups in Africa, reflecting the editor's view that ethnophilosophy is indeed a major philosophical preoccupation.

10. M. Towa, *Essai sur la problématique philosophique dans l'Afrique actuelle.*

11. Hountondji, *African Philosophy: Myth and Reality,* 161.

12. Helaine Minkus, ''Causal Theory in Akwapim Akan Philosophy,'' in Wright, *African Philosophy: An Introduction,* 127.

13. See P. F. Strawson, *Individuals: An Essay in Descriptive Metaphysics.*

14. John Skorupski, *Symbol and Theory,* 218.

15. These notions are to be found in the writings of Rattray, who was the first ethnographer to give a written account of Asante ideology, and they can be confirmed by discussion with people in Asante today; see R. S. Rattray, *Ashanti,* 46. They are discussed also by Wiredu in Wright's *African Philosophy: An Introduction,* 141, and Kwame Gyekye in ''Akan Language and the Materialism Thesis'' and more recently in his *African Philosophical Thought.*

16. Indeed the literature on Akan ideas does not often distinguish among the various Twi-speaking Akan cultures; that it is potentially different schemes that are being compared is thus an issue that has not usually been raised.

17. Ben Oguah, ''African and Western Philosophy: a Comparative Study'' in Wright, *African Philosophy: An Introduction,* 170.

18. Ibid., 177; compare Gyekye, ''Akan Language and the Materialism Thesis.''

19. But my stepgrandmother was a very active Methodist and would probably have taken me to be asking only about the Christian soul: about which she would, however, probably have believed the same.

20. The interpretation of proverbs out of context is by no means a straightforward business; see the introduction to *Bu Me Bε: The Proverbs of the Akan* (Enid Margaret Appiah, Anthony Appiah et al., forthcoming.)

21. I say "most" because Kwasi Wiredu is a monist and Kwame Gyekye a dualist: but each of them is the product, of course, of an extensive Western training.

22. Diop, *The African Origin of Civilization,* xiv–xv.

23. Ibid., xvi.

24. The work of Diop, which I am about to discuss, challenges the claim to Greek originality: unlike their other claims, this one seems to me plausible and worth examining, and the best case for it, so far as I know, is in Martin Bernal's recent *Black Athena.* I think one of the most important lessons of Bernal's work is that it makes a strong case for the centrality of racism—directed against both "Negroes" and "Semites"—in the rewriting of the official history of the Greek miracle that occurred in the European Enlightenment; a rewriting that rejected the ancient commonplace that the Greeks learned much from Egypt. Bernal does not count as an Egyptianist, for me, because he does not make his argument the basis for a view about what contemporary black intellectuals should care about. He is simply concerned to set the record straight.

25. My feelings on this topic may be connected with my having had a British secondary education in which the role of classics in maintaining class differentiation was difficult to ignore!

26. There is, incidentally, something paradoxical about the insistence that we must work with the great *written* texts of philosophy in Africa. For if we are trying to get away from European stereotypes, then surely the view that all interesting conceptual work is written and the property of an individual, and that all interesting analysis has to be of written texts is one that we should discard faster than many others?

27. I am not meaning to imply that this is the only place where philosophy in this sense occurs. I mean only that the kind of philosophy I have in mind occurs typically in universities.

28. Robin Horton, "African Traditional Religion and Western science," 159.

29. Towa also offers an acute analysis of the motivations for this strategy; *Essai sur la problématique philosophique dans l'Afrique actuelle,* 26–33. "The concept of philosophy thus enlarged is coextensive with the concept of culture. It is achieved by way of a contrast to animal behavior. It is thus differentiated from such behavior but it remains indistinguishable from any other cultural form at all: myth, religion, poetry, art, science, etc."

31. Ibid., 26.

31. Wright, *African Philosophy: An Introduction,* 27.

32. Wiredu, *Philosophy and an African Culture,* 38.

33. Ibid.

34. Ibid., 41.

35. Ibid., 47.

36. Ibid., 41.

37. Ibid., 47.

38. Ibid., 1, 4.

39. Ibid., 43. It is important, in the light especially of his more recent work in the explication of Akan philosophical ideas, to be clear that Wiredu does not reject as traditional or superstitious *all* African modes of thought. Indeed, as he was kind enough to point out to me in commenting on a draft of this chapter, on the last paragraph of p. 42 he explicitly denies this; and on p. 50 he writes: "particularly in the field of morality there are conceptions not based on superstition from which the modern Westerner may well have something to learn. The exposition of such aspects of African traditional thought specially befits the contemporary African philosopher."

40. Hountondji, *African Philosophy: Myth and Reality,* 39.

41. Ibid., 45.

42. Ibid., 97.

43. Ibid., 98. "Science," here, means systematic knowledge, and is used in the French sense; we anglophones need to know at least thhhis much about "Continental" philosophy if we aren't to misunderstand our francophone brethren!

44. Hountondji, *African Philosophy: Myth and Reality,* 33.

45. Ibid., 168.

46. Ibid., 104.

47. Hountondji has—for example, in a talk at the African Literature Association meeting in Dakar, Senegal, in April 1989—accepted this point, insisting now that his original *prise de position* was *polemical.* In a situation where African philosophy was supposed to be exhausted by a descriptive ethnophilosophy, it is understandable that his point—that this was by no means all there was to philosophy—was overstated, as the claim that ethnophilosophy had nothing to do with philosophy.

48. Wiredu, *Philosophy and an African Culture,* x.

49. Some of the most interesting work that could be classified as African philosophy does not proceed from the problematics I have been discussing at all. Certainly, V. Y. Mudimbe's *The Invention of Africa,* a powerful inquiry into the contours of Africa in Western modernity, is exemplary of the kind of richly textured explorations of cultural life that are the inevitable task of a contemporary African philosophy.

Old Gods, New Worlds

1. J. F. Thiel, *La situation religieuse des Mbiem,* proverbe 5, 171. The French translates as follows:
What we eat—the ancestors have shown us.
Gloss: "We recognize what is edible because the ancestors have shown it to us. We simply follow the ancestors."

2. I might have chosen the word *posttraditional* here, but, as I argue in Chapter 7, it may be as well to reserve *post* as a prefix for a more specific purpose than that of meaning simply "after."

3. Rattray, *Ashanti,* 147–49. I have varied his translation occasionally.

4. Try asking a Catholic priest in rural Ireland or in Guatemala for an explanation of each step in the Eucharist.

5. This point is made clearly in John Skorupski's excellent *Symbol and Theory.*

6. Clifford Geertz, *The Interpretation of Cultures,* 90.

7. Wiredu, *Philosophy and an African Culture,* 42.

8. Achebe, Interview.

9. Oscar Wilde, *Phrases and Philosophies for the Use of the Young,* 418.

10. Robin Horton, "Spiritual Beings and Elementary Particles—A Reply to Mr Pratt," 30.

11. "One approach to the phenomena of magic and sorcery would be to suppose that we find ourselves facing a symbolic language. . . . A man who flies through the air, who changes himself into an animal, or who makes himself invisible at will . . . cannot be anything but a coded language whose key we have simply to discover. We would then be reassured." M. P. Hegba, *Sorcellerie: Chimere dangereuse . . . ?* 219.

12. Horton, "Spiritual Beings and Elementary Particles," 31.

13. ". . . symbolic and esoteric language is highly honored in our society." Hegba, *Sorcellereie,* 219.

14. John Skorupski has persuaded me that Durkheim does indeed offer this apparently crude argument; see Skorupski's *Symbol and Theory,* chap. 2, for an excellent discussion.

15. This account was suggested to me in conversation with Ruth Marcus. This conception of rationality belongs to a family of recent proposals that treat a concept as being defined by the *de re* relations of agents to the world; see, for example, Grandy's account of knowledge in Hugh Mellor, ed., *Prospects for Pragmatism*. It is thus true on this view that a person's beliefs can be objectively irrational, even though they are subjectively justified. As Gettier showed, a belief can be justified and true, but not a piece of knowledge, because the justification fails to be appropriately related *de re* to the facts; see Edmund L. Gettier III, "Is Justified True Belief Knowledge," 281–82. Similarly, I want to say a belief can be reasonable (subjectively), but irrational (objectively). Since questions of rationality, therefore, raise questions about how other people stand in relation to reality; and since these questions cannot be answered while leaving open, as I wish to do, questions about who is right, I shall talk from now on about reasonableness rather than rationality. Someone is reasonable, on my view, if they are trying to be rational: if they are trying to act so as to maximize the chance of their beliefs being true.

16. Evans-Pritchard, *Witchcraft, Oracles and Magic among the Azande*, 202.

17. Richard Miller, *Fact and Method*.

18. Evans-Pritchard, *Witchcraft, Oracles and Magic among the Azande*, 201.

19. Ibid.

20. Ibid., 199. By "mystical" notions Evans-Pritchard means, as he says, "patterns of thought that attribute to phenomena supra-sensible qualities which, or part of which, are not derived from observation or cannot logically be inferred from it, *and which they do not possess*" (p. 229, italics mine). It is the italicized phrase that does all the work here: the rest of this definition simply means that mystical predicates are theory-laden, which means, if recent philosophy of science is correct, that they are, in this respect, like every other empirical predicate; see N. R. Hanson, *Patterns of Discovery*, and (for some reservations) Ian Hacking, *Representing and Intervening*, 171–76. (Hanson's term is "theory-loaded" but I—and others—use the expression "theory-laden.")

21. Evans-Pritchard, *Witchcraft, Oracles and Magic among the Azande*, 201–3.

22. Uri Geller is believed by some people to have what are called "paranormal" powers: the ability, for example, to bend spoons "by the power of his mind."

23. See Karl Popper's *Conjectures and Refutations* and T. S. Kuhn's *The Structure of Scientific Revolutions*.

24. Horton's most famous paper is his "African Traditional Religion and Western Science." All my thought on these questions has been stimulated and enlivened by reading and talking with him, and so many of the ideas I shall be offering are his that I make now a general acknowledgement.

25. "While neither failing to recognize their limits nor restraining the march towards progress, theoretical understanding [science], and liberation, we must admit that African explanations of the phenomena of magic and sorcery are rational. Our popular beliefs are certainly disconcerting, sometimes false; but would it not be a serious methodological error to postulate irrationality at the beginning of the study of a society?" Hegba, *Sorcellerie*, 267.

26. Wiredu, *Philosophy and an African Culture*, chap. 3.

27. Horton, "African Traditional Religion and Western Science," 64.

28. Ibid., 51.

29. See Daniel Dennett's *The Intentional Stance*.

30. See Evans-Pritchard, *Witchcraft, Oracles and Magic among the Azande*, chap. 2.

31. Wilson, *Rationality*, 153.

32. Catherine Coquery-Vidrovitch, "The Political Economy of the African Peasantry and Modes of Production," 91.

33. Barry Hallen, "Robin Horton on Critical Philosophy and Traditional Thought."

Wiredu, of course, does not deny the existence of skeptics in traditional cultures. See pp. 20–21, 37, 143 of *Philosophy and an African Culture*.

34. Ibid., 82.

35. Ibid., 82.

36. Karl Popper, "Towards a Rational Theory of Tradition."

37. Hallen, "Robin Horton on Critical Philosophy and Traditional Thought," 83.

38. M. Griaule, *Dieu d'eau: Entretiens avec Ogotemmeli.* (And we might add, despite Horton's comments in the manuscript "African Thought-patterns: The Case for a Comparative Approach," that after Kuhn the "openness" of science is also in question; see D. Gjertsen, "Closed and Open Belief Systems.")

39. Barry Hallen and J. Sodipo, *Knowledge, Belief and Witchcraft.*

40. This work is in the paper "Traditional Thought and the Emerging African Philosophy Department: A Reply to Dr. Hallen."

41. This is not to say that they do not have the concepts necessary to understand the idea of an experiment, merely to say that they are not interested in disinterested experimentation simply to find out how things work. For the Azande are very aware, for example, that an oracle needs to be run carefully if it is to be reliable. They therefore test its reliability on every occasion of its use. There are usually two tests: *bambata sima* and *gingo;* the first and second tests. Generally, in the first test, the question is asked so the death of a chicken means yes and in the second so that death means no; but it may be the other way round. Inconsistent results invalidate the procedure. The Azande also have a way of confirming that an oracle is not working; namely to ask it a question to which they already know the answer. Such failures can be explained by one of the many obstacles to an oracle's functioning properly: breach of taboo; witchcraft; the fact that the *benge* poison used in the oracle has been "spoiled" (as the Azande believe) because it has been near a menstruating woman.

42. Evans-Pritchard, *Witchcraft, Oracles and Magic among the Azande,* 202–4.

43. Gellner proposes "a low cognitive division of labour, accompanied at the same time by a proliferation of roles" as "crucial differentia between the savage and the scientific mind" in *Legitimation of Belief,* 158.

44. Discussion of the significance of this fact is one of the most exciting areas in the philosophy of language; see, for example, Hilary Putnam's "The Meaning of Meaning" in his *Mind, Language and Reality.*

45. William Lecky, *History of the Rise and Influence of the Spirit of Rationalism in Europe,* 8–9.

46. "Every African who wanted to do something positive had to begin by destroying all these old beliefs which constitute the marvelous where there is only a natural phenomenon: volcano, virgin forest, thunder, the sun etc." Aké Loba, *Kocoumbo, l'etudiant noir,* 141.

The Postcolonial and the Postmodern

1. Yambo Ouologuem, "A Mon Mari."

2. Susn Vogel et al., *Perspectives: Angles on African Art* (New York: The Center for African Art, 1987); by James Baldwin, Romare Bearden, Ekpo Eyo, Nancy Graves, Ivan Karp, Lela Kouakou, Iba N'Diaye, David Rockefeller, Willian Rubin, and Robert Farris Thompson, interviewed by Michael John Weber, with an introduction by Susan Vogel.

3. Ibid., 11.

4. Ibid., 138.

5. Ibid., 29.

6. Ibid., 143.

7. Ibid., 131.

8. I should insist this first time I use this word that I do not share the widespread negative evaluation of commodification: its merits, I believe, must be assessed case by case. Certainly critics such as Kobena Mercer (for example, in his "Black Hair/Style Politics,") have persuasively criticized any reflexive rejection of the commodity form, which so often reinstates the hoary humanist opposition between "authentic" and "commercial." Mercer explores the avenues by which marginalized groups have manipulated commodified artifacts in culturally novel and expressive ways.

9. Once Vogel has thus refused Kouakou a voice, it is less surprising that his comments turn out to be composite also. On closer inspection, it turns out that there is no single Lela Kouakou who was interviewed like the other cocurators, Kouakou is, in the end, quite exactly an invention: thus literalizing the sense in which "we" (and, more particularly, "our" artists) are individuals while "they" (and "theirs") are ethnic types.

10. It is absolutely crucial that Vogel does not draw her line according to racial or national categories: the Nigerian, the Senegalese, and the African-American cocurators are each allowed to be on "our" side of the great divide. The issue here is something less obvious than racism.

11. Vogel et al., *Perspectives: Angles on African Art*, 23.

12. Margaret Masterman, "The Nature of a Paradigm," 59 n. 1; 61, 65.

13. Jean-François Lyotard, *The Postmodern Condition: A Report on Knowledge*.

14. *Post-* thus images in modernity the trajectory of *meta* in classical metaphysics. Originating in the editorial glosses of Aristotelians wishing to refer to the books "after" the Philosopher's books on nature (physics), this "after" has also been translated into an "above and beyond."

15. Brian McHale, *Postmodernist Fiction* (New York: Methuen, 1987), 5.

16. Scott Lash, "Modernity or Modernism? Weber and Contemporary Social Theory," 355.

17. Trilling, *The Opposing Self*, xiv.

18. Fredric Jameson, *The Ideologies of Theory: Essays 1971–1986*, vol. 2, *Syntax of History*, 178–208; 195.

19. Ibid., 195.

20. Ibid., 195, 196.

21. Ibid., 105.

22. Habermas is, of course, a theorist *against* postmodernism.

23. Max Weber, *The Protestant Ethic and the Spirit of Capitalism*, 13.

24. All that Weber was insisting was that these new charismatic leaders would have thier charisma routinized also.

25. Reinhard Bendix, *Max Weber: An Intellectual Portrait*, 360.

26. Max Weber, *The Theory of Social and Economic Organization*, 358–59.

27. Weber, *The Protestant Ethic and the Spirit of Capitalism*, 194.

28. See "Science as a Vocation," in *From Max Weber*, 155.

29. It is this tendency that leads, for example, in the case of nineteenth-century British utilitarians such as John Stuart Mill, to the view that we can identify a single goal—"the greatest good of the greatest number" conceived of as maximizing happiness or "utility."

30. Oscar Wilde, "The Decay of Lying: An Observation," ih *Intentions*, 45.

31. Jonathan Ngaté, *Francophone African Fiction: Reading a Literary Tradition*, 59.

32. Miller, *Blank Darkness*, 218.

33. Ngaté, *Francophone African Fiction*, 64.

34. Ngaté's focus on this initial sentence follows Aliko Songolo, "The Writer, the

Audience and the Critic's Responsibility: The Case of *Bound to Violence*," cited by Ngaté, *Francophone African Fiction*, 64.

35. Yambo Ouologuem, *Le devoir de violence*, 9. "<u>Nos yeux</u> boivent l'éclat du soleil, et, vaincus, s'étonnent de pleurer. Maschallah! oua bismillah! . . . Un récit de l'aventure sanglante de la négraille—honte aux hommes de rien!—<u>tiendrait aisément dans</u> la première moitié de ce siècle; mais la véritable <u>histoire</u> des Nègres <u>commence</u> beaucoup plus <u>tôt</u>, avec les Säifs, en l'an 1202 de notre ère, dans l'Empire africain de Nakem, . . ."

36. André Schwartz-Bart, *Le dernier des justes*, 11. Cf. nn. 35 nad 36. "<u>Nos yeux</u> reçoivent la lumière d'étoiles mortes. Une biographie de mon ami Ernie <u>tiendrait aisément dans</u> le deuxième quart du xxᵉ siècle; mais la véritable <u>histoire</u> d'Ernie Lévy <u>commence</u> très tôt, dans la vieille cité anglicane de York. Plus précisément: le 11 mars 1185."

37. Ouologuem, *Le devoir de violence*, 12.

38. Soyinka, *Myth, Literature and the African World*, 100.

39. Ibid., 105.

40. Ouologuem, *Le devoir de violence*, 102. Yambo Ouologuem, *Bound to Violence*, translated by Ralph Mannheim, 87.

41. Ibid., 6.

42. Here we have the literary thematization of the Foucauldian *Invention of Africa* that is the theme of Valentin Mudimbe's important recent intervention.

43. Ouologuem, *Bound to Violence*, 181–82, 207.

44. It would be interesting to speculate as to how to account for an apparently similar trend in African-American writing and cultural theory.

45. V. Y. Mudimbe, *L'Écart*, 116.

46. V. Y. Mudimbe, *Entre les eaux*, 75.

47. " 'Tu vas trahir, m'avait dit mon supérieur,' lorsque je lui avais fait part de mon projet.

'Trahir qui?'

'Le Christ.'

'Mon Père, n'est ce pas plutôt l'Occident que je trahis? Est-ce encore une trahison? N'ai-je pas le droit de me dissocier de ce christianisme qui a trahi l'Evangile?'

'Vous êtes prêtre, Pierre.'

'Pardon, mon Père, je suis un prêtre noir.' " V.Y. Mudimbe *Entre les eaux*, 18.

48. Mudimbe, *Entre les eaux*, 20.

49. "L'Eglise et l'Afrique comptent sur vous."

50. Mudimbe, *Entre les eaux*, 73–74.

51. Mudimbe, *Entre les eaux*, 166.

52. Ibid., 189.

53. See Richard Rorty's *Contingency, Irony and Solidarity*.

54. Ouologuem, *Le Devoir de Violence*, 110.

55. Ibid.

56. Ibid., 111. Ouologuem, *Bound to Violence*, 94–95.

57. Ouologuem, *Le Devoir de Violence*, 112. Ouologuem, *Bound to Violence*, 95–96.

58. Sara Suleri, *Meatless Days*, 105.

59. I learned a good deal from trying out earlier versions of these ideas at an NEH Summer Institute on "The Future of the Avant-Garde in Postmodern Culture" under the direction of Susan Suleiman and Alice Jardine at Harvard in July 1989; at the African Studies Association (under the sponsorship of the Society for African Philosophy in North America) in November 1989, where Jonathan Ngaté's response was particularly helpful; and, as the guest of Ali Mazrui, at the Braudel Center at SUNY Binghamton in May 1990. As usual, I wish I knew how to incorporate more of the ideas of the discussants on those occasions.

Altered States

1. Akan proverb. (Proverbs are notoriously difficult to interpret, and thus, also to translate. But the idea is that states collapse from within, and the proverb is used to express the sentiment that people suffer as a result of their own weaknesses. My father would never have forgiven the solecism of trying to explain a proverb!)

2. In *Politics and Society in Contemporary Africa*, 81, Naomi Chazan, Robert Mortimer, John Ravenhill, and Donald Rothchild cite from *Afriscope* 7, no. 4 (1977): 24–25, a figure of 150,000 "professionally qualified people" in sub-Saharan Africa.

3. See D. G. Austin, *Politics in Ghana 1946–1960*, 48.

4. Ethiopia, which was never a colony, is one of the world's oldest unitary states, but the modern boundaries of Ethiopia include Eritrea and the Ogaden, both of them essentially granted to the Ethiopian empire by Western powers.

5. Nkrumah, *Autobiography of Kwame Nkrumah*, 153.

6. Peter Duignan and Robert H. Jackson, eds., *Politics and Government in African States 1960–1985*, 120–21.

7. Samir Amin, "Underdevelopment and Dependence in Black Africa: Origins and Contemporary Forms."

8. Chazan et al., *Politics and Society in Contemporary Africa*, 41.

9. Twi is the generic name for the language spoken (with some variations in accent and vocabulary) in most of the Akan portion of Ghana; the language of Asante is Asante-Twi.

10. This is not to ignore the role of the structural adjustment program (SAP) in strangling the labor movements, which in some places constituted one of society's major antagonists to the state. The SAP has, as intended, played a part in making life easier for capital in other ways as well.

11. In Britain, Mrs. Thatcher's opposition to full European monetary union and a single currency, for example—an opposition that played a part in her departure from the prime ministership—was plainly connected with a sense (threatening in the extreme to anyone with Mrs. Thatcher's sympathies with monetarism) that this would reduce the options for British national monetary policy.

12. Reference to "the essential faith of citizens in Ghana and elsewhere in the established judicial system"—in Chazan et al., *Politics and Society in Contemporary Africa*, 59—is one of the few points where I am bound to say I find their analysis unconvincing.

13. I have found very helpful the theoretical elaboration of these patterns in Chazan et al., *Politics and Society in Contemporary Africa*, chap. 3 on "Social Groupings."

14. We should not, however, ignore the role of asymmetries of power in the Kumasi and other places in the state's periphery, in structuring who benefits from these arrangements.

African Identities

1. Achebe, Interview.

2. See, for example, Robert Harms, *Times Literary Supplement*, 29 November 1985, 1343.

3. Tzvetan Todorov, "'Race,' Writing and Culture." You don't have to believe in witchcraft, after all, to believe that women were persecuted as witches in colonial Massachusetts.

4. Gayatri Spivak recognizes these problems when she speaks of "strategic" essentialisms. See *In Other Worlds*, 205.

5. The violence between Senegalese and Mauritanians in the spring of 1989 can only be

understood when we recall that the legal abolition of racial slavery of "Negroes," owned by "Moorish" masters, occurred in the early 1980s.

6. David Laitin, *Hegemony and Culture: Politics and Religious Change among the Yoruba*, 7–8.

7. Ibid., 8.

8. This passage continues: "Increasingly also Lingala and Swahili came to divide functions between them. Lingala served the military and much of the administration in the capital of the lower Congo; Swahili became the language of the workers in the mines of Katanga. This created cultural connotations which began to emerge very early and which remained prevalent in Mobutu's Zaire. From the point of view of Katanga/Shaba, Lingala has been the undignified jargon of unproductive soldiers, government clerks, entertainers, and, recently, of a power clique, all of them designated as *batoka chini*, people from down-river, i.e. from Kinshasa. Swahili as spoken in Katanga was a symbol of regionalism, even for those colonials who spoke it badly." Johannes Fabian, *Language and Colonial Power*, 42–43. The dominance of Swahili in certain areas is already itself a colonial product (*Language and Colonial Power*, 6).

9. Similarly, Shona and Ndebele identities in modern Zimbabwe became associated with political parties at independence, even though Shona-speaking peoples had spent much of the late precolonial period in military confrontations with each other.

10. Laitin, *Hegemony and Culture*, 8. I need hardly add that religious identities are equally salient and equally mythological in Lebanon or in Ireland.

11. That "race" operates this way has been clear to many other African-Americans: so, for example, it shows up in a fictional context as a central theme of George Schuyler's *Black No More;* see, for example, 59. Du Bois (as usual) provides—in *Black Reconstruction*—a body of evidence that remains relevant. As Cedric J. Robinson writes, "Once the industrial class emerged as dominant in the nation, it possessed not only its own basis of power and the social relations historically related to that power, but it also had available to it the instruments of repression created by the now subordinate Southern ruling class. In its struggle with labour, it could activate racism to divide the labour movement into antagonistic forces. Moreover, the permutations of the instrument appeared endless: Black against white; Anglo-Saxon against southern and eastern European; domestic against immigrant; proletariat against share-cropper; white American against Asian, Black, Latin American, etc." Cedric J. Robinson, *Black Marxism: The Making of the Black Radical Tradition*, 286.

12. See Robinson *Black Marxism*, 313.

13. John B. Thompson, *Studies in the Theory of Ideology*, 62–63. Again and again, in American labor history, we can document the ways in which conflicts organized around a racial or ethnic group identity can be captured by the logic of the existing order. The financial support that black churches in Detroit received from the Ford Motor Company in the 1930s was only a particularly dramatic example of a widespread phenomenon: corporate manipulation of racial difference in an effort to defeat labor solidarity. See, for example, James S. Olson, "Race, Class and Progress: Black Leadership and Industrial Unionism, 1936–1945"; and David M. Gordon et al., *Segmented Work, Divided Workers*, 141–43, and Fredric Jameson, *The Political Unconscious*, 54.

Epilogue: In My Father's House

1. Joe Appiah, *Joe Appiah: The Autobiography of an African Patriot*, 103.

2. Ibid., 202–3.

3. Ibid., 368.

4. On the way to the palace, a couple of notes on the terminology surrounding chieftaincy may be in order. The symbol of chieftaincy in Akan cultures, including Asante, is the stool. The Asantehene's stool is called the Golden Stool; his queen mother's is the Silver Stool. These are *symbolic* representations of chieftaincy and, unlike a throne in Europe, they are not sat upon in the ordinary course of things, being thought of rather as repositories of the *sunsum,* the soul, of a chief's village, town, area, or nation. Indeed, the Golden Stool has its own palace and servants. We speak in Twi (and in Ghanaian English) of the stool, the way an English person might speak of the throne, when referring to the object, the institution, and, sometimes, the incumbent chief or queen mother.

Any person of high status, male or female, including one's grandparents, other elders, chiefs, and the king and queen, may be called "Nana."

A chief—Ɔhene—is named for his place: the king of Asante is the Asantehene, the chief of the town of Tafo, the Tafohene; and the queen mother—the *Ahemma*—is called the Asantehemma or the Tafohemma. Not all chieftaincies are hereditarily restricted to a particular matriclan; some are appointive. Thus the *Kyidomhene,* the chief of the rearguard, associated with major stools, is appointed (for life) by his chief.

5. Appiah, *Joe Appiah,* 2–3.

6. Ibid., 200–201.

Bibliography

Achebe, Chinua. "The Novelist as Teacher." In *African Writers and Writing,* edited by G. D. Killam. London: Heinemann, 1973.

——. Interview with Anthony Appiah, D. A. N. Jones, and John Ryle, *Times Literary Supplement,* 26 February 1982. [Some passages cited in the text are from my own unpublished transcription of the full interview, which was edited for this briefer published version.]

A. W. H. Adkins. *Merit and Responsibility in Greek Ethics.* Oxford: Oxford University Press, 1960.

Amadiume, Ifi. *Male Daughters, Female Husbands.* London: Zed Books, 1987.

Amin, Samir. "Underdevelopment and Dependence in Black Africa: Origins and Contemporary Forms." *Journal of Modern African Studies* 10, no. 4 (1972):503–24.

Anderson, Benedict. *Imagined Communities: Reflections on the Origin and Spread of Nationalism.* London: Verso, 1983.

Appiah, Joe. *Joe Appiah: The Autobiography of an African Patriot.* Westport, Conn.: Praeger, 1990.

Appiah, K. A. "How Not to Do African Philosophy." *Universitas* 6, no. 2 (1979):183–91.

——. "Modernisation and the Mind." (Review: Wiredu, *Philosophy and an African Culture.*) *Times Literary Supplement,* 20 June 1980, 697.

——. "An Aesthetics for Adornment in some African Cultures." In the catalog *Beauty by Design: The Aesthetics of African Adornment,* edited by Marie-Therèse Brincard, 15–19. New York: African-American Institute, 1984.

——. "Stricture on Structures: On Structuralism and African Fiction." In *Black Literature and Literary Theory,* edited by Henry Louis Gates, Jr., 127–50. New York: Metheun, 1984.

——. Review: Hountondji, *African Philosophy: Myth and Reality. Queens Quarterly* (Winter 1985):873–74.

——. "Soyinka and the Philosophy of Culture." In *Philosophy in Africa: Trends and Perspectives,* edited by P. O. Bodunrin, 250–63. Ile-Ife: University of Ife Press, 1985.

——. "Are We Ethnic? The Theory and Practice of Emerican Pluralism." *Black American Literature Forum* 20 (Spring–Summer 1986):209–24.

——. "The Uncompleted Argument: Du Bois and the Illusion of Race." In *"Race," Writing and Difference,* edited by Henry Louis Gates, Jr., 21–37. Chicago: University of Chicago Press, 1986.

——. "Racism and Moral Pollution." *Philosophical Forum* 18 (Winter–Spring 1986–87):185–202.

——. "A Long Way from Home: Richard Wright in the Gold Coast." In *Richard Wright: Modern Critical Views,* edited by Harold Bloom, 173–90. New York: Chelsea House, 1987.

——. "Old Gods, New Worlds: Some Recent Work in the Philosophy of African Traditional Religion." In *Contemporary Philosophy: A New Survey.* Vol. 5, edited by Guttorm Fløistad, 207–34. Amsterdam: Martinus Nijhoff, 1987.

————. "Thought in a Time of Famine." (Review: Gyekye, *An Essay on African Philosophical Thought.*) *Times Literary Supplement* (July 29–August 4, 1988):837.

————. "Racisms." In *Anatomy of Racism,* edited by David Goldberg. Minneapolis: University of Minnesota, 1988.

————. "The Conservation of 'Race.'" *Black American Literature Forum* 23 (Spring 1989):37–60.

————. *Necessary Questions.* New York: Prentice-Hall, 1989.

————. "Race." In *Key Words in Contemporary Literary Studies,* edited by Frank Lentricchia and Tom McLaughlin, 274–87. Chicago: University of Chicago Press, 1990.

————. "Tolerable Falsehoods: Agency and the Interests of Theory." In *Some Consequences of Theory,* edited by Barbara Johnson and Jonathan Arac. Baltimore: Johns Hopkins University Press, 1990.

————. "Soyinka's Myth of an African World." In *Crisscrossing Boundaries in African Literatures,* edited by Kenneth Harrow, Jonathan Ngaté and Clarisse Zimra, 11–24. Washington, D.C.: Three Continents Press and the African Literature Association, 1991.

Appiah, Peggy and K. A. Appiah. *Bu me bɛ: The Proverbs of the Akan,* forthcoming.

Arnold, A. James. *Modernism and Négritude.* Cambridge, Mass.: Harvard University Press, 1981.

Austin, D. G. *Politics in Ghana 1946–1960.* Oxford: Oxford University Press, 1964.

Barthes, Roland. "Reflections sur un manuel." In *Enseignement de la littérature,* edited by Tzvetan Todorov and Serge Doubrovsky, 170–77. Paris: Plon, 1971.

Beaujour, Michel. "Genus Universum." *Glyph* 7 (1980):15–31.

Bendix, Reinhard. *Max Weber: An Intellectual Portrait.* London: Methuen University Paperback, 1966.

Berger, Harry, Jr. "Bodies and Texts." *Representations* 17 (Winter 1987):144–66.

Bernal, Martin. *Black Athena.* Vol. 1, *The Fabrication of Ancient Greece 1785–1985.* New Brunswick, N.J.: Rutgers University Press, 1987.

Bloom, Harold. *A Map of Misreading.* New York: Oxford University Press, 1975.

Blyden, E. W. "Study and Race." In *Black Spokesman: Selected Published Writings of Edward Wilmot Blyden,* edited by Hollis R. Lynch. London: Frank Cass, 1971.

————. *Christianity, Islam and the Negro Race.* 1887. Reprint. Edinburgh: Edinburgh Univeristy Press, 1967.

Brotz, Howard, ed. *Negro Social and Political Thought.* New York: Basic Books, 1966.

Butler, Marilyn. "Against Tradition: The Case for a Particularized Historical Method." In *Historical Studies and Literary Criticism,* edited by Jerome J. McGann. Madison: University of Wisconsin Press, 1985.

Cartwright, Nancy. *How the Laws of Physics Lie.* Oxford: Oxford University Press, 1983.

de Certeau, Michel. *Heterologies: Discourse on the Other.* Translated by Brian Massumi. Minneapolis: University of Minnesota Press, 1986.

Césaire, Aimé. *Cahier d'un retour au pays natal.* Paris: Présence Africaine, 1971.

Chase, Cynthia. "Translating Romanticism: Literary Theory as the Criticism of Aesthetics in the Work of Paul de Man." *Textual Practice* 4.3 (Winter 1990):349–75.

Chazan, Naomi, Robert Mortimer, John Ravenhill, and Donald Rothchild. *Politics and Society in Contemporary Africa.* Boulder, Colo.: Lynne Rienner Publishers, 1988.

Chinweizu, Onwuchekwa Jemie, and Ihechukwu Madubuike. *Toward the Decolonization of African Literature.* Enugu: Fourth Dimension Publishing, 1980.

Cole, H., and D. Ross. *The Arts of Ghana.* Los Angeles: University of California, 1977.

Coquery-Vidrovitch, Catherine. "The Political Economy of the African Peasantry and Modes of Production." Translated by Jeanne Mayo and reprinted in *The Political Economy of*

Contemporary Africa, edited by Peter C. W. Gutkind and Immanuel Wallerstein, 94–116. Beverly Hills, Calif.: Sage Publications, 1976.

Crummell, Alexander. "The Relations and Duties of Free Colored Men in America to Africa." In *Negro Social and Political Thought,* edited by H. Brotz, 171–80. New York: Basic Books, 1966.

———. "The Race Problem in America." In *Negro Social and Political Thought,* edited by H. Brotz, 180–90. New York: Basic Books, 1966.

———. "The English Language in Liberia." In *The Future of Africa: Being Addresses, Sermons Etc., Etc., Delivered in the Republic of Liberia.* 1862. Reprint. Detroit: Negro History Press, 1969.

Dennett, Daniel C. *The Intentional Stance.* Cambridge, Mass.: Bradford Books, 1987.

Dieterlen, M., ed. *La notion de personne en Afrique noir.* Paris: Editions du CNRS, 1973.

Diop, Cheikh Anta. *The African Origin of Civilization: Myth or Reality.* New York and Westport, Conn.: Lawrence Hill and Company, 1974.

Douglas, M. *Purity and Danger.* New York: Praeger, 1966.

Du Bois, W. E. B. *Black Reconstruction: An Essay Toward a History of the Part which Black People Played in America, 1860–1880.* New York: Russel and Russel, 1935.

———. "Races." From *The Crisis,* August 1911. Reprinted in *Writings in Periodicals Edited by W. E. B. Du Bois.* Vol. 1, *1911–1925.* Compiled and edited by Herbert Aptheker. Milwood, N.Y.: Kraus-Thomson, 1983.

———. "The Conservation of Races." American Nagro Academy Occasional Papers, no. 2, 1897. Reprinted in *W. E. B. Du Bois Speaks: Speeches and Addresses 1890–1919,* edited by Philip S. Foner, 73–85. New York: Pathfinders Press, 1970.

———. *Dusk of Dawn: An Essay Toward an Autobiography of a Race Concept.* New York: Harcourt, Brace and Company, 1940. Reprinted with an introduction by Herbert Aptheker. Milwood, N.Y.: Kraus-Thomson, 1975.

Duignan, Peter, and Robert H. Jackson, eds. *Politics and Government in African States 1960–1985.* London and Sydney: Croom Helm; Stanford: Hoover Institution Press, 1986.

Eagleton, T. *Literary Theory: An Introduction.* Oxford: Basil Blackwell, 1983.

Eddington, A. *The Nature of the Physical World.* Cambridge: Cambridge University Press, 1928.

Evans-Pritchard, E. E. *Nuer Religion.* Oxford: Oxford University Press, 1956.

———. *Witchcraft, Oracles and Magic among the Azande.* Abridged, with an introduction by Eva Gillies. Oxford: Oxford University Press, 1976.

Fabian, Johannes. *Time and the Other: How Anthropology Makes Its Object.* New York: Columbia University Press, 1983.

———. *Language and Colonial Power.* Cambridge: Cambridge University Press, 1986.

Fanon, Frantz. *The Wretched of the Earth.* New York: Grove Press, 1968.

Feyerabend, P. *Against Method.* London: New Left Books, 1975.

Gates, Henry Louis, Jr. *"Race," Writing and Difference.* Chicago: University of Chicago Press, 1986.

———. *Figures in Black.* New York: Oxford University Press, 1987.

———. The Signifying Monkey: A Theory of Afro-American Literary Criticism. New York: Oxford University Press, 1988.

———, ed. *Black Literature and Literary Theory.* New York: Methuen, 1984.

Geertz, Clifford. *The Interpretation of Cultures.* New York: Basic Books, 1973.

Gellner, Ernest. *Legitimation of Belief.* Cambridge: Cambridge University Press, 1974.

Gettier, Edmund L. III. "Is Justified True Belief Knowledge?" *Analysis* 23.6 (June 1963):121–23.

Gjertsen, Derek. "Closed and Open Belief Systems." *Second Order* 7.1 (1980):5–69.

Goody, J. *The Domestication of the Savage Mind*. Cambridge: Cambridge University Press, 1977.

Gordon, David M., Richard Edwards, and Michael Reich. *Segmented Work, Divided Workers: The Historical Transformation of Labor in the United States*. Cambridge: Cambridge University Press, 1982.

Greenblatt, Stephen. *Renaissance Self-fashioning: From More to Shakespeare*. Chicago: University of Chicago Press, 1980.

Griaule, M. *Dieu d'eau: Entretiens avec Ogotemmeli*. Paris: Editions du Chêne, 1948.

Guillory, John. "Canonical and Non-canonical: A Critique of the Current Debate." *ELH* 54, no. 3 (Fall 1987):483–527.

Gyekye, Kwame. Review: Mbiti, *African Religions and Philosophy*. *Second Order* 4, no. 1 (1975):86–94.

———. "Akan Language and the Materialism Thesis." *Studies in Language* 1, no. 1 (1977):237–44.

———. *African Philosophical Thought*. Cambridge: Cambridge University Press, 1987.

Habermas, Jürgen. *The Philosophical Discourse of Modernity: Twelve Lectures*. Cambridge, Mass.: MIT Press, 1987.

Hacking, Ian. *Representing and Intervening: Introductory Topics in the Philosophy of Science*. Cambridge: Cambridge University Press, 1983.

Hallen, B. "Robin Horton on Critical Philosophy and Traditional Thought." *Second Order*, no. 1 (1977):81–92.

Hallen, Barry, and J. O. Sodipo. *Knowledge, Belief and Witchcraft: Analytic Experiments in African Philosophy*. London: Ethnographica, 1986.

Hanson, N. R. *Patterns of Discovery: An Inquiry into the Conceptual Foundations of Science*. Cambridge: Cambridge University Press, 1958.

Harrow, Kenneth, Jonathan Ngaté, and Clarisse Zimra, eds. *Crisscrossing Boundaries in African Literatures*. Washington, D.C.: Three Continents Press and the African Literature Association, 1991.

Hartman, Geoffrey. *Wordsworth's Poetry, 1787–1814*. New Haven: Yale University Press, 1964.

Hebga, Meinrad P. *Sorcellereie: Chimere dangereuse . . . ?* Abidjan: INADES, 1979.

Heisenberg, W. *Philosophic Problems of Nuclear Science*. New York: Pantheon, 1952.

Hobsbawm, Eric, and Terence Ranger, eds. *The Invention of Tradition*. Cambridge: Cambridge University Press, 1983.

Horsman, Reginald. *Race and Manifest Destiny: The Origins of American Racial Anglo-Saxonism*. Cambridge, Mass.: Harvard University Press, 1981.

Horton, R. "God, Man and the Land in a Northern Ibo Village Group.: *Africa* 26, no. 1 (1956):17–28.

———. "The Kalabari World View: An Outline and Interpretation." *Africa* 32, no. 3 (1962):197–220.

———. "Ritual Man in Africa." *Africa* 34, no. 2 (1964):85–104.

———. "African Traditional Religion and Western Science." *Africa* 37, nos. 1 and 2 (1967):50–71, 155–187.

———. "A Hundred Years of Change in Kalabari Religion." In *Black Africa: Its Peoples and Their Cultures Today*, edited by John Middleton, 192–211. London: Collier-Macmillan, 1970.

———. "Spiritual Beings and Elementary Particles—A Reply to Mr Pratt." *Second Order* 1, no. 1 (1972):21–33.

———. "Lévy-Bruhl, Durkheim and the Scientific Revolution." *Modes of Thought*, edited by R. Horton and R. Finnegan, 249–305. London: Faber and Faber, 1973.

————. "Paradox and Explanation: A Reply to Mr. Skorupski." *Philosophy of Social Sciences* 3 (1973):231–56.

————. "Understanding Traditional African Religion: A Reply to Professor Beattie." *Second Order* 3, no. 1 (1976):3–29.

————. "Traditional Thought and the Emerging African Philosophy Department: A Comment on the Current Debate." *Second Order* 6, no. 1 (1977):64–80.

————. "Tradition and Modernity Revisited." In *Rationality and Relativism,* edited by S. Lukes and M. Hollis, 201–60. Oxford: Basil Blackwell, 1982.

————. "African Thought-patterns: The Case for a Comparative Approach." Unpublished manuscript.

————. "Traditional Thought and the Emerging African Philosophy Department: A Reply to Dr. Hallen." Unpublished manuscript.

————. "African Thought Patterns: The Case for a Comparative Approach." Unpublished manuscript.

Horton, R., and R. Finnegan, eds. *modes of Thought.* London: Faber and Faber, 1973.

Hountondji, P. *Sur la philosophie Africaine.* Paris: Maspero, 1976.

————. *African Philosophy: Myth and Reality.* Translated by Henri Evans with the collaboration of Jonathan Rée, with an introduction by Abiola Irele. Bloomington: Indiana University Press, 1983.

Hume, David. "Of National Characters" (1748). In *Essays and Treatises on Several Subjects.* Vol. 1, *Containing Essays, Moral, Political and Literary,* 194–210; nn. 507–21. Edinburgh: Bell & Bradfute, & W. Blackwood; & T. Cadell; Longman, Hurst & Co.; J. Cuthell; J. Nunn; Baldwin, Craddock & Joy; Jeffrey & Son; John Richardson; Sherwood & Co.; G. B. Whittaker; R. Saunders; J. Collingwood; W. Mason; & J. Duncan, London, 1825.

Hunter, George K. *Dramatic Identities and Cultural Tradition: Studies in Shakespeare and His Contemporaries.* Liverpool: Liverpool University Press, 1978.

Irele, Abiola. "In Praise of Alienation." An inaugural lecture delivered on 22 November 1982 at the University of Ibadan, Nigeria, by F. Abiola Irele, professor of French and head, Department of Modern Languages. Privately printed, n.d.

Jameson, Fredric. *The Political Unconscious.* Ithaca, N.Y.: Cornell University Press, 1981.

————. *The Ideologies of Theory: Essays 1971–1986.* Vol. 2, *Syntax and History.* Minneapolis: University of Minnesota Press, 1988.

Joyce, Joyce. "Who the Cap Fit." *New Literary History* 18, no. 2 (Winter 1987):335–44.

July, Robert K. *The Origins of Modern African Thought.* London: Faber and Faber, 1968.

Kagamé, Alexis. *La Philosophie Bantou-Rwandaise de l'etre.* Brussels: Memoire in 8 de ARSOM, N.S. Vol. XII.1, 1956.

Kallen, Horace M. "The Ethics of Zionism." In *The Maccabaean,* New York, August 1906.

Kambouchner, Denis. "The Theory of Accidents." *Glyph* 7 (1980):149–75.

Killam, G. D., ed. *African Writers on African Writing.* London: Heinemann, 1973.

Kohn, Hans. *The Idea of Nationalism.* New York: Collier Books, 1967.

Kuhn, Thomas. *The Structure of Scientific Revolutions.* 2d ed. Chicago: University of Chicago Press, 1962.

Laclau, Ernesto, and Chantal Mouffe. *Hegemony and Socialist Strategy.* London: Verso, 1985.

Laitin, David. *Politics, Language, and Thought.* Chicago: University of Chicago Press, 1977.

————. "Linguistic Dissociation: A Strategy for Africa." In *Antinomies of Interdependence,* edited by J. G. Ruggie. New York: Columbia University Press, 1983.

————. *Hegemony and Culture: Politics and Religious Change among the Yoruba.* Chicago: University of Chicago Press, 1986.

Lash, Scott. "Modernity or Modernism? Weber and Contemporary Social Theory." In *Max Weber, Rationality and Modernity,* edited by Scott Lash and Sam Whimster. London: Allen and Unwin, 1987.

Lecky, William. *History of the Rise and Influence of the Spirit of Rationalism in Europe.* Vol. 1. New York: D. Appleton & Company, 1914.

Le Page, R. B., and A. Tabouret-Keller. *Acts of Identity: Creole-Bases Approaches to Language and Ethnicity.* Cambridge and New York: Cambridge University Press, 1985.

Lithown, R. "Bodunrin on Theoretical Entities: A Critique." *Second Order* 5, no. 2 (1976):76–84.

Loba, Aké. *Kocoumbo, l'etudiant noir.* Paris: Flammarion, 1980.

Lukes, S., and M. Hollis, eds. *Rationality and Relativism.* Oxford: Basil Blackwell, 1982.

Lyotard, Jean-François. *The Postmodern Condition: A Report on Knowledge.* Vol. 10 of *Theory and History of Literature.* Translated by Geoff Bennington and Brian Massumi. Minneapolis: University of Minnesota Press, 1988.

MacDougall, Hugh B. *Racial Myth in English History: Trojans, Teutons, and Anglo-Saxons.* Montreal: Harvest House; Hanover, N.H., and London: University Press of New England, 1982.

MacIntyre, Alasdair. *A Short History of Ethics.* New York: Macmillan, 1966.

———. *After Virtue: A Study in Moral Theory.* Notre Dame: University of Notre Dame Press, 1987.

———. *Whose Justice? Which Rationality?* Notre Dame: Univesity of Notre Dame Press, 1988.

de Man, Paul. *Allegories of Reading.* New Haven: Yale University Press, 1979.

———. *The Resistance to Theory.* Minneapolis: University of Minnesota Press, 1986.

Masterman, Margaret. "The Nature of a Paradigm." In *Criticism and the Growth of Knowledge,* edited by Alan Musgrave and Imre Lakatos, 59–89. Cambridge: Cambridge University Press, 1970.

Maynard-Smith, John. *The Theory of Evolution.* 3d ed. London: Penguin, 1975.

Mazrui, Ali. "The Patriot as an Artist." In *African Writers on African Writing,* edited by G. D. Killam, 73–90. London: Heinemann, 1973.

Mazrui, Al-Amin M. "Ideology or Pedagogy: The Linguistic Indigenisation of African Literature." *Race and Class* 28, no. 1 (Summer 1986):63–72.

Mbiti, John S. *African Religions and Philosophy.* New York: Doubleday, 1970.

McHale, Brian. *Postmodernist fiction.* New York: Methuen, 1987.

Mellor, D. H., ed. *Prospects for Pragmatism: Essays in Honour of F. P. Ramsey.* Cambridge: Cambridge University Press, 1981.

Mercer, Kobena. "Black Hair/Style Politics." *New Formations* 3 (Winter 1987):33–54.

Miller, Christopher. "Theories of Africans: The Question of Literary Anthropology." In *"Race," Writing and Difference,* edited by Henry Louis Gates, Jr., 281–300. Chicago: University of Chicago Press, 1986.

———. *Blank Darkness: Africanist Discourse in French.* Chicago: University of Chicago Press, 1985.

Miller, Richard. *Fact and Method.* Princeton: Princeton University Press, 1987.

Montrose, Louis. "Of Gentlemen and Shepherds: The Politics of Elizabethan Pastoral Form." *ELH* 50 (1983):433–52.

Moore, Gerald. *Twelve African Writers.* Bloomington: Indiana University Press, 1980.

Moore, Gerald, and Ulli Beier, eds. *Modern African Poetry.* 3d ed. New York: Penguin, 1985.

Moses, Wilson. *The Golden Age of Black Nationalism: 1850–1925.* Hamden, Conn.: Archon Books, 1978.

Mudimbe, Valentin Y. "African Gnosis. Philosophy and the Order of Knowledge: An Introduction." *African Studies Review* 28, nos. 2 and 3 (June/September 1985):149–233.

———. *Entre les eaux*. Paris: Présence Africaine, 1973.

———. *Le Bel immonde*. Paris: Présence Africaine, 1976.

———. *L'Écart*. Paris: Présence Africaine, 1979.

———. *L'Odeur du père*. Paris: Présence Africaine, 1982.

———. *The Invention of Africa*. Bloomington: Indiana University Press, 1988.

Nei, M., and A. K. Roychoudhury. "Gene Differences between Caucasian, Negro and Japanese Populations." *Science* 177 (August 1972):434–35.

———. "Genetic Relationship and Evolution of Human Races." *Evolutionary Biology* 14 (1983):1–59.

Ngaté, Jonathan. *Francophone African Fiction: Reading a Literary Tradition*. Trenton, N.J.: Africa World Press, 1988.

Ngugi wa Thiong'o. *Homecoming*. New York: Lawrence Hill and Company, 1972.

———. "The Language of African Literature." *New Left Review* 150 (1985):109–27.

———. "Interview with Ngugi wa Thiong'o by Hansel Nolumbe Eyoh." *The Journal of Commonwealth Literature* 21, no. 1 (1986):162–66.

Nkrumah, Kwame. *Autobiography of Kwame Nkrumah*. London: Panaf Books, 1973.

Oguah, Ben. "African and Western Philosophy: A Comparative Study." In *African Philosophy: An Introduction*, edited by Richard Wright, 195–214. Washington, D.C.: University Press of America, 1979.

Olson, James S. "Race, Class and Progress: Black Leadership and Industrial Unionism, 1936–1945." In *Black Labor in America*, edited by M. Cantor, 153–64. Westport, Conn.: Negro Universities Press, 1969.

Ouologuem, Yambo. "A Mon Mari." *Presence Africaine* 57 (1966):95.

———. *Bound to Violence*. Translated by Ralph Mannheim. London: Heinemann Educational Books, 1968.

———. *Le devoir de violence*. Paris: Editions du Seuil, 1968.

p'Bitek, O. *Religion in Central Luo*. Nairobi: East African Publishing House, 1971.

———. *Song of Lawino and Song of Ocol*. Nairobi: East African Publishing House, 1972.

Pêcheux, Michel. *Language, Semantics and Ideology*. New York: St. Martin's Press, 1982.

Popper, Karl, *Conjectures and Refutations: The Growth of Scientific Knowledge*. New York: Basic Books, 1962.

———. "Towards a Rational Theory of Tradition." In *Conjectures and Refutations:* New York: Basic Books, 1962.

Pratt, Mary-Louise. *Toward a Speech-act Theory of Literary Discourse*. Bloomington: Indiana University Press, 1977.

———. "Reply to Harold Fromm." In *"Race," Writing and Difference*, edited by Henry Louis Gates, Jr., 400–1. Chicago: University of Chicago Press, 1986.

Pratt, V. "Science and Traditional Religion: A Discussion of Some of Robin Horton's Views." *Second Order* 1, no. 1 (1972):7–20.

Putnam, Hilary. "The Meaning of 'Meaning.'" In *Mind Language and Reality. Philosophical Papers*. Vol. 2, 215–71. Cambridge: Cambridge University Press, 1975.

Rajchman, John. "Habermas's Complaint." (Review: Habermas, *The Philosophical Discourse of Modernity*.) *New German Critique* 45 (1988):163–91.

Randles, W. G. L. *L'ancien royaume du Congo des origines à la fin du XIXᵉ siècle*. Paris: Mouton, 1968.

Rattray, R. S. *Ashanti Law and Constitution*. London: Oxford University Press, 1929.

———. *Ashanti*. London: Oxford University Press, 1955.

Reed, Adolph, Jr. "Black Particularity Reconsidered." *Telos* 39 (Spring 1979):71–93.

Renan, E. "Qu'est-ce qu'une nation." In *Oeuvres complètes*. Vol. 1, 887–906. Paris: Calmann-Lévy, 1882.

Robinson, Cedric J. *Black Marxism: The Making of the Black Radical Tradition*. London: Zed Books, 1983.

Rorty, Richard. "The World Well Lost." *Journal of Philosophy* 69 (1972):649–66.

———. *Contingency, Irony and Solidarity*. Cambridge: Cambridge University Press, 1988.

Sartre, Jean-Paul. "Orphée Noir." In *Anthologie de la nouvelle poésie Nègre et Malagache de langue Francaise*, edited by Leopold S. Senghor. Paris: Presses Universitaires de France, 1948.

Schuyler, George. *Black No More*. New York: Negro Universities Press, 1931.

Schwartz-Bart, André. *Le Dernier des Justes*. Paris: Editions du Seuil, 1959.

Senghor, Leopold S. *Chants d'ombre*. Paris: Editions du Seuil, 1964.

Sheldrake, Rupert. *A New Science of Life: The Hypothesis of Formative Causation*. London: Blond & Briggs, 1981.

Skorupski, John. *Symbol and Theory*. Cambridge: Cambridge University Press, 1976.

Smith, Paul. "A Question of Feminine Identity." *Notebooks in Cultural Analysis* 1 (1984):81–102.

Snowden, Frank. *Blacks in Antiquity*. Cambridge, Mass.: Harvard University Press, 1970.

Sollors, Werner, *Beyond Ethnicity: Consent and Descent in American Culture*. New York: Oxford University Press, 1986.

Songolo, Aliko. "The Writer, the Audience and the Critic's Responsibility: The Case of *Bound To Violence*." In *Artist and Audience: African Literature as a Shared Experience*, edited by Richard Priebe and Thomas A. Hale, 126–40. Washington, D.C.: Three Continents Press, 1979.

Soyinka, Wole. *Death and the King's Horseman*. London: Methuen, 1975.

———. *Myth, Literature and the African World*. Cambridge: Cambridge University Press, 1976.

Spivak, Gayatri C. *In Other Worlds: Essays in Cultural Politics*. New York and London: Routledge, 1988.

Spiller, G., ed. *Papers in Inter-Racial Problems Communicated to the First Universal Races Congress Held at the University of London, July 26–29, 1911*. London: P. S. King & Son, 1911. Republished with an introduction by H. Aptheker. Secaucus, N.J.: Citadel Press, 1970.

Strawson, Peter F. *Individuals: An Essay in Descriptive Metaphysics*. London: Methuen, 1959.

Suleri, Sara. *Meatless Days*. Chicago: Chicago University Press, 1989.

Taine, Hippolyte A. *History of English Literature*. Translated by H. Van Laun. London: Chatto & Windus, 1897.

Thiel, J. F. *La situation religieuse des Mbiem*. Ceeba Publications, series 2, vol. 1. Bandundu, Zaire: Centre d'Etudes Ethnologiques, n.d.

Thompson, John B. *Studies in the Theory of Ideology*. Berkeley: University of California Press, 1984.

Todorov, Tzvetan. "'Race,' Writing and Culture." In *"Race," Writing and Difference*, edited by Henry Louis Gates, Jr., 370–80. Chicago: University of Chicago Press, 1986.

Todorov, T., and Serge Dubrovsky, eds. *Enseignement de la littérature*. Paris: Plon, 1971.

Towa, M. *Essai sur la problématique philosophique dans l'Afrique actuelle*. Yaoundé: CLE, 1971.

Trilling, Lionel. *The Opposing Self: Nine Essays in Criticism*. New York: Viking Press, 1955.

———. *Sincerity and Authenticity*. Cambridge, Mass.: Harvard University Press, 1971.

Vogel, Susan et al. *Perspectives: Angles on African Art*. By James Baldwin, Romare Bearden, Ekpo Eyo, Nancy Graves, Ivan Karp, Lela Kouakou, Iba N'Diaye, David Rockefeller, William Rubin, and Robert Farris Thompson. Interviewed by Michael John Weber, with an introduction by Susan Vogel. New York: The Center for African Art, 1987.

Wallerstein, Immanuel. *Historical Capitalism*. London: Verso, 1983.

Weber, Max. *The Protestant Ethic and the Spirit of Capitalism*. Translated by Talcott Parsons. London: Unwin University Books, 1930.

———. *The Theory of Social and Economic Organization*. New York: Oxford University Press, 1947.

———. *From Max Weber: Essays in Sociology*. Edited by H. H. Gerth and C. Wright Mills. London: Kegan Paul, 1948.

———. *Ancient Judaism*. Glencoe, Ill.: The Free Press, 1958.

———. *Economy and Society*. 3 vols. Edited by Gunther Roth and Claus Wittich. New York: Bedminster Press, 1968.

Westphall, Jonathan. *Colour: Some Philosophical Problems from Wittgenstein*. Oxford: Basil Blackwell, 1987.

Wilde, Oscar. *Intentions*. London, 1909.

———*Phrases and Philosophies for the Use of the Young,* in *The Annotated Oscar Wilde,* edited by H. Montgomery Hyde, 418–19. New York: Clarkson N. Potter Inc., 1982.

Williams, Bernard. *Ethics and the Limits of Philosophy*. London: Fontana, 1985.

Williams, Raymond. *Marxism and Literature*. Oxford: Oxford University Press, 1977.

Williams, William Carlos. *In the American Grain*. 1951. Reprint. New York: New Directions, 1956.

Wilson, Bryan, ed. *Rationality*. Oxford: Basil Blackwell, 1970.

Wiredu, J. E. (Kwasi). "How Not to Compare African Thought with Western Thought." In *African Philosophy: An Introduction,* edited by Richard Wright, 166–84. Washington, D.C.: University Press of America, 1979.

———. *Philosophy and an African Culture*. London: Cambridge University Press, 1980.

Wright, Richard, ed. *African Philosophy: An Introduction*. 2d ed. Washington, D.C.: University Press of America, 1979.

Index